Additional Praise for *Born in Flames*

"*Born in Flames* shatters the myth that Bronx residents burned their own neighborhoods in the 1970s. Bench Ansfield reveals how a 1960s-era privatized fire insurance reform policy—redlining in disguise—fueled mass-scale landlord abandonment and arson for profit during a decade of financial crisis, not just in the Bronx but nationwide. Amid the devastation, residents led one of the largest urban rebuilding efforts in U.S. history. Elegantly written and deeply researched, this groundbreaking history lays bare the roots of today's housing crisis."
—Johanna Fernández, author of *The Young Lords: A Radical History*

"*Born in Flames* is a searing and incisive exploration of the intersection of race, capitalism, and urban devastation in the late 20th century. Bench Ansfield masterfully unearths the hidden histories of landlord arson and the financialization of urban space, illuminating how racial capitalism set fire to American cities. Challenging conventional narratives of urban decline, Ansfield offers a profound analysis of the way policies meant to rectify inequalities instead deepened them, and how marginalized communities fought back against the destruction. A vital contribution to understanding how the fires of the past continue to shape the injustices of the present."
—Elizabeth Hinton, author of *America on Fire: The Untold History of Police Violence and Black Rebellion Since the 1960s*

"Bench Ansfield has written an extraordinary history of the American city in the late twentieth century. Beautifully written and drawing on meticulous archival work, *Born in Flames* illuminates the economic and social logic that has led to the emergencies of our time."
—Kim Phillips-Fein, author of *Fear City: New York's Fiscal Crisis and the Rise of Austerity Politics*

"Racial inequality persists because it was insured. In this beautifully written work, Bench Ansfield is the first to uncover crucial links between the 1970s wave of urban arson and the subsequent rise of finance in the United States. One of the very few essential books on the recent history of racial capitalism in the United States, and a revelatory and unusually creative history of race and risk."

—Jonathan Levy, author of *Ages of American Capitalism: A History of the United States*

"*Born in Flames* tells a gripping story of how our cities came to be—by way of power, capital, and fire. In this expansive account of the arson wave, Bench Ansfield gives us a diligent history lesson, but also a provocation about our current conditions, highlighting what we have yet to learn from the episodes detailed in the book. This book does what so many neglect, introducing the reader to not just the policies and power brokers, but also to the regular people of the Bronx, who revolted against the profiteers who conspired to burn their homes."

—Tara Raghuveer, founding director, Tenant Union Federation and KC Tenants

BORN
IN
FLAMES

BORN IN FLAMES

THE BUSINESS OF ARSON AND THE REMAKING OF THE AMERICAN CITY

BENCH ANSFIELD

W. W. Norton & Company
Independent Publishers Since 1923

Copyright © 2025 by Bench Ansfield

All rights reserved
Printed in the United States of America
First Edition

For information about permission to reproduce selections from this book, write to
Permissions, W. W. Norton & Company, Inc., 500 Fifth Avenue, New York, NY 10110

For information about special discounts for bulk purchases, please contact
W. W. Norton Special Sales at specialsales@wwnorton.com or 800-233-4830

Manufacturing by Lakeside Book Company
Book design by Chris Welch
Production manager: Louise Mattarelliano

ISBN 978-1-324-09351-0

W. W. Norton & Company, Inc.
500 Fifth Avenue, New York, NY 10110
www.wwnorton.com

W. W. Norton & Company Ltd.
15 Carlisle Street, London W1D 3BS

10 9 8 7 6 5 4 3 2 1

For Bruce

And for all those in the struggle for housing justice

CONTENTS

INTRODUCTION: Race and Risk in the Burning Years . . . 1

PART I: RISK

ONE: The Crisis of Insurance and the Insuring of the Crisis . . . 19

TWO: The Brownlining of the Bronx . . . 47

PART II: REVERB

THREE: To Torch a Fireproof Building . . . 73

FOUR: "We Went to Bed with Our Shoes On Every Night" . . . 101

FIVE: A Triangular Trade in Risk . . . 133

PART III: REVOLT

SIX: Out of the Shadows and into the Streets . . . 161

SEVEN: Fighting Fire with FIRE . . . 193

EIGHT: Corrective Capitalism . . . 225

EPILOGUE: The Ashes of History . . . 255

Acknowledgments . . . 265
New York FAIR Plan Loss Experience . . . 273
A Note on Arson Statistics . . . 275
Sources Consulted . . . 277
Notes . . . 281
Credits . . . 331
Index . . . 333

BORN
IN
FLAMES

INTRODUCTION

Race and Risk in the Burning Years

The Blacks represent a kind of insurance for humanity in the eyes of the Whites.

—FRANTZ FANON, 1952[1]

Sixth grader Roberto Ramirez holding his burning brick outside Intermediate School 52, in the South Bronx. On the roof, he'd painted "rent late" (1982).

The fallen brick sat at the edge of an abandoned lot, staring up at Roberto Ramirez like a question mark. Ramirez, a sixth grader in the Bronx, had been instructed by his art teacher to search for "found objects," and his eyes gravitated toward this small chunk of a crumbling tenement. The assignment was to envision the objects "as something else," so Ramirez pictured the brick as a tiny building that was still standing. He took a paintbrush to its rough exterior, and after carefully outlining the building's matchbox windows, he filled their frames with fire. Not all of them, though—only the windows on the upper floors. He knew that in the Bronx, fires started at the top.[2]

Ramirez's technique quickly caught on among the other kids in his class, and before long the eleven- and twelve-year-olds had produced a series of fifty flaming miniatures. It was 1982, and they drew what they knew: life in a firestorm. Another student, John Mendoza, and his family had been burned out of their apartment three times by arsonists, an experience as routine as it was calamitous. Yet what the students didn't know, beyond the rumors children sometimes absorb, was why fire was so prevalent in their neighborhood. For an explanation, they looked to their new art teacher, Tim Rollins, a white conceptual artist with ties to the downtown art scene. As an outsider in the Bronx, Rollins had no satisfying answers, so he decided on a field trip. "We go down to the Fire Department," he recalled, and "the firemen see these ten crazy kids and me come stomping in and asking, '*Why are there so many fires?*'" The firefighters offered only vague replies. The students left the station dejected, but in the mystery Rollins spotted a teaching tool. He asked the sixth graders to inscribe an explanation on the bricks, and marveled, "We got 70 different reasons." Ramirez, for one, blamed tenants who were behind on rent: he wrote "RENT LATE" on the building's roof. His classmate claimed that "junkies burned the buildings down," while another wrote, "NO HEAT."[3]

The students were left with concrete bricks in lieu of concrete answers. What they were attempting to do was give the bricks a history. The project became known as the *Bricks* series, and it was the first in a decades-long, intergenerational collaboration called Kids of Survival (or K.O.S.), so

Untitled (brick), by Tim Rollins and K.O.S. at the Whitney Museum of American Art.

named because "we were broke but not broken." One of the *Bricks* now sits in the permanent collection of the Whitney Museum of American Art.[4]

The question haunting the *Bricks* series to this day is why the students suggested "70 different reasons" for the conflagration that upended their lives and engulfed their neighborhoods. How could the toll from the fires have been so colossal and its source so opaque?

+++

SEVEN YEARS EARLIER, in April 1975, a different act of painting offered some insight. Smearing black pigment onto their hands and faces, landlord Imre Oberlander and his associate Yishai Webber prepared to torch one of the former's six buildings in the South Bronx. The white incendiaries believed blackface would offer them cover, like a perverse kind of safety gear. At four a.m. on a Friday morning, the two men cruised down South-

Imre Oberlander (center) and his associate Yishai Webber (left) were among the first landlords indicted for arson conspiracy in the 1970s Bronx. They were caught driving in blackface, with two unexploded firebombs in their car. They were convicted of criminal possession of a weapon in the third degree, and Oberlander was sentenced to five years of probation.

ern Boulevard en route to the targeted building. They hoped the twilight would provide further protection, but when they drove past a police car, their broken taillight caught the attention of the officers on patrol. Pulling them over on the wide thoroughfare, the policemen saw two Hasidic men from Williamsburg made up in blackface, one wearing a wig, and proceeded to search the car. They found two "firebombs"—crude incendiary devices made out of gasoline, gunpowder, and a timing device.[5]

Oberlander became one of the first landlords charged in connection with the decade's "epidemic of arson," as the *New York Times* had begun to call it. Though the Bronx, in particular, had been burning for years by this point, authorities remained so oblivious to the root causes that they initially suspected Oberlander and Webber of being spies en route to the Soviet diplomatic compound, ten miles away, at the opposite end of the borough. It is true that the firestorm involved vast conspiracies, transnational dealings, and a doctrine of containment, but it all had little to do with the Cold War. What drove the arson wave was profit. Oberlander had collected $125,000 (nearly $750,000 in 2024 dollars) in insurance payouts from twenty-one separate fires between 1970 and 1975. All his claims were "paid off without a murmur from the insurance company," railed Bronx District Attorney Mario Merola, warning without hyperbole that this was just "a drop in the bucket."[6]

Between 1968 and the early 1980s, a wave of landlord arson coursed through cities across the United States, destroying large portions of neighborhoods home to poor communities of color. From Boston to Seattle, tens of thousands of housing units burned (this is a conservative estimate); the most affected neighborhoods lost up to 80 percent of their housing stock.

A fire in the upper floors of a Bronx apartment building in 1980. Fires in the top corner apartments were telltale signs of arson.

Yet historians have largely neglected the burning of the nation's cities, and popular memory has commonly confused the 1970s arson wave with the well-documented but far less destructive urban uprisings of the previous decade. The 1960s rebellions—most famously Watts in 1965, Newark and Detroit in 1967, and everywhere after the assassination of Martin Luther King Jr. in 1968—were born of Black (and in some instances Puerto Rican) outrage over the persistence of white supremacy despite the tangible gains of the civil rights movement. In most cases set off by an incident of police violence, the rebellions represented a collective revolt against not just overpolicing but the daily persecution of Black communities in the form of unequal employment, housing, education, and more. Though these events were often deemed "senseless riots" devoid of a coherent politics, they were formidable and far-reaching—though fledgling—insurgencies. Historians typically describe this era as stretching from Birmingham in 1963 to the nationwide uproar following MLK's murder in 1968, although important recent work has tracked the rebellions into the 1970s.[7]

Whether measured in dollars or lives lost, the destruction caused by the uprisings of the 1960s pales in comparison to the arson wave of the 1970s. In 1967, the most violent year of the decade, the number of dead were counted in the tens and the insurable losses totaled $75 million. By contrast, at least five hundred people died of arson annually across the United States during the 1970s, and by 1980 the *New York Times* was estimating that arson caused $15 billion in total annual losses. Admittedly, these are crude and fraught barometers of historical significance. The rebellions had immense political implications on a national scale, and they justifiably loom large within the popular imagination. The 1970s blazes were perhaps too common, too consistent with existing iniquities, to draw the same kind of attention.[8]

The latter decade was defined not by insurrection but by indemnification, though the two were connected, as we will see. The 1970s conflagrations bring into view the untold history of the racially stratified property insurance market, a key force in the making and remaking of American cities. Although fire usually requires only oxygen, heat, and fuel, the crucial ingredient during that decade was state-sponsored fire insurance, initiated by federal fiat *in response to* the 1960s uprisings. The reform effort was supposed to put an end to insurance redlining, which had left entire swaths of the American city uninsured or underinsured due to the race and class of their residents. Yet increased access to second-rate fire insur-

The Bronx lost approximately 20 percent of its housing stock to fire and landlord abandonment between 1970 and 1981. The worst-hit neighborhoods hemorrhaged upwards of 80 percent of their housing units. Map adapted for *Born in Flames* by Molly Roy and Jonathan Tarleton.

ance, when paired with state cutbacks and ongoing mortgage redlining, incentivized landlord arson on a vast scale.

While telling a national and international story, this book centers on the Bronx, known in these years as the "arson capital of the world." The Bronx lost approximately 20 percent of its total housing stock to fire or abandonment between 1970 and 1981—around one hundred thousand units, nearly the equivalent of the number of housing units in today's Richmond, Virginia, or Reno, Nevada. Destruction on this scale, unfathomable as it may be, should not be seen as evidence of the Bronx's exceptionality. The arson wave hit cities across the country, in every region. Coast to coast, Black and Brown tenants were blamed for the fires. Yet the evidence is unequivocal: the hand that torched the Bronx and scores of other cities was that of a landlord impelled by the market and guided by the state.⁹

That hand was also, in the case of Imre Oberlander, covered with dark pigment. Who was the audience for this four a.m. racial masquerade? Was it the building's tenants, the block's bystanders, the beat cops? Whomever they imagined as potential witnesses, Oberlander and Webber were performing a well-rehearsed script of Black and Brown incendiarism. The specter of the Black firesetter, in particular, is older than the United States itself. For the two white arsonists, the racist trope was something to exploit. The landlord and his accomplice believed it could deflect blame and prevent them from being identified. They applied blackface as though it, too, were a form of insurance.¹⁰

Oberlander and Webber may have also seen blackface as a shield against a different bigotry—that of "Jewish lightning." The stereotype of the arsonist Jew was a vestige of medieval anti-Semitism that was modernized by fire insurers in the mid-nineteenth century, when underwriters at Aetna, the Hartford, and other notable firms warned against issuing policies to "Jew risks," in part because of Jews' supposed proclivity for fraud. The slur still stings, and a few Jewish New Yorkers active in the fight against landlord arson in the 1970s spoke to me about their experiences only because of my own Jewish background. What became clear in the course of researching this book is that the stereotypical arsonist, whether in its anti-Semitic or anti-Black variant, fulfilled a similar function: distracting from the larger power structures at work. In the 1970s, the Jewish slumlord became a potent symbol of Black exploitation, but in fact the redlining banks and insurance companies had, to different degrees, discriminated against both Black and Jewish communities.

The irony in Oberlander and Webber's blackface gambit was that the two men ended up getting caught precisely *because* their performance of Blackness was both too convincing and too implausible. That is, their apparent Blackness may well have played a role in the police officers' decision to pull them over, and their thinly veiled whiteness—upon closer inspection—almost definitely prompted the search of their car.¹¹

Few landlord arsonists actually made a habit of wearing blackface, because few had a need for it. The arson wave was made possible by *financial* masquerade—an array of insurance and real estate practices that obscured accountability and diffused risk—combined with official neglect and the presumed criminality of the Black and Brown tenants held culpable for the fires. Instead of blackface, landlords often chose more cunning disguises, such as hiring paid "torches," usually neighborhood teenagers, to do the burning for them. But that was just the opening scene of a multi-act white-collar revue, one that featured Hollywood studios dishing out Bronxploitation films, journalists vilifying the supposed welfare arsonist, underwriters flooding cities with subpar coverage, insurance executives feigning impotence, real estate players attacking rent control, criminologists theorizing about broken windows, lawmakers gutting the fire service, and pundits yammering on about riots and pyromaniacs. All sang the same chorus, drowning out dissenting voices as well as the true origins of the arson wave. Blackface was not necessary when there was such a vibrant tradition of briefcase minstrelsy.

+++

THE TORCHING OF wide swaths of the American metropolis may strike some as a bizarre event in the distant past. Yet it is very much part of how our cities came to be. Long neglected by historians, the 1970s arson wave vividly reveals late-twentieth-century shifts in political economy that still shape our lives. Out of its embers was forged the metropolis we know today: one defined by volcanic real estate booms, economy-cratering busts, and an ongoing decline in housing stability. The world in which a solidly built home could generate more value by ruination than habitation is the same world in which homelessness, eviction, and foreclosure have become defining aspects of urban life.[12]

The story of landlord arson is not a cautionary tale of capitalism gone awry, of a few bad apples, of uncaring policymakers, of government overreach, or of a grittier bygone era. To frame it as a singular, sensational episode of the past is to gloss over its continuities with—and its role in creating—the structures of the present. Warning against such "spectacularization of black pain," Saidiya Hartman counsels that "shocking displays too easily obfuscate the more mundane and socially endurable forms of terror." The arson wave renders visible much that is hidden in plain sight, historically and to this day.[13]

Over the last fifty years, housing insecurity and real estate volatility have come to define our cities, and though there are many causes, none is more significant than financialization, which surged in the years after 1968. Financialization is the process by which an economy that was once organized around the making and trading of physical commodities becomes increasingly oriented around the profits from financial activity. This pattern is not unique to our times; it has been a fixture of declining empires since sixteenth-century Genoese merchants opted for the trading of money over the trading of goods. The ascendance of high finance over manufacturing and the commodity trades marked the beginning of the end for the Dutch, British, and then American imperial expansions—it was everywhere a "sign of autumn," in historian Fernand Braudel's memorable phrasing.[14]

In the United States, the triumph of high finance in the 1970s and 1980s was predicated on a profitability crisis among large domestic manufacturers and, in response, the federal government's shift toward deregulation and market-based governance. Manufacturers were suffering the effects of stiffer international competition and skyrocketing inflation. To curb the inflationary spiral, in 1980 the Federal Reserve hiked the federal funds interest rate to an unprecedented 20 percent, which increased borrowing costs for firms, cutting into their bottom lines and soon leading to further layoffs and rising unemployment. As the United States began a general transition into a net importer of goods for the first time in a century, corporations backed away from their long-term investments in factories and a well-paid, though racially segmented, workforce. Instead, they came to favor short-term, immediate returns that could be reported on quarterly earnings calls. Multinational corporations were remade in the image of Wall Street, and meanwhile global capital poured into New York banks in search of U.S. dollars, the peg for financial globalization. As the accountant-cum-CEO of U.S. Steel put it, the firm was "no longer in the business of making steel" but was, rather, "in the business of making profits." For corporations, liquidity—the ability to easily convert an asset into cash value—was king.[15]

The high finance we know from the nightly news and the silver screen is found on the fiftieth floor of a glass-encased skyscraper and in the cacophonous pits of a stock exchange, fueled by adrenaline, greed, and cocaine. The image we have is set a thousand feet in the air, its spoils and scandals a world apart, even if they eventually touch the rest of us. But this is not the only face of financialization, nor necessarily the one that sheds the most light on the crises of the present. The arson wave opens up a view of financialization from the ground up and far from the fray of Wall Street.

History teaches us that arson can be an indicator of macroeconomic flux. A week after 1911's Triangle Shirtwaist Factory fire, trade unionist Rose Schneiderman bellowed to an audience of mourners, "The life of men and women is so cheap, and property is so sacred!" That infamous New York fire, which was suspected of being incendiary, killed 146 garment workers, many doomed to death by the factory owners' policy of locking the doors to the exits and stairways. The fire prompted a referendum on working conditions under industrial capitalism, and Schneiderman's indictment of property's exaltation at workers' expense won broad currency. The Triangle fire was a watershed in American politics, galvanizing a reform movement that, in turn, helped catalyze the New Deal.[16]

The Triangle Shirtwaist conflagration is remembered for unearthing contradictions that seethed under the surface of a nascent Fordism, the regime of mass production and mass consumption that drove the U.S. economy from World War I through the 1970s. What that fire was to Fordism, the 1970s arson wave was to financialization. Whether called post-Fordism or neoliberalism or financialized capitalism, the new era was characterized by global capital mobility, market triumphalism, transnational supply chains, the rise of service work over mass production, and a drastic reduction in economic security for the average worker. Corporate firms fled for the U.S. South, the suburbs, and beyond the nation's shores, pulled by a non-unionized and often migrant-based labor force, and pushed by the newly sacrosanct injunction to prioritize shareholder value above all else.[17]

If the Triangle Shirtwaist fire helped seed the New Deal order, the legacy of the 1970s inferno is one of unfinished struggle and ongoing immiseration. In the flames we can catch glimpses of redlining's long shadow, of the dawn of the subprime, of freedom dreaming and tenant might. The fires tell a story of the transliteration of race into the language of risk, of financial abstractions made tangible in the char of the roof and the scald of the hand.

Born in Flames argues that the firestorm was made possible by the interplay of two epoch-defining transformations: the rise of the aptly named FIRE (finance, insurance, and real estate) industries on the one hand, and the nation's shifting racial politics amid the civil rights struggle on the other. Although these two developments are almost always framed as discrete and unrelated, they were in fact entwined. The framework of racial capitalism is helpful in revealing their points of intersection. Racial capitalism is the idea that racial hierarchy and capitalist accumulation are entangled—and have been since the dawn of chattel slavery and Indigenous dispossession. "Capitalism requires inequality and racism enshrines it," writes geographer Ruth Wilson Gilmore. This book uses racial capitalism to explain this dynamic in the age of financialization.[18]

The stock image of the 1970s American city features an urban economy in decline. It is rarely acknowledged that there were profits to squeeze from the destruction of the metropolis, particularly in neighborhoods of color. The ascendance of the FIRE industries on the heels of the civil rights movement created conditions primed for plunder, especially in cities suffering from the flight of white residents and well-paying jobs. "Instant liquidity," as one arsonist for hire described it in his testimony before Congress, was the real estate equivalent of Wall Street's liquidity preference: the priority placed on an asset's ready convertibility into cash. What made buildings liquid was property insurance expansion, presented as a means of racial justice and redress. Which is to say that race underwrote the gains enjoyed by landlords.[19]

For those looking to make a quick buck, the Bronx and other communities of color possessed a peculiar asset: the powerful alibi of racial pathology. The presumption of Black and Brown criminality blotted out the fact of dispossession so completely that, all these decades later, the vague impression that Bronxites burned down their own borough endures, while the vast fortunes made were forgotten. The peril of getting caught perpetrating fraud thus transferred to its victims, where it has long remained.

+++

PART I OF this book charts the post-1945 development of the racially stratified market of property insurance, which introduced comprehensive homeowners policies in the suburbs while redlining the central cities. Insurance became accessible to poor neighborhoods of color in U.S. cities only after the 1960s uprisings, the result of a quiet upheaval in actuarial conventions and insurance regulation. Property damage from the rebellions had been relatively modest, but insurance companies were resistant to covering losses on the few policies they retained in the affected neighborhoods. With insurers threatening to fully withdraw from cities once and for all, in 1968 the federal government established and sponsored a program to bail out the insurance industry. Co-opting the language of the civil rights movement, lawmakers framed the program as a racial justice measure that would stamp out redlining. In return for federal riot reinsurance, insurers agreed to cease redlining areas like the Bronx by offering a new line of state-sponsored property insurance, called the FAIR (Fair Access to Insurance Requirements) plan. But contrary to the program's branding, the high cost and poor coverage made it most accessible to those with significant stores of capital—namely, absentee landlords, the majority of whom were white. In place of farther-reaching reforms, the program shored up urban property at the expense of the renting masses.

With the FAIR plan, the state found a mechanism for responding to deep-seated social problems via a market-based financial remedy. Race and location were formally barred as underwriting guidelines by the 1968 legislation. The program made insurance an entitlement of propertied citizenship, and lawmakers hoped that it would thus help quell Black militancy. But as a financial framework, risk could no more be emptied of racial thinking than property insurance could rectify the inequities of the city. In questions of property, risk and race are subject and verb.

Instead of redistributing insurance access in meaningful ways for the residents of once-redlined neighborhoods, the FAIR plan's high-cost, low-value insurance set the stage for further ruin. The ensuing deluge of insurance access marked a step away from insurance redlining, but it fell far short of what so-called greenlining promised: financial inclusion as a racial justice remedy. I introduce the term "brownlining" to capture this blend of red and green—how the FAIR plan increased access to property insurance in communities of color, but on discriminatory terms. The sedimented relationship between insurance redlining's residual presence and the FAIR plan's abrupt infusion of substandard insurance created specific and highly combustible conditions.

Even as FAIR's expansion of insurance to formerly redlined neighborhoods heralded a redefinition of racialized risk, it worked to indemnify landlords from economic precarity. That is, fire insurance became available to landlords in once-redlined neighborhoods just as jobs, capital, and social services retreated. Part II explores how landlords turned to arson not necessarily out of malice but out of calculated interest. With the urban real estate market facing a crisis of profitability, landlords' buildings became most valuable *after* they went up in flames. Insurers, for their part, were able to absorb the resulting losses through a number of arcane industry techniques, all legal, which took full advantage of financialization's distorting effects. One such scheme enabled insurance companies to diffuse liability across transnational financial circuits spanning from the Bronx to Britain to Brazil—a triangular trade in risk.

The only buildings that did not burn were those that could not generate profit: public housing. In yet another irony, that enduring symbol of urban failure happened to be a far safer place to live than private rental buildings. During a decade that saw the United States swear off state-sponsored urban renewal, the arson wave was, in a sense, a free-market slum-clearance program. As in the better-remembered urban-renewal programs of the 1950s and 1960s, the market-made bulldozer precipitated massive displacement and community rupture. Yet in an era of municipal fiscal crises and state cutbacks, the blazes provoked little state action until the end of the 1970s.

The lack of a government response to the fire problem triggered a groundswell of community organizing throughout the Bronx and in many other cities across the nation. Part III chronicles the anti-arson movement's interracial experiments in tenant organizing, urban homesteading, community development, and computerized early warning systems, which ultimately helped stop the burnings. These efforts, including Boston's Symphony Tenants Organizing Project and the Northwest Bronx Community and Clergy Coalition, have been overlooked for far too long. In the Bronx, the very tenants mobilizing against the arson wave became its scapegoats when the borough was made into a global symbol of the nationwide "urban crisis." Residents' struggles against the fires thus extended into the battlegrounds of culture, as with hip-hop anthems like Rock Master Scott & the Dynamic Three's "The Roof Is on Fire" (1984) and the protests against Bronxploitation films like *Fort Apache, the Bronx* (1981). Against that backdrop, the fiery fixations of 1970s popular culture, from "Disco Inferno" to *The Towering Inferno*, take on new meanings. Even the era's social science, in particular the psychological concept of "burnout" and the criminology of "broken windows," was shaped by the arson decade. By the early 1980s, the renters of the Bronx and other cities across the country had succeeded in pressuring lawmakers and insurers to take action. Yet once the profit was taken out of arson, residents were made to grapple with both the devastated landscape and the enduring, racialized narratives of urban crisis left in its wake.

+++

THE STORY TOLD here is one of contingency and continuity, violence and struggle, and, above all, the entanglement of race and risk. I have borrowed the book's title from Lizzie Borden's 1983 cult film of the same name. In the dystopian New York of the film, the state fails to safeguard the city's most vulnerable, forcing women to band together in anti-rape bike brigades and other direct-action campaigns. Their efforts become more militant when the protagonist, a radical student at Lehman College, in the Bronx, is martyred by the forces of racism and misogyny that persist after a socialist revolution. "We are born in flames," wails the titular song, a chorus that echoes into our own era.[20]

Part I

RISK

ONE

The Crisis of Insurance and the Insuring of the Crisis

> What oxygen is to the air, insurance is to the economic and social life of our time.
> —JOHN BAINBRIDGE, 1952[1]

> All the things I was trying to escape...
> such things as dealing with insurance companies if I want fire insurance.
> —JAMES BALDWIN, 1964[2]

Insurance adjusters served as capitalism's first responders. This General Adjustment Bureau brochure, released after the Watts uprising in 1965, celebrated adjusters as heroes.

When the Watts rebellion erupted in August 1965, insurance men beat the National Guard to the scene by a full day. As specialists in the assessment of loss, adjusters entered the still-smoldering Los Angeles neighborhood with a single mission: to gauge the insurable damages. The proximate spark for the uprising had been the violent arrest of a Black motorist the previous day, but decades of racist policing and discrimination in housing, employment, and education had laid the kindling. The unrest stretched for six days. Among the rebellion's many other effects, it set in motion a series of shifts in the insurance industry that continue to be felt today.

With the arrival of the National Guard, a curfew was announced, and the specialists with the General Adjustment Bureau (GAB), a national agency providing adjustment services to member companies, withdrew and regrouped. When the curfew was lifted a few days later, a private squadron of adjusters from around the country stood at the ready. As a GAB brochure boasted, "Except for troops, police and firemen, they were the first non-residents to enter the area after the start of the riots. In fact, they made their first trip into Watts on fire vehicles." Hitching a ride on government vehicles, the insurance personnel were, in a real sense, capitalism's first responders.[3]

It bears asking why a private insurance firm would feel it necessary to send in workers "to adjust losses even before winds die down, waters recede, or snipers are rooted." What was it about property insurance that made it so vitally essential for the capitalist economy? And what sort of threat was posed by the urban uprisings to an industry that regularly handled hurricanes and earthquakes? These were among the questions that led President Lyndon Baines Johnson to convene an investigative panel in August 1967, at the high tide of the nationwide rebellions. Huddled in the Indian Treaty Room, in a building adjacent to the White House, the committee of dark-suited men counted among its ranks two governors, an assistant attorney general, and captains of industry. Later, fielding questions from the press, former governor of Pennsylvania William Scranton disclosed that the group was under "heavy pressure" to devise a path forward from the uprisings and the explosive state of American racial politics. The committee set off at a feverish pace, conducting some three thousand interviews nationwide before submitting its report to President Johnson six months later. Its conclusions would help set the course for U.S. cities over the coming decades.[4]

This was not the National Advisory Commission on Civil Disorders—better known as the Kerner Commission, after its chair, Governor Otto Kerner Jr. of Illinois—which had been established by LBJ two weeks earlier. The Kerner Commission was quickly "hailed as a definitive inquiry into America's troubled race relations." Blaming institutionalized white supremacy for the uprisings, the best-selling *Kerner Report*, published as a 708-page paperback in 1968, is often remembered for a single line: "Our Nation is moving towards two societies, one black, one white—separate and unequal." In holding white society accountable for the unrest, the report veered far from the moderate bromides LBJ had envisioned, and accordingly, "he viewed its assessment of urban social realities as unreasonable and too radical." Though the release of the *Kerner Report* was a media spectacle—Marlon Brando read from it on late-night television—most of its recommendations were ignored, with the major exception being its proposals to augment police power. Until recently, the *Kerner Report* has largely been remembered as a path not taken.[5]

By contrast, the panel that gathered in the Indian Treaty Room on August 23, 1967, largely skirted the media spotlight, and its proposals cruised straight into the legislative record. The President's National Advisory Panel on Insurance in Riot-Affected Areas had actually been appointed by LBJ and the Kerner Commission after they decided "that a separate and expert group could deal more expeditiously with the insurance problems of urban core residents and businessmen." It, too, was named after its chairman, Governor Richard Hughes of New Jersey, who had called the Newark rebellion of 1967 "a criminal insurrection against society, hiding behind the shield of civil rights"—a far cry from the sympathetic tenor of the *Kerner Report*. In hindsight, perhaps the White House opted to delegate the insurance issue to a separate panel because the nation's urban property was too critical to entrust to Kerner's lightning rod of a commission. Whatever the case, the two investigative bodies took dramatically divergent paths.[6]

The Hughes Panel completed its report, *Meeting the Insurance Crisis of*

Our Cities, in January 1968, and by August, its recommendations had been quietly codified into law. During its investigation, the appointed lawmakers and industry executives had singled out property insurance redlining in what had been labeled "riot-prone areas" as both a cause and effect of the uprisings. Their proposed corrective was the creation of new statewide companies called FAIR plans (Fair Access to Insurance Requirements), which they billed as a progressive remedy for insurance redlining. These public-private insurance companies would be backed by the federal government and overseen by individual states. In exchange for their mandatory participation in the high-risk insurance pools, private insurance firms would be offered federally sponsored riot reinsurance—or financial backup—on losses resulting from future uprisings. FAIR plans were introduced as a racial justice measure, but in reality they hawked substandard policies with poor coverage and exorbitant premiums.

One of only a handful of federal legislative responses to the uprisings, the advent of the FAIR plans marked a new mode of state crisis management in the face of widespread social unrest and political and economic volatility. In the 1970s, as finance eclipsed manufacturing and industrial relocation transfigured U.S. cities, the new insurance program secured property while promising financial inclusion to Black and Brown neighborhoods. Yet the strange career of the FAIR plan reveals that the expansion of property insurance was not only incapable of indemnifying against the brutalities of racial capitalism but was in fact bound to amplify them.

+++

ON AUGUST 19, 1967, Philadelphians awoke to discover that their city's insurance had been canceled. That morning, the *Inquirer* reported that the Philadelphia Housing Authority (PHA), the largest landlord in Pennsylvania, had found itself suddenly uninsured. In a climate of "riot jitters," the Mutual Fire, Marine and Inland Insurance Company informed the housing authority that the three-year insurance contract it had signed just a month prior was null and void. Some *Inquirer* readers might have been surprised to learn that a large government agency could be at the mercy of the private property insurance market, but this is how the economic infrastructure of contemporary American cities was built. The housing authority's forty housing projects and one thousand rehabbed houses, valued at $118 million, relied on private insurance for protection from common hazards like fire. Now the future of these properties, home to tens of thousands of Philadelphians, was suddenly in doubt. Mutual Fire did not offer an official justification for its decision, but none was necessary. All agreed that "fear of riots" had prompted the cancellation. What was confusing was the timing: it had been years since Philadelphia had experienced the type of large-scale civil unrest that preoccupied insurers. Even more mystifying was how a federally subsidized government agency could be deemed uninsurable and considered an unworthy risk.[7]

The Philadelphia Housing Authority was far from an exceptional case. A 1968 federal inquiry into cancellations unearthed a widespread pattern of insurance redlining in neighborhoods of color. Redlining was nothing new, of course, and thanks to the tireless work of organizers and scholars, we now know a great deal about its history and legacy. But redlining has been overwhelmingly understood as a mortgage-specific phenomenon. Research into how, since the 1930s, the Federal Housing Administration (FHA), the Home Owners' Loan Corporation (HOLC), and private financial firms systematically appraised the racial composition of neighborhoods in determining the allocation of mortgage loans has been the cornerstone of twentieth-century U.S. urban history. Yet for all its breadth, this work tells us little about how a government agency itself could be a target of redlining.[8]

Insurance redlining is in fact its own beast; it is not just a mirror image of redlining in the mortgage market. Despite all the scholarly scrutiny of FHA mortgage insurance, which protected lenders against the possibility of default on mortgages, it remains an open question how the availability of property insurance—or its absence—dictated the racialized flows of mortgage capital across U.S. cities in the years after the Second World War. Given that property and casualty insurance has long been a basic and integral component of the mortgage credit system, this is a glaring omission. In fact, because property insurance was a prerequisite for mortgage loans, the history of redlining in the housing market cannot be fully understood without examining the role played by property insurers in steering mortgage financing toward certain risks and away from others.

There are four distinct periods in the history of property insurance from the turn of the twentieth century up to the 1980s. Until the late 1940s, the industry operated much as it had throughout the nineteenth century, with firms specializing in the indemnification of single hazards, like fires or floods, coverage for which had to be purchased from separate companies. Patterns of insurance deregulation and suburban housing development in the post–World War II metropolis brought about the Jim Crowification of the property insurance industry. This era saw the advent of comprehensive, high-value insurance policies in the suburbs and the corresponding constriction of the insurance market in the urban core. The racially tiered insurance market, in turn, gave rise to the redlining of communities of color, where insurance access became either unattainable or exorbitantly expensive and undependable. The uprisings of the mid-1960s brought the tensions of the tiered insurance market to a boiling point, marking a short-lived third stage during which panicked insurers threatened to abandon U.S. cities once and for all. Federal and state legislative interventions sought to halt the flight of insurers by establishing the statewide FAIR plans in 1968. The fourth period was ushered in by these programs, which, paradoxically, both expanded insurance access and deepened the racialized divides of the stratified insurance market. By 1969, the insurance landscape of Philadelphia and scores of other U.S. cities had been transformed, though some things stayed the same. That year, no less a civic institution than the Philadelphia School District was stripped of its insurance coverage; it fell upon the Pennsylvania FAIR plan to step in as the insurer of last resort.[9]

+++

THE HISTORY OF the modern American home is, to a large extent, the history of property insurance. Over the course of the nineteenth century, fire insurance became an essential backbone of urban capitalism during the period when cities were most prone to extensive conflagration. More than a hedge against fire, insurance helped underwrite the expansion of credit and the private property regime. In 1910, a high-profile investigation into the fire insurance industry declared that the credit system itself was "founded on the institution of insurance."[10]

By the post–World War II housing boom, fire insurance was fully entwined with the housing market. One senior economist at the Department of Housing and Urban Development (HUD) stressed "the importance of property insurance to the extension of credit for (1) the construction of new property, (2) for the financing and improvement of existing property, and (3) the rehabilitation of existing property. Without insurance, these activities, and indeed all business activity would stagnate." When the modern thirty-year mortgage was institutionalized by the Federal Housing Administration in the 1930s, lenders refused to offer financing without proof of indemnity against fire and other basic hazards. Property insurance supplied the mortar as the United States constructed, brick by brick, its chosen identity as a nation of homeowners.[11]

Through the early twentieth century, most property insurers were restricted to selling only one "line"—or type—of insurance. If a homeowner wanted to insure against both fire and vandalism, for instance, they would have to go to two separate companies. The growth of multiple-line insurance followed the 1945 passage of the McCarran-Ferguson Act, which enshrined the system of state—as opposed to federal—regulation favored by the industry. Insurers were thus able to "pit states against each other," threatening to withdraw from those that failed to foster companies' optimal regulatory environment. What's more, insurer representatives swelled the ranks of state insurance departments, effectively empowering the industry to regulate itself. Thanks to this regulatory capture, the industry was, in the words of one of its own, "freed from [the] shackles" of regulations that prohibited multiple-line insurance. The insurance industry was virtually the only major sector of the economy to evade the watchful eye of New Deal regulators.[12]

The loose regulatory environment coincided with the postwar suburban housing boom, which brought windfall profits to construction firms, banks, and mortgage lenders. But property insurers found themselves sitting on the sidelines in the late 1940s. With their financial products tailored for high-density U.S. cities, they were unprepared for the new housing landscape. For single-line insurers, underwriting low-density neighborhoods populated by single-family homes was less profitable than insuring the multi-family apartment houses of the city, which could fetch higher premiums with less overhead. In order to adapt to the rapidly growing suburban terrain, explained an economist with the U.S. Fire Administration, "a marketing strategy was required which would create economies of scale. The homeowners' policy was the answer."[13]

By insuring against multiple different perils at once—including fire, theft, and liability—homeowners policies revolutionized the property insurance industry. First legalized in New York State in 1949, homeowners insurance (as multi-line insurance quickly came to be known) offered more comprehensive protection to insureds than any property insurance previously available. Because numerous protections were bundled together, the premiums cost much less than they would have if each line of insurance were sold separately. Yet the benefits to insurance companies were patently clear: by bundling multiple lines, insurers earned higher premiums overall because consumers could now be convinced to insure against hazards that did not particularly imperil them. A Floridian's homeowners policy, for example, might insure against damage caused by ice and snow. The homeowners insurance policy was a new financial instrument for a new suburban landscape, and its growth in the postwar years was nothing short of explosive. In 1950, property insurers wrote only $30,000 in homeowners premiums, a sum that grew to $1 billion in 1962 and kept climbing.[14]

If property insurers tailored the homeowners policy to the suburban single-family home, stand-alone fire insurance became a sort of threadbare hand-me-down thrust upon the residential and commercial properties of U.S. cities. The industry soon designated pure fire insurance—once the only game in town—to be a "residual market," and that moniker captured the second-rate protection afforded by these policies. As reported by the Federal Insurance Administration, "the old fire insurance business was quickly converted into a residual class of business and the residual property insurance market came into being." Upending earlier thinking, insurers now came to consider the urban grid "relatively riskier" than new builds in lily-white suburbs. The reappraisal was informed by both race and the higher density of development in cities, which increased the "susceptibility to loss from the spreading of fire from an adjacent structure." Fire insurance became more and more expensive in the urban core even though the coverage it provided was spottier than the homeowners policies available in the suburban market. In the face of white and capital flight, city dwellers were left shortchanged and underinsured.[15]

These twin processes—the advent of comprehensive policies in the suburbs and the corresponding constriction of the urban insurance market—produced a racially tiered insurance market. Like its well-studied cousin the racially stratified housing market, the tiered insurance market entrenched existing racial segregation in the metropolis. Those who owned property in communities of color found it to be progressively more difficult to buy insurance. Separate and unequal, these areas had become a "market of last resort" that insurers "systematically bypassed." When property owners in these residual markets did manage to secure insurance, their policies were far more expensive, less comprehensive, and less reliable than the coverage offered to their suburban counterparts, sometimes exceeding the standard rates by as much as 400 percent.[16]

The birth of homeowners insurance in the suburbs was thus also the birth of insurance redlining in the cities. By 1960, "the wholesale red-lining of large urban areas by insurers virtually removed all hope of obtaining insurance," recounted one federal study. Insurers instructed their underwriters—the specialists who evaluate the hazards and price of insuring a particular risk—to pay close attention to the neighborhood and location of a building in determining whether to provide coverage. One 1964 bulletin issued by Aetna management directed its underwriters to draw "a *red line* around the questionable areas on territorial maps," paying particular attention to the "blighted areas," "the redevelopment operations," and the "economic makeup of the area." A 1964 memo from a vice president of the Travelers Insurance Company similarly instructed underwriters that "location of risk be afforded prime underwriting consideration," adding that they must "emphasize the importance of insuring only risks with locations situated in stable, better neighborhoods."[17]

As property insurers abandoned the city, a neighborhood's racial makeup became more decisive in the underwriting process. But companies hedged against accusations of racism by using novel terms such as "high-risk areas" and "knock-out areas." Sylvia Downer, a Black insurance broker from Brooklyn, decoded these euphemisms in a 1967 hearing on insurance redlining: "In New York these are called K.O. areas—meaning knock-out areas, in Boston they are called redline districts. Same thing: don't write the business. The companies explain their policy by describing these areas as blighted, substandard, disadvantaged, high-risk and by other such clichés. . . . I am inclined to believe that there is a good deal more to this policy determination than the coincidence that these areas are almost exclusively inhabited by Negroes and Puerto Ricans."[18]

Insurance redlining had a stranglehold effect on such "knock-out areas." When insurers restricted the availability of property coverage on a block or neighborhood basis, real estate transactions there slowed to a halt, and loan applications for repairs or renovations were destined to be declined. In an insurance desert, cautioned Philadelphia mayor James Tate in 1967, financial life in general would shrivel and wilt: "Far from being the result of blighting influences, the inability to obtain adequate and reliable insurance is in itself a serious cause of blight." Not only housing but commercial activity, too, was at risk. As a Newark insurance agent observed, "The inability to provide insurance in the Newark area causes many businesses to relocate, discontinue their operation, and the general area to become blighted." In short, the withdrawal of property and casualty insurance threw a wrench into the routine workings of urban capitalism. "A neighborhood without insurance," warned the New York Urban Coalition, "is a neighborhood doomed to death."[19]

How property insurance redlining affected homeowners and business owners of color is easy enough to see. More complex is grasping what it meant for Black and Brown tenants and consumers, who constituted a disproportionate share of the rental population in most cities. The most direct manifestation of redlining on their lives was the tightening of the nascent renter's insurance market, making it difficult for tenants to protect their belongings. But it also influenced the behavior of landlords. The unavailability of property insurance—or its exorbitant cost—was among the factors that led landlords to cut services, scale back on maintenance, and begin "milking" their buildings for rental payments. Because so much of the redlining literature is focused on the mortgage market, we risk overlooking how insurance unavailability curbed landlords' ability to access loans for renovations and repairs. The effects on tenants could be disastrous. Many watched in dismay as their heat was cut off, their plumbing became unreliable, and other essential services lapsed.[20] Although insurance served to protect the interests of property holders, the industry's withdrawal from U.S. cities was thus felt most acutely by poor communities of color, despite their lower rates of homeownership.

Insurance redlining should be understood as one crucial link in a chain that has become known as the "urban crisis": the confluence of industrial relocation, white and Black middle-class flight, the corresponding loss of a city's tax base, ruinous urban renewal projects, blockbusting, the withdrawal of social services, and the arrival of Puerto Ricans and Black and white southerners into cities hemorrhaging manufacturing jobs. The term "urban crisis" came into vogue amid the great rebellions of the 1960s, and ever since, it has often been reduced to them. When the uprisings get cast as the dramatic climax of the urban crisis, the events that followed become little more than an overdetermined epilogue. In the process, insurance redlining and its connections to the crisis have been forgotten.[21]

The fire-ravaged skylines of the 1960s left such an enduring mark on American culture that they have obscured the far more destructive and more protracted arson wave of the 1970s, a phenomenon with deep ties to the insurance market. Crucially, the uprisings of the 1960s do not simply overshadow the arson wave in popular memory; rather, these two distinct phenomena were and are frequently conflated as being one and the same. In 1970, a few years after the uprisings had ebbed and the arson wave had begun, presidential adviser Daniel Patrick Moynihan warned Richard Nixon that fires had become "endemic" to Black neighborhoods: "Fires are in fact a 'leading indicator' of social pathology for a neighborhood. They come first. Crime, and the rest, follows. The psychiatric interpretation of fire-setting is complex, but it relates to the types of personalities which slums produce." And a 1974 report commissioned by the Law Enforcement Assistance Administration argued, falsely, that "the rapid increase in incendiary rates that is noticeable for at least the past 20 years seems to be related to rises in the political, spite, and vandalism types of fires." The conflation persists, including among historians. As Bronx-based community organizer Harry DeRienzo reflected in 2008, "Even now, many people believe that the people who lived in the South Bronx and other inner city areas across the nation actually burned their own homes."[22]

The two eras were indeed linked, just not the way many assume. Although the arsons of the 1970s were not for protest but for profit, the governmental and corporate reaction to the 1960s uprisings had set the stage. Property insurance was the thread that braided together the tumultuous 1960s and what became, for U.S. cities, the disastrous 1970s. While those connections have been overlooked by historians, they were a concern for legislators in the era of the Kerner Commission and Lyndon Johnson's Great Society. Some lawmakers even singled out insurance redlining as a cause of the 1960s uprisings. For Senator Philip Hart of Michigan, "one of the things which makes for unrest" was the policy of "instructing representatives of insurance companies to get into the business of race." Though Hart's indictment of the insurance industry was notable for being relatively explicit, his concern was shared by lawmakers in both parties. And this concern can be traced directly to the industry's response to the uprisings.[23]

+++

BY 1967—their fifth consecutive year—the urban revolts had sent the property insurance industry into a tailspin. After a summer that saw the most destructive of the decade's uprisings roil Newark and Detroit, Seymour Smith, vice president of the Travelers Insurance Company, warned, "We cannot economically cope with the potentials of massive destruction resulting from drastic social upheaval and the breakdown of law and order." Differentiating between "acts of God," like hurricanes—which, in an era predating the public discourse around climate change, were presumed to arise solely from natural causes—and these socially produced catastrophes, Smith insisted, "I doubt if there is any individual in this room that really knows or has a strong ability to completely predict what is going to happen in the nature of social change. It is the completely unknown that is staggering our industry." For an insurer to lose faith in its predictive capacity is akin to a fortune teller losing their crystal ball. Prediction is the very stuff of insurance; without it, Travelers and its competing firms would be rudderless.[24]

Describing the rebellions as a "cloud [that] hangs over" the insurance industry, Smith positioned them as beyond the pale of insurability. Yet, partly because much of the industry had already redlined U.S. cities, the insurable losses stemming from the uprisings were negligible compared to far more destructive "acts of God." And insuring against "fire losses due to riot" was nothing new for the industry. Something else besides dollar losses or underwriting norms was at work.[25]

One reason the rebellions so unnerved the property insurance industry was that all the commotion threatened to draw the attention of federal regulators. Since 1945, when the McCarran-Ferguson Act terminated a brief period of federal regulation and replaced it with a patchwork of state insurance departments, the industry had worked feverishly to maintain the system of state regulation. Having wriggled out of Washington's grasp, insurers enjoyed extraordinary immunity from federal anti-trust laws. But charges of insurance redlining threatened to rouse state and federal regulators from their slumber. By 1967, insurance companies in numerous states had already grappled with local accusations of redlining. Hanging over property insurers was the ever-present threat of regulations that would encroach upon the autonomy of companies' underwriting departments.[26]

On a more primal level, the uprisings had sent the industry into what is best described as a racialized panic, convulsing the international insurance market. Days after the Detroit uprising, the London *Times* estimated—hyperbolically—that "rioting in major U.S. cities threatened property and liability companies with their worst claims losses in history," surpassing the $715 million in losses from Hurricane Betsy in 1965. (Betsy's losses were later estimated to be over $1 billion, a first for a natural disaster in the United States.) Only a few weeks passed before firms learned that these predictions were grossly exaggerated, but the damage had been done. The London *Times* story struck fear into the hearts of the U.S. insurers, which were acutely aware of the paper's proximity to Lloyd's of London, the world's oldest and largest market for reinsurance (a practice that enables insurers to pass along some of their liabilities to other insurance companies, thus reducing their exposure to risk). As feared, the article prompted Lloyd's to cut off its supply of reinsurance. Any withdrawal from the United States on the part of Lloyd's of London was sure to send shock waves through the entire industry: in an era that saw an increasingly globalized financial sector, 30 percent of the U.S. property insurance market was dependent on Lloyd's.[27]

The shock waves hit and quickly reverberated. State insurance departments received widespread reports that insurers were cutting the already scant supply of property insurance in U.S. cities. For Newark's Morris Spielberg, the director of a neighborhood merchants association, these cancellations spelled doom for local businesses. "The insurance companies are swiftly and firmly putting us out of business—one by one," he told the Newark *Star-Ledger*. "As far as the retail business community is concerned, these are the real after-effects of the riots." Spielberg blamed insurance cancellations for the closure of nearly forty stores in his area and noted that Black-owned businesses were disproportionately targeted: "The worst hit merchants are the Negroes. The Negro merchant in most cases has absolutely no coverage and can't buy it." An owner of a local barbershop despaired: "I'm a Negro. What are my chances of getting insurance in this area?"[28]

In the summer of 1967, facing the likelihood of a final mass exodus of insurance from U.S. cities, many state insurance departments implemented a ninety-day mandatory freeze on policy cancellations. Though there were reports of insurers violating the freeze, this measure gave the industry some time to more closely review the magnitude of the losses. Before the ashes had settled in Newark and Detroit, insurers hurriedly dis-

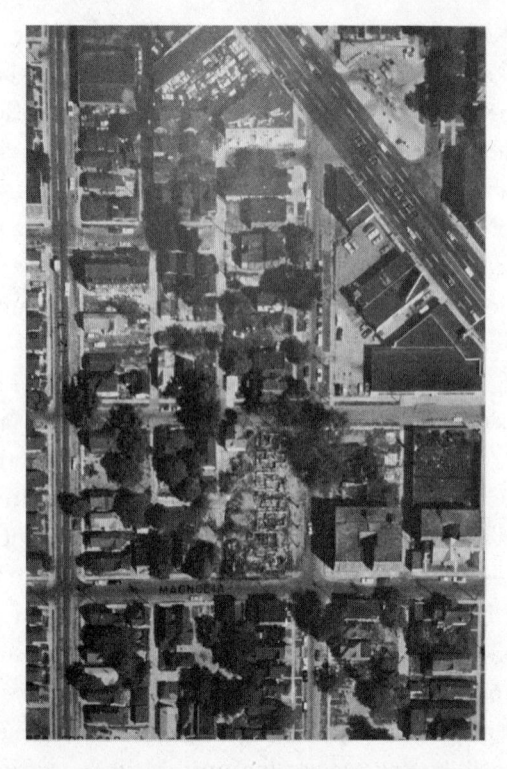

Seeing like an insurer: aerial photographs enabled the insurance industry to quickly appraise the damage from uprisings in cities like Detroit, sometimes while they were still underway.

patched claims adjusters to survey the damage. By 1967, adjusters with the General Adjustment Bureau were already experienced in this realm, having cut their teeth in Watts and elsewhere. In Detroit, the adjusters were not immediately permitted to enter the affected areas, so the bureau developed "an innovation in the prompt assessment of property damage—the mapping of a disaster area through the use of aerial photography." On July 25, while the rebellion was still underway, GAB arranged for photographs to be taken from altitudes of fifteen hundred to three thousand feet. The photographs were like an insurantial X-ray. They revealed what it meant to see like an insurer, with housing abstracted from its residents and property stripped down to its raw, depopulated form.[29]

Following this flurry of adjustment activity, insurers soon realized that the initial damage estimates reported by the London *Times* had been overblown; nonetheless, the reappraisal did little to shake Lloyd's or the broader industry's resolve to retreat from the urban market. The insurance losses from the summer of 1967 totaled less than $75 million, about *one-tenth* of the $715 million figure first proposed. In the final analysis, uprising-related losses made up only about 1 percent of insurance premiums written nationally in 1967, compared to 20 percent from Hurricane Betsy, two years earlier. "Yet no hurricane or series of hurricanes or threat of future hurricanes has produced an insurance crisis of the proportions that now face us in the aftermath of the riots," observed David Dykhouse, Michigan's commissioner of insurance.[30]

What, then, can account for the industry's panicked desire to flee from the American city once and for all? Monetary loss alone cannot explain the impulse. A Michigan insurance regulator conceded as much: "The problem from the point of view of the insurance industry was not so much that it could not absorb its liability under the fire policy." Instead of "unbearable dollar losses," what the "riots did produce was a loss of faith in the efficacy of past experience as a guide to future losses." That is to say, the threat posed by the uprisings was less about underwriting losses than about the recalibration of racialized risk.[31]

Industry professionals define insurance as a contract that promises financial protection against specific risks. But insurance is also a mode of narrating history and a means of speculating on the future. The reactions of the property insurance industry to the uprisings thus have much to tell us about how the underwriter of American capitalism perceived the meaning of Black rebellion as both a historical phenomenon and a possible future. For insurers, what was most terrifying about the rebellions was their potential to persist. Surveying the U.S. urban landscape in 1967, what they saw was the nation's property under threat from unremitting Black revolt. An executive from Travelers predicted, "There is little to indicate that urban social unrest is subsiding." James Bentley, head of the National Association of Insurance Commissioners, shared a similar assessment: "The frightening thing is that the insurance industry today apparently has an actuarial conviction that riots are going to continue."[32]

Proceeding from this "actuarial conviction," the insurance industry's prognostications took on a decidedly dystopian cast, projecting Black revolt for the foreseeable future. Such projections offer us a vivid glimpse of racial capitalism in this moment of upheaval. The prospect of ongoing rebellion needed to be quantified, and within that actuarial assessment we can witness racial hierarchy and the imperatives of capital accumulation becoming entwined. How would Black resistance get converted into dollars and cents? And how would that translation of mass struggle into the language of property be used to indemnify capital interests against future threats?

The collective fury animating the uprisings had forced the insurance industry to adjust its calculus of urban risk. Whereas before 1967, insurance companies had approached the issue with a degree of resignation, the events in Detroit and Newark tipped the actuarial balance, and insurers reframed the uprisings as fundamentally uninsurable hazards. The trade publication *Best's Weekly* claimed that the rebellions were "manifestly beyond the realm of underwriting" because the insurance contracts "never contemplated a situation such as Watts or Detroit." The uprisings were distinguished from natural disasters like hurricanes or routine perils like residential fires. Unlike such natural or mundane threats, the rebellions brought "social losses" that were ostensibly outside the underwriting responsibilities of the industry. The commissioner of insurance for California argued that "the very fact of its unpredictability" made urban revolt "something that an underwriter cannot cope with, and an actuary cannot rate."[34]

The industry may have claimed that insurance contracts never imagined a Watts or Detroit, but riot insurance had been a standard coverage since the labor upheavals of the early twentieth century. Insurers first began offering it following the attempted 1914 bombing that targeted John D. Rockefeller in retribution for his role in the Ludlow Massacre of striking mineworkers and their families in Colorado. The bombing gained notoriety when it was linked to the Industrial Workers of the World and prominent anarchist Alexander Berkman, leading insurers to begin selling protection from explosions. Labor unrest over the course of the next decade, especially during the strike wave of 1919, generated further demand for such policies. In 1943, riot coverage was added into New York's basic fire insurance policy, which set the standard for all other states.[35]

The insurance industry had billed its riot insurance coverage as protection against popular unrest, as one method the owners of property could use to insulate capital from the claims of labor. The relative paucity of large-scale, unsanctioned property destruction from the 1920s to the early 1960s spared most insurers from incurring sizable riot-related losses during these four decades. In the 1960s, when the hazard that these policies were designed to protect against finally arrived, many insurers sidestepped liability by redefining the uprisings as uninsurable. For an insurance industry already extricating itself from the urban market, the rebellions gave them a final push.

The result was actuarial retribution: insurance cancellations were rife, redlining surged, and the racially tiered insurance market hardened. In late 1967, Carrie B. Johnson, who owned a drugstore and an adjacent liquor store in predominately Black North Omaha, Nebraska, received cancellation notices from a number of insurers that had underwritten her stores for decades. One such letter explained, "Due to the location of your store ... and the more than probably uncontrollable damage which might occur at any time, due to riot, we do not feel that we can carry insurance in this case." Acknowledging that Johnson had been "an excellent insured," Alliance cited "the location of your store" as the basis for canceling her insurance, effectively informing Johnson that she had been redlined.[36]

+++

ONCE THE UPRISINGS had been deemed ineligible for indemnity, the industry pushed the financial burden onto the state. "This is fundamentally a social problem for which the government has a heavy responsibility," telegraphed the president of the American Insurance Association (AIA) to policymakers on August 12, 1967, two weeks after the Detroit rebellion. What the AIA was seeking was tantamount to a federal bailout. Its proposal, a federal riot reinsurance program, would empower the Department of Housing and Urban Development and the U.S. Treasury to collect contributions from insurance companies and create an untaxed fund indemnifying the industry against large riots. With Lloyd's of London having retreated from the U.S. market, insurers wanted the federal government to secure the nation's property against uprising-related losses. The U.S. Treasury would be the backstop in the event of major unrest in the future.[37]

The industry had little trouble shepherding the federal government in the direction of riot reinsurance. Its conduit was the Hughes Panel, which convened for its first meeting just over a week after the AIA's telegram. Six more closed-door sessions followed. Governor Hughes, the son of an insurance broker and prison guard, had vowed to draw "the line between the jungle and the law" during the Newark rebellion, and although the panel postured as a progressive body, it ultimately shored up property rights above all else. Despite conducting some three thousand interviews—most of them in the renter-dense cities of Boston, Cleveland, Detroit, Newark, Oakland, and St. Louis—the researchers were unapologetic about speaking only to "owners of dwellings but not tenants." That data was then translated into policy by the panel, which not only counted insurance executives among its members but had a staff consisting largely of insurance personnel. Almost inevitably, their recommendations aligned closely with the interests of the insurance and real estate industries. The proposals were made law within six months, enacted by the Urban Property Protection and Reinsurance Act as part of the Housing and Urban Development Act of 1968. The first head of the Federal Insurance Administration, established by the same legislation to oversee the program, acknowledged the industry's success in steering its outcome: "Reinsurance . . . was essentially proposed by the industry, to and through the Hughes Panel, to the Congress."[38]

Of the twenty-five largest property insurers in the country, twenty-three joined the riot reinsurance program within the first two months. The eagerness to accept governmental assistance was something of a historical oddity, as we've seen. According to one Hughes Panel staffer, "The industry, usually fearful of federal involvement, seemed to beckon to the Colossus on the Potomac with open arms. . . . Some cynics have described their descent on Washington as the most successful poor peoples' march in history." Insurance executives and members of the Hughes Panel were surprisingly candid about the industry's hope for federal assistance. At one early Hughes Panel meeting, Frank Wozencraft, assistant attorney general and a member of the panel, was asked if he wanted the federal government involved. He answered bluntly, "Not the government—just its money."[39]

When property insurers transferred their liabilities onto the federal government, they not only off-loaded their contractual responsibilities but conveniently ignored the role their own redlining had played, and continued to play, in deepening metropolitan inequality. Yet by advocating for federal relief through the Hughes Panel, insurers risked airing their dirty laundry, thereby exposing themselves to unwanted regulations. Even though a majority of the Hughes Panel staff were industry personnel, insurers still attempted to keep the investigation on a short leash. In at least one instance, the industry was charged with sabotaging the panel's work. In November 1967, commission staffers were to meet with roughly one hundred Detroit homeowners whose insurance had been dropped. Less than a quarter of the confirmed attendees showed up. "Inquiry Suspects Sabotage," read the front-page headline in the *Michigan Chronicle*, reporting that registered attendees had received phone calls falsely notifying them of the meeting's cancellation.[40]

Petty machinations would go only so far. The industry's broader solution was to wrest control of the regulatory wheel and steer national policy itself. A grand bargain was struck: property insurers purportedly agreed to cease redlining "riot-affected areas" in exchange for federal reinsurance for the uprisings. As Governor Hughes articulated the compromise, "Only after the industry and states have initiated affirmative action to solve the first problem of making adequate insurance available, should the possibility of federal government financial backup be considered with respect to the second problem." Hughes's use of the term "affirmative action" was intentional—the concept had been popularized by JFK in a 1961 executive order establishing the forerunner to the Equal Employment Opportunity Commission. But the industry's acquiescence to anti-redlining legislation was in fact an attempt to neutralize the redlining debate before public outcry might provoke more dramatic change.[41]

Thus the Hughes Panel became the means for warding off more stringent legislation, by setting the terms through which the industry would formally renounce its redlining practices. As panel member A. A. Roberts counseled his colleagues in the industry, "Investigations in Washington and the state capitals should not be viewed with alarm but should be viewed as presenting opportunities to find new solutions to problems that have plagued us for too long."[42]

+++

ONE OF THE "new solutions" Roberts had in mind was the public-private insurance company that the Hughes Panel named the Fair Access to Insurance Requirements plan. Established on a statewide basis, FAIR plans (each participating state had its own insurance facility, or "plan") were enacted into federal law by the same piece of legislation that introduced riot reinsurance. The Urban Property Protection and Reinsurance Act, which one analyst deemed "the most significant insurance legislation adopted in this century," was designed to end redlining by requiring insurers to assess each risk individually, without regard to location. FAIR plans were forbidden from considering conditions extrinsic to the property in question, such as "past area riots, general neighborhood decay, or the atmosphere of unrest." Essentially, the FAIR plan was fashioned as an actuarial "affirmative action" for properties that had been relegated to the residual market and thus disqualified from accessing insurance at reasonable rates. What the FAIR plan did not do was eliminate the residual market itself; FAIR plans' high-cost, low-coverage policies were most affordable to absentee landlords with sizable capital reserves. Nor did FAIR plan legislation prohibit insurance companies in the private, voluntary market—the majority of insurers—from redlining. Instead, FAIR plans actually enabled private insurance companies to hasten their departure from U.S. cities by soaking up the policyholders purged by retreating insurers. In numerous states, FAIR plans remain the largest property insurers to this day.[43]

The blueprint for the FAIR plan was the Hughes Panel's report, *Meeting the Insurance Crisis of Our Cities*, which positioned insurance access as a salve to the wounds of the metropolis. "Insurance is essential to revitalize our cities," the report began. "It is a cornerstone of credit.... Communities without insurance are communities without hope." The panel's report characterized insurance as a fundamental right of property owners. Upon its release, President Johnson endorsed this view, asserting, "Insurance is a basic necessity for responsible property owners and is vital to the rebuilding of our cities." Betty Furness, Johnson's special assistant for consumer affairs, expanded on this idea, designating property insurance as a civil rights issue: it "is almost a matter of life and death.... If the residents of our ghettos cannot obtain adequate insurance at reasonable rates, they are condemned to a life without security."[44]

Linking insurance access to the achievement of Black citizenship and the growth of Black businesses, the FAIR plan was a tactic of counterinsurgency. In a moment of surging Black radicalism, insurance could offer a mechanism of mollification and a tool of incorporation. As *Newsday* put it, "A fire insurance policy means more to a ghetto resident than a promise of protection against loss by fire. It is a necessary ingredient in self improvement."[45]

By 1971, there were FAIR plans in twenty-six states, most of them along the coasts and in the Midwest; plans have also been established in Puerto

Meeting The Insurance Crisis Of Our Cities
A Report by The President's National Advisory Panel on Insurance in Riot-Affected Areas

The January 1968 report of the Hughes Panel. Its proposals were implemented by Congress within six months.

Rico and Washington, D.C. FAIR plans "pooled" the registered property insurance companies operating in a given state, all of which were required to participate. The resulting pool created a new corporate entity that spread the risks and rewards of insuring the residual market among the state's licensed insurers. Although federal legislation launched the program and federal riot reinsurance was the reward for insurer participation, FAIR plans were designed to reflect "creative federalism, insurance style," with relatively nominal federal involvement, according to a staffer with the Michigan Governor's Commission on Insurance Availability in Urban Core Areas, which created a precursor of the state's FAIR plan: "The Panel sought to avoid the disturbance of existing patterns of state and federal regulation, and even the appearance of coercive regulation itself."[46]

A state's FAIR plan was no ordinary insurance company; it was both nominally public and a private proxy for the insurance industry. FAIR plans were public in the sense that they were answerable to state insurance departments, followed a set of federal mandates, and served as vouchers for insurers to enroll in the federal reinsurance program. At the same time, they were financially backed by private firms, each of which possessed a stake proportional to its share of the statewide insurance market. A FAIR plan merged the total underwriting capabilities of all the insurers in a state, welding them into a new corporate mold. The pool then evenly distributed the liabilities and gains of the residual market that insurers had previously spurned. If the industry was forced to renounce redlining, it would do so without disrupting the distribution of profits; indeed, it would do so without disrupting the racially tiered insurance market at all. Even so, FAIR plans should not be mistaken for an elaborate accounting trick. They were actual, physical corporate entities with private workforces that could number in the hundreds. And they were governed by boards of directors handpicked by the state's largest insurance companies.[47]

In sum, for an industry on the defensive in the late 1960s, the FAIR plan was an ingenious gambit, advancing the interests of property insurers in at least four areas. For one, it was a public relations strategy, a means of deflecting criticism of the industry's handling of uprising-related claims and its decades-long withdrawal from U.S. cities. As one of FAIR's architects, A. A. Roberts, explained in an editorial urging industry support of the program, "our public image leaves something to be desired." Roberts linked the PR strategy to a second benefit of the program: its ability to redirect the redlining debate away from government-administered solutions and toward an industry-led initiative. He warned, "We will be on trial in the months ahead. It cannot be emphasized too strongly that we must offer positive solutions to the vexing problems we face." But the FAIR plan was not only a bulwark against bad press or government oversight; it was also a source of industry enrichment, albeit an indirect one—it entitled insurers to federal riot reinsurance at a time when other sources of reinsurance had dried up. And finally, FAIR plans could charge their customers higher rates than were generally permissible by state insurance departments, which set the price of insurance.[48]

The Urban Property Protection and Reinsurance Act of 1968 thus proved to be, as the *Chicago Law Review* noted, "a boon to the insurance companies, according to legal scholars." Yet insurers tended to "claim FAIR plan losses drain profits," an argument that the newly created Federal Insurance Administration found to be "without merit." An FIA study showed that "insurer profitability in FAIR plan states for fire insurance, including FAIR plan experience, exceeds the profit levels in non–FAIR plan states." This did not mean that individual FAIR plans turned a profit; for much of the 1970s, they did not. But when FAIR plans experienced losses, they were spread evenly across all companies operating in a state, with no company suffering a competitive disadvantage relative to another. What's more, insurers had the ability to hot-potato any losses to consumers. "It's pretty obvious that they pass the losses on to private policy holders," observed an official in the Government Accountability Office.[49]

+++

IN NEIGHBORHOODS THAT the FAIR plans were designed to assist, the impact was, in many cases, nothing short of cataclysmic. Far from eliminating the residual market, the plans sanctified its existence. FAIR plans absorbed the policyholders cast aside by insurance companies as the latter continued their retreat to the edges of the metropolis, gesturing toward their participation in the program as they closed their underwriting books to neighborhoods of color once and for all. In 1978, the Federal Insurance Administration itself acknowledged that the FAIR plans had accelerated the industry's disinvestment from U.S. cities, enabling insurers to redline with impunity. In the words of the FIA, the FAIR plans had furnished "an escape valve" through which property insurers continued to flee to the suburbs. Within a few years, it was clear that the FAIR plans not only failed to disrupt the fundamental workings of the racially tiered insurance market but had actually served to deepen its divides. As one Chicago-based community organizer testified before the U.S. Senate in 1980, "Residents of my neighborhood now commonly refer to the Illinois FAIR Plan as 'back of the bus' insurance."[50]

And like the Jim Crow bus, the FAIR plans' lines of demarcation were variable and erratic. To delineate the target zones for its insurance program, the Hughes Panel had introduced new terminology: the "riot-prone" or "riot-affected" area. What exactly was a "riot-prone area"? The panel failed to offer any working definition, but in practice, it was synonymous with urban Black and Brown neighborhoods. In Chicago, for instance, 90 percent of the Illinois FAIR plan policies were concentrated in the city's predominantly Black South and West Sides, as of 1979. This held true on a national scale, according to the FIA: "There is a strong correlation between FAIR plan writing and the racial composition of a neighborhood."[51]

The idea of riot-proneness was a way to demarcate Black and Brown neighborhoods using the clinical jargon of risk. For the insurance industry, riot-proneness was an inherent trait of Black communities, and thus a core liability of the U.S. metropolis. But insurers could not say that outright. By 1968, the overt racism of Jim Crow had become taboo and required new avenues of expression. The language of risk offered a realm where racial discrimination could survive in legally and socially acceptable form. In some ways, this was not new. Risk had long been racialized; life insurers had used race-based premiums since the early days of the industry, and the invention of a statistical link between Blackness and criminality was the handiwork of a Prudential actuary in 1896. But with the dawning of a new "color-blind" consensus in response to the legal and legislative victories of the civil rights movement, the importance of risk as a marker of race grew, and it spread outside the insurance industry. Consider which populations are usually implied by "at risk" or "high-risk" or "risky"—phrases now ubiquitous in the education and criminal legal sectors—which map difference with terms lifted out of an underwriter's manual. Even being deemed a "worthy risk" can have profound and treacherous effects, as Keeanga-Yamahtta Taylor captures in the phrase "predatory inclusion."[52]

A few years after the establishment of the FAIR plans, the terms "riot-prone" and "riot-affected" were retired from the industry's lexicon amid a "waning fear of civil unrest," as the New York FAIR plan put it. When the uprisings dwindled after the early 1970s, insurers' "actuarial conviction that riots are going to continue" was shown to be nothing more than false fortune-telling. But the industry's remedy to that flawed prognosis—the FAIR plan—endured.[53]

By the end of the 1970s, a new term would gain currency within FAIR plans across the nation. The FAIR plan "is committed to insure buildings in *arson-prone areas* with high degrees of vacancy or even total vacancy," noted the vice president of the New York plan. Within a few years of the Hughes Panel's report, the "arson-prone area" had almost imperceptibly replaced its "riot-prone" forebear, a process enabled by the conceptual slippage between the two eras, the two dynamics. It was in propelling the arson wave that the FAIR plans would claim their greatest impact on U.S. cities.[54]

It is worth noting that the Hughes Panel was warned that the FAIR plans would benefit landlords and hurt their tenants. Frank Farwell, a member of the panel, cautioned that with the FAIR plan's imprudent underwriting, "you are telling somebody who owns a tenement that if you put a torch to it you can sell it to the insurance company." Farwell's premonitions went unheeded, and the Hughes Panel failed to incorporate robust anti-arson measures into its FAIR plan proposals.[55]

That the dynamic set in motion by the Hughes Panel was far from inevitable can also be seen in the host of alternatives proposed to the panel during its deliberations. As the Illinois AFL-CIO wrote to the panel, "The answer or solution to civil rights disorders is steady employment. Anything less than that will not solve the problem." In its letter to the Hughes Panel, the Rhode Island AFL-CIO advised against a privatized solution to the insurance crisis: "If we can produce electricity through a publicly owned power corporation (The TVA)... then why can we not create a national publicly owned insurance company to take those risks which profit-seeking companies turn down?"[56]

The Hughes Panel never seriously considered a publicly administered program, a striking departure from the FAIR plan's legislative sibling, the National Flood Insurance Program, which was made law by the same act of Congress in 1968 and which involved heavy federal subsidies to homeowners along the nation's coastlines. According to George Bernstein, the first administrator of the FIA, which was established to oversee the dual programs, the National Flood Insurance Program was "an insurance program in name only.... It is a delusion to believe that the National Flood Insurance Program is anything but a federally subsidized trade-off under which something called 'insurance' is substituted for disaster relief." Whereas the FAIR plans furnished high-cost, low-value insurance policies that further decimated urban landscapes, the NFIP underwrote a flurry of new construction on the nation's coasts. One historian has shown that "the nation's fastest-growing counties" in the 1970s tended to be on the coasts, and the FIA itself found that "developers were advertising the existence of flood insurance as an incentive to move into flood prone areas." While the federal government refused to directly underwrite the rebuilding of the nation's cities in the aftermath of the uprisings, its subsidies to homeowners on the nation's coastlands reached astronomical levels. In 1980, Bernstein reported that the NFIP entailed an annual administrative cost of

$500 million and exposed the federal government to $70 billion in potential property loss.[57]

In effect, the National Flood Insurance Program bankrolled the buildup of coastal property, a full third of which consisted of second homes. In other words, the NFIP was, like many other federal housing programs, a subsidy to white homeowners. What distinguished it from the Federal Housing Administration, the GI Bill, and other midcentury housing programs that subsidized white homeownership is that the NFIP owed its existence to programs intended to aid neighborhoods of color: the FAIR plan and riot reinsurance. Calls to introduce federal flood insurance had echoed around the halls of Congress since the days of the Truman administration, but the proposed legislation had proven too divisive. The NFIP passed in 1968 only due to the Hughes Panel's legislative momentum. As Bernstein reflected, "The flood insurance program would never have been enacted without riot reinsurance." Though the FAIR plan had been branded as an "affirmative action" to end redlining, the National Flood Insurance Program was in fact a much more generous government subsidy. As of 2022, the program's debt was $20 billion and counting, a burden shouldered by taxpayers and produced by unsustainable, often luxury coastal development.[58]

The birth of the NFIP roughly coincided with the emerging scientific consensus that anthropogenic climate change poses an existential risk to low-lying coastlines and floodplains worldwide. Yet in the United States, there is probably no federal policy more decisive than the NFIP in spurring development on land all but destined to succumb to sea level rise. Between 1970 and 2010, the population of coastal areas rose by 40 percent; every single new mortgage written in the floodplains required flood insurance.[59]

When set against the reckless scope of the National Flood Insurance Program, the narrowness of the FAIR plan comes into view. As one op-ed directed at Chairman Hughes counseled, "There is, of course, a way to insure 100-percent protection. That would be to eliminate the causes of riots, thus eliminating the riots and the damage that follows. After all, when did a town with full employment and decent housing for all its residents have a riot?"[60]

Given that the majority of rebellions found their spark in episodes of police violence, the Hughes Panel's apparent indifference to police conduct is especially glaring. Granted, the subject fell more explicitly under the Kerner Commission's purview. But considering that insurance rates had long been tied to the performance of the local fire service, an underwriter's evaluation of a police department's proclivity to violence would not have been so far-fetched. Encouraging such appraisals might have created a financial disincentive to police violence: a viable if imperfect strategy for rigging racial capitalism *against* the police power that sustains it. There did exist a precedent for this type of underwriting assessment. Following the policing killings of seventeen Black Detroiters during a brutal episode of civil unrest in June 1943, a group of Black businessmen formed "an insurance company that will insure clients against police brutality." The coverage offered by the company was geared toward "the Negro who, because of his militancy in behalf of his race, is often the target of a policeman's pistol or nightstick."[61]

For the Hughes Panel, the locus of risk was not to be found in the "policeman's pistol or nightstick" but in the racialized maelstrom of the "riot-prone area." It was a fateful cartographic error. The Hughes Panel's understanding of "the insurance crisis" would have real, material impacts on the American city. Insurance companies operate by quantifying fear, and the uprisings had triggered sheer hysteria. One result was the FAIR plan, which offered a political solution to the dangers besetting property and capital in the late 1960s. But as the nation entered a new decade, it became clear to industry veterans that with FAIR, "we have jumped out of the frying pan into the fire."[62]

TWO

The Brownlining of the Bronx

The Bronx is next.
—SONIA SANCHEZ, 1968[1]

Firefighters battle an all-hands blaze on Ogden Avenue near Yankee Stadium in 1974. Five families were displaced by the fire.

"We would rather walk the street, you know, at night than go inside our apartments," Hedy Byrd told the Senate Subcommittee on Investigations during four days of hearings on "arson for hire" in 1978. As a mother of four children, Byrd had traveled from Harlem to Washington, D.C., to "represent most of the mothers in my neighborhood who have young kids and are concerned" about the "fear inside your home, thinking that someone is going to come to set the place on fire." Having survived two arson fires in fifteen months, both of which remained unsolved, Byrd's fears were well-founded. In early 1977, her family was evicted by an incendiary blaze at their apartment building in the Morris Heights section of the Bronx. It took a few months for her to locate a new permanent home, but eventually they landed in the Sugar Hill neighborhood of Harlem. "For the first time in several years, I felt my children were living in safe housing," she recalled. Things seemed so stable that she decided to really settle in, purchasing her children brand-new beds on an installment plan.[2]

The family lived in the new home for eight fireless months before "the sound of breaking glass" interrupted their morning routines one day in May 1978. Panicked, Byrd ran to the window of her fourth-floor apartment and saw "flames shooting up from the lower floors." With the fire raging below them, she grabbed her nine-month-old and hurried her older children up the stairs and onto the roof. But during their frenzied evacuation, she lost track of her three-year-old son, Eric, and darted back down the smoke-filled stairwell to find him crying for help. Crawling on all fours, Hedy and Eric climbed back up the stairs, "gagging on the smoke until we reached the roof." Thanks to a neighbor, they figured out how to cross onto the roof next door, and they managed to escape. But everything they had was lost, including costly items purchased on credit. The beds were gone, yet Byrd's debt would not rest, and she was forced to keep up with the monthly payments. The city offered little in the way of relief besides putting the family up in a "very cramped" and temporary shelter hotel three miles away, far from their schools, friends, and fledgling social worlds. "It is very difficult, if not impossible to explain the trauma my children and I have gone through since being burned out," Byrd told the senators. Twice displaced, she and her family found themselves in free fall, and with little government support, they were expected to use their own parachutes. Under racial capitalism, the parachute was a fire insurance policy. But Byrd didn't have one.[3]

The New York FAIR plan, which had quickly become the dominant insurer in Black and Brown neighborhoods like Harlem and the South Bronx, would only sell policies to her landlord, not to tenants like her. The coming of the New York FAIR plan, beginning in 1968, did nothing to help fire refugees like Hedy Byrd. Yet it had transformed the insurance landscape surrounding her. For property owners, the arrival of the FAIR plan marked a dramatic departure from the redlining era. Supporters praised it as the antidote to redlining and the beginning of a new age of equitable insurance—an optimism captured by the term "greenlining," which would come into use in the mid-1970s. But in reality, the FAIR plan's policies left the racially stratified property insurance market intact, offering inadequate coverage at expensive rates. For policyholders, FAIR insurance could be thought of as "subprime" insurance: it cost far more than conventional insurance policies available to the suburban consumer, but did not include standard coverages like theft and liability.

The result was insurance brownlining—the convergence of redlining and greenlining—which expanded access to property insurance on unfavorable terms. Like one map superimposed on another, brownlining overlaid the successive eras of racial capitalism, with financialization layered atop the racial cartography of redlining. The timing was everything, especially in the Bronx, where the FAIR plan's influence was felt most acutely. Brownlining descended on the Bronx at the precise moment that the landlords who purchased FAIR policies were up in arms about the falling rate of rental profits, a lethal synchrony that exacerbated an already volatile real estate market.

+++

BEFORE THE BRONX burned beyond recognition, it burned on paper. Four years before Hedy Byrd's first fire, in September 1973, the borough received an ominous warning. In front of city hall, a group of Bronx landlords crowded around Ruben Klein, the president of the Bronx Realty Advisory Board, as he took a match to a rolled-up map of the borough. It was political theater; Klein used the map as a torch to ignite a four-by-five-foot

A pamphlet advertising the New York FAIR Plan, or the New York Property Insurance Underwriting Association, which began writing insurance policies in 1968. By 1970, it had become the largest underwriter of fire insurance in New York.

cardboard diorama of the Bronx. The aggrieved landlords had gathered in protest of the city's "rent controls which have been imposed on us for the last 30 years." The owners, whose organization represented twenty-five hundred apartment buildings, were dramatizing what they insisted would befall the borough if the city's rent-control regulations were not repealed. Unfortunately for Klein, the wind was not on his side, and after two attempts, the only thing he managed to burn was his own fingers. The diorama went unscathed; it ended up confiscated by the NYPD, which saddled Klein with a pair of summonses. The city government had done more to protect the miniature Bronx than it did the real thing.[4]

In hindsight, it is nearly impossible to interpret the demonstration as anything other than an overt threat, though Klein himself maintained that it was purely "symbolic." In any case, the choreographed stunt raises a number of questions. Why did the landlords insist that Bronx housing was a tinderbox? And if the owners of Bronx property saw a powder keg, what did its insurers, its arbiters of risk, see? Most importantly, what forms of protection could property insurance offer a city in crisis?[5]

In the 1970s and 1980s, a generation of campaigning politicians, well-meaning journalists, bottom-feeding filmmakers, lowlife landlords, scheming champions of law and order, and other pundits, speaking mostly as outsiders, used the borough's tribulations to advance agendas that did little to improve life in the Bronx. The image of the Bronx familiar to most Americans today is the same one they conjured while the borough was still aflame: a landscape of dilapidated buildings, a bacchanal of senseless crime, and people thought to be ravaging their own homes. As it did then, this crude effigy continues to stand in the way of comprehending the burning years and the urgent lessons they hold for us now.

How to name the forces that devastated the borough without shoring up those same tropes? The standard arc of the crisis narrative begins with the supposed glory days of the early to mid-twentieth century. It was in this era that the borough's tenemented expanse first became home to Jewish, Irish, Italian, and other ethnic white communities seeking a better quality of life than they had found in lower Manhattan's dense enclaves. The Bronx as it is known today was largely built in this period, during the three decades after it attained borough status, in 1898, and opened its first subway line, in 1905. Its ubiquitous five- and six-story walk-up apartments sprouted up almost overnight atop soil that had not long before grown grains and vegetables for Manhattan. According to the real estate interests that governed the borough, the purpose of the new Bronx was to furnish "dwellings for its citizens who labor outside of the borough." Land that had once supplied Manhattan's foodstuffs now reproduced its workforce. The Bronx functioned as a sprawling bedroom community for one of the fastest-growing cities in the world.[6]

With few exceptions, histories of the Bronx betray an Edison-bulbed nostalgia for this earlier era. We could call the genre the Bronx pastoral, and it is defined by an anguished wistfulness for "the way it was," which—not incidentally—is the tagline of *Back in the Bronx* magazine, a nostalgia rag that has published more than one hundred quarterly issues since 1992. The magazine and its kindred texts, including books like *The Bronx in the Innocent Years, 1890–1925* and *Boulevard of Dreams: Heady Times, Heartbreak, and Hope Along the Grand Concourse in the Bronx*, rejoice in bygone days of "egg creams, movie matinées, and stickball in the street." These works imagine a Bronx of limitless upward mobility, a place that served as a "staging ground for the American Dream," especially for Jewish residents, who made up 49 percent of the borough in 1930. For the first- and second-generation immigrant families who filled its apartment houses, a move up to the Bronx brought not only a change in address but a shift in one's race and class coordinates as well. During the first half of the twentieth century, the borough was a way station on the road to whiteness.[7]

The snapshot mourned in these accounts was taken before significant numbers of Black and Puerto Rican residents settled in the borough, which is to say before the onset of white flight. The Bronx pastoral commemorates racial exclusion. As late as 1940, Black and Puerto Rican residents represented only around 2 percent and 4 percent of the Bronx's population, respectively. Much of the western and northern portions of the borough remained "closed to black residents . . . right up to the early 1960s." While some authors writing in this tradition acknowledge the borough's history of exclusion, the tendency to frame the first half of the century as the Bronx's "innocent years" brands its later decades with an air of racial decline. In turn, the destruction of vast swaths of the Bronx in the 1970s is recalled as a moral outrage only to the extent that it represents, for its former inhabitants, a betrayal of their lost idyll. In a 1992 *New York Times* profile of the "Bronx of Yore," police officer Charles Medwin lamented, "This used to be a little piece of prosperity, but they destroyed it." He elaborated on that idea: "They burned it, welfared it, gouged it and then Co-op City finished it." But who were "they"?[8]

When the part of the villain is assigned to a single role, it is most often played by New York planning czar Robert Moses, who was the hand behind a host of projects that together transfigured the borough. Thanks to Robert Caro's famous book about Moses, *The Power Broker*, the Cross Bronx Expressway is typically identified as the opening salvo in the administrative assault on the Bronx. *The Power Broker*'s deep probing into how the Cross Bronx Expressway carved a "One Mile" incision across the torso of the Bronx in the 1950s is still remembered as a prime example of the violent excesses of urban renewal. Displacing thousands and tearing at the fabric of Jewish community life in East Tremont, the thoroughfare reduced the neighborhood's "very good, solid housing stock" to a mass of "ravaged hulks." Meanwhile, the New York City Housing Authority, also under Moses's thumb, constructed in the southern part of the borough what was once the "largest concentration of public housing anywhere in the country." Given renewal-era slum-clearance projects in Harlem, East Harlem, and San Juan Hill (also Moses ventures), Bronx public housing developments drew northward thousands of Black and Puerto Rican residents fleeing housing insecurity in Manhattan.[9]

For the borough's Black and Brown newcomers, the Bronx—especially what would soon become known as the South Bronx—was initially embraced as a refuge from Manhattan's bulldozers and segregated districts. "As housing went down in Harlem and El Barrio and in Brooklyn, the City brought people here," remembered Richard Tancl, a public school teacher who moved from East Harlem in 1964. "That's where the housing was," he recalled. "It was beautiful then." A generation earlier, Robert Gumbs and his family had left Harlem for the South Bronx for similar reasons: better housing and clearer skies. They made their 1941 move at the urging of the family doctor, who counseled that "the air was cleaner" in the northern borough. In the decades between Gumbs's and Tancl's respective arrivals, the South Bronx was distinguished by its relative absence of white resistance to Black and Brown in-migration. With its ethnic white resident base steeped in leftist unionism, the area was less inclined toward segregationist vitriol. Through the 1950s, the South Bronx could claim to be a beacon of interracial solidarity. It was here that activists with the Forest Neighborhood Committee successfully fought for the desegregation of Forest Houses, touted as the city's first integrated public housing development.[10]

But these experiments in desegregation were happening at the same time as the flight of Jewish, Irish, and Italian Bronxites, which took off in the 1940s and accelerated in the 1950s. At its peak in the 1970s, the exodus saw the borough bleed out three hundred thousand residents, one-fifth of its population. In most elegies of the borough, the death knell is sounded by the late-1960s opening of Co-op City in the far northeastern Bronx. Co-op City is the largest housing cooperative in the world, and as yet another Moses-backed project, it catered exclusively to the middle class, 80 percent of whom were white when it opened its doors. Although it was built to *contain* white flight, Co-op City is widely blamed for hastening the deterioration of the Grand Concourse, the Park Avenue of the Bronx, with one observer remarking, "It just siphoned people out of there like a vacuum cleaner."[11]

Accounts of these events often risk overemphasizing Moses's urbicidal footprint. The Bronx-raised critic Marshall Berman cautions that Moses "turned potential long-range entropy into sudden inexorable catastrophe." That is to say, Moses "left it forever unknown" whether the neighborhoods he tore down "would have collapsed or renewed themselves from within" were it not for his outsized mark on the built environment. There were, in fact, larger forces at work. What happened in the Bronx in the second half of the twentieth century was also happening in other New York City boroughs and in many other American cities. Industrial relocation to the suburbs and the Sunbelt saw New York City—like cities across the Northeast and Midwest—hemorrhage half a million manufacturing jobs from the late 1950s to the mid-1970s. And as it did elsewhere, mortgage redlining took its toll from the 1930s onward, cutting off oxygen to the Bronx real estate market and sending its buildings into a long cycle of disinvestment.[12]

The resulting loss of the tax base was a key factor in New York City's fiscal crisis, which came to a head in 1975 when the city's largest creditors—the banks that purchased its debt in the form of municipal bonds—refused to continue loaning it money. In order to regain access to the bond markets, the city was forced to submit to the austerity regime of the Municipal Assistance Corporation (MAC) and the Emergency Financial Control Board (EFCB), state-convened bodies that stripped the city of its governing autonomy and placed it in the hands of the financial elite. A new era in urban governance had begun, and New York City became a crucible for austerity politics. The unrivaled social services that had once distinguished the city now withered as its public workforce shrank by seventy thousand employees in just three years. Under the authority of MAC and the EFCB, with New York City teetering on the edge of bankruptcy and the stream of federal dollars into welfare and anti-poverty programs drying up, the Bronx became a shock absorber. Health care, education, sanitation, and other essential services, already in dire straits, descended to desperate levels. Even the once-untouchable fire department faced severe cuts; fifteen hundred firefighters were laid off between 1974 and 1977, and the resulting staffing shortages had ruinous consequences in the Bronx. "For many New Yorkers," writes historian Kim Phillips-Fein, "the city's willingness to cut back on fire protection was the most shocking aspect of the fiscal crisis."[13]

In 1976, Roger Starr, commissioner of the Housing and Development Administration, introduced the notion of "planned shrinkage," also known as urban triage. Starr urged the city to withdraw essential services like schools, health-care facilities, and subway stations from neighborhoods experiencing population loss, thereby pressuring the remaining residents to move to more densely populated areas. Starr's crosshairs fell on the South Bronx: "Large parts of the Bronx south of the Cross Bronx Expressway are virtually dead," he wrote. "They have been so reduced in population that block after block of apartment houses stand open to wind and sky, their windows smashed, their roofs burned, their plumbing pilfered." Predictably, Starr's prescriptions for the Bronx and other parts of the city stirred up immediate controversy, prompting his departure from city government. Despite Starr's brief tenure, chroniclers of the borough's crisis years have tended to emphasize planned shrinkage as the defining state and municipal policy in the 1970s Bronx.[14]

Yet things were not quite that simple. Although the borough certainly suffered under the governmental cutbacks in the wake of the fiscal crisis, it is a mistake to conflate state disinvestment with the premeditated decimation of the Bronx. There is little evidence of a sinister cabal plotting to eviscerate the Black and Brown sections of New York City. A conspiracy just wasn't necessary. All it took to destroy the borough was the fierce churn of racial capitalism at a moment of systemic crisis. The decisions of individual policymakers mattered, yes—but the disinvestment from the Bronx was much more haphazard, partial, and *un*planned than the notion of planned shrinkage implies. For one, planned shrinkage does little to explain how the Bronx came to be allocated one-third of all federally subsidized Section 8 housing units introduced in New York City between 1975 and 1980. And, as housing scholars have observed, it cannot account for the ways Roger Starr himself "helped steer remaining government subsidies into [housing] renovation programs, despite his quip about planned shrinkage."[15]

A more nuanced analysis was offered by a resident of the Bronx's 163rd Street named Carlos. His last name unprinted, Carlos told a journalist in 1975, "[Policymakers] don't think the area can be saved. They figure we're lost, so they might as well spend money somewhere else.... They're just waiting for the South Bronx to destroy itself." Indeed, the state's involvement in the borough—at least until the late 1970s—was characterized more by inaction, abandonment, and miscalculation than deliberate administrative intent. If the state did leave its fingerprints, it did so with the FAIR plan.[16]

+++

WHEN ROBERT B. COOPER, a Bronx real estate and insurance broker, learned of the Hughes Panel in October 1967, he wrote a letter voicing his support of its mission. Having sold property insurance in the Bronx for years, he was well acquainted with the problems of insurance availability in neighborhoods of color. "The small property owners in the ghetto areas are being rob[bed] by all insurance companies," he wrote. "Coverage for fire will cost a ghetto property owner from 4 times the manual [or normal] rate to 10 times the manual rate," a disparity that "only happens in black & Puerto Rican areas." Outraged over how these industry practices affected his brokerage and his neighborhood, Cooper asked, in all caps, "I ASK YOU SIR IS THIS FAIR?" The Hughes Panel dismissed Cooper's proposed solution, an assigned risk plan, which would challenge insurance redlining head-on by compelling insurers to cover all risks, albeit at elevated rates.[17]

Within a year of mailing his letter, Cooper would have learned that his advice went unheeded, and the Hughes Panel had instead opted to establish statewide FAIR plans. In his home state, the resulting entity was the New York Property Insurance Underwriting Association (NYPIUA). Enacted into law by Governor Nelson Rockefeller on April 8, 1968, after securing strong bipartisan support, the NYPIUA immediately and indelibly transformed the property insurance market in New York City, where over 80 percent of its business was concentrated. A year and a half after its launch, the NYPIUA stood as the largest underwriter of fire insurance policies in New York, issuing four times as many policies as the second-largest firm.[18]

Against the backdrop of the fiscal crisis and austerity politics, the growth of the NYPIUA and the state-backed residual market for property insurance is all the more striking. Its rise offers a dramatic contrast to the simultaneous downsizing of many other municipal, state, and federal government institutions, complicating historical narratives about this pivotal decade in U.S. political history. The 1970s represent an inflection point, an era when the already stunted welfare state began to atrophy. Through a process of marketization—also called neoliberalism—functions previously performed by government were turned over to the private sector. Meanwhile, as the welfare state contracted, the carceral state ballooned. With the rise of mass incarceration, the state turned to punitive policies, as opposed to (or sometimes in combination with) social services, to manage unemployment, homelessness, capital flight, and the growing inequalities of the age.[19]

Where did the FAIR plan fit in these twin processes? Rather than advancing a punitive or progressive political agenda, it picked up the slack of a social safety net riddled with holes and going limp. The program was a stopgap: as the United States entered a prolonged period of welfare retrenchment, the FAIR plan indemnified real estate and property insurers against the social and economic shocks of the urban crisis. Though the program responded to a similar set of pressures as the burgeoning carceral state, it aimed to generate security not through retributive policies but by protecting the financial interest of property. It was a regressive form of welfare state expansion, broadening the entitlements of citizenship for a chosen few: property owners. And because of the dynamics of property ownership in the Black and Brown neighborhoods it intended to serve, the primary recipient of its coverage was most often the landlord class. At the same time, the program served insurers by securing the elasticity—and the inequities—of the residual market. In this way, the reinsuring of the Bronx was an instance not of the welfare state but of the financialized state.[20]

Increased access to property insurance was no substitute for a robust social welfare system, especially for Bronxites, most of whom were renters, not owners. The FAIR plan's high-cost, low-value policies appeared at the same moment that the welfare state was being hollowed out, and while it was not intended to serve as a replacement for a broader system of social welfare, it represented one of the few direct legislative responses to the 1960s uprisings. This irony was not lost on insurers. As the chairman of the Massachusetts FAIR plan remarked in 1976, "The paradox is that while government may extricate itself to one degree or another" from so-called riot-prone neighborhoods, "FAIR Plans are forced to remain and even broaden their offerings of coverage." Absent a far-reaching legislative program, and amid cutbacks to the traditional safeguards of urban order, such as municipal sanitation and the fire service, the FAIR plan, in areas like the Bronx, proved to be a weak protector of property, and an even weaker guardian of neighborhood well-being. "Communities without insurance are communities without hope," the Hughes Panel had warned in 1968. The ensuing decade established not only that insurance access did little to improve the lives of tenants in FAIR-dense neighborhoods like the Bronx but that it could in fact bring new levels of destruction upon them.[21]

+++

WHEN THE NYPIUA opened its doors on October 28, 1968, it was immediately inundated with applications. It had placed a onetime advertisement in a few dozen newspapers around New York State, including *El Diario*, the *Amsterdam News*, and the *New York Times*, but was still caught off guard by the demand. In its first ten weeks of operation, the NYPIUA received almost fifty-five thousand applications, with ten thousand applicants flooding in during one particularly busy week. Although the NYPIUA represented a pool of all property insurers operating in New York State, it was a separate corporate entity, with its own Wall Street offices and staff. As with other property insurance in the state, most New York FAIR plan policies were sold by third-party insurance brokers representing the insured. To keep up with demand, the NYPIUA was compelled to quickly hire and train three hundred employees. By 1974, it had captured over 25 percent of all fire and extended-coverage insurance in New York State. The New York superintendent of insurance noted that the vertiginous rise of the NYPIUA "reflects a substantial backlog of needed insurance coverage by property owners who were unable to obtain adequate coverage in the normal market." Put differently, the NYPIUA's rapid growth was perhaps the clearest measure of the sweeping scope of insurance redlining in New York leading up to 1968.[22]

While the NYPIUA claimed an unusually outsized share of the market—it took in 23 percent of all FAIR plan premiums collected nationally in 1977—its growth was in step with FAIR plan expansion across the country. In 1976, the twenty-seven FAIR plans in operation wrote a combined total of roughly $19 billion of insurance, equivalent to $105 billion in 2024 dollars. By 1979, over one million properties across the nation, many of which had dozens of units, were covered by FAIR plans. As the federal insurance administrator noted the following year, the growth of the FAIR plans, first established to provide insurance in "riot-affected" areas, "has taken place during the very time when the threat of major riots has apparently receded and the insurance industry has enjoyed some of its most profitable years."[23]

In New York City, the coming of the NYPIUA meant the total overhaul of the urban property insurance market. But there, as elsewhere, increased access to insurance did not spell the demise of the redlining era. In a twist that would not become evident to the broader public until the late 1970s, the advent of the NYPIUA brought both expanded access to insurance coverage and the engorgement of the residual, second-rate market. This was the defining characteristic of insurance brownlining, which hastened the flight of the private property insurers that had already been abandoning the city. Now they could use their mandatory participation in the FAIR plan as a justification for their ultimate departure. The NYPIUA took the place of private insurers, peddling subpar insurance for exorbitant prices, and doing so at scale. Brownlining meant the return of fire insurance to neighborhoods formerly thought to be "uninsurable," but instead of dismantling the residual market, the NYPIUA was built on top of its foundations.

The NYPIUA offered no coverage to renters in these years, and as Hedy Byrd's experience made plain, the tenants of the Bronx stood to gain little when their landlords secured policies. As Bronxites watched their neighborhoods undergo cuts to fire protection, health care, sanitation, and other services, the arrival of the NYPIUA did nothing to attenuate—let alone counteract—these austerity measures. For the renters of the Bronx, the NYPIUA could not even be counted as palliative care.

Through a cruel irony of history, the Bronx was perhaps more sharply affected by its actuarial designation as a "riot-prone area" than any other place in the country—even though it had been largely untouched by the uprisings of the 1960s. The NYPIUA became the largest registered insurance company doing business in the riot-*unaffected* Bronx. The borough was not alone in suffering such an indignity. As Juanita Gear of National People's Action testified before the Senate Subcommittee on Insurance, "The FAIR Plans, once designed for only those risks in specifically defined riot affected areas, are now the major insurer of good risks in neighborhoods that were not then and never have been subject to extreme environmental risks [riots]." Of course, the absence of mass rebellion in the Bronx had not shielded the borough from insurance redlining. In the years leading up to the uprisings, "brokers reported that insurance... was not available in the black sections of Queens and the South Bronx." As the 1960s wore on, the market would only get tighter.[24]

After the inception of the NYPIUA, the relatively few Bronx buildings and neighborhoods that had maintained their coverage from the normal market during that turbulent decade lost their insurance over the course of the next. The NYPIUA's policies flooded in just as the borough began showing "creeping signs of total deterioration," in the words of longtime resident and activist Hetty Fox. With the Bronx visibly in decline, private insurance companies were eager to hasten their exit. By 1977, two insurance brokers were lamenting that "almost the entire Bronx is redlined and this 'fever' is spreading quite rapidly into other areas that were once considered the cream of the market." The NYPIUA scooped up the actuarial jetsam as it was "dumped" (the industry's term) by what became known as the "voluntary market"—as distinct from the "involuntary" FAIR plan. The pattern was replicated across the country. According to Chicago's Juanita Gear, FAIR plans were "being used not as an insurer of 'last resort' but as an insurer of 'first resort.'" In the Bronx, the NYPIUA captured somewhere between 50 percent and 90 percent of the property insurance market within two years of its launch. In the space of a few years, the NYPIUA had quietly become a major player in the management of urban risk.[25]

+++

WHAT WERE THE immediate effects of this rapid growth? The insurance policies offered by the NYPIUA were defined by their flagrant lack of coverage against theft, burglary, and liability risks—that is, injury to other people or damage of their property. As the Northwest Bronx Community and Clergy Coalition warned Bronxites, the NYPIUA offered "less coverage" with "no theft, no liability!" Most property owners in the borough therefore went without those coverages, at a time when the New York Police Department and the mass media were sounding the alarm over the increase of reported property crimes. Given their heightened financial vulnerability, property and business owners were thus incentivized to rely more on the police and the carceral state to protect against such perils. As a study of Bronx businesses by Fordham's Institute for Urban Studies presciently warned, "If firms cannot obtain sufficient insurance protection against the possibility of fire, burglary, vandalism, and the like, then the

City will have to augment police patrols and otherwise enhance the area's security." And indeed, in the decades to come, the NYPD ushered in the broken windows era, with the maintenance of order and the protection of property against even the slightest infractions becoming the paramount objectives of the police.[26]

The unavailability and unaffordability of crime insurance complicates a recent tendency among some scholars to hold Black leaders accountable for facilitating the rise of mass incarceration. According to this argument, in the 1970s, middle-class Black communities waged campaigns for heightened policing and tougher sentencing that proved decisive in the construction of the modern carceral state. But as the history of insurance shows, when Black and Brown owners of capital were unable to indemnify themselves against a broad range of threats to their property, they were deprived of what had become a significant financial entitlement of property ownership. White property owners in the suburbs, where comprehensive property insurance was first developed, enjoyed as much. If property owners in redlined areas turned toward the punitive policies of the expanding carceral state, they did so partly to mitigate their systemic overexposure to urban risk.[27]

The brownlining of the Bronx also played a role in hastening industrial flight in the borough. Between 1969 and 1979, the Bronx lost 40 percent of its manufacturing firms and two out of every five factory jobs. Companies cited the unavailability or exorbitant cost of property insurance as one of the chief obstacles to doing business in the borough. In 1977, when the Cedardale Drug Company, a wholesaler that had operated out of the Belmont neighborhood for three decades, found its insurance canceled, its owner, Sol Lederman, wrote urgently to the borough president, "I find that I am slowly and surely being driven out of the Bronx. . . . We cannot exist without proper insurance protection." Cedardale Drug's insurance, which had been written in the voluntary market, had been revoked despite its excellent safety profile: located in a fireproof brick building, the drug wholesaler was outfitted with both sprinkler and security systems, and it had not incurred any fire losses in its thirty years of operation. Yet as Lederman suspected, "This has no relevance to the fire insurance companies who are only interested in the fact that we are located in the Bronx." Cedardale was banished from the voluntary market and forced to seek second-rate, yet far costlier, coverage from the NYPIUA. "We have to be placed in a

[NYPIUA] 'Pool' and the maximum insurance we can receive is $200,000," Lederman noted; this was "completely inadequate" given the wholesaler's $750,000 of merchandise. Cedardale Drug's experience was typical. When the People's Development Corporation, a community organization, conducted a survey of Bronx businesses in the late 1970s, it concluded that "the chief problem that businesses have to deal with after high taxes and energy costs is the almost total inability to get insurance, particularly insurance against theft."[28]

But even in New York's boom times in the early twentieth century, the Bronx was never a manufacturing center on the scale of Manhattan or Brooklyn. Its major economic function has long been housing the city's workers, most of whom commuted to jobs outside the borough. Even in 1974, amid unprecedented depopulation, it would have been the sixth-largest city in the United States (by population) if it were counted as an autonomous municipality. Accordingly, the Bronx was nowhere more affected by brownlining than in its housing sector.[29]

In the mid-1970s, government officials estimated that landlords across New York City were abandoning between twenty thousand and sixty thousand units each year. The South Bronx was more scarred and mangled by this process than any other area in the city. Abandonment was not commensurate with arson, but it was the precondition for the fires to come. And insurance brownlining played a significant role in landlords' decision to walk away from their buildings. As the cost of NYPIUA insurance policies steadily climbed, landlords saw their premium payments taking an increasingly disproportionate share of their rental income. In isolation, the soaring price of insurance may not have triggered abandonment, but when combined with other disruptions to the profitability of rental real estate, it could be the final straw.[30]

The ruinous surge of landlord abandonment in the 1970s remains one of the more enigmatic episodes in the city's history. As planner Peter Marcuse observed in 1988, "There are probably more explanations for abandonment in the South Bronx than there are abandoned buildings in the South Bronx." Although it coincided with the city's fiscal crisis and was exacerbated by cuts to municipal services like sanitation and inspections, the phenomenon of mass abandonment cannot be reduced to a by-product of the fiscal crisis, for it first drew the attention of policymakers a full ten years before the city's brush with bankruptcy. Nor did abandonment correlate with the age, design, or condition of a neighborhood's housing stock. South Bronx housing tended to be structurally sound, well endowed with public transit infrastructure, proximate to Manhattan, newer than many of the city's buildings, and equipped with modern amenities like elevators—all of which should have generated demand.[31]

Despite the relative health of the Bronx's housing stock, abandonment had become common sense for the borough's landlords by the start of the 1970s. As one study concluded, "Abandonment, as a possible course of action, seemed to have been accepted by almost all the landlords interviewed." In its defense, the real estate industry pointed the finger at its decades-old foe: the city's rent-control apparatus. By the 1960s, landlords had launched a formidable campaign to abolish rent control. As housing abandonment became a more pressing concern over the next fifteen years, landlords deployed it as a warning sign, claiming it was the outcome of overly restrictive rent regulations. This was the context for Ruben Klein's attempted dioramic immolation on the steps of city hall. Landlords represented by Klein's Bronx Realty Advisory Board argued that their insufficient rental incomes forced them to walk away from their buildings—or worse. In turn, they promised that ending rent control would mean the end of abandonment. "Everything would straighten out within six months in a free-enterprise system," insisted landlord Lee Sterling, who appeared in a *New York* magazine profile brandishing a sign that read: "END N.Y.C. RED NAZI RENT CONTROLS." If rent control were eradicated, he added, "There'd be no slums. And buildings wouldn't be abandoned."[32]

In the landlords' crusade against rent control—a struggle that continues today—the specter of housing abandonment was a convenient rallying cry, but it rang hollow. The Upper West Side of Manhattan had many rent-controlled buildings, but it didn't experience the successive waves of abandonment and arson that hit the South Bronx, the Lower East Side, and many parts of Brooklyn. Moreover, abandonment bedeviled even avowedly free-market cities like Houston that had none of the vestiges of New Deal rent protections. Landlords in New York City also conveniently ignored the fact that 49 percent of South Bronx landlords were not charging the maximum allowable rents for their properties. In one of the most authoritative studies of the abandonment problem, the Women's City Club of New York discovered "little or no correlation" between rent control and abandonment. The building with the highest rents in one neighborhood was abandoned, while over half the area's occupied buildings were charging below-market rents.[33]

In fact, housing abandonment was precipitated by the landlords themselves. And yet the owners, not their tenants, set the terms through which the issue was popularly understood: as a matter of governmental overreach. Tenants' voices have largely been absent from historical accounts, though renters were far from silent. Tenant and housing organizations were taking root at a furious pace in these years, and their campaigns posed a sustained challenge to landlord claims. One such organization, Homefront: Citywide Action Group Against Neighborhood Destruction and for Low-Rent Housing, formed in 1974 after a gathering of two hundred housing activists and intellectuals from across New York. In 1977, at the height of the problem, Homefront released a 140-page report, *Housing Abandonment in New York City*, which remains one of the most incisive studies of the phenomenon to date—and yet is widely forgotten.[34]

To grasp why landlords would walk away from their buildings, Homefront asked how landlords typically turned a profit from real estate. Rental income, the authors found, "is only one aspect of housing investment and by no means the major one." Residential real estate could also serve as a tax shelter, since the Internal Revenue Service considered a building's depreciation to be a deductible business expense. The deduction applied even when a building appreciated in value, and it could be so substantial as to offset taxes owed for rental income. Even more lucrative were the future gains to be made through the resale or refinancing of a rental property. The revenues earned by selling a structure that had appreciated in value relative to its purchase price are straightforward enough. More roundabout was cash-out refinancing, a principal source of profit for landlords. As George Sternlieb, former director of the Center for Urban Policy Research at Rutgers University, observed, "Most of the return on residential real estate comes not from the operations of the building per se, but from the capacity of the owner to remortgage his building. He thus recaptures amortization which frequently has severely limited his cash flow over a period of years." In other words, landlords' profits typically hinged less on monthly rental income than on the equity of their investments and their relationship to the tax code.[35]

It was not New York's rent controls that disrupted the profit margins of rental real estate but, rather, the mounting toll of bank and mortgage lender redlining, state disinvestment, and white and capital flight. "The roots of abandonment," Homefront explained, "stem from doubts about the possibility of realizing ... future resale/refinancing profit." Such doubts were a direct product of mortgage redlining practices in the postwar decades. According to a 1973 report by the National Urban League on mortgage redlining in the Bronx, "as the number of blacks and Puerto Ricans ... increased, the number of mortgages made decreased." Where redlining reached, abandonment often followed, and like its precursor, abandonment progressed along the racialized grooves first carved by the Home Owners' Loan Corporation and the Federal Housing Administration starting in the 1930s. The colossal scale of abandonment in the Bronx was in direct proportion to the bank and mortgage lender disinvestment that preceded and dovetailed with it. For instance, the share of North New York Savings Bank's mortgages written in the Bronx plunged from 88.4 percent in 1960 to 18.2 percent in 1970. The figures got even more dismal over the course of the next decade. Only thirty-two Bronx mortgages were granted in 1975 by Dollar Savings Bank, the borough's largest and the country's fifth-largest savings bank—and this number represented just 7.4 percent of the Bronx-based bank's total mortgage portfolio. That same year, the Bronx borough president reported that a mere 10 percent of the assets owned by the five largest banks in the Bronx were invested in the borough. Yet, in an astounding asymmetry, 80 percent of these banks' deposits came from Bronx households.[36]

Why did the lion's share of capital generated by Bronx residents and deposited into Bronx banks flow out of the borough? And where did it go? In our own age of online banking, these questions may seem quaint, but they carry real historical significance. Savings banks and savings and loan associations had traditionally reinvested a majority of their deposits in their local communities through mortgages and other investments. In 1966, Albany loosened laws prohibiting mutual savings banks from investing in mortgages outside New York and adjoining states. Then, after 1968, the state began allowing its savings banks to invest in commercial paper and federal funds. Together, these deregulatory initiatives enabled unprecedented capital flight. Bronx workers continued to deposit their earnings in their local banks, but these moneys were being rerouted to suburbs, Sunbelt states, and newly sanctioned financial ventures. The outflow of capital squeezed the Bronx mortgage market, making it difficult for landlords to refinance or resell their properties.[37]

When a "landlord's hopes of future gain are dashed," Homefront concluded, the bottom line suddenly becomes wholly determined by the difference between rental income and operating expenses. Accordingly, landlords began to cut corners, falling behind on tax payments and allowing building maintenance to lapse. "This is where the notorious milking process comes in—owners hold onto more of the rental income by putting less into maintenance," until eventually, they opt to "get out." What for landlords might have been a straightforward strategy of maximizing profits was, for tenants, a source of ailing bodies and sleepless nights. "Milking" a property meant extracting value out of burst pipes, unabated mold, asthmatic children, leaky roofs, untended boilers, and pneumonic families. The residents of 3836 Bailey Avenue endured the entire winter of 1974 without heat, writing on a balmy Friday in May that "sickness still prevails among families, one man still under doctor care with T.B." At 1995 Davidson Avenue, residents like Mrs. Barclay had to go without any water at all, meaning she could not even flush her toilet. "Half of the ceiling is missing" in her bathroom, she noted, but her landlord was nowhere to be found. David Teichner, the owner of Roosevelt Gardens, a large apartment complex on the Grand Concourse, "used a gun-carrying assistant to help collect rents," even while he "neglected maintenance and repairs and failed to provide heat." A landlord like Teichner saw his building as a boat bound for the bottom of the sea; the residual rent was all its captain sought to save before abandoning ship.[38]

It was against this backdrop that spikes in overhead costs from higher insurance premiums could make the difference between a landlord staying afloat a bit longer or going under. Bronx borough president Robert Abrams emphasized this point in his 1978 report "The Insurance Industry: It Redlines Too." Abrams shared the case of Morton Olshan, a landlord whose annual insurance premiums on two fifty-eight-family buildings skyrocketed from $1,945 in the voluntary market to $15,180 with the NYPIUA, a 680 percent increase. Upon learning of the premium hike, Olshan resigned himself to the necessity of selling the buildings. "Of all the other increases in management expenses, the increase of insurance rates has hit us the hardest," he groaned. This was the fallout of insurance brownlining, and as the New York Urban Coalition warned, it reverberated far beyond the Bronx: "The lack of affordable insurance has ... become a substantial factor in the abandonment of the state's housing stock and the destruction of its neighborhoods."[39]

New York City was not alone in this plight. A survey in Newark in the early 1970s found that "when landlords were given a list of possible problems in operating and maintaining their properties to rate, insurance was the single largest volunteered response," behind only mortgage redlining. In 1967, the Hughes Panel had drawn the same conclusion when considering the national situation, linking the inaccessibility of insurance to the decision to relocate or abandon a property. A decade later, Joyce Fortunato, a Bronx insurance broker, witnessed the common sequence of events up close: "The price of insurance is ... a factor in causing people to abandon their buildings." Writing to the New York Department of Insurance, she protested her inability to place her customers with companies in the voluntary market: "Fire insurance is impossible to obtain in the Borough of the Bronx, forcing individuals to insure their property through the Fair Plan, who[se] premiums are far from fair."[40]

"Far from fair" was putting it mildly: by the mid-1970s, NYPIUA rates were, on average, four to five times higher than those in the voluntary market. The NYPIUA's inflated rates were a result of its self-rating system, which based the cost of its policies solely on the pool's own loss experience. For every property insurer in New York State except the FAIR plan, premium rates were determined from the industry-wide loss experience— which had the effect of leveling the cost of insurance across disparate geographies and populations. When the FAIR plan "pooled" together its policyholders, it not only recast the spatial segregation that already divided the metropolis but created a new instrument for segregating its policyholders in the financial world. This was Jim Crow, insurance-style, and as late as 1977, the president of the NYPIUA, Richard G. Brueckner, rationalized it this way: "We defend self-rating. *The bad risks should be made to pay.* Nobody wants to pay for somebody else's insurance." What Brueckner elides here is that paying "for somebody else's" risks is the bedrock principle of insurance—a principle that could apparently be set aside when it came to Black and Brown neighborhoods.[41]

+++

GIVEN THE DELICATE profit margins of Bronx real estate in the 1970s, who could pay for the NYPIUA's exorbitant policies? In one broker's telling, "The only people who can afford the FAIR plan are those who are planning to have a fire." As the cost of insuring with the NYPIUA shot up over the course of the 1970s, those most likely to purchase FAIR plan policies became absentee landlords far removed from the well-being of their buildings and tenants.[42]

According to the basic theory of insurance, underwriting decisions about which risks can or cannot be covered—and at what price such coverage is sold—should incentivize owners to safeguard their property to the best of their ability. That is, it should make economic sense for those with a stake in a given property to mitigate the hazards facing that property, for they will presumably be rewarded by their insurer with lower premiums and more complete coverage. Describing this core tenet, J. Carroll Bateman, the president of the Insurance Information Institute, noted in 1977, "Historically, the withholding of property/casualty insurance has been a *disciplinary device* for the business or individual involved.... The withholding or the withdrawal of insurance tended to force more responsibility for improvement by the person or institution involved."[43]

The advent of the FAIR plans put this fundamental idea to the test. "The development of involuntary markets negates this principle," Bateman insisted, "for they continue to provide insurance coverage in the face of conditions that argue against such protection." Indeed, the FAIR plans disrupted the system of incentives upon which the insurance "principle" was constructed. One sign that the FAIR plans were failing to serve as a "disciplinary device" was their remote relationship with housing repair. In 1978, the director of the Property Insurance Plans Service Office (PIPSO)—the trade association representing all FAIR plans across the country—admitted that "there is little evidence that the insurance payments are being used by policyholders 'to rehabilitate the depressed sections or urban areas within FAIR Plan areas.'" That same year, the director of the Illinois FAIR plan conceded that even when applicants were penalized with surcharges for safety violations, "repairs are usually not made and the owner just continues to pay the higher premium." Reports on the New York FAIR plan were even more egregious. The New York Urban Coalition uncovered that when an inspector discovered safety violations in an applicant's property, the NYPIUA had no procedure for relaying those infractions to the policyholder. This meant that the NYPIUA was in the habit of levying surcharges without ever communicating to the owner that the violations were observed or the penalties imposed. The insurer seemed to have all but abandoned the role of incentivizing policyholders to keep up their properties.[44]

This malfunction in the insurance principle reflected the growing disconnect between the financial protection afforded by property insurance and the physical condition of the insured property itself. The insurance contract, argues one theorist, "does not ensure things, it ensures a form of value." Even the most comprehensive property insurance did not promise to protect the safety of a given building; it could only secure the property against the possibility of financial loss. Property insurance was designed to mitigate risk, not eliminate it. As a Bronx insurance watchdog pointed out, "It insures the financial interest and not the physical structure. The insurance industry is neutral on whether the claim is reinvested in the damaged property or not." How insurers could tolerate this widening gulf between the physical structure and its financial value, between material protection and financial indemnity, is ultimately a historical question about financialization, one that is taken up in the following chapters.[45]

For Bronx tenants, the insurance industry's apathy about what their landlords did with the money paid out for a fire or a leak was salt in the wound of housing precarity. That there was no stipulation requiring insurance proceeds to be reinvested in the damaged building—a provision that would be legally within the rights of insurers to include—was perhaps the starkest measure of the vast gulf between the FAIR plan and the communities it was created to serve.

Bemoaning the failure of the FAIR plan to improve the lives of those it ostensibly sought to help, one senior adjustment executive in New York remarked, "The intention was that by providing insurance through the Fair Plans a substantial contribution would be made to the revitalization of the inner cities. It appears at times that the real beneficiary has become the slum landlord who, after making an insurance claim for the amount of repairs, walks away from the property leaving a burned out building, which in turn leads or contributes to the deterioration of the neighborhood." Brownlining had most rewarded those landlords with the weakest allegiance to their buildings and tenants.[46]

With its links to housing abandonment, industrial relocation, and overexposure to urban risks, the FAIR plan had strayed far from the stated hopes of its architects, the members of the Hughes Panel. Granted, part of its failure was contingent on the hollowing out of the social safety net. The program had the misfortune of getting its start at the same moment the welfare state began to atrophy. It had no chance of filling in for the social services being slashed at every level of government, particularly in the Bronx, where these cuts became especially drastic during the fiscal crisis. All the NYPIUA was equipped to do was indemnify the financial interest in property. But it was in its emphatic protection of property owners—as opposed to the protection of tenants or even the properties themselves—that fault can also be laid at the door of the FAIR plan itself. The infusion of subprime insurance access served only to soften the blow that rampant disinvestment by mortgage lenders and the state inflicted on the borough's landlords. Across the 1970s, the policies sold by the NYPIUA came to have less and less of a direct relationship with the safety and well-being of their corresponding properties. In the growing space between the building and the policy, between the property and its protection, between the thing and the abstraction dwelled the tenants of the Bronx, stranded in the brown-lined American city.

Part II

REVERB

THREE

To Torch a Fireproof Building

I'm an ordinary guy
Burning down the house

—TALKING HEADS, 1983[1]

The roof, the roof, the roof is on fire

—ROCK MASTER SCOTT & THE DYNAMIC THREE, 1984[2]

The slow violence of landlord arson and abandonment, as documented by Camilo José Vergara's rephotography series of Vyse Avenue at East 178th Street in 1980, 1983, and 1986.

Adrian "Popo" Vega was a handyman for a building being milked. He had been hired for this oxymoron of a job by Carmine Lanni, a landlord with a pattern of buying hard-up buildings, collecting maximal rent, and cutting services while keeping up with his insurance payments. Accordingly, Vega served more as rent collector than repairman, compensating for the shortage of billable hours with a set of side hustles. The felony on the young man's record for military desertion only further circumscribed his career prospects, given the dismal employment landscape of the 1970s Bronx. These were far from boom years for repairmen in the borough, but in 1976, Vega's boss presented him with a new opportunity in the form of a five-gallon container of gasoline. Vega's earning potential in housing repairs was minuscule compared to what he could net in what had become a growth industry: arson for profit.[3]

Lanni enlisted Vega to be a "torch," tasking him with burning down the five-story building he owned at 1895 Belmont Avenue, in the East Tremont neighborhood. Lanni had taken out a hefty fire insurance policy from the NYPIUA, and he reportedly promised Vega half the proceeds from the claim. It would not be a small sum. The NYPIUA "would have paid a minimum of $40,000 on the dilapidated Belmont Ave. building and up to $250,000," marveled the *Daily News* a few years later.[4]

Even the $40,000 minimum potential settlement would have been a windfall for Lanni, who had recently acquired the mortgage from North Side Savings Bank for a mere $5,000. North Side Savings was in the middle of dumping many of its Bronx mortgages for pennies. "Even though the overwhelming majority of North Side's depositors live in the Bronx," inveighed the Northwest Bronx Community and Clergy Coalition (NWBCCC), the bank "has written off the future of the Northwest Bronx by its redlining policy." As the bank liquidated its Bronx liabilities, it enacted policies to preclude any future investment in the borough. "North Side Savings Bank will not even consider mortgage applications for 3-Family homes, for buildings built before WWII, and for apartment buildings with less than 35 units," an indignant NWBCCC reported, noting that the policy disqualified 90 percent of housing in the community.

In sharp contrast, the bank was readily granting home loans in suburban Westchester County.[5]

The gulf between the $5,000 valuation by the redlining bank and the $250,000 in coverage by the brownlining insurer put 1895 Belmont Avenue in a peculiar yet not uncommon position. To borrow from Arthur Miller's Willy Loman, the building was "worth more dead than alive." Its lopsided valuation tells a story, one that takes us from the stairwells of the Bronx to the ledgers of insurance companies and to the ethical quandaries of hired torches like Popo Vega. From these scenes emerges a panorama of the financialization age. In the 1970s, just as New York City was cementing itself as the center of the global FIRE industries, it was crowned the fire capital of the world. The two distinctions were linked. In the Bronx, financialization entailed not only the excess buildup of substandard, state-sponsored insurance but also the insurance industry's readiness to swallow the attendant arson-related losses. These developments marked a striking shift from the insurance industry's historic investments in fire safety and the safeguarding of property. What FIRE capitalism brought to the 1970s Bronx—as it did in other racially defined "riot-prone" areas across the nation—was a market for insurance that encouraged not fire protection but fire risk.[6]

+++

POPO VEGA WAS a professional handyman, but he made an amateur torch. In the predawn hours of August 29, 1976, he hauled a five-gallon container of gasoline up to a vacant apartment on the fifth floor of 1895 Belmont Avenue. Lanni had instructed Vega to torch the top-floor apartment and ensure that the roof caught fire, thereby exposing the building to the downpours of late summer. The job was not so much to burn *down* the building as to maximize the monetary damage. Accordingly, Vega doused the floor, ceiling, and walls of the unit until the stench was overpowering. Standing back to strike a match, he failed to account for the buildup of fumes in the enclosed space. "Instead of a nice steady fire, he produced an explosion that practically blew him out of the window," the *Daily News* would later recount. "Shaken and scorched, [he] fled down the fire escape and headed for the open spaces."[7]

Vega had bungled the job. His fire failed to catch, and what's more, his hurried exit had left witnesses: 1895 Belmont was still an occupied building. Despite cutting tenant services, Lanni had not yet driven out all his renters. The seventeen families that still lived in 1895 Belmont were awoken by the five a.m. explosion, and thanks to the loud blast, they all escaped unscathed. Before evacuating, several tenants peered out their windows and observed the man they knew as their rent collector fleeing the scene. Vega's blunder brought his story out of the shadows and into the public eye. The vast majority of New York City's 13,752 verified structural arsons in 1976 went uninvestigated by the police and fire departments and unreported by the media. But because Vega botched the job and left material witnesses, the fire at 1895 Belmont entered the historical record and remains legible to us all these years later.[8]

After the tenants identified Vega to the New York Police Department, a team of detectives pursued him across the city for three months. Winter was already rolling in by the time they caught him, at which point he confessed to having burned several buildings for Lanni. In exchange for a reduced sentence, he agreed to wear a wire and record conversations with his employer. And before long, Lanni gave Vega another shot, drafting him to burn 2025 Valentine Avenue, a building valued at $100,000 that Lanni had acquired from Dime Savings Bank for a piddling $7,000. Caught on tape, Lanni was arrested and sentenced to fifteen years in prison—a stiffer punishment than most convicted arsonists received. This disparity owed to the Bronx district attorney's success in linking him to multiple fires. Lanni was revealed to belong to a circle of six landlords operating an arson-for-hire business out of a Bronx storefront. "It was common knowledge on the street that if a person wanted a building burned, he could contact someone at the landlords' store," reported a local journalist. The arson ring's real estate portfolio was extensive; when the DA's office followed the paper trail, it connected the landlords to fifty buildings. Many of these had been purchased at rock-bottom prices from small-time landlords who wanted out of the Bronx. Lanni and his ilk were known as "finishers," for their climactic role in a disinvestment process that often preceded them. The arson ring was directly tied to seventeen commissioned fires, "but we know there were many more," said a detective on the beat. For landlords, the spoils of arson were manifest—Lanni was known to cruise through the South Bronx in a pink Cadillac.[9]

The investigation into Lanni's syndicate brought one of the first high-profile indictments of an arson ring in the 1970s Bronx. District Attorney Mario Merola boasted that it was "one of the biggest arson conspiracies in the city's history," a line he would reprise again and again throughout the decade. The spectacular character of these syndicates made them fodder for media outlets looking for stories of urban decay and violence, and for prosecutors searching for high-profile convictions. Eye-catching though they were, the arson rings were far from representative of the arson industry as a whole.[10]

Most landlord arsons in the Bronx, especially in the first half of the 1970s, were not the product of organized crime but were, rather, carried out by small-time landlords who understood that they could squeeze far more insurance money from their buildings than they could rental income or equity. Even DA Merola, who had much to gain from indictments of large criminal syndicates, admitted as much before a 1977 Senate panel. Asked whether organized crime was the source of the arson-for-profit problem, Merola responded, "We have not found that to be so. Most of it is by business people who are frustrated or trying to get out from under." The U.S. Fire Administration similarly reported that "small scale fraud, although less spectacular, probably occurs far more frequently" than large-scale arson rings.[11]

New York City's Arson Strike Force (ASF) pointed out that the representative case was a smallholding landlord who acquired a building with intentions to remain within the licit economy but struggled to break even. The ASF shared the story of an unnamed Puerto Rican landlord who "had worked 30 years on two jobs in order to purchase a small building in the South Bronx." At long last, he had saved enough money to buy the building as a present for his wife. But by the time he acquired the property, the neighborhood was suffering from public and private disinvestment, and he had trouble keeping it at full occupancy. The strains of operating a failing business drove a wedge between him and his wife, and they filed for divorce. In desperation, he "looked around for someone who said he would burn the building down." Though it was far more typical, his story was more disquieting than Carmine Lanni's, which featured a shady villain straight out of central casting. Perhaps that's why it was the large arson rings that entered the archival record in the most vivid detail. In other words, we know the most about the least-representative arsonists. That they got caught at all only makes them more exceptional. If they hadn't, they would have joined the masked majority who evaded detection and left no trace in the archive. Still, if used carefully, Lanni's story can help reveal more ordinary, hard-to-see truths about the everyday workings of finance, insurance, and real estate in the 1970s city.[12]

+++

CARMINE LANNI'S HIRING of a torch like Popo Vega was standard practice in arson-for-profit schemes, big and small. By contracting torches, who were typically young men or boys of color living near the targeted building, landlords could insulate themselves from prosecution; it was exceedingly difficult to incriminate anyone but the person who struck the match. In the rare case that anyone was arrested for arson, they were likely to be among the city's most vulnerable residents: young, of color, and poor. In 1983, for instance, close to 80 percent of those arrested for arson in New York City were Black and/or Puerto Rican. Two-thirds were under thirty years old, and most lived below the poverty line. Young teens were frequently hired, and after New York's Juvenile Offender Law was passed, in 1978, those aged thirteen to fifteen were tried as adults. Torches took on virtually all the risk of arson for profit, receiving in return only a sliver of the rewards. Commissions could vary widely, from less than $10 to over $1,000 per fire.[13]

To be a young person in the 1970s Bronx was to be shut off from most socially sanctioned means of earning money. With unemployment skyrocketing, an estimated 25 to 30 percent of working-age South Bronx residents were without a job in 1977. For the young torches who made up the rank and file of the arson industry, the money they could scrape together burning buildings was a significant enticement. And it was substantial enough to warrant the risks involved. Lorine Padilla recounts that she was a young woman "living in the street" with her brothers when the owner of a building on Tiffany Street "approached my brothers to burn two buildings in that block. They agreed, and then they approached me. If you give us $250, that's a lot. It's more than our moms could ever afford to give us." Padilla knew it was dangerous work, but she told herself that her involvement would help keep her brothers safe: "If I go with them—you know, help them—and watch the cops, I had this crazy notion that at least I'm keeping them out of prison."[14]

A similar dynamic was at play for Angelo Colon, a twenty-one-year-old who was offered between $100 and $150 to set fire to a laundromat at 39 East 213th Street. In April 1975, Colon had been approached by his uncle Miguel Rodriguez, who worked as the superintendent at the laundry.

"Boy Tells of Setting Fires Here for $3" read the caption adjoining this photograph. Those hired for arson jobs were called torches, and they were usually young men or boys of color who lived close to the targeted building. Torches were far more likely to be arrested than the landlords who commissioned them. Of his work as a torch, one boy interviewed for a 1975 *New York Times* profile said plainly, "I don't do it for fun. I do it when they hire me."

Rodriguez had himself been propositioned by his employer at the laundromat, Roberto Bonet, who hoped to cash in on a $20,000 insurance policy. We can only speculate about how Rodriguez might have felt about the order to arrange the torching of his own place of employment, and whether he was conflicted about bringing his nephew, half his age, into the scheme. He lived two doors down from Colon, and when he broached the idea, Rodriguez promised to make it easy for the young man. He drew his nephew a map of the laundromat and took him to the store to show him precisely where the fire was to be set. With these assurances, Colon agreed to take the job. At midnight on April 15, he and his sixteen-year-old girlfriend, Virginia Rivera, bought a five-gallon can of gasoline and lugged it to the laundromat. Rivera served as a lookout as Colon splashed the interior with gasoline. But the blaze soon got out of hand, spreading to seven nearby stores and drawing the attention of law enforcement, who arrested Colon and Rivera, and later Rodriguez.[15]

Arson workers created their own code of ethics to navigate the fraught terrain of firesetting. One fifteen-year-old torch interviewed by the *New York Times* explained, "If some people live there, I wouldn't do it. There might be babies in the apartments." The teenaged boy admitted to setting forty to fifty fires but defended his motives: "I don't do it for fun. I do it when they hire me." For many torches, the job of firesetting was chosen from a position of constrained agency and, hence, was freighted with all the ambivalence and anguish of survival work. When Lorine Padilla was asked whether there was a building she regretted torching, she sighed and said, "Every single one." Another torch, this one working in Philadelphia, testified before Congress that he had been duped into the job by his boss and landlord, who led him to fall behind on rent by not accepting installment payments and encouraging him to roll over his debt. The landlord then presented arson as the only way to make good on what he owed. "I was really desperate to pay him back," the torch said of the arrangement, which had begun when he was just sixteen.[16]

To do their jobs effectively, torches required training and practice. Getting the timing right was essential for stealth. Torches needed to synchronize their fires with the comings and goings of any remaining residents, along with pedestrians and car traffic. Because the goal was most often for the fire to burn as long as possible before the fire service arrived, the ideal timing was when the city was sleeping. Arsons were most frequently set between four p.m. and four a.m., peaking in the hours between eleven p.m. and one a.m. Stealth was key not only for prolonging the life of the fire but also for making it appear accidental. Amid personnel cuts to the FDNY, only fires that were undeniably suspicious were investigated by fire marshals. Those that slipped under the radar of fire marshals enabled perpetrators to avoid legal consequences and insurer withholding. Torches drew from a diverse tool kit to maximize damage and minimize suspicion. Many used towels, newspapers, or rope as a fuse, soaking them in gasoline or kerosene to give them a head start in escaping the building. Another method was to disarm the safety controls of a building's gas water heater before blowing out its pilot light. This forced flammable gas to waft through the building until it came into contact with the pilot light of a kitchen stove, igniting a blast.[17]

Much of the housing stock of the South Bronx was composed of fireproof walk-ups, and it took much more than a box of matches to destroy it. "Those buildings couldn't have been knocked down by heavy artillery," the city's deputy chief fire marshal said. For some buildings, he added, "fifty to seventy fires were required." Indeed, burning these structures was an arduous and piecemeal process, with multiple fires set in various sections of a building over the course of weeks or months. Walls of brick and floors of cement and reinforced concrete meant these structures rarely burned to the ground. The aim was instead to "total" them in the eyes of insurance adjusters, and, accordingly, torches aimed to inflict maximum monetary damage.[18]

Most started right where Vega did with 1895 Belmont: in the cockloft, or the recess between the ceiling of the top floor and the roof. Destruction of the roof was calamitous, in that it exposed the entire structure to water damage. The old-school Bronx hip-hop crew Rock Master Scott & the Dynamic Three was deadly accurate when they shouted, "The roof, the roof, the roof is on fire!" at the close of their classic 1984 anthem. We should understand the song to be unnervingly literal, and, indeed, the arson economy was a product of the same conditions of "organized abandonment" that gave shape to early Bronx hip-hop. For torches, the job was to let "the motherfucker burn" after lighting up the cockloft. "Once the roof went, the building was considered uninhabitable," verified the Bronx DA. Because top floors were often the first to be vacated by tenants, these fires posed less risk to other people, and their distance from the street reduced the chances of immediate detection. With their collateral smoke and water damage, such fires could have the additional advantage of pressuring remaining residents to leave the building. For that reason, it was common for torches to begin with a relatively small fire, a warning shot signaling that it was time for tenants to find a new home. Once the building was uninhabited, the torch would cascade the fire downward, often using the stairwell as a "natural flue." By this point, the aim was to inflict maximal damage as quickly as possible. "To hasten the destruction of the building," explained the National Fire Protection Association, "the arsonist may cut or bore holes in walls or floors, or open doors and windows to ventilate the fire and create greater draft conditions."[19]

The job of the torch was wretched, violent work. It was also skilled work. To complete their task without getting injured, torches had to become proficient with fire science and the fundamentals of building construction and property insurance. They were the demolition workers of the informal economy.

+++

THOUGH THE TORCHES incurred most of the legal and bodily risk involved with firesetting, it was the landlords who determined which buildings burned, and when. Predicting which buildings were at risk for arson was a difficult undertaking for tenants and investigators throughout the 1970s. In 1981, after a two-year study, the Arson Strike Force finally released a detailed portrait of what made a building prone to arson. The archetypal building, it found, was a midsized five-story walk-up tenement located on a corner and owned by an absentee landlord. Some 80 percent of arson fires in New York City occurred in residential housing, and they were much more common in multi-unit buildings than in one- or two-family homes. Almost half of torched buildings had been in tax arrears for more than a year, "an indication of great negligence by circumstance or design." These buildings were also likely to have suffered a previous fire; 63.5 percent of arson-affected structures had sustained at least one fire in the past two years—often "of suspicious origin." High rates of vacancy were likewise closely correlated with arson-proneness. None of this was especially surprising, but when the ASF reviewed the data, it discovered a paradox: those buildings most prone to arson happened to be those built to be fireproof. "Here the intentional nature of arson is clear: with fire safety systems built in, only planned, deliberate fires would be expected to erupt." As we will see, this data proved extraordinarily useful for anti-arson organizations. But it can tell us only so much about what drove the arson wave. To better answer that question, it is most instructive to ask which buildings *didn't* burn.[20]

The only type of building spared by the decade's arson wave was public housing. Indeed, the most decisive factor determining a given building's susceptibility to arson was whether it was owned by the state or private enterprise. The New York City Housing Authority (NYCHA), the agency responsible for administering public housing in the city, was nearly completely untouched by fire. As the Bronx DA reported, "When the profit is taken out of arson there are no fires. A good example of this is the record of the New York City Housing Authority (the largest landlord in the world) where there have been *virtually no structural fires.*" Some 169,663 families were housed by NYCHA in 1977, the year that the report was filed, yet the city's largest landlord could claim an "almost total absence of fires."[21]

Structural Arson in New York City

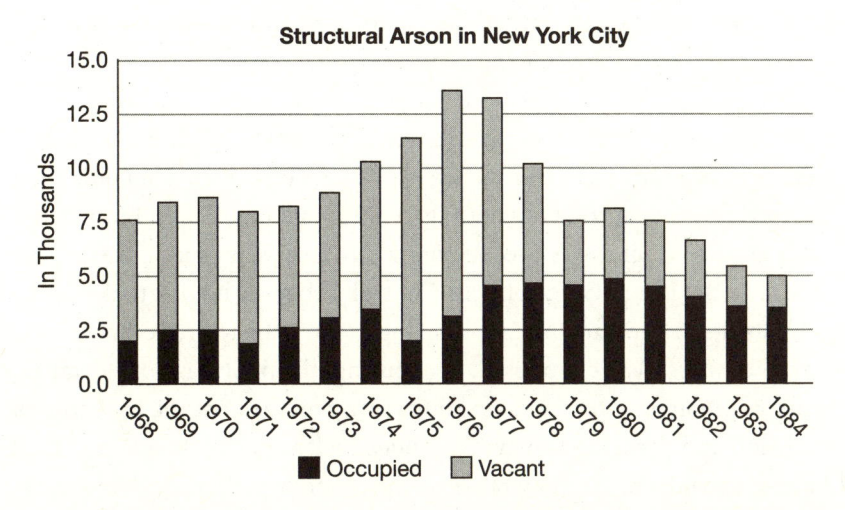

For much of the 1970s, rates of arson in vacant buildings far outpaced those of occupied buildings, according to a study conducted by the New York City Arson Strike Force.

It is difficult to imagine a more damning indictment of the private market for rental housing. State-owned housing proved so immune to fire that it remained unscathed even when it was literally adjacent to buildings being set aflame. In one four-block area surveyed by the Bronx DA, the only buildings undamaged by incendiary fires were "nonprofit buildings," or what housing activists call social housing. This immunity owed to the fact that "no profit can be realized from burning down a Housing Authority building." Similarly, the New York City Department of Housing Preservation and Development—which became, by some measures, the city's second-largest landlord in the late 1970s, when it began taking possession of abandoned and tax-delinquent properties—was largely unaffected by arson. In stark contrast, the privately owned buildings participating in the federally subsidized Section 8 program, which replaced public housing as the nation's solution to affordable housing after 1974, "had higher arson rates than buildings not in the program." That is, Section 8 housing—the privatized substitute for social housing—was even more prone to arson than the average building in the private market. That social housing alone escaped the decade's plunder highlights just how contradictory the state project was in these years, when the government-sponsored FAIR plan was the spark and public housing the retardant.[22]

The arson wave should be understood as the perverse conclusion of the disinvestment process; it was a redlining map drawn in flames. The blazes were acts of extraction, commissioned or carried out by landlords on a redlined financial terrain not entirely of their making. "South Bronx landlords are like California's prospectors a hundred years ago," observed an official in the Bronx Office of Rent Control. "They rushed in, took out the gold, and left a ghost town." Emphasizing the scorched-earth economics at play, the *Village Voice* proposed, "In housing, the final stage of capitalism is arson." Watching the city's housing stock burn against the backdrop of recession and fiscal crisis may have indeed felt to residents like "the final stage of capitalism." The downturn in the economy was more than a backdrop for the arson wave—it was a springboard. From 1973 to 1974, during the first year of a global recession prompted by an OPEC oil embargo, rising inflation, and President Nixon's elimination of the gold standard, fire losses incurred by insurance companies increased by 75 percent. Bronx economist Gelvin Stevenson situated the spikes in fire losses within this macroeconomic situation: "Fires are countercyclical. When the economy is improving, fires diminish in number and severity. When the economy turns down, fires increase."[23]

More than tax arrearage, prior fire history, vacancy, or the recession, the condition of possibility for the arson wave was the inverse relationship between the amount of insurance taken out on a building and that building's valuation by the real estate market. For landlords, the coverage available from the NYPIUA stood in stark contrast to the ongoing disinvestment by banks and mortgage lenders. The resulting asymmetry created what I call an *insurance gap* between how a building was valued by insurers (in this case, at exaggerated rates derived from brokers or the owners themselves) and its valuation by mortgage markets (at rock-bottom prices). The presence of a wide insurance gap actively altered the business strategies of landlords, imposing a new economic calculus of "rent it or burn it."[24]

Historically, two principal frameworks have been used to describe the twisted economic logic at play here. In the world of insurance, the scenario is called a "moral hazard," which is said to exist if the presence of insurance alters behavior in damaging ways. In order to avoid moral hazards—situations when the very fact of the insurance contract might *increase*

"You're the accountant, should I rent it or burn it?"

An insurance gap was present when there was a wide spread between a building's valuation by the mortgage markets and its valuation by insurance companies. This cartoon captures the economic calculations of landlords while deploying anti-Semitic tropes in its portrayal of the landlord and the accountant.

the likelihood of an adverse event—insurers rely on prudent underwriting, actuarial precision, and careful adjustment of losses. To succumb to a moral hazard is, in the eyes of insurers, to breach the insurance contract and, more broadly, to tear the moral fabric of society. Moral hazards are figured as aberrations: they exist outside the proper workings of property insurance, which is implicitly or explicitly imagined to be a fundamentally *moral* enterprise.[25]

A more crass term for the same scenario is "Jewish lightning," as well as its analogues "Burnheimer," "Burnstein," "Smokenstein," "Blazenheimer," and "Swindlebaum." As discussed in the book's introduction, such anti-Semitic tropes have circulated since the Middle Ages. Like anti-Semitism more broadly, the stereotype has a long and sordid history of feeding off societal misgivings about finance's increasing centrality in economic life. The portrayal of Jews, especially Jewish bankers, as dishonest and usurious parasites was a defining facet of Nazi ideology. Nazism successfully diverted a Depression-era critique of capitalism into a venomous suspicion of financial abstraction, which was configured as a Jewish conspiracy.

"Jewish lightning," premised on the notion that Jews are swindlers, likewise sublimated a populist distrust of financial exploitation and trickery into base anti-Semitism.[26]

Even as Jews were popularly reduced to incarnations of financial evil, the world of finance produced its own breed of anti-Semitism. In the middle of the nineteenth century, the American fire insurance industry updated the medieval trope of the arsonist Jew, casting it in actuarial terms with the phrase "Jew risk." As one prominent agent wrote in the pages of the *New York Herald*, Jews "have blistered and swindled the Insurance Companies most unmercifully, and doubtless will continue to do so as long as unrestricted insurance is granted them." Where "moral hazard" depoliticizes insurance fraud and exonerates the industry, "Jewish lightning" racializes a political and economic problem. Needless to say, a new framework is needed, and the concept of the insurance gap can fill the explanatory void.[27]

The history of insurance redlining and brownlining shows us that entering into an insurance contract is never a neutral act. Insurance is, at its core, an apparatus for spreading and sharing risks; industry judgments about which risks are pooled together, who receives what type of coverage, and at what rates they are covered are all political decisions. As historian Jonathan Levy argues, the coming of the insurance age created "risk communities" that "plucked individual lives out of their local worlds, spawning webs of statistical interdependence between them." Off-loading risk onto a broader pool of policyholders forged a new "we," albeit an invisible one. And the risk pools into which policyholders were placed, though abstracted from the physical world, reflected and reconfigured the social contours of that world.[28]

Brownlining may have "plucked" individuals out of their "local worlds," but the "webs" that joined FAIR policyholders together were deeply shaped by the raced, classed, and geographic characteristics of the insured risks. In the Bronx, the property owners who purchased NYPIUA coverage from their insurance agents and brokers were as segregated in their "risk community" as their properties were in the physical world. As a result, the insurance policies sold by the NYPIUA were expensive and second-rate. Yet for the many landlords who made up the pool, the policies nonetheless helped them hedge against the large-scale destabilization of the Bronx real estate market.

Unlike the moral hazard framework, which suggests aberration, the insurance gap better captures the dynamic at work. The value of real estate in the United States—as appraised by insurers and mortgage markets—is both a measure and a maker of racial hierarchy. The prevalence of the insurance gap in the 1970s was a function of both low valuations by real estate markets (a corollary of mortgage redlining) and overinsurance (a by-product of insurance brownlining). In the case of Carmine Lanni's stake in 1895 Belmont Avenue, the disparity between the building's $5,000 selling price and its insured value of up to $250,000 produced an insurance gap of as much as fifty times the building's valuation by the primary mortgage market.[29]

The insurance gap was a systemic issue in properties underwritten by the NYPIUA during the 1970s. In one study of 20,162 properties, 12,517 buildings—or 62 percent—were overinsured; that is, they were insured by the NYPIUA for an amount greater than what they had been purchased for (purchase price should be understood here as a rough measure of the properties' market value). Some degree of overinsurance is not atypical, even in the private market. But over a quarter of NYPIUA properties were insured for more than two times the purchase price, and 1,455 buildings were insured for more than *six times* the purchase price (see "New York FAIR Plan Loss Experience" on page 273 for detailed figures). There was a strong correlation between the magnitude of the insurance gap and the frequency and extent of property damage. Buildings with a sizable insurance gap (greater than a factor of two) were over three times more likely to incur a loss than those without a gap. And the larger the insurance gap, the larger the property damage. In short, damage to property was far more likely and many times more destructive for buildings with a significant insurance gap than those without, indicating that when a building was overinsured, it was also overexposed to fire and other perils. These correlations point unequivocally toward fraud.[30]

The pervasiveness of the insurance gap was not limited to the Bronx. A 1978 report by the comptroller general of the United States criticized the FAIR plans of Illinois, Maryland, Massachusetts, Pennsylvania, and Washington, D.C., for "providing insurance in amounts that property owners desired." And in 1980, then-senator Joseph R. Biden decried the tendency of insurance companies nationwide to "indiscriminately overinsure and settle property insurance claims without investigation." That property insurers would countenance insurance policies that so clearly fostered fraud was a striking departure from the industry's historical treatment of fire risk. What sort of metamorphosis was this that left the industry with such a brazen willingness to underwrite high-risk policies and then shell out when the buildings burned down? What responsibility, if any, did the industry have to prevent fire and fraud?[31]

+++

FROM THE LATE nineteenth century to the middle of the twentieth century, during an era of breakneck urban and industrial expansion, the fire insurance industry and the fire service grew in tandem. When the insurance industry entered its boom times at the turn of the twentieth century, it wholeheartedly embraced fire prevention, sponsoring and giving shape to urban fire departments as they gradually transitioned away from volunteer units to paid forces. Beginning in the 1890s, the partnership between the National Board of Fire Underwriters and the National Association of Fire Engineers was a testament to the increasingly symbiotic relationship between insurers and firefighters. This union precipitated a transformation in construction materials and methods, jump-starting the new century's breakthroughs in fire safety.[32]

As Howard Tipton, the first United States fire administrator, remarked in 1972, "Historically, the American fire services and building codes and standards groups have strong ties to the fire insurance industry. Early fire departments were organized and financed in many instances by insurance companies to protect their insured buildings and to act as salvage crews. Building and fire prevention codes as well as research into the causes of fire developed principally out of the keen interest of the insurance industry to minimize fire losses." These building codes had a pronounced impact on the American city, inaugurating the age of fireproof construction (of which the Bronx was a typical example). Moreover, insurance rates for a given municipality were tied to the record of the area's fire service, securing the link between the two. A new age of fire safety was born, and the great citywide conflagrations of the nineteenth and early twentieth centuries, which had leveled Chicago in 1871 and San Francisco in 1906, became a thing of the past. With the fire insurance industry throwing its weight behind fire prevention, the fire rate and fire losses each plummeted by almost 50 percent between 1910 and 1940.[33]

In the decades following 1945, fire insurance and fire safety began slowly moving in opposite directions. As U.S. property insurers diverted their capital away from cities and created the racially tiered insurance market, they invested less in fire prevention, since the low density of suburbs made them resistant to major conflagration. By 1972, Tipton could report that within the insurance grading schedule, a survey that helped determine premium rates, only 7 percent of "deficiency points"—measuring the level of fire safety—were concerned with fire prevention. By 1977, the National Fire Protection Association had determined that these safety metrics were arbitrary and often uncorrelated with actual fire rates or casualty numbers. In the midst of an industry-wide retreat from the American city, insurers had retreated from their prior commitment to urban fire protection.[34]

For its part, the fire service also moved away from a prevention approach during the postwar era. By the early 1970s, less than 5 percent of most fire department budgets was dedicated to prevention measures like code enforcement, with the rest consumed by fire-suppression efforts. When the National Commission on Fire Prevention and Control released its landmark 1973 report, *America Burning*, this mismatch in priorities was determined to be partly to blame for the nation's astronomical fire rates. "Appallingly," the report began, "the richest and most technologically advanced nation in the world leads all the major industrialized countries in per capita deaths and property loss from fire." *America Burning* prompted the federal government to overhaul its role in preventing and fighting fires, leading to the 1974 formation of the National Fire Prevention and Control Administration (NFPCA, later renamed the U.S. Fire Administration), the first federal agency of scale dedicated to fire safety.[35]

Yet the NFPCA merely recapitulated the errors of the prior, decentralized fire regime. When the agency was established, the South Bronx and many other urban areas across the country were at full blaze, but arson barely registered as an official concern. Instead, the NFPCA focused on fire safety issues relevant to suburban and exurban America. During its first fire safety education conference in 1975, not a single session of the three-day program concerned arson. Instead, attendees could expect sessions such as "The Prevention of Electrical Burn Injuries" and "Children and Forest Fires." And not once was arson mentioned in President Gerald Ford's proclamation accompanying the NFPCA's 1976 Fire Prevention Week, released during the absolute peak of the nation's arson wave. That year, President Ford declared

The 1973 publication of *America Burning* led to the formation of the National Fire Prevention and Control Administration, the first federal fire safety agency.

a national disaster for only a single fire, one that displaced a total of eighteen families in Bartlesville, Oklahoma, home to just thirty thousand people. The arson at Carmine Lanni's 1895 Belmont Avenue building would have—on its own—been responsible for relocating seventeen families. And this was but one of some ten thousand arsons that hit New York City annually in the mid-1970s.[36]

One can draw at least three troubling conclusions about the state of fire safety in the 1970s. First, the suppression of fire had been thoroughly divorced from its indemnification. Second, both the fire insurance industry and the fire service had withdrawn from the business of fire prevention. And as late as 1976, the peak year of incendiary fires in the Bronx and elsewhere, arson remained a low priority for insurers and the federal fire bureaucracy alike. Together, these developments meant that the insurance industry and the municipal government marched through the 1970s with next to no capacity to confront the mounting firestorm.[37]

+++

"NEGLIGENCE" IS TOO kind a word to describe the insurance industry's role in the arson wave. "Complicity" and "collusion" are more apt. As one FDNY fire marshal told Senate investigators, "Things were bad before, but once the FAIR plan started and anyone could get insurance, everything started burning." The underwriting divisions of many FAIR plans—a job function typically associated with prudence and vigilance—seemed to be bizarrely exempt from the actuarial standards of the industry. One of the New York FAIR plan's own vice presidents admitted that the NYPIUA "did not inspect all the properties it insured." And even when it did, the NYPIUA's inspectors were "often reluctant to go in high crime areas," resulting in inspections "carried out from behind the windshield of a car." It was no surprise that many of the buildings insured through the NYPIUA were later shown to be completely vacant, and thus at a much greater risk for arson.[38]

Gloria Jimenez, the federal insurance administrator, conceded in 1980 that FAIR plans across the United States "have insured buildings that probably are uninsurable by anybody's standards. It's hard for me to understand why the insurance industry would do such a thing." Jimenez offered this admission following years of denying any correlation between the FAIR plans and the arson problem. Pointing out that most FAIR policyholders did not produce losses, Jimenez and the FIA had consistently claimed that firesetting was an industry-wide scourge that afflicted all insurers equally. But by 1980, the link was indisputable, and the FIA was doing damage control. "I have been going all over the Nation," she emphasized, "telling [insurers] that the Congress never intended that they were to insure each and every building; that the buildings should be insurable." Jimenez was trying to make clear that FAIR plans were under no statutory mandate to insure every applicant. Nevertheless, their underwriting record suggests that the insurance pools were in the practice of doing just that (though, crucially, often at exorbitant rates). Observed an NYPIUA executive, "We're insuring risks that no intelligent underwriter would insure." Similarly, in Illinois, the FAIR plan was reportedly accepting ninety-nine out of every one hundred applicants. As a federal inquiry confirmed, "Many

Fair Access Plan officials believe that the Plans are encouraging arson-for-profit by providing insurance coverage to almost everyone requesting it." The report singled out the NYPIUA in particular, faulting it for providing "property owners any amount of coverage they want without regard to property values." In the Bronx, the DA came to the same conclusion: "The Fair Plan has the inadvertent effect of promoting arson."[39]

Still, the question is *why*. Why would an industry that prides itself on its ability to discriminate between risks engage in such indiscriminate underwriting? The question is all the more bewildering given the substantial sums of money at stake. As the arson wave surged in the mid-1970s, the underwriting losses incurred by the NYPIUA rapidly accumulated. In the Bronx, the average loss to the New York FAIR plan from an arson fire was $11,374, and in 1974 alone, the NYPIUA paid out $10 million on policies in the South Bronx—despite collecting only $3.5 million in premiums from the area. By 1977, the NYPIUA had amassed underwriting losses totaling $68.5 million, with the national toll exceeding $275 million for all FAIR plans. Were the NYPIUA a typical private corporation, a deficit like this would have been a death blow.[40]

But the NYPIUA was not a fully autonomous corporation—it was an association of all registered property insurers operating in New York State. As a result, it was able to distribute these losses across the dozens of companies that made up its membership, in proportion to each company's share of the statewide market. No single company would have to suffer an incapacitating portion of the deficit. In the words of Michael Jacobson, deputy director of the city's Arson Strike Force, "the cost of funding the N.Y.P.I.U.A. is a burden the industry is happy to bear." Even though the industry's down-market insurance products catalyzed the conflagration, "these high arson rates are not visible on [insurance companies'] profit ledgers." For the individual companies constituting the FAIR plan, arson did not significantly eat into the bottom line. Its deficits were tolerable—especially when we recall the program's role in keeping federal regulators at bay by safeguarding the state-based regulatory system preferred by the industry.[41]

The question nonetheless remains: Even if the NYPIUA allowed its participating insurance companies to mitigate the loss claims generated by its profligate underwriting, and even if insurers were bent on avoiding federal regulation, why would they have tolerated such unnecessarily high losses?

Property insurance is the business of managing and dispersing losses; accordingly, the question of the economics behind the arson wave is less one of *why* than *how*. How did insurers distribute and hedge the losses emanating from the centers of U.S. cities?

First, insurers passed along arson losses in the form of premium hikes. According to one of the U.S. General Accounting Office officials who prepared the report on arson and the FAIR plans, "It's pretty obvious that [insurers] pass the losses on to private policy holders." That is to say, the FAIR-related losses incurred by private insurance companies could be recouped by jacking up the premiums for customers in the voluntary market. Bronx DA Merola called attention to this practice before Congress, noting that insurance companies "view fire losses as a business cost and just pass it on to the consumer." The deputy director of the Arson Strike Force put a finer point on it: "A certain level of fire losses may even be essential since it motivates people to buy fire insurance." As frustration over insurer indifference to arson grew among law enforcement and the fire service, this was a common refrain. "Insurance companies don't care about fires," a fire marshal told *Newsweek*, explaining that they "generate a demand for more insurance and higher rates." Sure enough, by 1977, arson-related losses were devouring a third to a half of all premiums earned by insurers; to keep up with these mounting losses, companies needed to keep hiking rates. In 1980, the *Times* editorial board warned its readers of the implications of this practice: "As long as insurance companies can freely pass on their arson losses to all other customers, they not only lack an incentive to resist the crime, they actually share in its profits."[42]

Second, insurers were able to recoup some of their losses by collecting on reinsurance policies. Reinsurance is a type of insurance coverage purchased *by* insurance companies to limit their exposure to large loss claims. Insurers turn to the reinsurance market to cede some of their liabilities to another company, thus indemnifying themselves in the event of major losses. When the tally of fire damages began to spiral upward in the 1970s, insurance companies used reinsurance to protect themselves from catastrophic risk.

The third factor at play was that it often made more business sense for insurers to issue rapid payouts to their policyholders than to investigate and challenge suspicious claims. Throughout the decade, insurance companies in many states were contractually bound to settle claims quickly and could be subject to costly lawsuits if they refused. As one anti-arson organization observed, "In many instances, a company may determine that it may be less expensive to compromise on a claim rather than incur the expense of an investigation, attorneys fees, court litigation, and, if a case is lost, the risk of the policyholder being awarded triple damages." This held true even if law enforcement concluded that the fire was incendiary; only when the policyholder was convicted of arson would insurers have a bulletproof legal basis for denying claims. Insurance companies were also reluctant to thoroughly investigate suspicious claims because they did not want to gain a reputation for being litigious or tightfisted. Due to these pressures, the property insurance industry remained notorious for avoiding investigation of loss claims until a series of reforms in the early 1980s. FAIR plans were particularly egregious in this regard, with Ohio congresswoman Mary Rose Oakar telling a Senate panel in 1979 that her state's FAIR plan does "very little investigation and they make out the check practically the next day. I am not really exaggerating when I say that. So it is an open invitation to people who are potential arsonists."[43]

But by far the most significant factor behind insurers' non-response to the large underwriting losses was an industry-wide shift in how profits were generated during an age of financialization. "How do insurance companies make their money?" asked Frank Logue, mayor of New Haven and an anti-arson reformer. "Increasingly they make it from income on investments. All those premium payments generate a huge cash flow." Logue was describing a quiet revolution in the business of insurance. For centuries, the profitability of a property insurer hinged on the ratio of losses to premiums earned—a formula called the loss ratio. In the 1970s, the wellspring of profits was found elsewhere: in the gains made by investing customer premiums in money markets, corporate and government bonds, mortgages, stocks, and other instruments. It became common for insurers to rake in upwards of 60 percent of their profits from dividends and capital appreciation of their investments. In 1976, for instance, stock insurance companies in New York State were hit by combined underwriting losses totaling more than $1.4 billion, but because their investments accumulated $3.25 billion in profits, the industry claimed a net profit of $1.48 billion, after taxes and dividend payments. "Instead of profitable underwriting," recounted two insurance vice presidents, firms were chasing "all the money we can get our hands on" to "invest it in this high return market."[44]

The shift in the industry's profit center reflected transformations in the broader economy. A decade characterized by oil shocks, recurrent recessions, the end of the gold standard, and major fluctuations in interest rates also saw insurance companies reimagine how they assigned and generated value. As an insurance scholar wrote in 1988, "Significant investment income is a recent phenomenon in the property and casualty insurance industry. Until the 1960s ... insurance companies made money on underwriting; investments were merely a way to protect capital and surplus from inflation." Financialization meant the bow of the economy was pointed toward capital markets, and the profitability of firms as disparate as Aetna and General Electric became increasingly contingent on their financial activities. For insurers, the underwriting function that had historically determined company profits became merely a means of raising capital—through premiums—for investment. By 1986, two students of the insurance industry could write in the *Nation*, "Contrary to popular belief, few insurers make money from insurance; that is, the premium dollars received seldom amount to a profit once losses and operating expenses are deducted."[45]

This shift toward financialization played out not only in the ledgers of insurance companies but also in the streets of U.S. cities. As interest rates skyrocketed over the course of the 1970s, "property and casualty companies began investing in short-term money markets and in the process were able to increase annual investment yields," wrote an industry researcher. The money market funds were brand-new—they sprouted up after 1970 to circumvent federal limits on bank interest rates, and they thrived amid the "piecemeal deregulation" of the decade. So long as an insurer kept inhaling premiums, it could almost guarantee profits through its investment arm. According to Urban Educational Systems, a Boston-based anti-arson organization, "The more premium income generated by a company (even income from questionable properties) the more premium income they have to invest." Cash-flow underwriting, as the technique was called, might have been counterintuitive, but it was extremely profitable, given the high interest rates of the period. As a senior official in the General Accounting Office explained to the perplexed members of the Senate Consumer Subcommittee, insurers willingly "sacrificed underwriting profit margins in order to generate cash for investment purposes."[46]

The industry's insatiable hunger for premiums meant lowering underwriting standards and tolerating higher underwriting losses, including those generated by the NYPIUA and subsequently absorbed by individual companies. As ASF deputy director Michael Jacobson concluded,

> Investigators and observers of arson-prone areas often wonder why bad risks are insured at all. . . . The problem here is that *what is insurable is an elastic concept*. What is plainly an unacceptable risk when investments are yielding 8% may be acceptable when investments can earn 25%. Investment climate and interest rates play as much of a role in determining what is or is not profitable to insure as does the nature of the risk.

When Jacobson sat down with me in 2017, thirty-two years after writing these words, his astonishment had not faded. "I think the fiscal dynamic was [that] they were making so much money on those premiums, Why do inspections? You know, there was no . . . financial or moral imperative to do inspections. So they'd hold the money, they'd make a ton of money on that money." Assured of a hefty profit margin, a firm approached underwriting losses with resignation. "Occasionally they'd give someone, you know, $40,000 on a $100,000 policy for a place that was worth nothing," he recalled. "It was just the Wild West. . . . It was sort of an explosion."[47]

The insurers' new business strategy yielded a financial windfall. The total assets possessed by the industry ballooned from $58.6 billion in 1970 to $197.7 billion in 1980, more than tripling, while the total premiums collected industry-wide grew from $32.9 billion to $95.6 billion. This growth was unprecedented in the postwar decades, and industry profitability was driven largely by whopping gains accrued through investments. Capital invested in short-term money markets, government securities, bonds, and stocks yielded annual rates of return on equity above 20 percent in 1977, 1978, 1979, and 1980. That these were the same years that the Bronx was in an acute stage of crisis was no coincidence. The fortunes reaped by an insurance industry concentrated in financial centers like lower Manhattan and Hartford, Connecticut, must be understood alongside the carnage in areas like the Bronx. In the infrastructure of 1970s racial capitalism, the FAIR plan was the bridge and the tunnel.[48]

From underwriting to investment, reinsurance to adjustment, all levels of the insurance industry were aligned in the 1970s to tolerate unprecedented arson losses. The net effect was that the fire insurance industry—extending beyond the FAIR plan—served more to exacerbate than to mitigate the risk of fire.

+++

THE BRONX IS not typically imagined as a site of financialization. In the popular imagination, the rise of finance took place under the fluorescent lights of Wall Street trading floors, in the corner offices of coked-up junk bond traders, and inside the algorithmic universe of a Bloomberg terminal. But the *where* of financialization was not just in lower Manhattan or the City of London; it was also in Morrisania in the Bronx. More precisely, it could be found in the uneven flows between them.[49]

The devastated landscape of the 1970s Bronx heralded the triumph of the FIRE industries just as surely as it did more familiar associations: industrial relocation, austerity politics, racialized poverty, capital flight. In the Bronx and elsewhere, fire insurance was unyoked from fire safety. Yet the incidence of fire continued to correlate with developments in the FIRE industries. Fire safety entered into a paradoxical relationship with the financial world: as the insurance and financial firms of Wall Street expanded their reach, a wave of incendiary fires erupted across the Bronx. During these years, property insurers were raking in record-breaking profits, the dynamics of which allowed them to look the other way when the NYPIUA's indiscriminate underwriting practices generated unprecedented losses. As its insurance policies proliferated across the Bronx, the resulting insurance gap spelled destruction for vast swaths of its real estate.

That landlords were responsible for the burning of the Bronx is indisputable. But in a sense they were merely actors cast in a larger production. The arson wave was a drama acted out in the theater of post-Fordism, on a stage set by the inequities of the racially tiered insurance market and the brownlining of the Bronx. Its villains were slumlords, yes, but the ultimate responsibility lay with the FIRE industries amid their ascent, cannibalizing themselves and generating insurance value out of real estate ruination. Tens of thousands of displaced tenants were caught up in this creative destruction, some of whom did not escape. The fate of their homes had been overdetermined by an insurance gap that made these buildings most valuable after they had gone up in flames. Here lay the housing blocks of industrial capitalism, battered by the changing winds of profit.

+++

WHEN CARMINE LANNI offered Popo Vega a second chance to torch one of his properties, the target was 2025 Valentine Avenue, a thirty-five-unit structure in the South Fordham area of the West Bronx. This one was personal for Lanni. The year was 1977, and tenants in the borough were banding together on a mass scale to fight against disinvestment. Organizers from the South Fordham Organization, a member group of the Northwest Bronx Community and Clergy Coalition, had spent months working with the tenants of 2025 Valentine Avenue. The building was falling into disrepair; its boiler, roof, front door, mailboxes, and intercom all needed to be replaced. The tenant association attempted to pressure Lanni to reinvest his rental income in the building that was generating it. But Lanni's business model was structured around the insurance gap, and the profits he could bring in through the building's demise far outpaced those he could earn through its upkeep. This was true despite the fact that, as the NWBCCC put it, the building remained a fundamentally "stable, sound, fully tenanted structure which produces more than adequate rents to meet expenses and provide a profit, according to another landlord who is watching the situation." Nevertheless, no amount of rental income could top the $93,000 profit Lanni stood to take home overnight in insurance proceeds.[50]

After Lanni was approached by the building's new tenant association, he "evidently became so aggravated that he gave the orders for the building to be torched," the NWBCCC later recounted. Lanni's arson-for-profit syndicate was already responsible for more than a dozen blazes, and he had become rather brazen in his methods. Enraged by the tenants' assertion of their rights, he reportedly announced within earshot of his renters his intentions to burn the building. But because Lanni's torch, Popo Vega, was wired up, prosecutors from the Bronx arson bureau did not even require the tenants' testimony to secure Lanni's conviction. Lanni was found guilty for both the arson on Belmont Avenue and conspiracy to burn 2025 Valentine.[51]

Incredibly, the building on Valentine Avenue remained under Lanni's ownership even after his conviction, though its management was assigned to a court-appointed administrator. It was ultimately Lanni's tax arrearage, not his arson conviction, that finally led the city to seize ownership of the building, in 1978. By then, the tenant association had long been the unofficial steward of the property. "We've managed the building for so long," noted resident Ida Robbins. In 1981, the tenants leveraged their "sweat equity" in the building—a claim to ownership accrued through years of uncompensated repairs and upkeep—for a buyout. They made use of the Tenant Interim Lease Program, initiated in 1978 to assist renters of city-owned buildings in converting their homes to jointly owned cooperatives. "It's a dream come true," exclaimed Robbins, who, as a member of the tenant association, had been instrumental in making the building "a showcase in an arson-plagued, deteriorating neighborhood." But while 2025 Valentine Avenue may have been a "showcase" building in a beleaguered area, its fate was in keeping with a larger pattern of the 1970s Bronx. For buildings left to the whims of the market, the greatest defense against arson was tenant organization.[52]

FOUR

"We Went to Bed with Our Shoes On Every Night"

Risk makes my back ache.

—ALICE WALKER, NEW YORK, 1977[1]

By 1980, when Perla de Leon captured this image, fire had become a daily presence in the lives of Bronx residents (Perla de Leon, *Good Morning Teacher*).

Anthony Rivieccio's first memory of moving to the Bronx in 1972 was watching the fires advance toward his neighborhood of Morris Heights. "What I remember most vividly is . . . maybe twice a week, three times a week you would run up to the roof of the building around 10, 11 o'clock at night, depending on the night of the week you would see a building burn." Rivieccio's mother, who was born in San Juan, Puerto Rico, had moved the family from Brooklyn to the West Bronx in order to be closer to her mother. That year, Morris Heights was still relatively unscathed by the fires, which were concentrated at the time in the southern reaches of the borough. But from the roof of their new building on West Tremont Avenue, twelve-year-old Rivieccio and his siblings stood transfixed by the wave of flames to the south.[2]

The mile-and-a-half expanse that lay between Morris Heights and the edge of the firestorm offered the sort of buffer that rendered the fires, at least through a child's eyes, merely fascinating. "We didn't understand it," Rivieccio said. "We would just look at it in amazement and on occasion even joke around about it." By 1974, Rivieccio had begun to notice that there was a movement to the fires: they were inching northward. Still, they remained an abstract threat. "I remember my biggest joke which almost—I know it's going to come back to haunt me—was I said one day, 'Oh, when the fires get closer, we'll come up here one night, we'll put on some marshmallows.'"[3]

Rivieccio was not alone in finding both levity and profundity in the flames. That impulse was behind a great deal of the era's popular culture. In 1974, the radio reverberated with the incessant cries of a fire engine as sirens launched the Ohio Players' "Fire" into its carnal, Billboard-topping bass riff. Lines like "I can tell by your game, you're gonna start a flame" and "I'm not gon' choke from the smoke" were worked out by dancers at clubs like upper Manhattan's Liquid Smoke, where partygoers whirled in a haze of strobe lights and (newly invented) water-based smoke machines—an ecstatic simulacrum of a building aflame. Disco was on the rise, synthesizing funk, soul, gay club music, and psychedelia into a genre defined as much by its fire-obsessed lyrics as its synthesizers and four-on-the-floor rhythms (consider the pyro-poetics of "Disco Inferno," "Hot Stuff," and "Night Fever"). Moviegoers, too, were transfixed by the flames, with *The Towering Inferno* becoming the second-highest-grossing film of the year. Audre Lorde captured the zeitgeist in more sober terms with her 1974 book of poetry, *New York Head Shop and Museum*, writing of "watching as flames walk the streets of an empire's altar." The Weather Underground described a similar scene in *Prairie Fire*, an anti-imperialist manifesto written in the wake of the U.S. napalm offensive across Southeast Asia. In a year when Americans were watching blazes on the big screen, reading about them in chapbooks and the underground press, listening to sirens on the hi-fi, and dancing in clouds of smoke at the disco, Rivieccio's droll spectatorship appears almost routine.[4]

But soon the fires reached him. "I went up to the roof one day to see the building across the street from me burn," he said. "And I thought about it, I thought about what I said.... What did I do? What I did was, I joined the Navy." Rivieccio enlisted as a seventeen-year-old, while still in high school. Having spent five years watching the fires lay waste to adjacent neighborhoods, he was well aware that their arrival threatened to annihilate the social worlds that made the Bronx home. With the arson wave at his doorstep, Rivieccio felt his only option was escape. "My way to get out was the U.S Navy," he recalled. Rivieccio served for four years, including a stint on a submarine in the Persian Gulf during the Iranian Revolution and hostage crisis.[5]

How did the risk of fire in a U.S. city become so great that a submarine stationed in the Persian Gulf could serve as a place of refuge? Rivieccio's decision to enlist in the Navy reveals the immense psychic toll the arson wave inflicted on Bronxites and city dwellers nationwide. The experience of watching the fires gradually advance toward one's neighborhood over the course of years became a ritualistic activity in the South Bronx, where more than thirty fires blazed every night. Spreading from building to building and block to block, and marching steadily northward, the fires often seemed to follow discernible geographic patterns. For Bronxites tracking the fires from the roofs and windows of their buildings, no maps were necessary to make sense of the broad progression of the flames from the southern end of the borough to points north, east, and west.[6]

It is difficult to overstate the profound rupture caused by the arson wave. Even before they overtook a neighborhood, the blazes—predictable as they were—cast a shadow over arson-adjacent communities. Witnessing the seemingly inexorable advance from a neighborhood in the fires' path was like finding one's feet stuck in the sand as a market-made hurricane approached landfall. The anticipation that one's home would, within months or years, be obliterated by fire was nothing short of traumatic. In the Bronx, fear, anxiety, and a sense of structurally produced precarity were pervasive. The conflagrations triggered the sympathetic nervous system on a collective level, activating a community-wide fight, flight, or freeze response. Later chapters of this book chronicle the organized articulation of the fight impulse, as embodied by tenant and block associations, anti-arson groups, and community development corporations. This chapter focuses on the more immediate, and intimate, reactions to the fires.[7]

As the blazes tore through American cities, tenants were forced to cultivate a bruising vigilance to survive. Arsonist landlords and their hired torches generally tried to avoid hurting people and, in fact, tended to warn renters ahead of time (though there were plenty of exceptions to this rule, as the prior chapter revealed). And because the fires followed somewhat predictable paths, residents were often braced for them even in the absence of such warnings. Tenants got in the habit of keeping a suitcase packed with their valuables near the front door. Parents instructed their children to wear shoes to bed. Expulsion by fire became routine. In the Bronx, it was not uncommon to hear of a family getting burned out of their apartment and relocated, only to endure a second or third fire-related eviction. As the borough hemorrhaged residents, the banality of dispossession became a central organizing principle of Bronx life. Landlords and pundits pointed to the enormity of the displacement problem as putative evidence that tenants themselves were to blame for the arson wave. Welfare recipients were burning down their own apartments, the story went, in order to qualify for a relocation subsidy or to be placed at the top of the waiting list for public housing. Though there were a small number of documented cases of welfare arson, the role it played in the arson wave was minimal, more smokescreen than spark. The cruel irony was that to survive the fires was to become their scapegoat.

+++

AS IT DID for Anthony Rivieccio, the arson wave made itself known to Bronxites long before it landed on a particular resident's block, announcing itself with a burst of auditory, olfactory, and visual intrusions. Rivieccio's penchant for fire watching was shared by his generation of Bronx youth. Ivan Sanchez was barely school-aged when he began observing the firestorm from the Kingsbridge section: "We were on another roof watching it. . . . I was probably about, maybe six or seven years old. And we watched this fire burn, and we watched people running down the fire escapes. But I saw fires all the time. You know, it was just nothing out of the ordinary back in those days." As a child, Shelley Sanderson also watched the fires, but did so from the relative safety of the Saint Mary's Park Houses. Public housing was a refuge, though she did not know it, and the proximity of the blazes frightened and confounded her. "I could look out my bedroom window and watch the houses on Cauldwell Avenue just go up in flames," she recalled. "There was no explanation except for discontent," and in the absence of a credible *why*, the young girl was left squinting at the impenetrable haze. "It was scary and it was sad and you just didn't know—you didn't know what to make of it. It was a time where you just didn't know what direction the world was going to go."[8]

Fire watching was a perverse and popular pastime in the 1970s Bronx, especially for the borough's youth.

For many, the burning years are remembered first and foremost for the smells, not the sights. Samuel Christian was a child when the borough was on fire, and three decades later he recalled that "there was so much smoke" that "when I smell smoke in the city sometimes it just brings back that memory." As Bronx DA Mario Merola wrote in his memoir, "When you got out of your car in the morning, you could smell smoke hanging in the air from the night before." Genevieve (Brooks) Brown likewise remembered: "You came home . . . you saw cars and houses burning and smelt smoke. It's like, how can you live this way?"[9]

For others, it was the looping scream of fire trucks that left the most lasting imprint. In 1975, Archbishop Terence Cooke noted with disgust that "the ominous wail of sirens has become a terrifying part of people's lives." Over the course of the decade, the sound was so common that, for some, it became almost imperceptible. As Father Louis Gigante, a Catholic priest and the founder of the South East Bronx Community Organization (SEBCO), reflected in 1983,

> We became so attuned to fire engines, we wouldn't even know they were on the block. A prime example. It was 3 o'clock in the morning, I got up, I was watching television. I went to the bathroom. There was a window right over the bowl and there's Fox Street—burning, fires. I said, what? I dressed, I went down, it's three o'clock in the morning watching the people get the people out. Engines all over the place. I said, when did they get here? I didn't hear a damn thing. They hadda go by my window. We heard so much of it, it just became another noise and you didn't notice it.

Merola put it in terms the Ohio Players might have appreciated: "the wail of the firetruck was practically the borough anthem." Merola, who was initially slow to respond to the arson wave but who in the mid-1970s became an anti-arson crusader, even credited the sirens with provoking his prosecutorial interest: "From my office on the sixth floor of the Bronx County Courthouse, I was hearing so many fire engines racing up and down the Grand Concourse that I finally asked, hey, what's going on?"[10]

Smoke billowed, sirens wailed, flames soared above the urban skyline—even when a fire was relatively contained, its sensory incursions were not. A resident's first brush with the blazes was for those reasons often experienced from afar. For all the chaos of fire, for all its associations with anarchy and lawlessness, the spread of arson seemed to follow a kind of logic. As an official with the U.S. Fire Administration told Congress, one study of Bushwick indicated that "you can actually watch the spread of arson, like a cancer, or like locusts, moving from neighborhood to neighborhood across that area." "In the Bronx," a different study concluded, arson "was repeated, house by house, block by block, for over ten years until half a million people had been driven from their homes." Another Bronx-based study confirmed the block-by-block nature of the destruction, finding that abandonment patterns—the precondition for arson—"tended to spread in the study site first from one building to its next-door neighbor and across back yards, and only later across streets."[11]

Nothing better illustrated the block-by-block movement of the arson wave than the label "South Bronx," a place-name that was itself forged from the fires. Until the late 1960s, the southern sections of the Bronx were known by their individual neighborhood names, such as Mott Haven, Morrisania, and Hunts Point. The continued in-migration of Black and Puerto Rican residents and out-migration of ethnic whites in the 1960s and 1970s coincided with a new title: the South Bronx, which followed the path of the fires as they spread outward from the southernmost sections of the borough, hastening white flight. By 1982, the *New York Times* had concluded that the South Bronx stretched all the way up to Fordham Road, a full four miles north of the 138th Street border of 1969. As one journalist put it, "When it became the 'South Bronx,' the South Bronx was doomed."[12]

As the newly christened South Bronx expanded, the name became a shorthand for describing the racial anxieties that accompanied the fires. The label seemed to encompass well-worn tropes of the decades of urban renewal and blockbusting (the practice of racial fearmongering by real estate agents cashing in on white flight), when the specter of "racial succession"—or desegregation—was seen as an existential threat to the integrity of white enclaves. Cancer metaphors proliferated. As the *New York Post* put it: "Like a cancer, the borders of the 'South Bronx' slowly keep spreading with the line of fires that are eating northward through the borough." The *Los Angeles Times* published a front-page feature headlined "Bronx—Landscape of Urban Cancer." The implications were clear: the cancer was not only the fires but the Black and Brown Bronxites associated with them. As the *New York Times* wrote, the Bronx's "social cancer is spreading; unless checked, it can destroy not just the rest of the Bronx, but the city itself.... The South Bronx is the American urban problem in microcosm."[13]

With the fires progressing in patterns visible to the naked eye, Bronxites learned to brace themselves for the flames' arrival. The warnings from landlords—worried about harming tenants or the heightened suspicion they would face if they did—often came just in time. Landlords or their lackeys sometimes issued the alert directly, perhaps slipping a note under their tenants' doors; one such message read, "Be out by 9 PM." According to an organizer who repeatedly witnessed this tactic, "that, along with word-of-mouth, was considered to be sufficient warning." Word of mouth was lifesaving gossip, and it went a long way in making a threat known. In the words of Genevieve Brown, "if you notice the history of all those fires in the Bronx, you had very few folks that got trapped in those fires. Somebody would tell the other one, 'There's going to be a fire set.' So most folks had a chance to get out." One senior citizen likely owed her life to one such knock at the door. "My mother was warned," remembers Joe Orange, whose elderly mother lived alone in the Morrisania neighborhood. "Someone during the day knocked on my mother's door and said, 'Ms. Orange, I think there's going to be a fire here today.'" Sure enough, that night, Joe got a call from a different neighbor of his mother's: the building was on fire, and "she was sitting in the street in a chair and a blanket."[14]

Still, tenants could not count on being tipped off; they had to maintain a constant vigilance to ensure their survival. Many recall putting their children to bed fully dressed. Prominent housing organizer Harry DeRienzo explained, "Fires are violent, frightening and deadly events made all the more terrifying when they become daily occurrences. During this time, many South Bronx children (such as my youngest stepson) went to bed with a set of street clothes under their blankets in case they had to flee in the night." The archives offer plenty of corroborating tales. José Ortiz was a fifth grader living with his mother and eight siblings in "the last remaining inhabited building" on his block on Crimmins Avenue (across the park from Shelley Sanderson's unscathed apartment in NYCHA's Saint Mary's Park Houses). Ortiz got in the habit of sleeping with his clothes on "just in case something happens." His friend Richard Ruiz, he shared, also "sleeps with his pants 'close by' because the superintendent in his building has twice found gasoline cans on the roof." Nearly three miles away, at the Roosevelt Gardens complex on the Grand Concourse, "fires remained a constant source of fear." One of its renters recalled, "We went to bed with our shoes on every night."[15]

A decent night's sleep was hard to come by. One renter described the emotional toll the heightened vigilance took on her: "Fear, panic, running out the building, grabbing your children, leaving your food on the stove. Sleeping with your clothes on. Scared. No place in the South Bronx to move to—you can't move here or there, except from ghetto to ghetto, with nothing but fire." The picture this renter paints helps explain why tenants might remain in a building or block with a high likelihood of arson: the available lines of flight extended only "from ghetto to ghetto, with nothing but fire." For Darney "K-Born" Rivers, a rapper and organizer who lived off the Grand Concourse,

> It seemed like just every second there was a fire. Some way or another, everywhere, no matter where you went, you couldn't escape it. My mom was saying, "There's a fire over here. I'm gonna send y'all to your aunt's house across town until this gets straightened up." It's burning over there. "I'm gonna send you somewhere else." It's burning over there. It was burning everywhere, man. The Bronx was burning so bad.[16]

The walls of fire restricting residential movement were unique to the 1970s, but they reinforced the existing constraints on mobility. Take the family of Richard Ruiz, who remained in their apartment of twenty-three years even after gas cans were twice discovered on their building's roof. The *New York Times* alleged that "they have no desire to move" because their rent was set at $65 per month. Yet in the very next sentence, the newspaper conceded that the family had previously attempted to move into public housing, "but gave up 'after waiting with no results.'" Circumscribed by the cost of rent and an underfunded public housing agency, the family's decision to stay looks less like an affirmative choice and more like making do. In the meantime, they would keep a watchful eye out for signs of arson, and twelve-year-old Richard would sleep with his pants at hand, just in case.[17]

+++

EVEN THE MOST painstaking vigilance could guarantee only so much security. According to one estimate, three hundred New Yorkers died in fires annually throughout the 1970s. With few exceptions, as their buildings went up in flames, their names and biographies did as well. The tenants who perished in the fires were not the sort of victims who made the news. Most were Black and Brown renters, which was consistent with nationwide patterns: in 1974, the rate of fire deaths for people of color in the United States was nearly three times that of whites. Even when they are found in the archival record, little information is available about them beyond their names, addresses, and cause of death. We know, for instance, that Elisa Falcone, fifty, died while trying to escape a fire set in the bodega below her apartment at 1168 Ogden Avenue. Jose Sepeda, forty-four, perished in the same blaze. The absence of a functional fire escape could be lethal. When a fire engulfed 3148 Perry Avenue early one summer morning in 1980, forty-eight-year-old George Montrose was forced to leap from his second-floor window, sustaining a fatal head injury. The perils of smoke inhalation were such that some could not even make it to the window.[18]

Survival came with its own costs. In 1975 alone, seven thousand New Yorkers, many of them firefighters, suffered fire-related injuries. Lung damage from asphyxiation could have lasting health impacts, and severe burns could leave survivors with "excruciating pain and disfigurement." More often than not, injuries took a less visible form. "Believe me," stressed longtime Bronxite Hetty Fox, "internally you can feel that heat." The psychic injuries of the arson wave began with the anxiety, fear, and sense of inescapability triggered by its encroachment. "It was like an angel of death," related Fox, "with a sword, moving from Vyse Avenue and slowly creeping up this way." When at last the fires arrived, these wounds only deepened. Hedy Byrd, a New York City mother of three, described being awakened by "the sound of breaking glass" and then enduring "the most harrowing few minutes of her life." Another mother, Rosetta Boyd, recalled opening her front door and being bombarded by a cloud of smoke:

> I fought my way through the blinding heat and black smoke. My children were lying motionless on their beds. I picked up my two

daughters, tucked them under my arms and carried them downstairs, calling for someone to get my sons.... The unconscious children were on the sidewalk, where they were given oxygen. The fire marshal who treated them told me if the children had been upstairs for several more minutes, they would have died of smoke inhalation.[19]

Fires caused a "catastrophic upheaval" in the lives of survivors, explained a specialist social worker in 1977, and the heavy psychological toll could "linger long after the flames of a torched building have been doused." This was especially true for children, who often suffered from depression, insomnia, anxiety, and nightmares in the aftermath of a blaze. Adults, too, were left haunted. "I did not get a full night's sleep for many long months," one survivor reported. For Robert Gumbs, who grew up in Morrisania, witnessing this process on his block "was very sad.... The whole character changed. There were fewer families. It was somewhat painful, quite honestly. So I stopped going around." Bronx-raised James Henderson worked as a firefighter in Highbridge, and watching his home borough burn down "was devastating—to see things, buildings, neighborhoods that you know people in, to see these buildings destroyed."[20]

Residents regularly described the loss of their apartment houses in dirgelike terms. Like Hetty Fox, former borough president Fernando Ferrer suggested that there was a spiritual depth to the collective mourning: "The devastation was nearly metaphysical, crushing not merely physical buildings but also people's spirits." The deep scars left by this grief—and its collective, rather than individual, lineaments—were made manifest in this elegiac poem by Morris High School student Jacquelin Espinal in 1979:

> Fire,
> Burning;
> Our fires,
> Our burning;
> Hope, a phoenix
> Rising from the ashes
> Of our buildings
> Our sorrows,
> Our lives

Having been burned out of her West Bronx apartment, along with her two children and her mother, Lucy Rodriguez "was too tired to weep." In this *Daily News* photograph taken hours after the fire had been extinguished by the FDNY, Rodriguez sits against the backdrop of what had been her living room, its contents drenched and destroyed.

Lucy Rodriguez's comments to a *Daily News* reporter just hours after her West Bronx apartment was torched also reveal the funereal dimensions of the losses. "I had a beautiful apartment. . . . I'm working all my life for nothing," she despaired. The contrast between her misfortune and the experience of the insured landlords was stark. "I worked there 19 years and now I have nothing," she observed while rummaging through "the charred ruins that only hours earlier had been her apartment." Her son, Alberto, who had lost both of his legs in a subway accident years earlier, was forced to flee their burning apartment so quickly that he was able to grab only one of his prosthetic legs. "I don't know what we are going to do now," he said.[21]

The despair was not necessarily less acute when the objects lost were not vital possessions. Chrystal Wade was in the seventh grade when fire—

and the accompanying water damage from the firefighters' hoses—hit her building:

> One Sunday we went to church and when we came back home we found that our home had been burnt down.... I'll never forget the big TV with the stereo inside and I used to play it to death. I had a record by The Marvelettes, "Watch out Mr. Postman." I played it until my father went crazy. He threatened to take out the cord if I played it one more time. It was devastating to me to come home and find that our home had been waterlogged.

For Wade, the immensity of her family's loss was encapsulated in the soggy cardboard sleeve of a Motown single. If the destruction of a mass-produced record can trigger the type of grief that still stings four decades later, what did it mean to lose a beloved dog, a family photo album, an heirloom quilt, a poet's notebook, an ancestor's ashes?[22]

Even in the best-case scenario—escaping the fire with one's family and essential possessions unscathed—the blaze was often merely the opening act in a drama of displacement. A good portion of arson's refugees in the South Bronx spent their first few weeks or months after the fire at the Fox Street Relocation Shelter, where, a *Daily News* reporter noted, "many arrive . . . with only the clothes on their backs." A large sign in the waiting area read, "TO ALL FIRE VICTIMS—THIS IS A ROOM FOR YOUR COMFORT." The shelter could house up to five hundred people in 117 apartments, and the average length of stay was four months. For many, the hope was to be placed in public housing. Those, like the Gonzalez family, who soon returned to the volatility of the private rental market were liable to end up right back in the shelter: "They have been in the center twice, having been burned out of their apartment last summer, then again on Saturday."[23]

Indeed, repeat displacement was a fact of life for many in the 1970s Bronx. The first fire often set in motion a chronic state of housing insecurity that was exacerbated by a tight rental market and an under-resourced public housing apparatus. As a Senate investigation documented, "some victims report a history of three, four, or more burnouts, each of them accompanied by fright, dislocation, and related financial stress." Margaret Murphy, an eighty-year-old resident of Shakespeare Avenue, had been repeatedly burned out of her apartment. "I have been moving from one side of the street to the other," she recounted. "I moved from apartments that got burned out, or where the water damage was so great I could not go on living there. I have been living in one place or another on Shakespeare Avenue for 13 years, and it cost so much money every time I move." Murphy's world was Shakespeare Avenue; because she needed a cane to walk, her neighbor did all her shopping for her. Of course she would do all she could to stay on that same street. And she was not an exception: a study by the New York Urban Coalition showed that the vast majority of fire refugees moved within five blocks of their old home. If their neighborhood happened to be on the front lines of the arson wave, repeat displacement was almost foreordained. From capital's embers, a new class of nomads was born.[24]

One of the paradoxes of the Bronx's housing stock in these years was that the areas hit hardest by arson were both abandoned *and* overcrowded. Charlotte Street, which became the borough's most infamous section after President Jimmy Carter paid it a high-profile visit in 1977, was known for its abandoned, burned-out, and demolished housing. But when the avail-

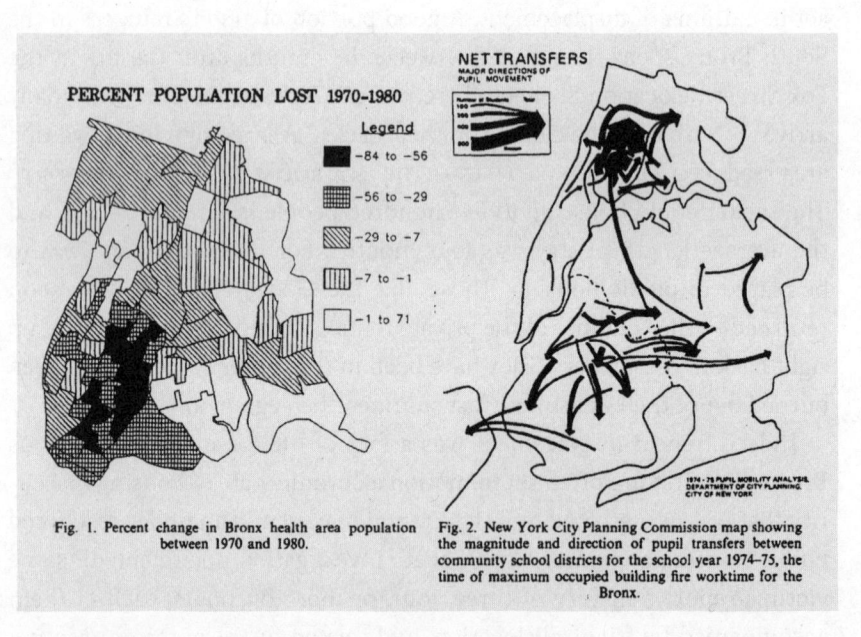

Fig. 1. Percent change in Bronx health area population between 1970 and 1980.

Fig. 2. New York City Planning Commission map showing the magnitude and direction of pupil transfers between community school districts for the school year 1974–75, the time of maximum occupied building fire worktime for the Bronx.

The map on the left illustrates the magnitude of population loss in the 1970s Bronx, while the map on the right charts the borough's diaspora via student transfers in 1974-75.

able housing stock contracted sharply, demand for apartments shot up. The result was that around Charlotte Street, Genevieve Brown recalled, "you had units wherein people were sleeping in bathrooms. They were just so crowded. You know, people were all over the place." Darney "K-Born" Rivers described another area with a "building [that was] halfway burnt down but people are still living in there. They living on the other half. Then you see this building on the next block, where half of the fifth floor burnt to the third. People still living on the second."[25]

The preferred destination for many fleeing Bronxites was outside the ever-expanding South Bronx. "Under these dire circumstances," observed housing activist DeRienzo, "nearly everyone with an option to move exercised it." Chrystal Wade witnessed the fire diaspora as a seventh grader: "That's when our neighborhood started to really change because my neighbors, they no longer wanted to live there because of fire. I think that was the primary reason—the fire. They didn't want to be involved in that." Some neighborhoods, like Morrisania, lost upwards of 50 percent of their residents between 1970 and 1980, although that figure was exceptionally high. In total, the Bronx hemorrhaged about three hundred thousand residents—or 20 percent of its population—over the course of the decade, with many people fleeing to neighboring Westchester County, Connecticut, New Jersey, or other corners of the city. Although the fire wave was but one of many factors behind this migration, one urban epidemiologist estimated that almost 80 percent of the borough's population change "can be explained by what we term a burn index."[26]

The scale of the movement captured in the maps opposite suggests that the 1970s ushered in a new, violent chapter in the history of housing precarity in New York City. For the renters of the Bronx, the decade witnessed levels of displacement on par with the most devastating urban-renewal projects of a prior age. The arson wave was no Cross Bronx Expressway, but its impact rivaled the bulldozers of Robert Moses.

+++

IT WAS NO coincidence that one of the era's new pop psychology terms was "burnout." When New York psychologist Herbert Freudenberger went searching for an evocative metaphor for the syndrome he was beginning to diagnose, he found it in the fire-ravaged building. "If you have ever seen a building that has been burned out," he wrote at the start of his internationally best-selling 1980 book, *Burn Out: How to Beat the High Cost of Success*, "you know it's a devastating sight." He continued: "As a practicing psychoanalyst, I have come to realize that people, as well as buildings, sometimes burn out." Freudenberger's epiphany came at the St. Mark's Free Clinic, where, in the early 1970s, he served as a volunteer counselor to the throngs of hippie youth who congregated in the East Village. He would arrive around six p.m., after putting in a full day at his private practice on Park Avenue. To get to St. Marks Place, he had to traverse an East Village pockmarked by burned-out buildings. Some areas, particularly blocks with a large number of Puerto Rican residents, lost more than half their housing during the decade. The peak hours for arson in these years fell just after midnight, right when Freudenberger tended to leave the clinic.[27]

In 1971, after a year of sixteen-hour days, the psychologist found himself unable to get out of bed, having succumbed to what he would soon term "staff burn-out"—a condition that he associated with overdedicated and overachieving professionals, especially care workers like himself. Years later, when Freudenberger related the experience for a broad audience, he reasoned from the ruins surrounding the clinic: "What had once been a throbbing, vital structure is now deserted." Not reducible to stress, depression, or exhaustion, Freudenberger's burnout was a symptom of high expectations that went unfulfilled. "The American dream is no longer a reality," he told the *Los Angeles Times* in 1982, "but many of us are still operating as if it were." If Freudenberger was looking for a symbol that could evoke those dashed dreams, he couldn't do much better than the burned-out building. Though he failed to acknowledge it in his own exploration of the term, those torched buildings had generated value by being destroyed. Freudenberger's burnout unwittingly suggested how depletion, even to the point of destruction, could be profitable.[28]

Despite its poignance, burnout had obscured the conditions that gave it meaning. Gone were the landlords and underwriters, the agents of government austerity, the torches, and the constellation of other forces that obliterated the built environment. Freudenberger even evicted from his analogy the tenants who had in actual fact been burned out. He described his prototypical patient in this way: "I came from a pretty good home, I went to school, settled into a career, married someone I loved, had children. We're a pretty successful family. Money, home, cars—but something is missing." In these early formulations, *Burn Out* was thus reserved for the well-to-do suburbanite: the by-product of accumulation, rather than dispossession. An indifferent worker putting in twelve-hour days on the assembly line was definitionally unfit for the diagnosis. "It would be virtually impossible for the underachiever to get into that state," Freudenberger wrote. That the tenants who had literally been burned out were deemed ineligible for the diagnosis was typical of an arson discourse rife with elisions, smokescreens, and amnesia.[29]

+++

WHEN THE ARSON wave is remembered at all, it is most often confined to the county lines of the Bronx. That the conflagration had national proportions, that it involved capital flows global in reach, that it touched neighborhoods like Manhattan's East Village and Boston's Fenway—these inconvenient details are swept aside. The overrepresentation of Bronx ruin has made it hard to see that the borough was not so much exceptional as exemplary. Even those who recognized the nationwide scope of the arson wave and pushed against Bronx exceptionalism were liable to present the borough as its point of origin. Testifying before a congressional committee, one researcher counseled, "Too often, people feel that arson is confined to areas like the Bronx. . . . This is not true. That behavior which is occurring in the Bronx has expanded and has infiltrated all of the cities throughout the country." Yet the South Bronx was far from ground zero of the arson wave.[30]

One method for tracking the national scope of the arson wave is to chart the proliferation of anti-arson agencies, squads, task forces, and neighborhood organizations in the 1970s. A virtually nonexistent phenomenon prior to 1968, anti-arson organizations like Cleveland's Near West Side Neighbors in Action and Salt Lake City Hands Up started appearing across the nation. Cities as far-flung as Anchorage, Alaska, and Wichita, Kansas, witnessed the emergence of such groups, some of which grew out of existing law enforcement bodies and others that resulted from ad hoc neighborhood mobilizations. So prevalent were these groups that the U.S. Fire Administration's *Arson Resource Directory*—a sort of anti-arson yellow pages—ran to more than 160 pages in 1980, cataloging anti-arson organizations in all but ten states.[31]

What transpired in the Bronx was exceptional only in terms of its scale. The NYPIUA generated an outsized share of the total underwriting losses

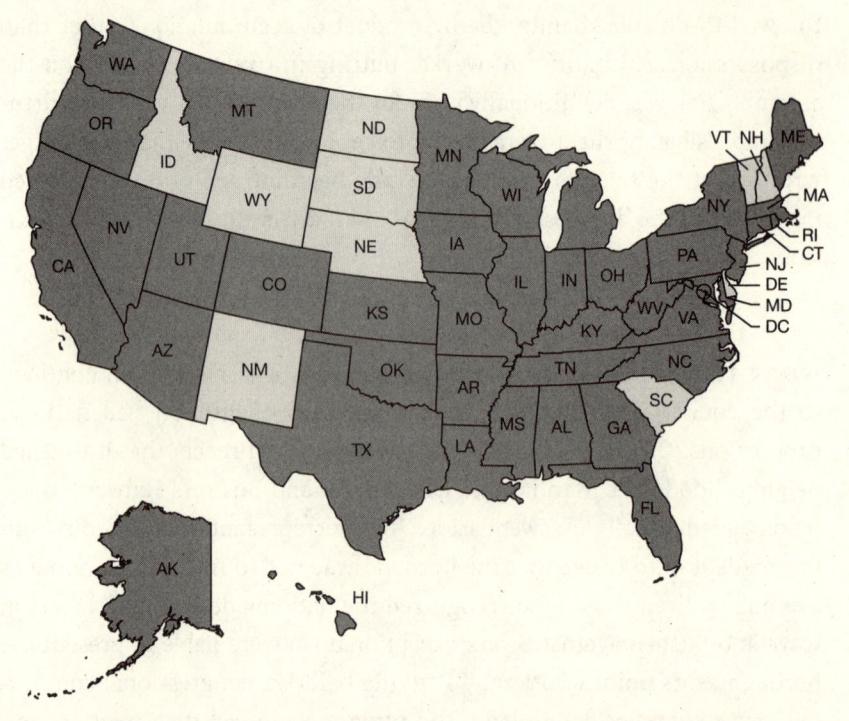

States with dark shading saw the formation of at least one anti-arson organization or task force in the 1970s. The U.S. Fire Administration kept a directory of these organizations, listing one or more in all but ten states.

sustained by all FAIR plans nationwide, much of that from Bronx fires. However, the NYPIUA's huge share of the deficits was not the result of the unique depravity of the New York situation but was, rather, the product of the city's mammoth rental market and the New York FAIR plan's particularly reckless underwriting practices. In 1975, the NYPIUA lost $16.1 million, which constituted 27 percent of losses sustained by all FAIR plans nationwide. Yet that still left a massive $42.7 million in net losses generated across the twenty-seven other statewide FAIR plans then in operation, losses also due primarily to what *Insurance Advocate* called the "unabated epidemic of arson." In Los Angeles, there was a 500 percent increase in arson between 1976 and 1981. Seattle, too, reported record arson rates, totaling $3.2 million in damage in 1974. In Detroit, it was estimated that arson destroyed ten thousand homes over the course of the decade. Even in the small municipality of Worcester, Massachusetts, 60 to 70 percent of all fires were thought to be incendiary.[32]

Many, but not all, of these arson fires can be attributed to the insurance gap and the FAIR plan. This was especially the case in rust belt states whose mortgage markets were suffering from disinvestment, industrial relocation, and white flight. In Massachusetts, at least 40 percent of arson fires in 1978 were FAIR-related, even though the FAIR plan wrote only 15 percent of property insurance in the state. In 1977, Boston fire commissioner George Paul went on the record with his concerns, telling the *Globe*, "I think the Fair Plan is the greatest single encouragement to arson." The manager of the Massachusetts FAIR plan openly fretted, "We're sitting ducks and there's not much we can do about it. We're just pouring money down the sewer." Other states did not fare much better. In Michigan, 35 percent of arsons in 1974 occurred in buildings insured through the state's FAIR plan. In Connecticut, 60 percent of fire losses in FAIR properties were logged as suspicious in 1976. And the Insurance Committee for Arson Control (ICAC) calculated that 52 percent of the *nationwide losses* from fires in FAIR-insured commercial properties were incendiary. Some states without FAIR plans also saw an uptick in arson. But FAIR plans may have had a hand in these fires as well: by supercharging the residual (or high-risk) market in the United States as a whole, they laid the kindling for the arson wave across the nation.[33]

As these statistics were publicized in the late 1970s, FAIR plans across the nation came under criticism from insurers and policymakers alike. One GEICO executive reflected, "FAIR Plans came about as a result of the riots of the 60s. They were hailed as almost a panacea for difficult-to-insure inner-city property. And the system worked—too well. Witness the arson problem." By 1980, Ohio senator John Glenn was cautioning the Senate Subcommittee on Criminal Justice that the FAIR Plan "has been exploited and subverted by absentee landlords and real estate speculators. It is often not honest, low income residents of inner cities who are utilizing FAIR plans, but rather fast writeoff absentee speculators and real estate hustlers who easily obtain coverage . . . and proceed to torch these properties and then collect insurance proceeds."[34]

The Bronx may not have been exceptional, but the United States was. The contrast in fire rates between U.S. cities and those of all other countries was appalling. "Tokyo, which has long been referred to as a paper city, does not have the frequency rate we have," noted a group of the nation's leading fire prevention officials, who drew a similar comparison to Cairo, Egypt. Likewise, in European cities that were also undergoing industrial relocation, arson rates were far surpassed by their U.S. counterparts. The nation's fire problem was so extreme that the National Commission on Fire Prevention and Control said in 1973, "the United States reports a [fire] deaths-per-million-population rate nearly twice that of second-ranking Canada."[35]

The singularity of the U.S. fire experience in the 1970s underscores just how historically contingent it was: if not for the insurance gap and the macroeconomic shifts that produced that gap, the rates would have been dramatically lower. And in New York City, the center of the global FIRE industries and the city with the highest fire rate in the world, these historical processes were put on smoldering display every night. Yet in the dominant narrative, the city's renters, not its rentiers, were to blame. Senator Daniel Patrick Moynihan of New York put this in the crudest terms: "People don't want housing in the South Bronx, or they wouldn't burn it down." The scale of the dispossession was here seen as proof of the profligacy of the dispossessed. As Bronx-born theorist Marshall Berman observed, "What a relief it must have been to think of the fires as something 'these people' were *doing to themselves*: then you wouldn't have to worry about whether the Bronx's troubles were somehow your troubles."[36]

+++

FOR MUCH OF its history, the social science of firesetting was really the art of scapegoating. The figure of the pyromaniac—the impulsive, pathological firesetter—dates to 1830s France, though the terms "arson" and "incendiarism" emerged around 1666 in connection with the Great Fire of London (which, significantly, also gave birth to fire insurance). The standard profile of the pyromaniac has morphed over time, almost always assuming a form that criminalizes bodies or behaviors deemed transgressive or out of place in a given historical moment. In nineteenth-century Europe, the firesetter manifested as a teenaged girl employed in domestic work far from family and home. Reflecting the anxieties of the early industrial economy, this figure was someone who had been corrupted by feminized wage work and the fragmentation of the agrarian, patriarchal family. She was also, according to the physicians constructing the ideal type, experiencing "disorders of menstruation." In the early twentieth century, the archetypal firesetter became the hypersexualized male. Sigmund Freud, especially in *Civilization and Its Discontents*, heralded this shift, presenting firesetting as a sort of masculinist fantasia of sexual and racial deviance. For Freud, incendiarism stemmed from a man's excessive and uncontrolled sexuality: "The warmth radiated by fire evokes the same kind of glow as accompanies the state of sexual excitation, and the form and motion of the flame suggest the phallus in action." He theorized that "in order to possess himself of fire, it was necessary for man to renounce the homosexually tinged desire to extinguish it by a stream of urine."[37]

Following Freud, the supposed queerness of firesetting has appeared time and again in the psychiatric literature. One study in the 1960s found that 54 percent of arsonists demonstrated some sort of "sexual maladjustment," with 44 percent of them marked as gay, bisexual, or exhibiting "heterosexual difficulty." Although by midcentury the connection between firesetting and sexual deviance was increasingly discredited, the linkage cropped up during the 1970s arson wave. A Massachusetts police lieutenant blamed "prostitutes, radicals, and homosexuals" for a series of fires in Boston's Fenway that were later proven to be arson for profit; the officer added, "I don't have to tell you, one of those [gay men] finds his lover in bed with somebody else, he'll just burn the whole place down." In New York City, the former deputy chief fire marshal urged arson investigators to conspicuously monitor suspected arsonists in the bathroom because "urination is a psychological form of sexual gratification for the pyromaniac, and it's impossible for him to function in front of other people." Even the administrator of the National Fire Prevention and Control Administration, fielding questions following a major fire in the Bronx, commented, "We know that there are arsonists who act out of vengeance, sex deviates [sic] who commit arson, and others who are simply seeking attention."[38]

The figure of the gay arsonist offered a convenient diversion from the historical truth that in the 1970s, gay clubs were frequent targets of arson attacks. The 1973 torching of the Up Stairs Lounge in New Orleans took the lives of thirty-two bar patrons, making it the deadliest attack on the gay community until the 2016 Pulse nightclub massacre, in Orlando. A similar, though far less lethal, fate befell the Gay Activist Alliance's New York dance club and offices in 1974. Affectionately called the Firehouse, the club went up in flames, even though it was literally housed in a decommissioned fire station.[39]

Martin Wong's epic painting *Big Heat* (1986) finds queer love in a hopeless place.

Ever ready to reclaim a homophobic slur, gay disco culture embraced fire (and firefighters) as primal and sensuous symbols of sexual liberation in the 1970s. When pioneering gay DJ Larry Levan needed to raise money for the construction of the legendary Paradise Garage nightclub in 1978, he threw a "Fire Down Below" party and projected clips of a warehouse blaze onto porn footage, all while blasting Karen Young's steamy hit "Hot Shot." Later that year, gender-bending icon Sylvester opened "Dance (Disco Heat)" with the flirty line "Got a match?" The painter Martin Wong, Sylvester's old collaborator from the drag troupe the Cockettes, immortalized the firefighter fetish in *Big Heat*, a large painting of two firemen kissing in the shadows of a towering burned-out tenement in the East Village. But reclaiming fire did not deliver protection from it. When the macho backlash against disco began in 1979, racist and homophobic hate was again written in flames. Mobs chanting "Disco sucks" piled and burned records at rallies all over the country. During the most famous of these, the Disco Demolition Night at Chicago's Comiskey Park, some forty thousand vinyl records were ritualistically burned by a crowd of fifty thousand.[40]

The association between gayness and firesetting largely fell out of fashion after 1980. That year, the National Gay Task Force confronted the stereotype head-on. The group denounced an arson investigation manual produced by the National Fire Academy that contended that gays and lesbians were particularly predisposed to arson. The manual noted that gay firesetters "retain a distinct predilection for arson 'initiated by hatred, jealousy or other uncontrolled emotions.'" In response to the public censure, Jimmy Carter's White House instructed the NFA to delete those passages.[41]

While the salience of sexuality as a cause of arson waned within popular and social-scientific understandings, race proved more enduring. In New York City, the conflation of Black communities and arson drew from a deep historical well, one that went back as far as 1712, when a group of enslaved New Yorkers launched an uprising by setting fire to a building owned by a local slaveholder. The revolt was quelled, but the fears it unleashed were not, and Black New Yorkers emerged from the episode as regular suspects in arson cases. Such fears climaxed in a 1741 witch hunt that resulted in the execution of dozens of Black men, thirteen by fire. More than a century later, during the 1863 draft riots, a different set of racialized fears—these rooted in working-class resentment among Irish Americans forced to fight for slavery's abolition in the Civil War—likewise proved combustible. The ensuing five days, during which rioters laid waste to Black New York, are best remembered for the Irish mob's burning of the Colored Orphan Asylum. With Black labor competition a key driver of Irish American racial animus, the event brought to life the fast-evolving strain of white supremacy in the industrializing North.[42]

In the following decades, as the scaffolding for Jim Crow was violently erected atop Reconstruction's ruins, the association of Blackness with incendiarism became central to the nascent disciplines of criminology and actuarial science. Perhaps no single person was more responsible than Frederick L. Hoffman, a progressive-era actuary for the Newark-based life insurance juggernaut Prudential. The quantitative language of statistics offered the actuary a potent, modern idiom for crystallizing the supposed link between Blackness and criminality. Hoffman's influential 1896 data tables attempted to prove this linkage, sorting by race those charged with various crimes. In a nation that criminalized Blackness, those incarcerated were disproportionately Black for every type of crime. But no category was more racially skewed than arson: 46 percent of those imprisoned for arson in men's prisons were Black, compared with rates in the 20 or 30 percentiles for other property crimes. Hoffman found these numbers remarkable, using them to praise fire insurers for their discrimination against Black customers in an age before formalized redlining: "The large proportion of colored among prisoners charged with arson attests to the wisdom of the recognized policy of fire insurance companies in restricting the amount of fire insurance obtainable by colored persons." The lynch mob translated these data tables into brute force. Between 1882 and 1903, 104 Black victims of lynching in the South were accused of arson, according to one count.[43]

The urban rebellions of the 1960s seared the notion of incendiary Blackness into the national psyche. "The urban riots of 1964–1968 could be thought of as epidemic conditions of an endemic situation," wrote then–Nixon adviser Moynihan in the "social pathology" section of his infamous 1970 memo "on the status of Negroes." Moynihan's coauthor and collaborator Nathan Glazer, who wrote frequently on the South Bronx, betrayed a similar obsession with "social pathology" in a set of musings about "the Puerto Ricans in New York." Transposing the stereotype from one racialized group to another, Glazer argued that "a good deal of Puerto Rican violence consists of crimes of passion involving members of the community only."[44]

The "crimes of passion" framework bled into the 1970s, and what could be called non-economic firesetting remained the dominant interpretation of the arson wave through much of the decade. "Arson for profit accounts for only about 10 percent of all deliberately set fires," insisted the *Boston Globe* in an article about the Bronx and New York City. "More often, arson is a 'crime of passion'—motivated by jealousy, revenge, vandalism and emotional disorders." The NYPIUA claimed the same in defense of itself when the *Daily News* published its scoop on landlord Carmine Lanni. "Nationwide, less than one out of every seven arson fires is set in an attempt to cheat an insurance company," the vice president of the NYPIUA said. "Actually, the vast majority of arson fires are ignited for purposes of revenge, as acts of vandalism or even for sexual gratification." A fire chief with the FDNY endorsed this view: "The youth in the neighborhood seem to get some enjoyment out of using some form of accelerant, usually gasoline." In 1977, years after the uprisings petered out, Dennis Smith, the author of the best-selling memoir *Report from Engine Co. 82* and the Bronx's—and probably the nation's—most famous firefighter, contended that for Black Americans, arson was "a form of social protest." For all that the journalistic establishment bungled its coverage of the arson wave, it was extraordinarily consistent on this point: the culprits for the nation's fires were the Black and Brown renting masses.[45]

"One thing that gave this situation an especially sinister twist," lamented Marshall Berman about his native borough, "is how many Bronx people came to see themselves as 'these people,' how many victims of suspicious fires came to think of themselves as prime suspects." Recounting her childhood years in the Bronx, Vivian Vázquez Irizarry reflected, "We did blame ourselves, 'cause that's what we internalized.'" The self-incrimination ran so deep that Vázquez Irizarry resolved to confront it head-on with the 2019 documentary *Decade of Fire*: "A lot of us still believe that we were to blame, cause that's the only story that ever gets told about the fires. But I could never let that go. What really happened to us here?"[46]

Although fires born of pyromania, protest, revenge, or recreation did indeed appear in the Bronx, there is no evidence to suggest they were more common there than anywhere else. "Yes, of course there's revenge fires, there's vandalism, but it's not that—this is not that," clarified the deputy head of New York's Arson Strike Force, Michael Jacobson. Part of the reason that non-economic arsons attracted more attention was their tendency to be overrepresented in statistical samples of convicted arsonists; put simply, these arsonists were more likely to get caught. Those who set fires out of vengeance, for instance, were likely to have acted "on the spur of the moment without regard to one's chances of being apprehended." In the words of one fire investigator: "We know the most about the least successful arsonists." What that meant was that researchers varied widely in their estimates of the percentage of arsons set for profit, with most falling in the 40 to 60 percent range in these years. Where researchers agreed was in the finding that fires set for financial gain were by far the most destructive type, with one study deducing that if a fire caused more than $5,000 in damage, it was likely arson for profit.[47]

In the blue-ribbon report *Arson in America*, released by the Senate Subcommittee on Investigations in 1979, arson for profit was cited as "the chief cause for the dramatic fire increase in urban areas." Yet arson for profit itself requires unpacking, since fires set for economic gain encompass a number of disparate types. In the Bronx and many other U.S. cities, the insurance gap was the primary causal force. According to the National Fire Prevention and Control Administration, this was certainly true in Boston, where "the fuel that keeps fires raging in [its] neighborhoods is insurance money." Even then-senator Joseph Biden, known at the time for his reactionary approach to law-and-order politics (he helped push Democrats toward racially targeted drug enforcement), pointed to white-collar insurance fraud as a "primary motive" for arson.[48]

A less common, but often more lethal, form of landlord arson had the purpose of spurring gentrification. Municipal tenant protections sometimes placed guardrails around redevelopment, which could incentivize rapacious landlords to pick up the torch. In Hoboken, New Jersey, and Boston's Fenway, landlords used eviction by fire to circumvent legal regulations that mandated two or more years of notice before a renter's unit could be converted into a condominium. Unlike many of the other types of arson analyzed in this book, this particular variant is still evident today in cities where hot real estate markets chafe against tenant protections.[49]

In another variant of arson for profit, building "strippers" scavenged abandoned or near-abandoned buildings in search of scrap metals they could sell on the secondary market. Strippers sometimes set fires to gain easier access to copper, bronze, aluminum, or lead piping concealed behind walls or between floors. At a scrap-metal vendor on 184th Street and Jerome Avenue in the Bronx, strippers could fetch 50 cents per pound of copper and 25 cents to 45 cents for brass. Sometimes they exploited firefighting practices to access the pipes and fixtures, since, as the *New York Times* reported, "firefighters will knock out the walls for them," thereby putting the pipes within reach. "Vertical mines are what we've got," quipped Fire Chief James M. Slevin. The firefighters were the drill and the dynamite to the tenement's ore.[50]

But if building stripping was an extractive microeconomy, it was ancillary to the primary markets of insurance, reinsurance, and mortgage credit.

Arsons set by strippers most often *followed behind* previous fires, feeding on the by-products of the insurance gap. Strippers "move in quickly at the first sign—often a fire in a single apartment," explained the *New York Times* in an exposé on the salvage economy. A similar sequence was recorded by arson investigators conducting an autopsy of a five-story walk-up on Fox Street in the South Bronx. The building had thrived for three decades of full occupancy before tumbling into a familiar tale of shady real estate transactions and landlord milking. Within six months of its latest sale, "the fires began. It started with a rubbish fire on the roof which spread to the cockloft. The two top floor families were forced to relocate. Even though the landlord made a substantial cash settlement with his insurance company, the fire damaged apartments were not repaired." Only *after* the landlord had collected a handsome insurance payout did the strippers arrive. "Bent on stripping the building and selling the material," the strippers "accounted for the next fire."[51]

+++

THOUGH THE SALVAGE economy offered a tantalizing news item, building strippers were far from the media's or the state's favorite scapegoats for the arson wave. That role was reserved for the welfare arsonist, a media-made effigy that was also—in exceptional instances—real. Blaming the welfare arsonist served as a pressure valve for a volatile real estate market. Yet although the figure's utility as a scapegoat is unequivocal, the welfare arsonist cannot be written off as simply a media fiction. Some Bronx tenants receiving welfare did indeed set fires to their own homes, though the evidence suggests their numbers were marginal. If we overlook their stories out of a commitment to debunking racist stereotypes, we miss a vivid illustration of the costs of survival.

To the extent that public discourse acknowledged the existence of an arson problem in the first half of the 1970s, the welfare arsonist was a convenient culprit at a time of welfare retrenchment. Even before Richard Nixon entered the White House in 1969, the brakes had already been slammed on the War on Poverty. The welfare arsonist emerged amid this great rollback of the welfare state, prefiguring the "welfare queen" rhetoric that would dominate domestic politics in the last decades of the century. Lamenting the Bronx's large number of welfare recipients was a standard journalistic motif, and it almost always had racial intimations. As the *Daily*

News reported, "A problem in the Bronx is the influx of blacks and Puerto Ricans, some of whom relied more on welfare than work, and the exit of an earning middle-class group made up of Germans, Irish, Jews and Italians." Obscured in such accounts was the role of the city's social service agencies in directing these migration patterns. "The South Bronx became a dumping ground for the social service agencies. We had a concentration of welfare clients in the South Bronx," observed Mike Nuñez, whose own family moved from the urban-renewal ruins of East Harlem to the Bronx's 158th Street in the postwar years. For their part, landlords were encouraged to welcome tenants receiving welfare assistance because the subsidized rent allowances often exceeded the caps set by the rent-control program.[52]

Those who raised alarms about welfare arson stressed two principal motives for setting one's own apartment on fire. First, for those waiting for a coveted unit of public housing, being displaced by fire sent their application to the top of the yearslong list. In 1975, the waiting list for the New York City Public Housing Authority officially had 145,000 families, though a NYCHA official estimated the "real need at 250,000 families." As the FDNY's most prominent fire marshal, John Barracato, told the *Times*, "if they appeared to be victims of a fire they would be given one of the highest priorities for public housing." Second, tenants displaced by fire received a few hundred of dollars in relocation subsidies per person. Both incentives were invoked in a defense of mortgage redlining by the president of Dollar Savings, the Bronx's largest bank:

> How can savings banks, the major source of mortgage funds in New York City, invest in neighborhoods where building after building is being burned out daily? The housing procedures of the welfare system encourage these burnouts and looting. Buildings are being "bombed out" and Welfare then feels obligated to relocate the tenants, refurnish their apartments and give the family an allowance for new clothing.

The New York State Welfare inspector general made the same argument, stating in 1977, "Some welfare recipients commit arson in order to collect funds for furniture replacements, escape an accumulation of rent arrears, and move into more desirable housing." Even critical historians today fall into such thinking.[53]

The archival record is decidedly thin when it comes to substantiating these claims. The most reliable source on the matter, New York City's Arson Strike Force (ASF), stated definitively, "We believe that far too many fires are blamed on tenants receiving public assistance." (It is worth noting that while the ASF could not establish a statistically significant link between welfare recipients and arson, one ASF study did discover a different housing program that was unmistakably connected to incendiary fires: the J-51 program, which offered tax abatements to landlords pursuing condo conversions.) Moreover, the city's relocation bureaucracy did not seem to churn any faster even when the arson wave was reaching its peak. In 1975, the *Times* reported, "Two of the agencies where [the fires'] impact is most likely to be felt, the New York City Housing Authority and the Division of Emergency Housing of the Department of Relocation and Management Services, report no major increase in their work as a result of the South Bronx fires." A housing authority representative even recorded a surprising 20 percent *drop* in housing applications from fire victims in 1975 compared to the same quarter in 1974, "despite the recent spate of fires in the Bronx." These statistics, noted a *Times* reporter, "do not seem to support the contention that there may be a trend among poor families, usually on welfare, to 'burn themselves out' to get to the top of the waiting list."[54]

Although its statistical significance was never borne out, the figure of the welfare arsonist was more than a mirage. The archives of the 1970s Bronx contain a number of documented instances of welfare recipients setting fire to their own homes in hopes of bettering their housing conditions. When I first encountered these cases, I brushed them aside as red herrings, given what I already knew about the scale of landlord arson. But as these tenants came into fuller view, I began to see that ignoring them would do a disservice to the story of the 1970s city.

In an internal report on "stress-induced arson," the ASF recounted the story of a Puerto Rican husband and father who moved to New York when he was eighteen. Amid the economic shocks of the 1970s, he came to the harsh realization that, in his words, "It's difficult [to find work] when a person doesn't know English. It's hard because I wanted to take care of my family." Unemployed and "forced to live off welfare received by his wife and children," the man found himself "in a situation of extreme duress." The precarity he faced around work was compounded by the "unbearable" housing conditions in his family's "dangerously deteriorating building." As he described it, "There was no steam, no heat. Both my wife and girl ... got sick. There were roaches and mouses running around. The rest of the apartments were empty." When he reached his breaking point, he made a calculated decision to "set a fire so that he and his family would be able to move ... to a [public] housing project." Against the odds, he was caught and convicted.[55]

Stuck in an infested, unheated, and nearly abandoned building, this father saw firesetting as a lifeline for his family. Nonetheless, fire marshals would classify his actions as yet another type of arson for profit, in the same league with—and subject to the same legal penalties as—a landlord arson scheme like Carmine Lanni's. Under racial capitalism, legal definitions of "arson for profit" and "profit" more generally flatten differences of history, scale, motive, and reward. But there is something categorically distinct between raking in an insurance windfall of $100,000 and extricating one's family from a living situation that is making them sick.[56]

The private market for real estate in the 1970s Bronx had veered so far from its professed objective of providing secure shelter that, for this man and his family, the clearest path to safety was *to set their home on fire*. He was not alone. In 1977, Bronx assemblyman Sy Posner, one of the first policymakers to take on landlord arson, described how welfare arson—to the extent that it occurred—emerged *in reaction to* insurance arsons: "This is how the scheme works. A landlord who plans on burning out a building first fills it with welfare recipients because he can charge higher rents and squeeze as much money as he can out of the building. ... Finally, he sets fire to the place." Only then do the remaining tenants, "seeing the handwriting on the wall ... set the fire a second time so they can be put on the priority list for relocation." In the perverse logic of the 1970s Bronx housing market, the surest way to escape the arson wave was arson itself.[57]

The gravitational force that gave shape to this system was the undeniable safety of public housing relative to the private market. In part because the scores of public housing developments in the Bronx experienced "virtually no structural fires," they were in extremely high demand. After her family's second displacement by fire, Hedy Byrd and her four children sought out public housing and "refused to move into another tenement" because they "were petrified that if we live in another tenement, it too will burn." As we've seen, one of the few ways to gain priority was to be displaced by fire, which was exactly what happened to the family of DJ Jazzy

Jay, an early collaborator of Afrika Bambaataa's who was instrumental in founding Def Jam Recordings. "We had a big fire," Jay recalled. "Man, it was awful. I'll never forget that, waking up in the middle of the night and everybody screaming, 'the building's on fire,' and then we moved to the Concourse Plaza Hotel [a shelter]. . . . I think we lived there for a few months until they finally placed us and the place they placed us in was Bronx River Houses." For Jay, arriving at Bronx River Houses brought a fateful introduction to his new neighbor and soon-to-be mentor, Afrika Bambaataa. For his family, the NYCHA-run facility offered refuge from the devastation of the surrounding neighborhoods. They stayed for decades. "Getting into the projects was . . . a big deal at that point in time," he remembers, his story disrupting the standard history of U.S. public housing, in which the 1970s mark its downfall.[58]

Once we recognize that setting fire to one's own home might have been the most expedient path to escape the ravages of the private real estate market, welfare arson begins to look less like another variant of arson for profit and more like the "stop, drop, and roll" cued up by an underfunded welfare state.

+++

THE GREAT INDIGNITY of the arson wave was that those whose lives were torn apart by the conflagration were also blamed for it. But while Bronxites themselves often overestimated the magnitude of welfare arson, the borough's archives are rich in tenant testimony implicating the systemic roots of the blazes. Before landlord arson became a major headline, one of the borough's congressional representatives noted, "there is a widespread feeling in the community that a conspiracy to defraud insurance companies is at work." The most sophisticated analyses of incendiarism, as chapter 7 will show, were leveled by the residents whose homes were destroyed by arson. As the sweat-equity activists of the Bronx's People's Development Corporation (PDC) theorized, "National and international shifts of private capital have inhibited the ability of private financial institutions and landlords to organize either the housing market or the labor market. This has resulted in a process of abandonment and arson on a scale unprecedented in the history of any American city." It was clear to the organizers of the PDC that Bronxites could count on neither private capital nor the state to solve the problems created by those very forces: "Private abandonment and government cutbacks have forced neighborhood residents to take control of their own destinies and chart the course of their future themselves."[59]

Yet even the most discerning witnesses would have trouble keeping up with the convolutions of capital. As Vivian Vázquez Irizarry recalled, "In the community, we knew that landlords were burning their buildings. We just didn't know how much money they made or how they got away with it." And deliberately so: those unfathomable sums evanesced with the flames that made them. But while the profits vanished rapidly from view, their wreckage lingers.[60]

FIVE

A Triangular Trade in Risk

> Do you really think you're insulated from
> the *Third World*?
>
> —TOM WOLFE, *BONFIRE OF THE VANITIES*, 1987[1]

> With such profound speculative dangers, why does
> capitalism tolerate fictitious capital in the first place?
>
> —DAVID HARVEY, *THE LIMITS TO CAPITAL*, 1982[2]

Martin Wong's 1984 painting *The Flood* casts the Statue of Liberty's iconic torch in brick and mortar, rising from a flooded tableau of moldering tenements. With a portentous sky overhead and a fire brigade in the foreground, Wong's canvas plays on the contrast between the desecrated state of U.S. cities and the nation's touted ideals of liberty and progress.

As darkness fell over New York Harbor on July 4, 1976, millions of revelers gathered at the water's edge to take in what the *New York Times* called "the biggest and most colorful fireworks display in the city's history." With the acrid aftertaste of Vietnam and Watergate lingering, the bicentennial promised a respite from imperial malaise—a day for waving the flag, not burning it. "Never had so many people watched a fireworks show," the *Times* recounted, almost in disbelief that, in a decade defined by war and scandal, the celebration appeared to be a success. The evening is best remembered for scenes of Lady Liberty bathed in a pyrotechnic glow, but there was another record-setting fireworks show on display that summer—one that, though largely unseen and forgotten, left a more lasting mark. In a perverse embodiment of "bicentennial fever," the absolute peak of the arson wave in New York City arrived just as the nation celebrated its two hundredth birthday.[3]

The Bronx's own Gil Scott-Heron had long kept a tally of American hypocrisy. Performing "Bicentennial Blues" during the Independence Day celebrations, the godfather of hip-hop took stock of the republic and counted only "Halfway justice / halfway liberty / halfway equality / it's a half-ass year." In the equation set up by Scott-Heron, the grand sum of these "halfway" truths was the blues tradition, at once a reaction to anti-Black violence and a history of struggle—a wound and a weapon. The blues was "born on the slave man's auction block" and "grew up in Nat Turner visions." By this bicentennial year, the blues was global: "bluesicians have gone all over the world carrying the blues message, and the world has snapped its fingers and tapped its feet right along with the blues folks." It didn't matter whether the time signature was 4/4 or 12/8; to Scott-Heron's ear, the blues always played in tempo with the "afterlife of slavery," as Saidiya Hartman dubbed the persistence of a deadly "racial calculus" long after emancipation. "The blues remembers everything the country forgot," the Bronx-raised singer seethed, enjoining his listeners to refuse the ritualized forgetting encouraged by the festivities.[4]

That same year, the liabilities of the arson wave would—like the blues—spread a form of Black pain beyond the United States, propelled by an increasingly transnational reinsurance industry. A decade earlier, Lloyd's of London, the reinsurance juggernaut, had fled the U.S. market in response to the uprisings of the era, helping to precipitate the creation of the FAIR plans. Now it suddenly washed back up on the shores of northeastern cities. Beginning in 1976, Lloyd's of London—by way of a series of intermediaries—started flooding the Bronx with insurance policies that undercut the high prices of the New York FAIR plan. The underwriters at Lloyd's did not want to carry all the liability for these risks, so they purchased reinsurance—a means by which insurers off-loaded some of their liability to other firms—from a Brazil-based reinsurer. With losses distributed across a chain of insurance firms, the return of Lloyd's pushed brownlining into overdrive, further stoking the flames on the ground.

The global flows of insurance followed a twentieth-century triangular trade, offshoring risk from the Bronx to Britain and Brazil. The hazards confronting a lone tenement in the Bronx reverberated across oceans, redistributing the risks forged at the core of twentieth-century racial capitalism. Like the triangular trade of earlier centuries, this one reworked the relationships between race, space, and finance. Haunting the 1970s routes of reinsurance were voyages like the 1781 expedition of the *Zong*, a British slave ship whose captain ordered 122 enslaved captives to be thrown overboard in response to overcrowding and disease. When the owners of the *Zong* attempted to collect maritime insurance on the murdered captives and the ten others who jumped out of fear or defiance, the abject horror of the episode galvanized the British abolitionist movement. The resonances with the twentieth-century triangular trade in risk are many: the *Zong* had previously been underwritten by Lloyd's of London, the ship sailed by the colony of Brazil before the massacre, and both cases sparked major political controversies.[5]

The twentieth-century triangular trade shown in the illustration on the next page depicts the flows of racial capitalism in a moment of increasing financialization. This particular circulatory system pumped vigorously from 1976 through 1978, leading to discounted premiums and even less oversight on fire risks in the Bronx. With a surplus of insurance capital saturating the borough, a number of large arson rings formed across the Bronx and New York City in 1976, eclipsing the small-time arson schemes more prevalent in the early 1970s. In that bicentennial year, arson for profit industrialized, generating a handful of vertically integrated enterprises

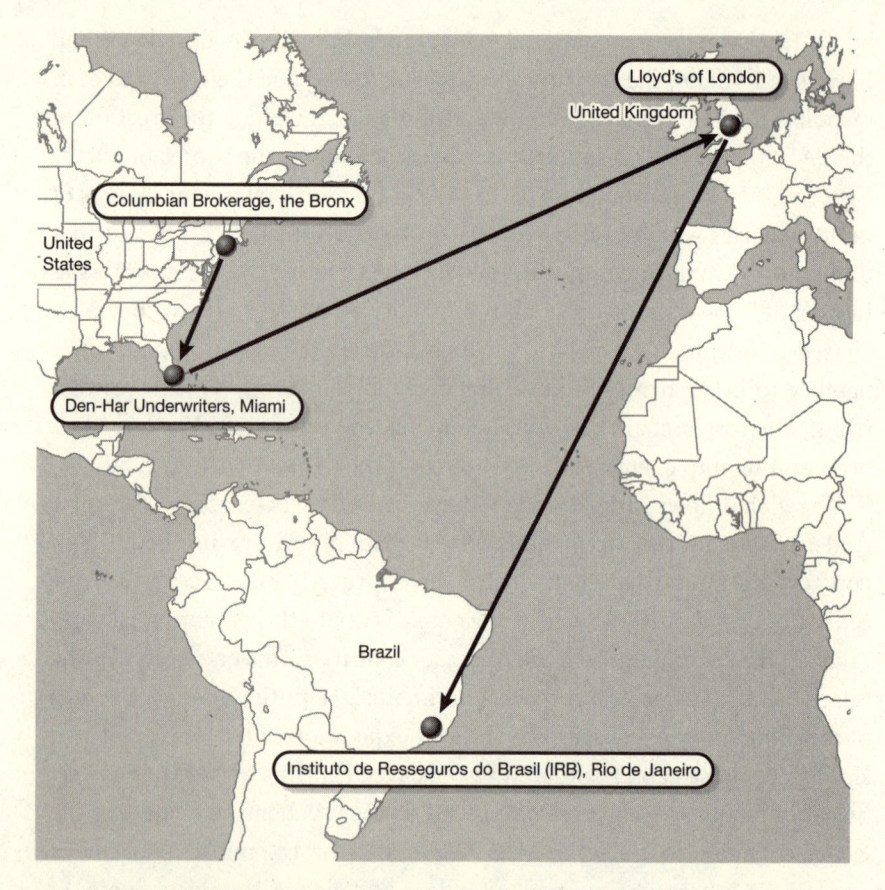

A twentieth-century triangular trade in risk.

that performed all services in-house. The membership of these arson rings could number in the dozens, involving insurance underwriters and adjusters, landlords, real estate agents, government workers, and torches. Their payouts far outpaced earlier ones, totaling in the millions.

The story of Lloyd's and the arson rings features no shortage of conspirators, but there is limited benefit in viewing the saga as a conspira*cy*. Though human hands lit those fires, they were set in motion by forces impersonal and far-reaching. The carnage followed from financial globalization, which accelerated in the mid-1970s and has remained a cornerstone of the global economy ever since. The triangular trade in risk was both a conduit and a consequence of that globalization. To reduce it to a conspiracy overlooks how much of the trade discussed here was just as legal as the eighteenth-century trafficking in human cargo.

The twentieth-century triangular trade spread risk across a global network of institutions and put off the reckoning for another day. Reinsurance worked to diffuse risk not only by stretching it across space but also by drawing it out over time. It could take years for claims to make their way across a chain of reinsurers; it was not until 1980 that a full accounting of losses was tallied. This liability lag was central to reinsurers' business model: it gave them a lengthy window during which they could invest their collected premiums. But a liability lag could also create vulnerabilities. The large arson rings of the late 1970s exploited the lag, and it took years for insurers to feel the pain. The losses of the Bronx careened from one side of the Atlantic to the other, but eventually the entire network of insurance collapsed. Never in its nearly three-hundred-year history had Lloyd's of London suffered such outsized losses. Yet that firm did not see the worst of it. As capital risk diminished for insurers, physical risk increased for people and the places they called home.

+++

WHEN LLOYD'S FLED the U.S. market for urban property insurance during the long, hot summer of 1967, it set in motion a crisis that, as we have seen, culminated in the establishment of FAIR plans. In New York City, the NYPIUA quickly grew to become the largest property insurer, a dumping ground for so-called riot-prone risks. What one critic termed "back of the bus" insurance had the effect of exacerbating the racial stratification of the property insurance market. Among the unforeseen consequences of their popularity among landlords and insurance brokers was that the FAIR plans lubricated the property insurance market as a whole. "Keeping the market elastic," the FAIR plan, ironically, paved the way for the return of Lloyd's of London to the U.S. urban market nearly ten years after it had exited.[6]

Soon after the NYPIUA's insurance coverage flooded New York City, it began to alter private insurers' calculus of urban risk. As early as 1971, the NYPIUA had the unanticipated effect of convincing some private insurers that, as the New York superintendent of insurance noted, "many properties, hitherto regarded as 'uninsurable,' could in fact be insured without disastrous results." This turnabout was occasioned by the NYPIUA's unexpected profitability that year. Its solvency was short-lived, though, and the NYPIUA ended up running a deficit almost every other year of the decade. Nevertheless, by 1972, some private insurance companies were siphoning off the highest-rated properties from the FAIR plan and placing them in the private market, a process the industry termed "depopulation." Between 1972 and 1973, all FAIR plans nationwide experienced a 43 percent drop in applications, according to an industry report that concluded that "'depopulation' is the key word" of the year. The New York Urban Coalition put it in more human terms, describing how the private market had "gotten jealous of the Pool's then profitable operation [in 1971], and decided to attract back some of the good risks they had rejected during the 1968 riots." This was certainly the case for the Hartford Insurance Company, which in the early 1970s "was seeking additional premium volume" to invest, leading it to "invite anyone with a FAIR Plan policy to bring it in." Within a few years, the Hartford had managed to snatch at least $10 million in premiums from the NYPIUA's pocket.[7]

The insurance industry spun the FAIR plans' "depopulation" as proof that it had succeeded in putting an end to the redlining era. Yet many FAIR policyholders simply traded one flavor of subprime insurance coverage for another. Specifically, many acquired property insurance in what was called the excess and surplus (E&S) line market, composed of companies that were unregulated by state insurance departments. Even states without FAIR plans experienced parallel growth of their E&S markets, leading industry experts to conclude that FAIR plans had stimulated the urban property insurance market nationwide.[8]

For all the criticism of the NYPIUA for reckless business practices, its reputation looked sterling compared to that of the average excess line company. Because E&S insurers were not officially licensed to do business in a given state, they were in the odd position of being both freed from rate regulations and restricted in their access to a state's market. Had state insurance laws been upheld, these companies would have been insurers of last resort, their products available only after a given risk had been denied coverage repeatedly by regulated, or "admitted," insurers, including FAIR plans. Such restrictions went unenforced, however, and surplus line companies in many states operated with impunity. In addition to price gouging, the E&S market had a reputation for shady dealings and poor oversight. Their high premiums equipped excess line insurers to "tolerate higher losses" than other companies, and investigators warned that the E&S market offered poor deterrence against arson. According to a New York City tenant organizer, "a disproportionate share of insurance fraud and tenant abuse originates with excess line insured properties."[9]

Excess line companies, itching to increase their premium income, sensed an opportunity to expand their customer base in the mid-1970s, when the rates of NYPIUA premiums skyrocketed. Earlier in the decade, when the NYPIUA was new on the scene, its policies were cheaper than those of excess line companies, which claimed only a marginal share of the property insurance market. By 1975, however, the rates of the New York FAIR plan were surging to four or five times suburban rates, and excess line companies swooped in under the cover of depopulation, cutting their prices to as low as one-third the rates charged by the NYPIUA. In the words of the president of the New York Metropolitan Brokers Association, "The Insurance Department contends that the policyholders are going to the voluntary [or private] market. What actually is happening is that these people are going to the excess market or doing without." Between 1975 and 1976, excess line companies increased their premium earnings by almost 300 percent, their growing market share coming at the direct expense of the NYPIUA. By 1978, E&S premiums had nearly caught up to NYPIUA writings, claiming at least $3 in premiums for every $4 collected by the NYPIUA.[10]

The best-known excess line insurer was Lloyd's of London. Though far more established and reputable than most E&S firms, Lloyd's was forced into the unregulated market by state protectionist regulations barring overseas or "alien" companies from entering the U.S. voluntary market. In late 1975, Lloyd's of London was nearing its three hundredth anniversary when it reentered the U.S. urban property insurance market. Lloyd's is not a single company but, rather, a marketplace composed of dozens of syndicates, each of which operates as an autonomous insurer. Founded in 1688 as a coffeehouse where merchants and shipowners could procure maritime insurance, Lloyd's played a central role in indemnifying the imperial expansions of European powers at the dawn of racial capitalism. As Eric Williams noted in his famous work *Capitalism and Slavery*, "In the early years, when Lloyd's was a coffee house and nothing more, many advertisements in the London Gazette about runaway slaves listed Lloyd's as the place where they should be returned." Lloyd's furnished

The Underwriting Room at Lloyd's of London, the oldest and largest insurance market in the world, where one of its syndicates was brought down by fraudulent insurance claims on Bronx fires, prompting a crisis of legitimacy at Lloyd's.

insurance on both enslaved bodies and the ships (like the *Zong*) that carried them. Its ascent as the preeminent marketplace for insurance thus hinged on the triangular trade. Over the centuries, Lloyd's expanded its horizons, and by the 1970s it was well known for insuring odd and difficult-to-place risks like nuclear reactors, the television rights to the 1980 Moscow Olympics, and even, as Michael Jacobson notes, "Jimmy Durante's nose and Betty Grable's legs."[11]

In addition to indemnifying individual risks in the American excess line market, Lloyd's sold reinsurance to U.S.-based insurers. Reinsurance is commonly described as insurance for insurance companies; insurers purchase reinsurance to neutralize their exposure to underwriting losses, which in bad years might exceed those companies' total assets. A reinsurance policy allows an insurer to hedge against unexpected loss by "ceding" a portion of its liabilities (and its premiums) to another firm.

In tandem with the financialization of other sectors, the reinsurance industry entered a period of massive global expansion during the 1970s, with risk becoming ever more dispersed and serpentine. There was nothing groundbreaking about reinsurance in this decade; it had structured and lent elasticity to insurance markets since the nineteenth century. But until the late 1960s, the reinsurance industry had been highly concentrated, modestly sized, and effectively old hat. "All that changed by the mid-1970s," explained a pair of social scientists writing in the *Nation* in 1986. "New companies, many based in Third World countries and some controlled by governments, began to flourish."[12]

While the 1990s are known as the globalization decade, it was really the 1970s that paved the way for the hyperglobalization of reinsurance and the financial industry at large. From 1944 until 1973, the international monetary system had been pegged to the U.S. dollar, which was directly convertible into gold. The Bretton Woods system, as it was called, represented the full ascendance of the United States to global economic dominance following World War II. But during the late 1960s, too many U.S. dollars were accumulating overseas due a host of factors: Vietnam War spending, an increase of imports relative to exports, the expansion of U.S. multinational corporations abroad, and the eagerness of U.S. banks to enter the London-based Eurodollar market, where they could benefit from higher interest rates than permitted by the Federal Reserve. Beginning in 1968, the gold-backed dollar endured crisis after crisis. In response, President Richard Nixon allowed the Bretton Woods system to collapse between 1971 and 1973, inaugurating our current era of floating exchange rates. The U.S. dollar remains the global reserve currency, but it is no longer convertible into gold.[13]

The fall of Bretton Woods made possible financialization in the United States and across the globe. Abandoning the gold standard "introduced both flexibility and volatility," writes the scholar of neoliberalism David Harvey. Domestically, that meant the removal of a significant restraint on federal budgets, enabling the deficit spending of the Reagan era and beyond. Meanwhile, foreign lending became the largest source of revenue for U.S.-based banks during the 1970s, and major markets in foreign exchange rates spurred the growth of novel and complex financial instruments involving derivatives, options, and futures. The mobility of capital was rapidly accelerating, with much of that capital coming from surging oil profits amid the OPEC oil embargo following the 1973 Arab-Israeli War. Thanks to a backchannel deal between the United States and Saudi Arabia, oil revenues—now understood to be "petrodollars"—were invested in New York banks, which then lent them back out to nations in the Global South. "Thus," explains scholar Saskia Sassen, "developing countries were a key element in the geography of financial activity, as both producers and consumers in international finance." So it was with the reinsurance sector, which developed strategic nodes all over the globe.[14]

With financial globalization came cultural shifts within the reinsurance business. The once-straitlaced industry took on a ruthlessness and a glamour more associated with other corners of the financial world. Reinsurers met annually at the Hôtel de Paris in Monte Carlo, becoming, as the finance reporter Lynn Brenner put it, "the high rollers, the big risk takers, the hams of the business." Glitz like this was possible only because of the skyrocketing growth in the reinsurance sector, as compared to all other lines of property and casualty insurance. Reinsurance premiums ballooned 323 percent between 1976 and 1985, compared with just 51 percent growth in fire and allied lines, and 138 percent growth for the average line of insurance.[15]

The reinsurance boom meant the bouncing of risks from one reinsurer to another, then to another, and on and on. A set of risks, having been bundled together, might "bounce 40, 50 times," explained an industry expert. "Today, risks are reinsured and retroceded so many times over, say reinsurers, that it is impossible to trace the ultimate recipient of the premium." The resulting webs of reinsurance represented the insurance industry's variant of the derivative, with risk spread thinly across firms located all over the world.[16]

Although the pinballing of risk meant forgoing some premium income, reinsurers benefited from being able to invest premiums for longer periods of time. It could take years for a claim to bounce its way through a chain of reinsurers. "In contrast," wrote Brenner, "to the primary insurer, who is subject to unfair claims practice regulations which speed up payment, the longer the lag, the more time the reinsurer has to invest the money." In some lines of reinsurance, like product liability, the lag time could stretch as long as twenty years. The "long tail," as it was known in the industry, was "one of the biggest inducements to get into the reinsurance business."[17]

For the better part of the 1970s, Lloyd's of London rode the reinsurance boom. The decade saw an unprecedented expansion in the membership of Lloyd's, with the number of Names—as Lloyd's terms its investors—tripling. This brought huge increases in underwriting capacity and a corresponding upsurge in profits. "The 1970s were years of high returns at Lloyd's," notes its institutional biographer, citing the 20 percent annual profits raked in by its high-performing syndicates. This was in striking contrast to many other industries, which were pulled down by the decade's oil shocks and stagflation. "For most of British business," remarked Godfrey Hodgson in his history of Lloyd's, "the 1970s were one long misery of raging inflation, endless strikes and labor disputes, falling shares of world markets, and vanishing profits. The insurance industry, in contrast, had ventured boldly into world markets, and had reaped a rich reward."[18]

Of those who "ventured boldly into world markets," Lloyd's of London was at the forefront, channeling its peerless underwriting capacity back into the same urban neighborhoods of color it had fled during the 1960s uprisings. But its timing could not have been worse. Its return to U.S. cities came just as fire losses were mounting to sums unthinkable during the summers of the 1960s. Lloyd's reentry into the market may have been the work of an actuary, but the effect it had on the 1970s Bronx suggested it was more of an accomplice.

+++

IN A SOUNDSCAPE defined by the relentless wail of sirens and the thumping bass of early hip-hop battles—what Bronx-born Melle Mel called "the sound of the whole world caught on fire"—it took more than a minor racket to pierce the Bronx night. Still, we can imagine the terror felt by East Tremont tenants in 1976 when twenty-five homemade gasoline bombs "ripped the roof off an occupied Bronx apartment building in the middle of the night," according to an investigation in the *Nation*. Awakened by the blast, the building's tenants had a clear path down the fire escape and stairwell, thanks to the torch's placement of the incendiary devices in the building's cockloft, just below the roof. Though all the residents made it out alive, the ensuing blaze caused injuries to several firefighters. The publicly available fire report attributed the cause and origin of the fire to the cockloft explosion, meaning that this fire defied the taxonomic odds and was unambiguously recorded as incendiary.[19]

Despite its classification as arson by the FDNY, the blaze was logged as accidental by the New Jersey–based adjuster in charge of calculating the total damage and settling the insurance payout. In his report to Lloyd's, which had underwritten the building, the adjuster said the fire was "caused by careless disposal of a cigarette in a garbage strewn elevator pit." Here was a building that had burned down in truly spectacular fashion, by way of a fire that was clearly marked by fire marshals as incendiary, and yet the insurer filed it as a simple sanitation issue. How could the evidence of arson be so patently clear and the insurance paperwork so far off base? The clerical discrepancy between a fire sparked by a cigarette and one detonated by twenty-five bombs somehow went unnoticed by Lloyd's claims personnel. On the adjuster's word, Lloyd's unhesitatingly paid out on the loss, issuing $21,000 to the policyholder in 1977 or 1978.[20]

According to the *Nation*, it was only when Frank Selemoncsak, the "repentant" torch who'd set off the bombs, "walked in off the street and made a detailed confession" that authorities connected the blaze with Lloyd's oversight and the subsequent payout—as well as with fifty other fires. That it took a torch's desire to clear his conscience for the scheme to come to light attests to the extraordinary conditions required for an arson ring to be exposed. What became known as the Gold ring was made up of six landlords and two torches, and their collective toll was obscene. At least nineteen buildings were torched by the landlords, many enduring multiple fires, which together injured forty firefighters and netted the owners a minimum of $1.2 million in insurance claims. A number of the buildings were still occupied at the time of the fires, though no tenants reported physical injuries—likely because the blazes were set in the cocklofts. At the center of the ring was Bernard Gold, an eighty-year-old insurance adjuster and landlord based in Queens and Florida. Gold's was a one-stop shop, handling everything from indemnity to ignition, building acquisition to insurance adjustment. He would be indicted in federal court for paying "bribes, gratuities and kickbacks" to other insurance adjusters, brokers, landlords, and torches.[21]

Its vertical integration notwithstanding, how did the Gold ring get away with shifting the blame for a twenty-five-bomb blaze onto a wayward cigarette and a junk-littered elevator shaft? How did Gold and Co. slip this cover-up past Lloyd's, thought to be "the greatest centre for insurance and reinsurance in the world"? The answer was the Sasse syndicate, whose lax underwriting standards were the basis of the business plan drawn up by Gold and his co-conspirators. When, in December 1975, the underwriting capacity of the Sasse syndicate began to spread through the Bronx and other northeastern cities, it became fuel to the FAIR-made fire. The property insurance coverage made possible by Sasse's entrance into the U.S. urban market "provided what must have been the most flexible insurance Bronx landlords had ever seen," observed the *Nation*.[22]

The story of that unscrupulous underwriting—what media outlets came to call the Sasse scandal—is the story of the arson wave at its grim, globe-spanning climax. Because a map of its complex roots and routes was commissioned by the United States Fire Administration, we have more detail on the Sasse syndicate and its associated arson rings than on any other arson scheme of the 1970s. The "highly confidential" (now declassified) fifty-page memorandum, written by arson researcher Alfred J. Lima, offers a revelatory, blow-by-blow account of the Sasse scandal.[23]

According to the Lima memo, the transnational circulation of Bronx-based risks looked something like this: A Bronx landlord walked into Columbian Brokerage at 2844 Westchester Avenue and purchased a fire insurance policy from a surplus-line insurer for a third of what it would cost with the NYPIUA. Columbian placed, or enrolled, the risk (let's call it Risk Bx) with Miami-based Den-Har Underwriters, known as an E&S insurer because it was not registered in, and was thus unregulated by, New York State. From its small Florida office, Den-Har was authorized to act as a "binding agent"—or remote underwriter—on behalf of Lloyd's of London syndicate 762. Named for its active underwriter, Frederick "Tim" Sasse, the Sasse syndicate was based out of the Lloyd's building in London, and it was the "anchor" for Risk Bx, meaning it was the original source of the insurance policy. But the syndicate did not want to carry all the liability for the risk, so it purchased reinsurance. Sasse bundled Risk Bx with dozens of similar risks and reinsured about half of its total liability with the Instituto de Resseguros do Brasil (IRB), a reinsurance firm based in Rio de Janeiro.[24]

The drama of the Lima memo revolves around the collision of seemingly disparate geographies. Tim Sasse oversaw a number of syndicates at Lloyd's, including syndicate 762. As its underwriter, Sasse was responsible for deciding which risks to indemnify with the capital reserves of the syndicate's 110 Names, or members. Sasse's Names were an august set, counting among their ranks Earl Fortescue, whose noble lineage extended back to the time of William the Conqueror, and Lord Napier, the private secretary of Princess Margaret. Among the "less wealthy members" of the syndicate was the famous opera singer Nigel Douglas, dubbed the "tenor of Lloyd's." Names had to be "elected" and were eligible for membership only if they possessed a minimum of £100,000 in assets (roughly $1 million in 2024 dollars). Securing one's status as a Name at Lloyd's was, for many, a way to preserve and capitalize on the vestiges of their aristocratic past. Because membership did not involve investment, per se, but instead required putting up one's assets as collateral for a syndicate's underwriting (and then amassing premium income), Lloyd's allowed Names to generate wealth from illiquid assets like estates.[25]

Tim Sasse was known as a lone wolf in the Lloyd's orbit. After a string of early successes, he no longer involved himself in the daily minutiae of underwriting, considering it "easy money." The racetracks were his passion; his crowning achievement was his horse's victory at the 1973 Prix de l'Arc de Triomphe, considered by many to be the world's most prestigious horse race. In 1969, he even wrote a book recounting his equestrian exploits, *Theme on a Pipe Dream: A Formula for Buying, Breeding, and Backing the Derby Winner*. The opening line: "In these days of the welfare state and high taxation, there is a special appeal and glamour added to the ever absorbing challenge of owning or breeding a champion race horse." Written during the swan song of the Keynesian welfare state, Sasse's "pipe dream" was of a market-dominant future that was closer at hand than he could have imagined. A decade later, amid the triumph of financialization, Tim Sasse's pipe dream slipped into an actuarial nightmare, and he won infamy for betting on the wrong horse.[26]

Sasse's underwriting technique relied heavily on "binding," or deputizing a third party with the authority to assume liabilities on behalf of his syndicate. His goal was to accumulate as much premium volume as he could, mostly by insuring small-scale risks. As one journalist put it, "This hands-off style produced large amounts of premium for little effort, but it also meant that the fortunes of the syndicate were in the hands of whoever produced the business." Sasse's luck ran out when his syndicate's fate landed in the hands of New Jersey's John Goepfert, a known insurance grifter who had already been in the crosshairs of the U.S. attorney of the Southern District of New York.[27]

In December 1975, Goepfert founded Den-Har Underwriters, taking a 30 percent share of the Florida-based company. Den-Har was specifically incorporated to write business on behalf of the Sasse syndicate, an arrangement that was brokered by a number of unsavory intermediaries, including a Coral Gables–based associate of Sasse's, Dennis Harrison, an English expat and Den-Har's namesake. Within the first month of business, Den-Har had attained binding authority from Sasse. The limit that Den-Har could underwrite on Sasse's behalf was twice the usual figure: $500,000 rather than $250,000 on any one risk. "In the binding authority from Sasse, [Den-Har] had something like a blank cheque," wrote a journalist on the Lloyd's beat. Although Lloyd's bylaws technically required a centralized review, or tribunal, of these types of binders, Den-Har started "binding risks for Sasse . . . without first being 'tribunalized.'"[28]

By January 1976, insurance brokers in New York and New Jersey were hawking Den-Har's insurance products, deliberately marketing them to the FAIR plans' customer base. As a streetwise insurance swindler, Goepfert was skilled at marshaling a "flood of business to flow into the channel" dug by Sasse and his colleagues. An ocean away, Sasse was slow to learn of Goepfert's dealings. Den-Har divided its book of risks into two categories, replicating the racially tiered insurance market within its excess line offerings. In its "Standard Portfolio," explained the Lima report, it sold "average quality risks emanating primarily from Florida." By contrast, its "Special Portfolio covers mostly risks in New York and adjacent states, many of them in areas of high fire risk." Goepfert stuffed the Special Portfolio full of the same risks that had previously been relegated to the FAIR plan's residual market, reinscribing the deep grooves of brownlining.[29]

Like the FAIR plan, Den-Har's insurance offered substandard coverage relative to the homeowners policies available in the suburbs. But Den-Har's policies were explicitly priced "on a basis designed to undercut the FAIR Plan rates of premium," often as low as one-third the cost of NYPIUA policies. Property owners were thus encouraged to "cancel their FAIR Plan policies and go with Lloyds." Taking advantage of the subprime market created by the FAIR plan, Den-Har expanded at a breakneck pace by raiding the FAIR customer base—an embodiment of the nationwide "depopulation" trend.[30]

Den-Har was pillaging the FAIR plan's premiums, which may have appeared to be good business, but in doing so it subjected itself to the liabilities of the racially tiered insurance market. "Most of the subsequent losses" were concentrated in the Special Portfolio, the Lima memo reported. As an underwriter, Den-Har was just as cavalier as the NYPIUA, insuring buildings for "agreed-upon" values (that is, at the behest of the insured). "Not only did the company charge low rates and care little about the condition of the buildings," detailed an investigative report in the *Nation*, "but it was also extraordinarily lax about looking into fire losses."[31]

The insurance gap that had emerged under the FAIR plan now widened. Landlords purchased buildings for $2,500 and then insured them with Den-Har for as much as $500,000. Take that disparity and multiply it a thousandfold: Den-Har wrote policies on more than thirteen hundred properties in 1976 alone. What these numbers meant was the unchecked obliteration of New York City's built environment and heightened peril for its renters. It was only against this backdrop that a cigarette and two dozen bombs might look indistinguishable on an adjuster's log sheet. The city's landscape was so consumed by fire that the arsons set by the Gold ring apparently did not need explaining, let alone mitigating. "What appears as a wasteland in the Bronx may be an acceptable loss in the board rooms of London or Lower Manhattan," concluded the *Nation*.[32]

As the anchor for Den-Har's reckless underwriting, the Sasse syndicate was able to countenance this enormous exposure to liability only by ceding some of the risk via reinsurance. In July 1975, before Sasse and Den-Har had forged a partnership, a broker at Lloyd's had arranged for Sasse's future writings to be reinsured by the Instituto de Resseguros do Brasil. IRB had been created and granted a monopoly on reinsurance by the Brazilian government in 1939 to help underwrite the growth of the nation's industrial sector. In the 1970s, when Brazil was ruled by a military dictatorship with grand economic ambitions, IRB began chasing after foreign capital. Amid the globalization of the financial sector, the reinsurer opened an office in London and began writing contracts with Lloyd's underwriters like Sasse (ventures like this would set the stage for Brazil's debt crisis in the 1980s).[33]

In the shipping lane of indemnity that linked Florida's Den-Har with London's Lloyd's, IRB's reinsurance was the wind and the current. Through secondary markets, reinsurance facilitated the diffusion of risk, stretching it out across several financial institutions. What property insurance did for mortgage markets, reinsurance did for the insurance industry more broadly: it kept the markets elastic. In the 1970s, as it was stretched ever thinner, reinsurance changed the relationships between people and places, investors and investments. With the liability lag and the yoking together of far-flung geographies, the act of reinsuring warped time and space. For IRB, this warping created information asymmetries that would eventually boomerang. But for a few years, the route from New York to Florida, then London to Rio, represented the mundane functioning of a distinctly postwar triangular trade in risk. In two years, more than $20 million in premium writings zigzagged from one Atlantic port city to another (over $100 million in 2024 dollars).[34]

Sasse's risk trade came to an abrupt halt in November 1977, when IRB finally caught word that "an explosive situation" was afoot. The Brazilian reinsurer had been tipped off by a Lloyd's broker that the Sasse syndicate was "in financial trouble." It would take almost three years for the full numbers to register, but already the Sasse syndicate had sought relief for losses exceeding $3 million. IRB was especially disturbed by the news coming out of New York and its possible connection to this mounting sum. Media coverage of the city's arson wave, particularly in the Bronx, had ballooned in 1977. Almost overnight, "Arson in the Bronx was big" for the pundit class, according to the *Washington Post*. News reports traveled around the globe, and IRB was paying attention. The Rio-based reinsurer began to suspect that "it had been the victim of misrepresentation," connecting Sasse's high losses to the reports of landlord fraud. When IRB notified Tim Sasse of its suspicions, Sasse got nervous about the prospect of losing his reinsurance. According to the Lima memo, he shot back: "Unless IRB pays the syndicate $500,000 within 24 hours ... Sasse will see to it that IRB is placed on the 'Yellow Sheet'"—essentially threatening to blacklist IRB from the world's largest insurance market. IRB caved to Sasse's imperial threat, shelling out the half million dollars as a "sign of good faith."[35]

In exchange for this partial payout, IRB demanded that Lloyd's conduct a thorough investigation before it would agree to pay another dime. After sniffing around for just a few weeks, Lloyd's leadership began to suspect wrongdoing and suspended the Sasse syndicate from further underwriting in December 1977. When the investigation wrapped up in March 1978, it corroborated IRB's "arson suspicions" and unearthed "alleged irregularities in the issue of the policies," including Lloyd's failure to fully vet Den-Har. IRB considered this evidence sufficiently incriminating to justify "instruct[ing] its counsel to void the reinsurance contract between it and Sasse." Just like that, Sasse was cut off from its reinsurance stream.[36]

With the Sasse syndicate defunct and IRB's reinsurance a thing of the past, Den-Har Underwriters was forced to cancel more than $100 million in insurance coverage, most of it concentrated in the Bronx and Newark, New Jersey. For the majority of these policies, thirty to sixty days of notice was given before the cancellation took effect. With the Lloyd's well having run dry, Bronx property owners were left with the same meager insurance options that had been available before Sasse's entry in 1976. But after years of Den-Har's cut-rate coverage, landlords were far from eager to return to the comparatively steep rates of the NYPIUA. Upon Den-Har's cancellations, Lima noted, local "brokers who placed this coverage panic[ked] and maintain[ed] that because of 'exorbitant' FAIR Plan rates in New York, owners will either abandon their property or go uncovered." More fearsome was the possibility that some owners will "use this time span [of thirty to sixty days] to torch their properties while they still have coverage." In the tinderbox Bronx of 1978, the likelihood of that scenario was less a question of if than of when.[37]

+++

IT WAS SUPPOSED to be an in-and-out job. The previous night, Luis Ayala had prepped apartment 4D of 2031 Seventh Avenue in Harlem, boring holes in the ceiling to expose the building's cockloft. This would be Ayala's twentieth arson, and though within his arson ring he was still considered an apprentice, he was on his way to being a seasoned torch. As he climbed up the building's poorly lit stairwell on the night of November 10, 1978, he had every reason to believe this job would go as smoothly as the others had. Clutching a ladder, a can of kerosene, and a black bag stuffed with rags, he silently ascended the empty stairway of the still-occupied building.[38]

What happened next was both freakish and fateful. Ayala lost his footing in the dark of the stairwell, dropping the red can of kerosene to the hard tiled floor. It fell with a crash so piercing that it echoed in the annals of Gotham's history. Though he still managed to set the fire, the chain of events precipitated by Ayala's fumble ended up exposing what was likely the largest arson ring in the city's history. Like the Gold ring, the Bald ring got its start in 1976, just as Den-Har's insurance products were landing in the Bronx. The landlords in the Bald ring took full advantage of Lloyd's presence, though we can only speculate as to whether the timing of the fire on November 10 was determined with the Lloyd's cancellations in mind. In 1978, the Bald ring was at its height, and like the Gold ring's, its downfall would begin at the bottom of the pecking order, with an unassuming torch.[39]

Moments after Ayala stumbled, "tenants were peering through apartment-door peepholes," recounted the *Times* years later. Spying Ayala's kerosene can and ladder, they recognized instantly that the building was set to burn, and they swiftly fled. It took only half an hour for the fire to engulf the roof before spilling down the stairwell and spreading to the other floors. By the standards of the arson industry, the blaze was a success: "the building burned through the night" and was deemed beyond repair. But as Ayala escaped in a black Chevrolet driven by his wife, one of the building's tenants ran behind the fleeing car, shouting at the Ayalas and jotting down the license plate. The tenant dutifully passed along the identifying information to the city's fire marshals, who paid one perfunctory visit to the Ayalas' Brooklyn address before dropping the investigation and letting the case go cold.[40]

For the Ayalas, however, the memory of being pursued in their black Chevy would not fade so easily. Convinced that "the police were hot on his trail," Luis Ayala asked Harry Rosen, his employer and the building's landlord, to buy his way out of town. Two days after the fire, Ayala, his wife, and their son flew to San Juan, Puerto Rico, on tickets purchased by Rosen. The plan was to hide out for two months and wait for the supposed investigation to blow over, but Luis Ayala's telltale heart throbbed with worry. Just two days after skipping town, he panicked and returned to Brooklyn to find out if the police were casing his house. Though initially relieved to see no law enforcement around, he was shocked to discover that Rosen had emptied his apartment. Confronting Rosen, Ayala "grew wilder" when the landlord "denied any knowledge of what had happened to his employee's possessions." Rosen responded by brandishing a pistol, and for Ayala that was the final straw. He went directly to Bedford-Stuyvesant's 81st Precinct, where he confessed: "I have some information on some fires." After three hours of testimony, it was clear to the Brooklyn cops that this was an interborough case with strong ties to the Bronx.[41]

Arriving at the precinct at two a.m., Barry Kluger, the assistant Bronx DA in charge of arson prosecution, enlisted Ayala as an informant. Ayala described an organization that numbered some two dozen people: retired police officers, real estate agents, at least four torches, a lawyer, and more than a dozen landlords. "The maypole of this circle of landlords," according to the *Village Voice*, was Joe Bald, a onetime rabbi, "fire broker," and owner of buildings all over the city. The effort to uncover the arson ring involved a wildly complicated, nineteen-month investigation that amassed twelve hundred pages in daily police reports.[42]

The Bronx DA's office began by "wiring up" Ayala and sending him out to inquire about new torch jobs from his employers. Donning a six-inch transmitter, Ayala accepted these risks in the hope that his cooperation would earn him leniency in his sentencing. But after his escape to Puerto Rico, hasty return to New York, and altercation with Rosen, Ayala had lost his credibility in the arson underworld. The circle of landlords who had supplied him with steady employment now wanted nothing to do with him. The prosecutors settled on plan B, dispatching Ayala to incriminate Edwin Julio Garcia, another torch in the same ring.[43]

Garcia and Ayala fit a similar profile: both were Latino handymen in their late twenties. Trained in the upkeep of buildings, Garcia and Ayala found themselves working for landlords who were structurally incentivized to run their properties into the ground. The lines between maintaining and torching a building were so blurred in the 1970s Bronx that Ayala's first experiences with arson were unwitting. He knew there was something suspicious about his instructions to climb up to the ceilings of vacant apartments and drill holes in them, but it wasn't until he surveilled one such building at night that he confirmed that he was unknowingly participating in a torch job. Sensing an opportunity for a pay raise and promotion, he confronted his employers and "demanded that he be taken into the ring." His arson apprenticeship began shortly thereafter.[44]

Ayala had little trouble implicating Garcia, who confessed to torching twenty-six buildings over a two-year period, beginning in 1976. Like Ayala, Garcia agreed to wire up, and in September 1979, he captured on tape an incriminating conversation with Harry Rosen and his deputy, Willie Rosen (no relation). Harry and Willie Rosen commissioned Garcia to burn down two apartment buildings in Brooklyn, supplying him with keys, a $150 cash advance, and $30 for gasoline.[45]

Within a month, the two Rosens were sitting in Barry Kluger's office listening to themselves conspire on tape. Harry reportedly yelled, "Shut it off!" before accepting his fate. He would be Kluger's ticket to the top of the arson ring: Bald, thought to be the most powerful "fire broker" the city had ever seen. Bald and his network of landlords had ushered in a new stage in the plunder of the Bronx. The large arson rings that took form after 1975 were something different from the small-time landlords who had turned to arson out of financial expediency in the first half of the decade. Achieving economies of scale by pooling torches, sharing information, and infiltrating insurance firms and law enforcement, these rings represented the industrialization of landlord arson.[46]

The injection of Lloyd's coverage—that is, the globalization of reinsurance in the 1970s—was a primary factor driving the formation of large arson rings. Bald and Co. purchased most of their insurance from the Sasse syndicate via Den-Har Underwriters, supplementing their coverage with policies from the NYPIUA. In maximizing their insurance revenues, arson rings like Bald's especially benefited from the ability to pass the title of a property between a set of straw owners, inflating its value with each transaction. One community anti-arson group warned, "Every time title is transferred, the owners increase the amount of the sale and, with it, insurance coverage.... This strategy can quickly result in overinsuring a property." The lax inspection standards for Sasse-insured properties did little to deter these practices.[47]

Straw ownerships made it nearly impossible for tenants, community groups, tax officials, or law enforcement to identify the true owner or beneficiary of a property. For years, Bald's system of straw ownerships helped insulate his arson ring from detection. If not for Luis Ayala's decision to turn himself in, it is difficult to imagine how the Bald ring would have been exposed. According to investigators, Bald and Co. "attempted to conceal true ownership of their holdings through a complex and sophisticated network of interlocking financial arrangements and paper enterprises." No fewer than forty-five shell corporations were unearthed by investigators, some with names like Boner Realty or Golem Realty Corporation (*golem* is Yiddish for "monster"), suggesting that the conspiring landlords considered themselves untouchable. With two former police officers on the payroll, they had every reason to believe they were.[48]

The Bald ring operated at scale, churning through Bronx buildings at a feverish pace. Within just a couple of years, it had torched some 250 buildings, netting approximately $5 million by 1980. Bald and his fellow landlords achieved these numbers in part by acting as "finishers" for struggling property owners. According to the Bronx DA, they would "buy buildings at deflated prices in deteriorating neighborhoods" from landlords who likely had no other buyers at the table. The bottom-feeders of the real estate industry, they offered an easy and legal way out for landlords who were not satisfied with their rate of return or were nervous about the long-term prospects of their property. Once it was in the hands of the ring, the property was sent through "a maze of corporate shells and dummy transfers."[49]

The arson ring, unrivaled in its scope, also proved to be unwieldy, and it fell apart with astonishing rapidity. When Harry Rosen made a deal to become an informant for the investigation into Joe Bald, he was agreeing to turn on his friend of twenty years. On January 18, 1980, Rosen walked hurriedly through the lobby of Bald's Brooklyn office, arriving to discover Bald acting shifty, convinced his office was bugged. Bald led Rosen to the men's bathroom, where he felt safer. In the false sanctuary of porcelain and tile, the two men agreed to split the insurance proceeds for 201 Marcy Place, a torched building they owned off the Bronx's Grand Concourse. Rosen's recordings gave the district attorneys of the Bronx and Brooklyn what they needed to bring charges against Bald and a dozen other landlords. After Bald agreed to act as an informant for other investigations into crooked landlords, he faced a reduced sentence of eight to twenty-five years. In the final analysis, the Bald ring could be linked to at least $25 to $30 million in insurance coverage, mostly purchased through Columbian Brokerage in the Pelham Bay neighborhood of the Bronx. Almost all of it landed on the books of Lloyd's Sasse syndicate, an ocean away.[50]

+++

JUST AS THE district attorneys were closing in on Bald's arson ring, the London police—prompted by the fallout from IRB's cancellation of the reinsurance contract—were "called in to investigate the books of the Sasse syndicate, the first time this has happened [at Lloyd's] in 50 years," according to the Lima memo. The Sasse scandal threw Lloyd's of London into a paroxysm of firsts. "For the first time in its 293-year-old history, the venerable insurance organization... is being taken to court by some of its own members," reported the *Financial Times*. This once-unthinkable legal action had been precipitated by the Sasse syndicate's $45 million underwriting deficit, at that point "the largest loss ever suffered by a single syndicate in Lloyd's history." As great as these losses were, the toll of the Sasse scandal was difficult to quantify on a balance sheet. "Lloyd's has been more shaken in the last few months than at any time since insurance men began to meet at Mr. John Lloyd's coffee house in the middle of the seventeenth century," marveled the *Guardian*. What Lloyd's was facing was a crisis of legitimacy.[51]

Even before Lloyd's had conducted a full-cost accounting of Sasse's losses, the syndicate's stateside misadventures were making headlines. In this post-Watergate moment, U.S. readers were gorging on tales of white-collar crime, and the decade of "financial fiction" was just getting underway. The striking juxtaposition between British noble houses and Bronx tenements was a business journalist's dream. "The village of Swinbrook in the Cotswolds is about as different from the fire-trap tenements of the South Bronx as one human habitation can be from another," Godfrey Hodgson told his readers about the estate of Sasse member Earl Fortescue. Of course, through the trade in enslaved Africans, investments in the segregation of the metropolis, and other historical legacies, the wealth of the British elite and the dispossession of poor Black and Brown Americans had long been inextricably linked. "The blues remembers everything the country forgot," Gil Scott-Heron insisted, and sure enough, by the 1970s such forgetting had hidden those ties from view. The Sasse affair merely unearthed them.[52]

What the media found scandalous about the Sasse syndicate's connections with the Bronx was not the scoop that landlords were setting their properties on fire en masse. The fact of arson, at least in coverage of the Sasse scandal, was greeted with wry resignation, as though it was an inevitability. As the *Guardian* put it, the Sasse syndicate "found itself providing fire insurance on property which was concentrated in the seedy run-down centres of American cities where arson is almost a way of life and American insurers stay out." Whose "way of life" was being identified here needed no specification; Black and Brown young people were the media's default scapegoats for arson. The article, like nearly every other write-up on Sasse, spoke of arson only in the abstract, failing to connect the flows of insurance to the actual buildings that were torched, let alone the tenants who were displaced.[53]

The namelessness of arson survivors and victims in the Bronx contrasted with the media fixation on how the Sasse scandal might affect the Names of Lloyd's. The moral outrage stemmed not from the decimation of entire communities of color by landlord arson but from the possibility that the Sasse syndicate's losses could bankrupt its noble members. With IRB having voided its reinsurance, Lloyd's syndicate 762 would have to foot the bill on its own. Astonishingly, though the syndicate had been suspended from further underwriting in December 1977, and IRB had canceled its reinsurance the following March, the Names involved did not learn that they were on the hook for Den-Har's losses until 1979. Due to Lloyd's idiosyncratic three-year accounting system—a complete accounting for 1976 was performed in late 1979—they did not know the full extent of the damage until 1980. What looked to be $8.5 million in losses in the summer of 1978 jumped to $13 million in July 1979, finally settling at the $45 million figure in February 1980. That burden was shouldered by only 110 Names; even for the British elite, this would be a lofty sum. One such Name, the opera tenor Nigel Douglas, owed £120,000 to cover the syndicate's losses, a debt that spoiled his plans to enroll his son at his alma mater, Eton, and forced him to cancel his membership at the Cavalry and Guards Club. While on tour, he had to stay in what he described as "extremely nasty" hotels.[54]

When the Names of Lloyd's syndicate 762 were asked to pony up $45 million for the losses of Den-Har Underwriters, they closed ranks and achieved another Lloyd's first. Sixty-three of the 110 Names refused to pay, and sued Lloyd's of London. This was, in the words of Lloyd's biographer, "a mutiny among the first-class passengers. It shook Lloyd's to the keel." According to the Lloyd's bylaws, joining a syndicate meant subjecting oneself to unlimited liability. In the hidebound world of Lloyd's of London, one journalist quipped, withholding payment or forsaking one's liability "just isn't done, old chap." A Name was supposed to accept such losses with lordly reserve. The lawsuit was so unprecedented in part because of the unusual, decentralized structure of Lloyd's of London. Since it was, as a business reporter explained, "not a monolithic organization but an agglomeration of many parts," Lloyd's was a slippery legal entity. It was coordinated by a central committee, but this body did not issue insurance; nor was it liable for the underwriting of its constituent syndicates. The committee had never been challenged by a syndicate in such a way before, and when the sixty-three Names announced their lawsuit, Lloyd's central committee brought a countersuit.[55]

In their lawsuit, the mutinous Names contended that Sasse had mismanaged the syndicate and violated the Lloyd's bylaws, and that therefore the Lloyd's Central Fund should pick up the tab. The Names charged that because Den-Har was not officially vetted by Lloyd's, the syndicate should not be liable for its losses. Although the Names' refusal to pay was itself in contravention of Lloyd's principle of unlimited liability, the litigants declared this principle void because the underwriting had proceeded in bad faith.[56]

For an insurance market that had made its name by steadfastly following through on payment for nearly three centuries ("Lloyd's most cherished tradition—that it always pays up," noted the firm's institutional biographer), the lawsuit was a doomsday scenario. To mitigate any further damage to its reputation, Lloyd's central committee caved in July 1980, agreeing to pay the lion's share of Den-Har's losses. The syndicate was suspended from writing insurance, and Tim Sasse was banned from Lloyd's for life. But, according to a finance reporter, "the chief casualty was faith in the old customs and ways of controlling the market." The Sasse scandal proved that lawsuits at Lloyd's could be fruitful, paving the way for the litigious Association of Lloyd's Members, which has been organizing Names and bringing legal actions ever since. It also played a role in Parliament's passage of the Lloyd's Act of 1982, which introduced accounting reforms and bestowed new powers on the Lloyd's coordinating council.[57]

In the years following the Sasse scandal, Lloyd's again withdrew from the U.S. market. In an odd bookend to its 1967 American exodus, Lloyd's of London's retreat in the mid-1980s came just as the arson wave was petering out. In this respect, its timing was mystifying. Sasse's fire insurance had arrived on American shores during the bicentennial year, at the height of the arson wave. With arson rates now rapidly falling, Lloyd's backed off. Its willingness to underwrite American risk seemed to bear little relationship to the physical state of American property. Here was demonstration on a global scale that the vicissitudes in fire insurance availability were governed by market forces far removed from measures of safety or risk.[58]

+++

THE SASSE CIRCUIT of reinsurance had diluted its own risk so much that the destruction of the Bronx did not register in London or Rio for years. As a biographer of Lloyd's put it, "One of the most striking aspects of this complicated story swirling around Tim Sasse is how quickly the damage was done and how long it took Lloyd's to realize what had happened, let alone do anything about it." As if pouring a vat of kerosene onto a raging bonfire, Sasse and Den-Har inundated the Bronx with cut-rate coverage for two full years before suspicions were aroused. Diffusing risk across time was a profit-maximizing technique that generally kept the insurance industry flush, granting it years with which to invest premiums. In Sasse's case, the time lag proved toxic.[59]

So, too, with the diffusion of risk across space. The web of reinsurers, despite promising to deliver the bounties of financial globalization, merely created a transatlantic shock absorber. Ask one of globalization's many critics how it affected a place like the Bronx in the late twentieth century, and the answer will likely involve deindustrialization, the offshoring of jobs, and rising unemployment. But financial globalization was directly implicated in the creative destruction of the built environment. And yet here we are, fifty years later, and the Sasse scandal and its many lessons are all but forgotten. When fire is naturalized on the basis of race, the *why* no longer demands an answer. To the extent that popular memory links fire in the 1970s to white-collar crime, the person wearing that white collar is most often a Jewish landlord. If we follow the money all the way up the chain, however, we end up in the lily-white estates of the British aristocracy.

In the end, the triangular trade in risk ensured that the destruction of the Bronx was felt around the world. By the time the financial hit was perceived by Sasse's earls and lords, much of the Bronx was lying in waste, many of its tenants already having suffered repeated rounds of displacement. What registered as slow violence on the balance sheets of London combusted with lethal immediacy on the streets and boulevards of the Bronx.[60]

Part III

REVOLT

SIX

Out of the Shadows and into the Streets

The Bronx is a revelation.
—PAUL NEWMAN, 1981[1]

Broken glass everywhere.
—GRANDMASTER FLASH AND THE FURIOUS FIVE, "THE MESSAGE," 1982[2]

Whether captured by a camera or a criminologist, the image of the Bronx was bound up with the turn to law-and-order politics during the 1970s. Though pundits clashed on the appropriate response to the borough's troubles, all agreed that the Bronx was a window onto the nationwide urban crisis.

Flanked by police cars and motorbikes, with three helicopters whirring overhead, the president's armored limousine arrived on the Grand Concourse unannounced. The White House had been planning Jimmy Carter's Bronx tour for weeks ahead of his October 5, 1977, visit, but even his host, New York City mayor Abe Beame, had been kept in the dark until that morning. Days before, the secretary of Housing and Urban Development, Patricia Roberts Harris, the first Black woman to serve in a presidential cabinet, had suggested to Carter that he steel himself: "The South Bronx is the end product of a process of decline and decay.... The area is unique only in that it is at the final stage of this process." But nothing could fully prepare the president for what he saw that autumn morning. As one of the few journalists to accompany Carter remembered, "The President seemed appalled by the extent of the destruction. It struck me that he must be thinking, 'How could you have let this happen to your city?'"[3]

Secretary Harris had anticipated the question, informing the rural Georgia–reared president that the Bronx's downfall had been precipitated by "social and economic forces." The first three she enumerated were "a marked shift to a poorer, less skilled, less educated population," "the physical deterioration of already old and inadequate housing," and "high density." For a Democratic administration already on the defensive for being slow to announce a national urban agenda after nearly a decade of Republican "benign neglect," Harris's diagnoses were hardly visionary. Nor were the instructions Carter issued when he stepped out onto Charlotte Street, a desolate stretch of half-demolished buildings that would emerge, as a result of his tour, as the visual epicenter of the nation's urban crisis. "See which areas can still be salvaged," he told Harris. "Maybe we can create a recreation area and turn it around. Get a map of the whole area and show me what could be done."[4]

In the aftermath of the president's tour, the Bronx became the blueprint for what the Carter administration billed as the "first comprehensive national urban policy." Yet Carter's urban policy fell far short of its stated ambitions. In the Bronx, the major infrastructural outcome of the president's visit was the trucking in of just 90 prefabricated single-family homes to Charlotte Street. Although Carter's tour did jump-start numerous funding streams for community development, it failed to enact the boroughwide overhaul it had promised.[5]

Nevertheless, the Bronx the president left in his wake would never be the same. The secrecy surrounding his visit was bad political strategy—one Bronx representative called Carter's failure to involve local legislators "shocking"—but despite the president's missteps, his tour made for potent political theater. After Carter's funereal rite, the Bronx became "a symbol of America's woes," an image that would go global, much like the Sasse scandal. Following in Carter's footsteps were busloads of tourists, largely from Germany and Japan, who went on guided tours of areas likened to the urban ruins of World War II. Calls for a Bronx Marshall Plan were put forth without irony. Still more buses, commissioned by "psychologists, sociologists, politicians, economists," and other researchers, facilitated a social-scientific pilgrimage to the borough. Charlotte Street, in particular, became a mecca for campaigning politicians, drawing Ronald Reagan, Ted Kennedy, Jesse Jackson, and Bill Clinton. Regularly dubbed "the worst ghetto in the nation" or even "the world," the Bronx became a destination for reporters and photographers documenting urban decline. As the *Times* editorial board wrote of Carter's trip, "the South Bronx [is] as crucial to an understanding of American urban life as a visit to Auschwitz is crucial to an understanding of Nazism." For most outsiders, the borough's ravaged landscapes were treated as evidence of cultural pathology. Criminalization would be the response, while residents' demands and counternarratives dissolved into background noise.[6]

Instead of a testing ground for a robust national urban policy, the Bronx became a laboratory of law-and-order urbanism. By the late 1970s, the borough's plight was increasingly used to justify carceral responses to social problems. Law-and-order liberalism was not new to the New York stage, but it became newly dominant in the late 1970s and early 1980s, helping to install Ed Koch in Gracie Mansion in the 1977 mayoral election. The 1960s search for "root causes" that had so preoccupied the Kerner Commission and urban liberals during the Great Society gave way to an understanding of "crime as the root cause of urban crisis," in the words of historian Elizabeth Hinton. With its fixation on broken windows and broken homes, law-and-order liberalism recalibrated social concern to favor a shallow depth of field and blur out the background context. After years of media neglect, the arson wave entered popular consciousness in this manner—with the troubles of the Bronx reduced to a series of perverse effects, their causes hidden from view.[7]

Bronxites cried foul as they watched their years of suffering get packaged into a circular set of narratives blaming them for their own hardships; before long, they took to the streets and the silver screen in protest. What ensued was a battle over the causes of the city's descent; the place of the police and the culture industry in addressing those causes; and, as ever, what protest tactics were acceptable from a movement of the criminalized.

+++

THE FIRES SMOLDERED for nearly a decade before attracting the type of media coverage and governmental action befitting a phenomenon of such scale. For years after the 1968 formation of the NYPIUA, arson was something of a niche story. In the Bronx, it was covered only locally and, at least until 1975, hardly at all. The federal response, meanwhile, was practically nonexistent. Only at the tail end of 1977, four years after the publication of the National Commission on Fire Prevention and Control's *America Burning* and the creation of a federal infrastructure for fire prevention, did Congress hold its first hearings on arson. By the time the policymakers and pundits grasped the epochal significance of the arson wave, it had already peaked in the Bronx.[8]

The inflection point came in 1977. In March, CBS aired *The Fire Next Door*, Bill Moyers's nationally televised TV documentary detailing the scale and scope of the Bronx arson wave. A few months later, the July 13 blackout in New York City offered a spectacular dramatization of Moyers's warnings. Touched off by a heat wave, a strained power grid, and a few fateful lightning strikes to the Con Ed power system, the twenty-five-hour blackout brought arson and looting in all five boroughs, with hot spots across the southern Bronx. The FDNY reported at least 168 fires in the borough that night (for the most part, their causes were undetermined), and some 473 stores were looted. For insurers, the damage was considerable. The NYPIUA alone recorded $7,547,677 in losses across the city. Electronics stores were hit especially hard—a boon to the fledgling hip-hop scene. As Grandmaster Caz recalled, "Everybody stole turntables and stuff. Every electronic store imaginable got hit for stuff. Every record store. Everything. That sprung a whole new set of DJs." Caz's collaborator Disco Wiz confirmed, "Before the blackout, you had about maybe five legitimate crews of DJs. After the blackout, you had a DJ on every block."[9]

Unlike the major uprisings of the 1960s, this one was not initiated by an episode of police violence, and its politics were thus more difficult to discern. Whereas the unrest of the 1960s was considered by many to be a political act—the "language of the unheard," in Martin Luther King Jr.'s oft-quoted formulation—what transpired during the 1977 blackout was largely dismissed as "ideologically empty." As the Ford Foundation put it in its definitive study, "the blackout looting was basically a welfare disturbance." In other words, "the prevailing tone of the looters was nonpolitical, and their purpose was to acquire items to fulfill personal needs or to sell to make money." Thus emptied of political significance, the events of July 13 and 14 would not necessitate even the most perfunctory soul-searching by those in power. Conservatives rushed to fill the interpretive void, blaming overly generous welfare policies, liberal permissiveness, and Black and Brown pathology. Historian Kim Phillips-Fein argues that conservative intellectuals spun the blackout as "a parable of liberal failure," thus emboldening austerity advocates across the nation.[10]

But to write off as "nonpolitical" the events of those hot July days was to release racial capitalism from culpability for the conditions that gave rise to the disorder. It required a particularly willful myopia to unsee the evidence that, as Phillips-Fein writes, "the blackout looting [was] an expression of the frustration of poor New Yorkers in the wake of austerity." The Ford Foundation's own exculpatory report, for instance, found that about two-thirds of those arrested for looting were unemployed, and that "the overwhelming majority" of looted stores were owned by white merchants who lived outside the neighborhood. Imagine hearing repeatedly that the most sought-after items were "baby food and pampers," and dismissing such actions as "nonpolitical."[11]

When the arson wave and the structural conditions that caused it are kept in view, the fires and looting of the 1977 blackout look less like aimless, self-seeking plunder and more like a collective reckoning. Most commentators suggest that the blazes were set by those swarming the streets, though we cannot know with certainty how many of the fires were in fact incendiary or accidental, set by tenants or set by landlords. What we do know is that the tenants of New York had, by the time of the blackout, endured a yearslong conflagration.

More than any other single event, the 1977 blackout can be credited with calling attention to the nationwide scourge of arson. "Until that blackout," noted the deputy coordinator of New York's Arson Strike Force, "fires were viewed as accidents rather than as crimes." The blackout accomplished in twenty-five hours what nearly a decade of blazes had not: it made the occurrence of fire in neighborhoods of color into something unfamiliar and worth interrogating. Never mind that landlords were, for once, probably not the main culprits. When investigators began recognizing individual fires as part of a yearslong pattern, landlords would emerge as the prime suspects. Within days of the blackout, Mayor Abe Beame announced the creation of the Mayor's Arson Task Force (later renamed the Arson Strike Force), which would play a pivotal role in stopping landlord arson. By the end of the month, the first attempt at an anti-arson bill had been introduced in the U.S. Senate.[12]

But perhaps the blackout's most direct legacy for the city's fire-scarred neighborhoods was spurring Carter's fateful trip to the Bronx. On July 24, Vernon Jordan, executive director of the National Urban League, pointed to the blackout as evidence that the Carter administration was not prioritizing the nation's cities. Jordan urged Carter to "signal to the nation his concern for the cities . . . by going to New York, by speaking with the looters and the looted in the South Bronx" and other affected areas. Though it took the president a few months to heed the call, Jordan's appeal is credited with inspiring Carter's tour of the Bronx. A week after Carter's visit, the image of the burning Bronx was further seared into the national imagination when nearly thirty-six million viewers watched as an aerial camera above Yankee Stadium panned away from Game 2 of the Yankees-Dodgers World Series and zoomed in on a large fire in an abandoned building nearby. Though announcer Howard Cosell never actually proclaimed that "the Bronx is burning," the mythology around that legendary phrase (spawning a *New York Times* bestseller and the ESPN series *The Bronx Is Burning*) is itself evidence that, in 1977, the South Bronx was transmuted into an enduring symbol of the urban crisis.[13]

After nine years of a largely unreported wave of arson for profit, it took a mass uprising to draw attention to the Bronx and the problem of insurance-induced arson. Minimized as "white-collar crime" or dismissed as residents burning down their own neighborhoods, arson did not become a pressing issue until the Black and Brown New Yorkers who had endured the firestorm rose up en masse. Their fury alarmed the powerful to a degree that landlord arson never had, and, in response, the state finally began to crack down on arsonist landlords. But for Bronx tenants, the trade-off of exposing the arson wave was that their borough became synonymous with it.

+++

THE SPECTACLE OF 1977 soon drew film studios to the borough. Within the space of a few years, feature films including *The Warriors* (1979), *Wolfen* (1981), *1990: The Bronx Warriors* (1982), *Wild Style* (1983), and *Escape from the Bronx* (1983) debuted, as did the documentaries *The Fire Next Door* (1977), *The Police Tapes* (1977), and *80 Blocks from Tiffany's* (1979). Bronxploitation had arrived. Most of the films were shot on location—a direct result of city hall's concerted efforts, beginning in 1966, to lure Hollywood to what one director called "the greatest back lot in the world." In a moment when New York was suffering from an "image crisis," the city's boosters saw homegrown film production as a means of counteracting Gotham's growing infamy. On one level, the scheme was wildly successful; in 1981, seventy-six films were shot on location, up from fifteen features annually in the mid-1960s. But the content of the films told a different story. What attracted Hollywood to New York and the Bronx was a sense of pervasive crisis and disorder—the polar opposite of the image promoted by the city's boosters. Few films illustrated these ironies more starkly than 1981's *Fort Apache, the Bronx*, which transposed the nation's frontier from John Ford's Monument Valley to the nation's newest monument of dispossession, Charlotte Street.[14]

The film's lengthy germination reveals how 1977 changed the borough's place in the nation's imagination. According to Time-Life Films, the script for *Fort Apache, the Bronx* was written in the early 1970s, based on the experiences of "two real-life cops who patrolled the South Bronx together." Acquired by a producer in 1973 for just $1,250, it was "shopped around" to studios for more than five years without success. But after 1977, the potential for monetizing the borough's suffering was newly apparent. In 1978, producer David Susskind, the host of nearly thirty seasons of *The David Susskind Show*, began piecing together the financing for Time-Life Films, and by the next fall the script had been acquired for more than $350,000. Not even the inflation rates of the 1970s could put a dent in a 27,900 percent return.[15]

With that kind of money behind the film, the producers aimed to cast a star in the lead role, and they landed Butch Cassidy himself. The heartthrob of a generation, Paul Newman had fallen into a slump in the second half of the 1970s, "by his own admission the low point in his career." His son had died of a drug overdose in 1978, and his latest films had been flops. "I made a couple of really bad ones back-to-back," he admitted. *Fort Apache, the Bronx* drew Newman in with a $3 million contract, but what really caught his eye was the chance to portray a badge-wearing antihero in an urban western. As he had proven with *Butch Cassidy and the Sundance Kid* (1969), the genre played to Newman's strengths as a "likable renegade." For his work in *Fort Apache, the Bronx*, Newman would be praised for his "most dramatic and realistic performance in years"; some credit it with getting his career "back on track."[16]

In a post-Fordist twist, the frontier was projected not onto the hinterlands of the city but onto its center. Although the Bronx was less than an hour's drive from Newman's home in Westport, Connecticut, he was aghast at what he saw there. Joining the procession of ruin seekers that started with Carter's 1977 trip, Newman took a Bronx tour led by former cops. He spoke of the experience as though he had landed on another planet, marveling, "The Bronx is a revelation. To realize that you live on its doorstep and never realize what's going on inside your own city came as something of a shock to me."[17]

Fort Apache, the Bronx chronicles the 41st Precinct in the late 1960s and early 1970s, when the officers' "sense that they are surrounded by violence" prompted them to adopt the nickname "Fort Apache." Newman plays NYPD Patrolman Murphy, a virtuous veteran cop stationed in a lawless precinct alongside crooked brethren. The project's initial billing emphasized what Murphy is up against: "A chilling and tough movie about the South Bronx, a 40-block area with the highest crime rate in New York. Youth gangs, winos, junkies, pimps, hookers, maniacs, cop killers and the embattled 41st Precinct, just hanging in there." The film's plot turns on the actions of its two female leads, Pam Grier, who plays a murderous sex worker, and Rachel Ticotin as Isabella, a selfless nurse who becomes Murphy's love interest. As scholar Pete L'Official points out, Grier's character, a "free-floating avatar of gratuitous death," is named Charlotte, an embodiment of the borough's infamous Charlotte Street. The movie opens with Grier's femme fatale sidling up to a squad car, shooting two cops at point-blank range, and then leaving their corpses to a band of preteen pillagers. The killing alarms the precinct's new commander, Captain Connolly (Ed Asner), who sets his men loose on the neighborhood. The heavy-handed approach incenses Murphy, whose remaining faith in the department is broken when he witnesses another officer throwing a boy off a tenement roof. Murphy finds solace in his new relationship with the unflappable nurse Isabella, but he remains tormented about whether to turn in his colleague. When Isabella overdoses, Murphy turns whistleblower, resigns from the force, and tells Connolly, "You can take the whole neighborhood and bulldoze it into the East River, and you and me with it." The final scene shows just that, the camera loitering on Charlotte Street and the wrecking ball.[18]

Although the film does not explicitly acknowledge its debts to John Ford's *Fort Apache* (1948) beyond its title, it adheres to the "standard cavalry/Indian paradigm," as scholar Richard Slotkin calls it. The besieged 41st Precinct is decorated with war bonnets, ceremonial pipes, totems, and other American Indian trophies. "This isn't a police station ... it's a fort in hostile territory," explains one deputy. The enemy is everywhere, but the role of the rebel natives is delegated in particular to the fictional South Bronx People's Party (SBPP), "disco revolutionaries" who "got federal money to open a storefront on Fox Street." A thinly veiled stand-in for the Young Lords Party, which had an office around the corner from Fox Street, the SBPP activists, according to one patrolman, "make a lot of hate-cop noises. They preach armed revolt, but they spend most of their time ballin' white chicks from Scarsdale." Lampooning the militancy of leftist organizations like the Young Lords, the Black Panthers, and the Black Liberation Army, the film conflates the three in a bumbling parody of Black and Brown radical movements. The South Bronx People's Party (named the Third World Action Group in the initial script) poses no real political threat, only a sexual one. When Captain Connolly suspects that the SBPP is behind the killing of two cops, its leaders eventually prove their innocence with a lewd alibi—they were at Sarah Lawrence College when the murders took place ("ballin' white chicks from Scarsdale"). In this way, the film both vilifies and disarms the radical groups of the era, which are reduced to little more than a rowdy fraternity, a lecherous caricature of the Young Lords Party.[19]

A standard-bearer for liberal causes, Newman was best known for his

A still from *Fort Apache, the Bronx* that depicts Bronxites rising up against the police in response to a raid of the fictional South Bronx People's Party.

roles in countercultural films like *Butch Cassidy* and *Cool Hand Luke* (1967), whose politics were a long way from the reactionary impulses on display in *Fort Apache, the Bronx*. An even more instructive comparison for our purposes is his earlier film *The Towering Inferno*, released in 1974. Newman plays Doug Roberts, the architect for San Francisco's new Glass Tower, the world's tallest skyscraper. Despite the sophisticated safety measures in Roberts's design, the developer and subcontractor cut corners and constructed a colossal fire trap. During the building's dedication ceremony, fires break out on multiple floors, trapping many luminaries inside. Roberts transforms from technocrat to hero, saving as many guests as he can manage. But at the end of the night, the death toll is still more than one hundred, a travesty brought about by the developers' disregard for fire safety. *Inferno* presents a stern public interest message within the frame of a disaster film; its suspicions of freewheeling developers and paid-off politicos fit well within the consumer-safety movement of the 1970s. The film broke box office records upon its release and prompted many municipalities to embrace new fire safety legislation.[20]

In *Fort Apache, the Bronx*, by contrast, fires exist as a seemingly natural feature of the Bronx landscape. Newman's character, Murphy, tells his partner, "Fires, you see a lot of fires. They look real good on the tube." The blazes do not just make for good TV viewing; they also put on a show for the neighborhood. When Murphy and his partner spot a young couple gazing at a fire from atop an apartment building, he jokes, "Hey it's a cheap date. Instead of going to the movies, they just walk up on the roof and watch the buildings burn." Although the film fails to explain who or what is causing the blazes, it depicts young Black men obstructing firefighters by "bombing" them with bricks and bottles from the roof. Gone are the developers of *The Towering Inferno*; there is not a landlord in sight. Fire is naturalized as an essential facet of Bronx life. "I feel as burned-out as those damn buildings down on Charlotte Street," Murphy mutters when defending his decision to turn in his badge. No further explanation necessary.

Fort Apache, the Bronx is strangely self-aware about the pathologies it assigns to Bronx residents, and the marketing team invoked its gritty realism as proof of the film's liberal credentials and investment in the communities it depicts. Only "by exposing these conditions," insisted executive producer David Susskind, would the film be able to "do something about the present day urban crisis." The filmmakers thus passed off the film's reactionary messaging as fully in line with liberal politics. Its demeaning portrait of the borough masqueraded as grit and tough love. "I feel I know this area as well as anybody can without actually living here," insisted one producer. Such a considered portrayal would, in Paul Newman's words, "be the positive catalyst needed to start a nationwide effort to rebuild the inner cities and better the lives of their inhabitants."[21]

The scene that the filmmakers regularly cited as demonstration of their good intent depicted the unprovoked killing of a teenage Puerto Rican boy by two of Murphy's colleagues. The decision to document gratuitous violence by the police purportedly showed the film's evenhandedness and set *Fort Apache, the Bronx* apart from a film like *Dirty Harry*, which critics panned as fascist agitprop. Newman told the press, "This is a tough movie. It's tough on whites, Blacks, Puerto Ricans and on lousy white cops. It is a tough, realistic script." This was law-and-order liberalism, and its contradictions were difficult to miss. The filmmakers proffered *Fort Apache, the*

Bronx as a tool for resolving the "urban crisis," even as they left viewers with a slash-and-burn fatalism ("bulldoze it into the East River"). Critics had reason to be confused. Writing in the *Village Voice*, Andrew Sarris, a self-identified liberal, worried that the film was gunning for a "center that cannot hold." One reason this tough-on-crime, tough-on-police formula was unconvincing was that it rested on a set of false equivalencies. The film may have dragged all parties through the mud, but the "cavalry/Indian paradigm" had the final word. Despite their failings, the police, some critics felt, remained "valiant holdouts against barbarism."[22]

The only realm where the film's treatment of the police succeeded as verité was on the set. Time-Life Films employed no fewer than thirty of New York's finest as security for the production, a force helmed by a twenty-year veteran of "the real Fort Apache, Precinct 41." The production also hired a forty-person auxiliary force of "yellow badges"—young Bronxites armed with walkie-talkies who patrolled the set. With that much muscle, "each member of the cast was assigned a bodyguard." A few months after the film's release, one such bodyguard, a former cop, was arrested and charged for his alleged involvement in an international cocaine ring. Memorabilia for *Fort Apache, the Bronx* was found all over his home.

Why, though, would a film set of one hundred require a seventy-person security force? The answer: the Committee Against Fort Apache.

+++

BRANDISHING SIGNS that read "PAUL NEWMAN—FROM LIBERAL TO RACIST FOR $3 MILLION" and "INDIANS ARE NOT SAVAGES—NEITHER ARE WE," thirty members of the newly formed Committee Against Fort Apache (CAFA) gathered along the Bronx's Third Avenue on the night of March 21, 1980. Although the film's shooting schedule had been kept secret for weeks, CAFA had been tipped off that the filmmakers had asked area storekeepers to stay open late that night. On a hunch, the protesters huddled together for hours in the rain before being rewarded for their endurance. When a caravan of police cars and trucks carrying film equipment drove down Third Avenue toward 149th Street, CAFA members surrounded the first car, forcing it to stop. They soon discovered that it carried the two leads of *Fort Apache, the Bronx*. Paul Newman "sat frozen at the wheel, looking straight ahead," while Rachel Ticotin, the Bronx-born actress who played the heroin-addicted nurse, "sank down in her seat." Two police escorts came running toward the crowd, clubs in hand. They managed to get Newman and Ticotin out without further incident, but for CAFA, the action was a success. The next day, the group was introduced to the world by favorable press coverage. One headline blared: "Uprising at Fort Apache."[23]

CAFA had taken shape weeks before, following the announcement of the film. But its swift formation was the result of earlier organizing against the 41st Precinct and its counterparts across the city. Even within the culture of gross misconduct that existed within the Bronx NYPD, the 41st Precinct had been singled out by police officials in 1978 as a "problem precinct" for its sanctioning of "excessive force." A dozen killings by police in the Bronx and other boroughs in the preceding year had created an especially charged atmosphere. Peter Funches, a Black Vietnam veteran, was brutally beaten to death by six policemen on a Bronx street in June 1979. A month later, Luis Rodriguez died in police custody hours after being beaten by Bronx police officers. Following the killing of Luis Baez in Brooklyn that August, the Black and Latino Coalition Against Police Brutality was created by organizations across the city "to unite our communities to fight the rise of police brutality and killings."[24]

When Time-Life Films announced its intention to shoot *Fort Apache, the Bronx* on location, activists who had already been organizing with the Coalition Against Police Brutality began mobilizing against the film. By 1980, Bronxites were attuned to how media portrayals fed into the ongoing decimation of the borough. Local activists saw the movie as an opportunity to "educate the community about [the] effects of media stereotyping and show links to [the] overall situation we face." Media savvy had been a hallmark of CAFA's forerunner, the Young Lords, an organization of mostly Puerto Rican and Black revolutionaries whose New York chapter waged a militant struggle for justice from 1969 into the early 1970s. CAFA was guided by the leadership of former Young Lords Diana Caballero and Richie Perez, among others. The group's first meeting was held on March 5, 1980, at the Bronx's Lincoln Hospital, which had been famously occupied by the Young Lords exactly a decade earlier in protest of the substandard health care being offered to Puerto Ricans and African Americans in the city. Though CAFA's mandate may seem comparatively narrow next to that of the Young Lords, it resurrected many of the hardball methods and movement-building strategies that had defined its predecessor.[25]

CAFA prioritized "mass outreach in community and mass mobilization" and used its opposition to the film as a vehicle to link Hollywood stereotyping to police violence, racialized austerity, and the false promises of liberalism. Within two weeks, the coalition had pulled in dozens of organizations across the city, including the Black United Front, United Bronx Parents, the Union of Patriotic Puerto Ricans, Women Against Pornography, and the Coalition of Asians to Nix Charlie Chan. One of its founding goals was building "higher levels of unity between the Puerto Rican and Black communities through common struggle." CAFA's bold and often triumphant campaign offers a dramatic counterpoint to the perception of late-1970s leftist movements as clumsy, sectarian attempts to defend past gains.[26]

Its coalitional approach earned CAFA instant clout, and five days after launching, the group succeeded in pressuring Time-Life Films to deliver a copy of the screenplay to United Bronx Parents, a sponsoring organization run by longtime Bronx activist Evelina López Antonetty. When its members read the script, CAFA's worst fears were confirmed, and the group "adopted the position that we would stop *Fort Apache* in the streets during its filming or we would stop it in the theaters." It began by sharpening its critique. Within two days, CAFA members had produced a white paper on how the film "stereotypes the Puerto Rican and Black peoples as violent savages, 'loose women,' and degenerates." The group's piercing analysis kept pace with developments within postcolonial theory and Black studies. "By the time the film is over, the impression has been created that *we* ourselves are inhuman," CAFA wrote, in a line that carried echoes of contemporaneous work by the scholars Orlando Patterson and Sylvia Wynter.[27]

In particular, CAFA argued that the film's denigrating portrayal of the Bronx rested on its depiction of Black and Puerto Rican women and families. "According to this film," wrote member Lourdes Torres, "we're all prostitutes and junkies. The only supposedly positive female role is a nurse who dies of a drug overdose." Families, too, are vilified for being, in the words of one officer, "on welfare for three generations." CAFA inventoried such racist and misogynist images, warning that the film "presents [them] as the total reality of our lives."[28]

For the members of CAFA, who had seen their neighborhoods burn and atrophy for over a decade, the stakes were clear: the group recognized *Fort Apache, the Bronx* to be an apologia for austerity and criminalization. In a press release, CAFA charged that "by portraying us as animals, by

In the summer of 1980, the Committee Against Fort Apache held frequent rallies and actions to protest and disrupt the filming of *Fort Apache, the Bronx*.

denying our humanity, [the film] will provide a rationale for the proposed budget cuts in health care, education and essential services that our communities are mobilizing against." In the same vein, a CAFA member group stressed, "Budgets of decaying American cities are being balanced on our people's bodies." Beyond condoning austerity measures, CAFA warned, *Fort Apache, the Bronx* worked to absolve police violence: "Fort Apache will also create a climate of support for the increased police killings our communities are experiencing."[29]

The unifying thread across the critiques was that the film would obscure the causes of the Bronx's troubles, instead zeroing in on their most sensational effects. CAFA pointed out how *Fort Apache, the Bronx* obfuscated the origins of the arson wave, shoring up narratives of Black and Brown incendiarism at the precise moment that landlord arson had become a prominent and politicized issue: "In Fort Apache there are no slumlords who refuse to make repairs and then burn their buildings for insurance money." In *El Diario*, the largest Spanish-language newspaper in New York, CAFA reiterated the charge that the film "gives the impression that the people of the South Bronx are themselves responsible for the horrid conditions under which they live." Neither "bankers who redline" nor "realtors who engage in arson for profit" are held accountable—instead, "we are."[30]

It would take only a few days for the filmmakers to regret their decision to share the screenplay with CAFA, calling it a "benevolent act" that the group had abused. On March 13, 1980, fifteen representatives from CAFA, including Richie Perez, met with Time-Life executives and demanded that production be halted. Producer Tom Fiorello, who had been born in the Bronx, was caught off guard. "I personally feel hurt," he said, awkwardly authenticating his Bronx roots by adding, "I love rice and beans, more so than I love spaghetti." The meeting only strengthened the coalition's resolve to thwart the making of the film.[31]

On March 24, CAFA scaled up its efforts, filing a class-action lawsuit against Time-Life Films for "group libel" and claiming damages of $1 billion. With legendary movement lawyer William Kunstler as their counsel, the suit was a bid for publicity, and it delivered. As Kunstler was filing (unsuccessfully) for an injunction to stop production inside the New York State Supreme Court in Manhattan, CAFA held a demonstration on the courthouse steps. The protesters were confounded when sixty to eighty Black and Puerto Rican high school students from the Bronx showed up to start a counterprotest. The students held up signs that read "FORT APACHE WILL HELP THE COMMUNITY" and "DON'T MIX OUR PEOPLE'S PROGRESS WITH COMMUNIST POLITICAL ADVANCEMENT." The CAFA leadership immediately suspected the studio of engaging in "dirty tricks." Members of the group approached the students and discovered that they knew little about the film. They showed the counterprotesters a few of the more demeaning excerpts from the script, and the students admitted that they had been put up to the stunt by the film's publicist: "promised fifteen dollars an hour for three hours," plus lunch and roles in the film. Before long, CAFA members convinced the students to swap sides and join their protest.[32]

As if on cue, the film's publicist, Bobby Zarem—of "I♥NY" fame—got out of a taxi and approached the crowd. The students cried out, "There's the guy with the money!" and ran toward him. "A wild chase began through the

Bronx students were hired by *Fort Apache, the Bronx*'s publicist to hold a counterprotest against the Committee Against Fort Apache (CAFA). When CAFA members gave the students a look at the screenplay, they abandoned the fake protest and began demonstrating against the film.

rotunda of the courthouse and back down the steps," reported *Artforum*. The students eventually caught up with him, knocked off his cowboy hat, and demanded payment. The NYPD intervened and Zarem escaped, but his plan "had backfired badly," Perez remembered with relish. The press ate up the story of the fake protest and the teenagers' change of heart.[33]

With Time-Life on the back foot, the film's key players reached for their surefire weapon: they invoked their liberal bona fides. Bristling at CAFA's charges of racism, producer David Susskind and director Dan Petrie cited their collaboration two decades earlier on the film version of Lorraine Hansberry's *A Raisin in the Sun*. "I want to assure the people of the Bronx that we are approaching the problems of their community in the same spirit which was brought to 'Raisin,'" Petrie wrote. In his formal deposition for the CAFA lawsuit, Susskind echoed Petrie. "My entire public and private life has been concerned with 'man's inhumanity to man,'" he testified. (Incidentally, "David Susskind's pretensions" made it onto Lorraine Hansberry's list of things "I Hate" in 1960.)[34]

In early April, Newman himself spoke out, orchestrating a press conference from the rubble of the Bronx, framed by a tableau of torched buildings. Exploiting the same mise-en-scène President Carter had a few years earlier, the method actor re-created the president's ham-fisted performance of compassion, addressing a crowd of bused-in reporters: "I have spent my whole life caring about what happened to the underprivileged. It is wrong for anyone to say that I would have anything to do with something that was racist." With his disavowal as their cue, four members of CAFA once again registered their dissent, interrupting Newman. Rattled by this attack from his left, Newman offered his "tough on lousy white cops" quip, which soon enough earned him an attack from the right. According to the president of the Patrolmen's Benevolent Association, a man the filmmakers could not afford to alienate, Newman was a "money-hungry mongrel." After uttering the anti-Semitic remark—Newman was Jewish—he called the actor a "bigot." Susskind issued an apology to the NYPD straightaway.[35]

In one bungled press stunt after another, the filmmakers failed to buff the film's progressive veneer—and here, perhaps, lay CAFA's most visible achievement. The group stripped the film of its pretense, drawing the violence and contradictions of law-and-order liberalism out in the open for all to see. CAFA had clocked the racial politics of the film from the start, noting in its first white paper, "The racism is more disguised. This is not a simple story of an openly reactionary cop like 'Dirty Harry.'" It took persistent pressure from CAFA to back the filmmakers into a corner and get them to show their teeth. "I don't like being called a racist pig," Newman snarled. "In the final analysis, *they're* the whores. Maybe they're looking for a political base."[36]

Although CAFA was not able to stop the film's production, it kept Time-Life Films on the defensive throughout the making and release of the movie. The group repeatedly disrupted the shooting schedule, and director Petrie admitted that he seriously considered moving the production out of the South Bronx. "I have often filmed under difficult circumstances, but none so disturbing and frustrating as that afternoon surrounded by people who thoroughly believed we were making a racist picture." Petrie ultimately made a few modifications to the script to mollify his critics, the most striking of which was a disclaimer at the start that read, "The picture you are about to see is a portrayal of the lives of two policemen working out of a precinct in the South Bronx, New York. Because the story involves police work it does not deal with the law abiding members of the community nor does it dramatize the efforts of the individuals and groups who are struggling to turn the Bronx around." The irony of this statement—coming from a film that caricatured and vilified the Young Lords—was not lost on CAFA.[37]

The coalition was unappeased by the concessions, launching a national boycott in anticipation of the film's premiere on February 6, 1981. By that point, CAFA had chapters in Jersey City, Boston, and even Albuquerque. It also formed relationships with partner groups across the country, including forty chapters of the Chicano student group MEChA, which had a strong presence on the West Coast. During its first week in theaters, *Fort Apache, the Bronx* drew protests across the nation. In Manhattan, hundreds marched on the Gemini II Theater, which was forced to cancel its screening of the film. The New York City Council's Committee on General Welfare even passed a resolution that called on the city to boycott the film, though the motion did not get through the full council. The cause fared better in Philadelphia, where the city council unanimously passed a resolution denouncing the film. Philly's theaters subsequently pulled the movie, which did not screen within the city limits for weeks.[38]

The controversy drummed up by CAFA cast a pall over the picture's opening. It earned only mixed, uneven reviews, and many critics "borrowed directly from CAFA's analysis." All told, the film failed to become the blockbuster the studio had expected, "making much less than had been anticipated," according to *Variety*. Time-Life, which was new to the movie business, left film production after disappointing returns from *Fort Apache, the Bronx* and two other films. Despite these victories, *Fort Apache* was far from the flop of CAFA's dreams. It was the nation's highest-grossing film for five weeks in a row (though it was the only big-budget new release during that period). In the end, the film was moderately profitable.[39]

In March 1981, CAFA organizers dissolved the coalition and redirected their energies toward kindred projects. The following month, a number of CAFA's central players, including Richie Perez and Diana Caballero, along with Juan González, helped launch the National Congress of Puerto Rican Rights (NCPRR) from the South Bronx. Looking back in 2022, González drew a straight line between CAFA's work and the "extraordinary mass organization" that was the NCPRR, which grew into "the leading group exposing the epidemic of police brutality against Latinos." For González, the movement had to confront police violence in its myriad forms—from prison cells to celluloid. This was perhaps CAFA's most enduring legacy: modeling how to cultivate a multiracial base of resistance against the intertwined physical and representational assault on the Bronx. In an era when leftist movements across the city and nation were in retreat, CAFA's genius for leveraging the power of images and culture prefigured later episodes in the city's movement history, including the work of ACT UP.[40]

On the eve of *Fort Apache*'s opening, listeners of WBAI-FM heard the chart-topping bass line of the Sugar Hill Gang's "Rapper's Delight," overdubbed with lyrics backing the boycott:

> Show the dignity of our life
> And we'll be glad to pay the price
> Cause if you turn around and mock it
> Gonna hit you right square in the pocket

With its chorus of "We're gonna run, jump, stomp / to the *Fort Apache* boycott," CAFA's "Fort Apache Bop" reached out to a younger generation of Bronxites. In a moment before hip-hop was recognized as a source of social critique, "Fort Apache Bop" injected politics into a song that those in the scene had written off as "a sham," a studio counterfeit. The track put a beat to CAFA's message, proving, in its own words, "the tremendous creativity and strength that mass struggle unleashes."[41]

But despite CAFA's tireless organizing, the image of the Bronx depicted in *Fort Apache* had staying power, in part because, by 1981, it was already well established. Soon enough, that image would be further reduced from a ruined landscape to something smaller and yet, for many, more evocative: the broken window.

+++

AFTER THE 1977 blackout and Jimmy Carter's visit, the Bronx had drawn a steady stream of journalists and photographers documenting decline. The arson wave made for good copy and shocking graphics, yet the blazes seldom made it to the front page of the *New York Times* or the *Wall Street Journal*. In place of the fires, media outlets, films, and artists seized on the image of the gaping window and empty-eyed tenement as signifiers of the Bronx's collapse.

By the late 1970s, descriptions and images of broken windows were fixtures of the opening paragraphs of articles about the Bronx, which presented the broken window as a marker of infrastructural, urban, and racial decline. Buildings were figured as infirm bodies, in the process of dying or already dead. Like the elderly, they were losing their eyesight, their windows onto the world. The *New York Times* wrote of the "blank eyes of the glassless windows of burned-out buildings overlooking the scene." In another article, the *Times* described "abandoned buildings, with smoke stains flaring up from their blind and broken windows." Robert Caro's chapter on the construction of the Cross Bronx Expressway in *The Power Broker* used these same tropes: "Windows, glassless except for the jagged edges around their frames, stared out on the street like sightless eyes." So pervasive was such imagery that it featured prominently in the 1980 presidential debates. Presidential candidate Ronald Reagan, haranguing his opponent for failing to live up to his 1977 promise to turn the Bronx around, spoke of his own recent tour of the borough: "I stood in the South Bronx on the exact spot that President Carter stood on in 1977. You have to see it to believe it, it looks like a bombed-out city. Great gaunt skeletons of buildings, windows smashed out, painted on one of them 'Unkept Promises,' on another, 'Despair.'"[42]

One of the most striking images of broken windows from the era appeared on the front page of the *Boston Globe* on January 7, 1979. Here a devastated South Bronx landscape furnishes the background for a bust of the newly named renewal czar, Ed Logue, who had been commissioned by New York City to head the borough's redevelopment efforts following President Carter's visit. Logue's mission, according to the article's author, was "to stem the cancerous spread of urban decay devastating the South Bronx, a community that is fast becoming a symbol of national shame." To illus-

> The man who helped to reshape Boston takes on the south Bronx —America's No. 1 urban problem

Ed Logue, who headed the South Bronx Development Organization, pictured in the *Boston Globe* on January 7, 1979.

trate this undertaking, the *Globe*'s graphic designers set Logue's eyes level with the dilapidated structures in the background, and the play between his eyes and the buildings is what animates the image. Logue's upward gaze, evoking hope and vision, is juxtaposed against the buildings. In contrast to Logue's glance upward into a better future, the buildings' "eyes" are weighted downward toward a pile of rubble. Some are pitch-black and indecipherable from the rest of the building, while others are eerily bright, suggesting that the camera can see straight through the structure. In either case, they signal that the apartment houses have utterly failed to provide shelter and safety.[43]

With their windows removed, the buildings are exposed as housing a hollow blackness that is set against the whiteness of Logue's skin. Like "gaping" and "blind" windows, such "black" or "blackened" windows appeared often in journalistic accounts. In the *New York Times*, one reporter wrote of a series of buildings that "look as if they had been blasted with cannon and burned over with napalm. All but a few windows are fire-blackened and vacant. Junkies haunt the reeking, ruined hallways." The *Baltimore Sun* described the Bronx as "acres of rubble, walled about by the burnt-out shells of tenements with their black, staring windows . . . beyond, it seemed, all hope." Syndicated *Los Angeles Times* columnist Jack Smith, writing about the Bronx, put it this way: "If you have ever walked past an abandoned apartment building, especially at night, you know it's an unnerving experience: The sinister black windows hide unimaginable horrors."[44]

These portrayals are consistent with longer histories of representing Black and Brown landscapes in ways that evoke racial horror. With the broken window, infrastructural decay was intertwined with social and racial degeneration, and the two lent meaning to each other. These images told a story of past intactness and present fragmentation, a nostalgic narrative premised on the contrast of the burning Bronx of the 1970s with the stabler, whiter Bronx of the early twentieth century. Commentators routinely lamented the passing of "the Bronx of the 1920s, 1930s, and 1940s," when it served, in the words of the borough's biographer, as a "staging ground for the American Dream" for the millions of ethnic whites who passed through en route to the middle class. Broken windows refracted those lost dreams; here, in a thousand pieces, were a past generation's hopes of upward mobility and American progress.[45]

Yet the windows of the Bronx never existed outside the brutalities of racial capitalism. The supposed golden age of the Bronx—the first decades of the twentieth century—had its own contradictions. "The growth of the Bronx during the last decade has been one of the marvels of city development in the United States," reported the *Real Estate Record and Builders' Guide* in 1912. As tenements shot up and mass transit crept northward, conditions aligned to allow landlords to "squeez[e] the most rent from the least space," easily yielding "10 to 25 percent annually on the initial capital investment." It was a landlord's market, shaken only by the presence of Communist tenant organizations that regularly coordinated rent strikes to protest rent hikes, evictions, and withdrawal of services. Striking buildings announced themselves by suspending banners from their windows bearing slogans like "DOWN WITH PROFITEERING LANDLORDS."[46]

In the 1970s and 1980s, media representations of broken glass glossed over these histories and left little room for an account such as Ella Baker and Marvel Cooke's "The Bronx Slave Market," a 1935 exposé about Black domestic workers in the Depression-era Bronx. Writing for the NAACP journal, *The Crisis*, Baker and Cooke surveyed domestic workers at a number of street corners that served as informal temp agencies. The Depression had brought ruin to the women who crowded these intersections, many of whom had lost stable positions when the wealthy white families that had employed them opted instead for working-class white women who had themselves fallen on hard times. Meanwhile, and "paradoxically," wrote Baker and Cooke, "the crash of 1929 brought to the domestic labor market a new employer class. The lower middle-class housewife, who, having dreamed of the luxury of a maid, found opportunity staring her in the face in the form of Negro women pressed to the wall by poverty, starvation and discrimination."[47]

Women labored in their new workplaces for meager wages, and among the most loathsome tasks was window cleaning. Baker and Cooke wrote of domestic workers left with few choices when employers asked them to "hang precariously from window sills, cleaning window after window." One of those interviewed, Millie Jones, protested, "I would do anything rather than wash windows." Workers' aversion to the task is understandable: the windows they were to wash could be up on the eighth, ninth, or tenth floors, affording panoramic views to their residents. Sleek, solid, and often adorned in Art Deco embellishments, these Bronx towers lured an emergent middle class of ethnic whites seeking a step up from the densely packed neighborhoods of East Harlem and the Lower East Side. One feature that set these buildings apart from the tenements of Manhattan was their higher ratio of glass to brick. It is easy to imagine how the fifteen-odd windows that distinguished their new apartments served as a point of pride.[48] But they were difficult to keep clean.

"The Bronx Slave Market" still resonates nearly a century after it was written because it guides us away from simple moralism and toward a set of questions about the windows' material conditions. Following Baker and Cooke, we must ask: How did the windows of the 1970s Bronx actually break? The majority fractured in one of four ways. Some fires triggered ruptures in the glass panes. Or firefighters, aiming to introduce ventilation and prevent a backdraft, smashed windows (residents often objected to these methods, calling them unnecessary and gratuitous). Third was the breakage from a source other than fire, whether by stone, bat, bullet, or some other agent. When deliberate, this was called vandalism, and it generally attracted the brightest spotlight of the four ways. And finally, there was demolition, which became increasingly common in the 1980s. Although contemporary forensic science would now be able to decipher the cause of a window's fracture, there is no way to speculate some forty years later about the prevalence of each type of injury. Suffice it to say that each of these occurred with great frequency.[49]

Nevertheless, resident vandalism—much like tenant arson—stood as the leading explanation for the broken windows of the Bronx. In 1982, Roger Starr, formerly the city's housing commissioner, wrote an op-ed for the *New York Times*, claiming that "an abandoned New York tenement with broken windows is like a corpse with open eyes." Despite government attempts to "discourage vandals from breaking in," he said, they persist, "starting fires, and terrifying neighbors until they move." Another government official, "who blames tenants and other local residents for vandalism," was quoted by the *Washington Post* as saying, "The buildings didn't come with holes in the walls." The Metro desk at the *Times* seemed to agree, reporting, "A new $6-million housing development in the South Bronx has been standing empty and ravaged by vandals for a year and a half, its smashed windows a symbol of . . . shattered hopes."[50]

This association between Bronxites and broken windows hid from view structural factors as well as alternate scenarios of fracture. It would achieve its greatest prominence in James Q. Wilson and George L. Kelling's seminal article "Broken Windows: The Police and Neighborhood Safety."

+++

PUBLISHED TO GREAT fanfare and controversy in a 1982 issue of the *Atlantic Monthly*, "Broken Windows" sent shock waves through social-scientific and law enforcement circles, recasting conversations about safety and crime across the United States and beyond. Wilson and Kelling's signal intervention was their argument that signs of disorder, such as subway graffiti or public drunkenness, push "law-abiding" residents toward vandalism and crime by reducing "community controls" against incivility. These signs of disorder further undermine community life by provoking "community fear" and suggesting the possibility of more injurious crime to come. In short, fear of crime—aroused by relatively mild manifestations of disorder—is cast as a primary cause of neighborhood deterioration. Accordingly, Wilson and Kelling claimed that the function of the police should be to cultivate a sense of safety and order, rather than fighting crime per se. Perceived safety could be achieved only by eradicating the visual cues of disorder.[51]

Enter the broken window: "Social scientists and police officers tend to agree that if a window in a building is broken and is left unrepaired, all the rest of the windows will soon be broken." If Wilson and Kelling's article were to be condensed into one sentence, that could be it. They substantiate the claim by gesturing toward a supposed social-scientific consensus around its validity. But in Wilson and Kelling's essay, only one empirical source shoulders the evidentiary burden of proving the connection between one broken window and "a thousand broken windows"—of proving, in other words, the connection between visual cues of disorder and neighborhood deterioration. That source was an experiment conducted fifteen years earlier in both the Bronx and Palo Alto by social psychologist Philip G. Zimbardo, best known for administering the Stanford prison experiment two years later.[52]

In 1969, Zimbardo, a Stanford professor raised in the Bronx, set about determining the relationship between community anonymity and vandalism. He and his research team installed a 1959 Oldsmobile in both the South Bronx and Palo Alto, removing the vehicles' license plates and raising their hoods to create the appearance of abandonment. The Bronx car served as a "comparison," with Zimbardo hypothesizing that it would not take long for Bronxites to dismantle it. He was correct; after only ten minutes, the informal economies of the Bronx made themselves known, and soon the car's battery, radiator, and other contents had been taken. Although the research team was surprised that the first "vandals" were not people of color but, rather, a "well-dressed" white family, Zimbardo considered his basic hypothesis confirmed: the lack of community cohesion in the Bronx produced a sense of "anonymity," which, in turn, generated antisocial behaviors.[53]

After the Palo Alto Oldsmobile went unscathed for a week, the research team moved the car to the campus of Stanford University, where they decided to "prime" it for vandals by taking a sledgehammer to its windows. Upon discovering that this act of destruction was "stimulating and pleasurable," Zimbardo and his graduate students "got carried away," pummeling the car and eventually overturning it. The passersby the experiment had intended to study had turned into observers of the action, and joined in only after the car was already destroyed. For Zimbardo, what happened in the Bronx and at Stanford suggested that crowd mentality, social inequalities, and community anonymity could prompt "good citizens" to act destructively. "Vandalism is a rebellion with a cause," he wrote.[54]

FIGURE 8
"Hit It Again, Harder, Harder!" The Awakening of Dark Impulses at Stanford University

Philip Zimbardo and his graduate students getting "carried away" on the campus of Stanford University.

By contrast, Wilson and Kelling found in Zimbardo's study proof that "one unrepaired broken window is a signal that no one cares, and so breaking more windows costs nothing." What is significant to note here is the work the Bronx performed in the making of Wilson and Kelling's theory. For 1982 readers, what separated the Bronx from Palo Alto went far beyond the three thousand miles that stretched between them. Barely any context was needed to evoke the familiar South Bronx images of arson, rubble, depopulation, and violence, and indeed, Wilson and Kelling gave little of their own: "Because of the nature of community life in the Bronx—its anonymity, the frequency with which cars are abandoned and things are stolen or broken, the past experience of 'no one caring'—vandalism begins much more quickly than it does in staid Palo Alto, where people have come to believe that private possessions are cared for, and that mischievous behavior is costly."[55]

In the opposition created by Wilson and Kelling, the Bronx and its residents were the "thousand broken windows" to Palo Alto's one. The danger was metastasis—the creation of many Bronxes—by way of small manifestations of disorder. In Wilson and Kelling's narration, one broken window had rendered "staid Palo Alto" lawless, a mirror image of what should have been its inverse, the Bronx. Here, in the introduction of the broken windows theory to the nation and the world, the Bronx served as a racialized landscape of death and destruction that threatened to encroach upon the rest of the country. The borough thus loomed over the *Atlantic Monthly* article as a possible future, one that could be prevented only by embracing the authors' proposed new regime of policing.

Crucially, when Wilson and Kelling put forward their theory, they did so while downplaying the significance of race. Broken windows policing was a deeply racialized policy program, yet Wilson and Kelling presented it as racially neutral, even progressive. "How do we ensure," they asked, "that the police do not become the agents of neighborhood bigotry?" That they posed the question at all suggests that the social scientists anticipated charges of racism, and their response—sensitivity training for law enforcement—was surely intended to establish their evenhandedness. But given that broken windows policing has played a decisive role in the hypercriminalization of people of color in the United States, it is notable that Wilson and Kelling sought to prove their "concern about equity" at all. As we saw with the advent of the FAIR plan and the "riot-prone area," the civil rights movement had transfigured how race was articulated. By the early 1980s, it was taboo to advocate for racially targeted policing, especially in a mainstream forum like the *Atlantic Monthly*. Yet race could speak loudly through the broken window without violating such taboos because the symbolism that linked the broken window to the decaying city was more difficult to denounce.[56]

Over the ensuing decades, the Bronx was made into a principal target of broken windows policing. The hyperpolicing of the borough was not a foregone conclusion in 1982, however. The officers of the 41st Precinct, for example, traded the Fort Apache moniker for "Little House on the Prairie" to reflect their minimal activity in the area in the late 1970s and early 1980s (ironically, exactly when *Fort Apache, the Bronx* was being made down the street). That all changed in the early 1990s, when broken windows policing was institutionalized. The adoption of broken windows led to the stop-and-frisk policy, which empowered the NYPD to interrogate and search anyone on the basis of "reasonable suspicion." The South Bronx soon began topping lists of the most heavily policed areas in the city. A 2011 survey of the neighborhood abutting Morris Avenue found that 69 percent of respondents had been stopped by the police in the previous twelve months, and of those, 82 percent were stopped more than once. In the nearby neighborhoods of Melrose and Mott Haven, 98.5 percent of those stopped in 2012 were people of color. Bronx precincts have regularly led the city not only in stops and arrests but in monetary settlements for police misconduct. In

A 2014 poster campaign by the Morris Justice Project in the Bronx directly refuted the logic of broken windows policing.

2019, 45 percent of the $67 million the city disbursed in taxpayer-funded legal settlements was paid to Bronx plaintiffs. The extreme levels of policing indicated by these numbers would, by the mid-2010s, play a catalytic role in the gentrification of the South Bronx. During that same period, Bronxites led and participated in increasingly powerful coalitions against broken windows policing. In 2014, the Morris Justice Project launched a public education campaign that plastered Bronx streets with posters refusing the broken windows paradigm. The messaging was clear: "This is not a broken window. This is our HOME."[57]

A decade before broken windows policing was adopted by the NYPD, the sealing of broken windows became municipal policy in the Bronx. In 1983, barely a year after the publication of Wilson and Kelling's *Atlantic Monthly* article, Mayor Ed Koch, who, according to his biographer, "thought [their] idea was brilliant," introduced a new program for the South Bronx. The Occupied Look program, coordinated by the city's fledgling Department of Housing Preservation and Development (HPD), installed vinyl decals over the borough's broken windows. As announced on the front page of the *Times*, "Scores of crumbling, abandoned tenements in the Bronx—part of a swath of blight that has become a national symbol of urban decay—will soon sport vinyl decals over their gaping windows depicting a lived-in look of curtains, shades, shutters and flowerpots." Citing budget shortfalls and cuts in federal support for cities, the HPD claimed that the trompe l'oeil decal program was the best it could do for the borough's crumbling housing stock.[58]

The program, though, did not target the entire borough, only the buildings facing the Cross Bronx Expressway, from which thousands of commuters encountered the South Bronx as they bypassed it. Robert Jacobson, director of the borough's City Planning Commission, explained the rationale: "The image that the Bronx projects—and projects to potential investors—is the image you see from that expressway, and our goal is to soften that image so people will be willing to invest.... Business people make decisions based on perception." Anthony Gliedman, the HPD commissioner, put it in more elliptical terms: "Perception is reality." The transition of the government's concern from cause to effect was complete.[59]

Predictably, Occupied Look sparked an immediate controversy, with critics condemning the city for trying to "paper over" social problems and applying "window dressing" to the South Bronx. Bronx graffiti artists reg-

The Occupied Look program installed vinyl decals over the broken windows of abandoned buildings. Here, Anthony Gliedman, the commissioner of the Department of Housing Preservation and Development (right), unveils a prototype in Brooklyn. In the Bronx, the decals were reserved for buildings that overlooked commuters on the Cross Bronx Expressway.

istered their protests with spray paint, tagging the decaled buildings with "THIS IS A DECAL" and "THIS IS A FAKE." As proponents shoved these criticisms to the side, one supporter drew upon a familiar source to bolster his argument. "There is a serious side to this, as we know who read, ravenously, everything written by James Q. Wilson of Harvard," wrote syndicated *Washington Post* columnist George F. Will in his defense of the Koch program. "In the lunar landscape of the South Bronx, decals, as a sign that indifference is not complete, are better, if just barely, than nothing." Occupied Look weathered the criticism and remained active for another three years. It was not until the late 1980s that the city began earmarking significant funds for the reconstruction of the borough, at which point many of the broken-windowed buildings were outfitted with new glass panes or simply demolished.[60]

In the words of neighborhood activist Hetty Fox, programs like Occupied Look "cater[ed] more to the traveling public than to the residents." Bronxites who had taken to the streets in protest of *Fort Apache, the Bronx* would not have been surprised. Bronx photographer David Gonzalez observed that the film, along with other "voyeuristic" portrayals, "obliterated any notion of real life as surely as any arsonist's fire or wrecking ball reduced apartment buildings to brick piles."[61]

SEVEN

Fighting Fire with FIRE

Catching the crook and putting him behind bars is
not going to solve the problem of arson.

—DAVID SCONDRAS, 1977[1]

How many arsonists in your city don't want you to read this?

Arsonists would like you to go on thinking there's "nothing you can do to stop them." Because when people start doing something the results are inspiring.

Once arson for profit entered public consciousness in the late 1970s, insurers like Aetna developed aggressive public relations strategies to position themselves on the right side of the war against arson. This ad ran in *Ebony*, *Newsweek*, and other periodicals in 1979 and 1980.

When Genevieve Brooks (later Brown) and her husband, Herbert Brooks, first moved to 1555 Seabury Place in 1962, the surrounding Crotona Park East neighborhood seemed so deeply rooted and tight-knit that she told herself, "Oh wow. I certainly won't have to move again." Since arriving in New York City from a sharecropping community in Anderson, South Carolina, where her great-grandparents had been enslaved, Gennie Brooks had gotten accustomed to moving every few years. When she landed on Seabury Place in the Bronx, her working-class neighbors were mostly Jewish; within a few years, they would join the mass exodus to Co-op City, in the far reaches of the borough, or to the suburbs beyond. With their departure, the upkeep of her building began to slip, and when Brooks approached her landlord with specific issues, he shrugged and told her dismissively "that I was the only one complaining." Undeterred, she looked to her neighbors for validation, and together they formed a tenant association to "speak with one voice." The pattern had been set: when her grievances were met with denial and dismissiveness, Brooks looked for allies and built a movement.[2]

Though Brooks and her neighbors successfully pressured their landlord to reinvest in maintenance, the surrounding buildings continued to fall into disrepair. When they called city agencies seeking blockwide assistance, they were again told that "we were the only one complaining," so Brooks resolved to organize a block association. She began simply—handing out brooms for street cleaning on Saturday mornings—and soon found that her most dedicated volunteers were the children of the largely Black and Puerto Rican neighborhood. "It's always some kids," she recalled. "You know you can do a lot with kids." Responding to the apparent hunger for youth-oriented programming, she launched the Seabury Daycare Center in 1970. Serving more than one hundred families, Seabury rapidly established itself as a neighborhood institution.[3]

And then the fires began. Brooks viewed the blazes through the eyes of the children in her care, who "were not able to have a good night's sleep. That is when we discovered we need to look at the housing crisis." Brooks had her ear to the ground and heard rumors that the fires were being deliberately set or commissioned by landlords. In 1973, she approached the fire department with her suspicions, but she was again dismissed: "The fire marshals insisted that it was the junkies or someone starting the fires." Where others may have been discouraged, Brooks again turned to organizing. Under the unlikely auspices of a day-care center, Brooks created what was probably the city's first community anti-arson organization, the short-lived Fire, Safety, and Educational Program. The program documented the blazes plaguing their immediate neighborhood, at one point counting fifty-six separate fires in a single two-week stretch. "We knew that arson was for profit," she recalled. "It wasn't that a junkie went to sleep in a building . . . it was a wholesale business for everybody. The landlords collected, I mean the owners collected from the insurance companies." In early 1974, Brooks presented the group's findings to the major players in Bronx politics, but she was once more brushed aside. "No one, but *no one*, was interested," Brooks recalled with dismay. Appalled by the lack of concern, she sought to raise broader awareness with an anti-arson education campaign. She invited the children of Seabury Daycare to compose slogans, which she printed on one thousand posters that spring and summer. "Fires are destroying our homes and ruining our businesses," read the posters, which were displayed all around the neighborhood, including nearby Charlotte Street. "Join with us to save our neighborhood."[4]

Gennie Brooks was at the vanguard of what eventually became a nationwide anti-arson movement, but she was a Black woman and a tenant taking on the Bronx's property owners and power brokers, and it would be years before she could build the collective power necessary to punch up in the direction of the borough's elite. In late 1974, she founded the Mid-Bronx Desperadoes, so named, she recalled, "because we were desperate." By the end of the decade, the Mid-Bronx Desperadoes would stand as one of the nation's highest-profile community development corporations. But from the vantage point of nearby Charlotte Street in 1974, there was little to suggest that the arson wave would meet a worthy foe anytime soon.[5]

Unless one knew where to look. Buried on the sixteenth page of the *Times* on September 2, 1974, was the announcement of the Bronx Arson Task Force, the first task force of the decade but certainly not the last. Although they didn't credit Gennie Brooks, the city's police and fire brass informed the public that on August 12, shortly after the Seabury poster campaign, "a task force made up of three police detectives and two fire marshals was appointed to try to find out what is behind the fires." And though the unit was left with "more questions than answers," its commander told the press: "We feel that perhaps there is some kind of a conspiracy here." Indeed, the task force would draft a two-page report, concluding "that there are large amounts of money involved in the burning of vacant buildings." As the investigators remarked, "nearly all the people interviewed," including tenants, community leaders, and prosecutors, "felt that many of the fires were started by paid arsonists." Though the task force was in operation only through October 8, it noted "a large reduction in the conditions leading to its formation"—that is, fires. The very presence of the task force had exerted a deterrent effect on landlords, who were accustomed to operating with impunity.[6]

In its short life, the first iteration of the Bronx Arson Task Force demonstrated both that the fires were being set for profit and that they could be curbed by state intervention. Despite these revelations, the task force's report—the first documented proof of large-scale arson for profit to come from the municipal bureaucracy—went unpublished, languishing for months in a filing cabinet before finding its way to the desk of another civilian crusader against arson, Reverend Neil A. Connolly, the vicar of the South Bronx.[7]

Again and again, grassroots mobilizations set the stage for robust state intervention against arson, only to be met with indifference, incompetence, or co-optation. Until the end of the 1970s, the government—with only a few exceptions—either did not intercede or actively compounded the conditions that kept cities burning. The same can be said of the finance, insurance, and real estate (FIRE) industries, which laid the kindling in the nation's brownlined neighborhoods, then allowed the fires to smolder for years before acknowledging their own incendiary role. Before the late 1970s, every level of government and every rung of the FIRE industries failed to intervene. Arson-affected communities took note. As arson survivor Hedy Byrd testified to the Senate Committee on Governmental Affairs in 1978, "I wanted to remind everyone here that people like me in New York, we are waiting to hear from you, to see just how you all can help us. We really need help in New York."[8]

If most of the political and economic institutions with the means to stamp out the fires were failing to do so, why did arson rates crest, then decline after 1976, before the combustibility of American cities had become a major social issue? The dominant answer since 1978 is the one offered by noted journalist Ken Auletta, who remarked that the fires were dropping off "only because there are so many fewer buildings left to burn." In the same key, an oft-cited epidemiological study of fire and public health in New York asserted, "What could burn did burn." Yet these claims are hard to support. The borough's standard walk-up was no tinderbox awaiting a spark; it was explicitly designed to be fireproof. And as devastating as the arson wave was, it left most buildings standing intact. By one commonly referenced estimate, the Bronx lost about 108,000 housing units to fire or abandonment between 1970 and 1981. Catastrophic, yes, especially where it was concentrated in the borough's southern end, but that figure represented no more than 21 percent of the Bronx's total housing stock.[9]

The arson wave came to an end only because those whose homes lay in its path mobilized and fought back, pressuring their legislators, landlords, and lenders—often with the help of their neighborhood clergy. When the tenants of the Bronx began organizing themselves, they identified the telltale signs of arson for profit and worked to shield their buildings and blocks against it. But no matter how powerful the tenant or block associations became, they could not win the war on arson without the state. The renters of the Bronx and other cities across the United States had to force policymakers in industry and government to take action. The fires would subside only when the profit was taken out of arson, and that required closing the insurance gap.[10]

+++

THE SMALL, HILLY neighborhood of Morris Heights in the West Bronx was, for a short period in the early 1970s, a refuge for families escaping the fires and abandonment ravaging the borough's southern end. With the Harlem River to the west, the elevated Jerome Avenue train line to the east, and the Cross Bronx Expressway carving out its southern border, Morris Heights was, as one tenant group put it, "cut . . . off from its neighbors on three sides." For its residents, many displaced from elsewhere in the borough, those environmental and infrastructural barriers were seen as a buffer against fiery encroachments from the south and east.[11]

That was certainly true for the Campbell family, who had been burned out of the Tremont area, to the east. The Campbells moved into a recently completed eighteen-story apartment building planned by Robert Moses, whose Cross Bronx Expressway lay just a few hundred feet to the south. Since the building was a state-sponsored Mitchell-Lama development—meant to be affordable for middle-income families—its owners had access to better financing options and tax abatements than did most Bronx landlords, which meant it was more likely to remain intact. For the Campbells' children, 1520 Sedgwick Avenue had the added benefit of a communal recreation room on its ground floor. On August 11, 1973, a teenaged Cindy Campbell threw a back-to-school party to raise money for a new fall wardrobe, renting out the building's rec room and commissioning her eighteen-year-old brother, Clive, to spin records. That night, DJ Kool Herc, as Clive was known, "noticed people was waiting for certain parts of the record," during which the dance floor seemed to come alive. On a whim, Herc began to loop his records, isolating and drawing out the songs' instrumental breaks. The response from the dance floor was ecstatic. This breakbeat style of DJing marked the birth of hip-hop, an innovation that evolved directly out of Herc's feedback with the dance floor. The wild moves unleashed by the new style of spinning records were dubbed *burning* (later known as breakdancing), a name that evoked the blazes that first brought Kool Herc to Sedgwick Avenue.[12]

The fires followed the Campbells into Morris Heights, opening up old neighborhood wounds. The construction of the Cross Bronx Expressway in the late 1950s and early 1960s had overcome residents' organized opposition and profoundly ruptured the community. When the blazes began in 1972–73, Morris Heights residents discovered not only that the Cross Bronx Expressway was an insufficient bulwark against arson but that its splintering of the neighborhood left it poorly prepared to defend against the fires. Yet before long, a new generation of tenant organizers would emerge. In the same years that the seeds of hip-hop were being sown at 1520 Sedgwick, another epochal formation was materializing on the adjoining streets and avenues. Like Kool Herc's breakbeat, the Bronx tenant movement of the 1970s was born of sustained experimentation and repetition, and it was similarly forged in the glow of the arson wave.[13]

In 1972, when the Morris Heights Neighborhood Improvement Association (MHNIA) was conceived, it identified itself as "the first organized cooperative community effort since the construction of the Cross Bronx Expressway." The stakes could not have been higher. As the son of one of its first organizers remembered, "Morris Heights was this attempt to stop the incursion of the epidemic of arson and devastation that had leveled much of the South Bronx as it headed north. And Morris Heights was sort of digging a trench in the forest fire kind of thing to try to hold a line against some of the practices that were promoting disinvestment and destruction." The man holding the shovel was Paul Brant, a Jesuit priest in training at Fordham University who was acutely aware of the forces arrayed against the neighborhood: "We were up against a stagnant bureaucracy and a real estate and banking complex which had written off that part of the Bronx."[14]

Brant, an unabashed "firebrand," threw the weight of the Catholic Church behind the ecumenical MHNIA, relying on church funds to hire two organizers who had been trained in the methods of Chicago activist Saul Alinsky. Using direct action to fight for concrete, winnable demands, the MHNIA adopted the Alinskyite technique of identifying strategic local targets for community campaigns. The group first took aim at the landlords of Morris Heights. "The community's more stable landlords were replaced by speculators," its organizers noted, warning that the owners' "intent was to milk the buildings and then abandon them." So intolerable was the management of the neighborhood's housing stock that the tenants of Morris Heights practically flooded into the MHNIA rolls when the group began organizing renters in 1973. "People are 'tired of moving,'" the association found. "Residents who have become involved in organizing their buildings and blocks exhibit a solid hope in preserving the community."[15]

That hope—as well as the frustration that often followed—was apparent in the sheer number of tenant and block associations formed over the following years. By 1976, the MHNIA had successfully organized 111 large buildings housing a total of 5,500 units. In many cases, tenants took over the management of their buildings through a municipal program that allowed them to petition for a receiver to assume management of abandoned buildings. The impact of these efforts was immediately clear. "It is possible, merely by walking through this area ... to tell which buildings are operated by tenant groups," the *New York Times* wrote of the MHNIA in 1977. "They are usually the ones without broken windows and with heat." The MHNIA also launched a number of security patrols, which equipped volunteers with walkie-talkies in an effort to deter, among other things, firesetting.[16]

But when even this flurry of block-level organizing did not slow the spread of arson and abandonment, Brant and his colleagues in the Bronx clerical community realized that they had been thinking too small. During a 1974 meeting of clergy from parishes in the borough's north and west sides, the priests swapped stories of losing parishioners due to fires. Grasping how widespread the problem was, one priest reportedly proclaimed, "Our problem here is survival. If those neighborhoods go up [in flames], our parishes go." The work of the MHNIA took on new salience. Adopting the Morris Heights group as both a model and a member, and Paul Brant as a guiding light, the priests of sixteen Northwest Bronx parishes decided to band together as the Northwest Bronx Community and Clergy Coalition. An ecumenical coalition of Catholic, Protestant, Jewish, Muslim, and non-religious Bronxites, the NWBCCC had its center of gravity in the Catholic Church, especially in its early years. Introducing the coalition to Fordham University in October 1974, Bishop Patrick V. Ahern, the episcopal vicar of the Bronx, described the effort as "unique in the American Church, both for its scope—and for its challenge—for every Catholic." Though there exists a long tradition of church involvement in beleaguered U.S. cities, the comment was not hyperbole. Within a year of launching, the NWBCCC had become "the most extensive grassroots organizing effort in the city." Its wingspan stretched across a quarter of Bronx County, representing some four hundred thousand people. The NWBCCC's ability to mobilize such a vast area was a consequence of the Catholic Church's commitment to the undertaking.[17]

As Brant saw things, the NWBCCC was an attempt to draw a line in the sand, and the fate of the entire borough was in the balance. "There's no hope for the southerly areas unless the northern areas win their fight to stop the spread of decay," he cautioned in 1975. In warning about the metastasis of the problems facing the South Bronx, Brant risked conveying the same racial logic that would undergird *Fort Apache, the Bronx* and the broken windows theory of policing. Many of the neighborhoods organized by the NWBCCC in the 1970s had experienced less white flight than their counterparts to the south. In the words of Harry DeRienzo, who cut his teeth organizing with the NWBCCC, the coalition "was intent upon stopping the 'South Bronx' with its violence and fires (and, perhaps, its residents), from spreading any further north." The progenitor of the NWBCCC, the MHNIA, itself began with an all-white board, though it soon integrated tenants of color into the leadership. Whether the NWBCCC exhibited racially exclusionary impulses in its initial years is difficult to gauge, largely because the struggle against disinvestment and the resistance to desegregation often shared a common rhetoric of contagion. When NWBCCC members warned of the possibility that "our neighborhood will become the next 'South Bronx,'" what were they signifying: the burning and disinvestment of Bronx apartment houses or the race and class of the tenants who lived in them? The answer, though muddled during the coalition's first years, becomes easier to decipher by the late 1970s and early 1980s, when the NWBCCC grew into the powerhouse of racial and economic justice organizing it remains as of this writing.[18]

In Morris Heights, Brant's line-in-the-sand ambitions were washed away by the arson wave's relentless advance. In its 1976 annual report, the MHNIA noted uneasily that "the rate of housing abandonment, though sharply curtailed through the efforts of MHNIA, continues to increase." The organization concluded that despite its impressive surge of tenant organizing, the demands on the group were "enormous and just short of overwhelming," all the more so because of "cutbacks in social program spending by the city, state, and federal government over the past four years." With the state and capital in full retreat, the organizers of the MHNIA had arrived at the hard truth that the tenants of Morris Heights were alone in trying to hold their neighborhood together. It proved an impossible task. The fires soon overtook its hilly streets, and by 1980, Morris Heights ranked among the most arson-afflicted neighborhoods in all of New York City.[19]

Morris Heights thus gave lie to the claim, frequently advanced by community development boosters, that the fate of urban neighborhoods in the post–War on Poverty decades was a question best left to their residents, over and against the state. "However unwelcome the notion was, history seemed to support the idea that government was powerless to save areas such as the South Bronx," wrote the influential planner Alexander von Hoffman. The story of Morris Heights cautioned against the notion that the state stood ever in the way of urban progress. Tenant power, even when built up methodically over a period of years, could not fend off the firestorm on its own. Though tenant organizing would play a pivotal role in suppressing the arson wave, it could not singlehandedly keep out a threat that was built into the financial foundations of the Bronx's brownlined neighborhoods. The arson wave was a function of real estate and insurance dynamics written into the deeds and contracts of the Morris

Heights housing stock. Stopping arson meant diminishing its profitability, and under racial capitalism, that was a role only state and corporate actors could perform. But it took tenants to force their hand.[20]

+++

A FEW MILES southeast of Morris Heights, the campaign to spur state action against arson was gaining steam. Following in the footsteps of Genevieve Brooks, the clergy of the Hunts Point and Longwood neighborhoods began to pressure their officials to mount a coordinated response to the intensifying blazes. In January 1975, a few months after the first Bronx Arson Task Force was disbanded, an officer in the 41st Precinct (of *Fort Apache* fame) forwarded its official report to Reverend Neil A. Connolly, the vicar of the South Bronx. Connolly was incensed to hear that even though the investigation conducted by the Bronx Arson Task Force "indicate[d] that conspiracy is a probable cause of many of the fires," the task force had been dissolved. He attempted to use his authority to renew investigative efforts, but he found the state bureaucracy unyielding. "When the South Bronx was really burning, we couldn't get the FBI or the D.A. to come in and investigate," he later recalled. Connolly first demanded a meeting with the U.S. attorney for the Southern District of New York, but he was stonewalled. "This does not appear to be a matter within this office's jurisdiction," the U.S. attorney replied. Connolly next brought his fight to the Bronx County Courthouse, confronting District Attorney Mario Merola and Borough President Robert Abrams with the threat of public condemnation by church leadership if they did not grant him a meeting.[21]

The tactic worked, and on March 13, 1975, Connolly, Father Louis Gigante, and other Bronx priests sat down with Borough President Abrams, DA Merola, and the heads of the police, fire, and welfare departments. An unconvinced Merola began the meeting by calling on Father Connolly "to present the case" that arson was a real problem. Connolly reviewed the conclusions of the disbanded Bronx Arson Task Force, asserting that insurance fraud and other forms of arson for profit were behind the blazes. NYPD chief Anthony Bouza and FDNY commander Francis Carruthers challenged Connolly, arguing that in fact, the task force had not discovered any conspiracy and that the fires "showed no patterns," but, rather, were "a result of a pervasive social condition that the task force couldn't solve." Connolly stood firm, and his persistent pleas won over the initially skeptical DA, who agreed "to sponsor a task force to investigate possible conspiracy in Bronx fires." The bureaucratic wall that Genevieve Brooks had run up against for years was finally showing some cracks, now that white clergymen were doing the pushing. With Merola on board, the tenants of the Bronx at last gained a capable ally in the government.[22]

Mario Merola claims an outsized presence in Bronx history; the borough hall and courthouse is named in his honor. As district attorney, Merola rose to fame as an anti-arson crusader, becoming such a mainstay of Bronx politics that he won reelection from the grave in 1987. Merola's 1972 election as district attorney of the Bronx coincided with the rising tide of arson, and he was in office when Gennie Brooks first sounded the alarm in 1973. Until his meeting with Reverend Connolly in 1975, however, he remained seemingly oblivious to the arson threat, and it was only after repeated interventions by tenants and their allies in the church that he took action.[23]

Two weeks after his decisive meeting with the clergy, Merola announced the formation of the new task force "to determine the true cost—both financial and social—of this epidemic of fires." The second task force lasted only slightly longer than the first; after two months it fell apart amid infighting between police and fire officials. Jurisdictional issues of this sort repeatedly stymied the government's ability to respond to suspicious fires. Which municipal officials possessed the authority to investigate arson: fire marshals, police, or a joint task force? Throughout the 1970s, from city to city, the authority for arson investigation passed from fire marshals (Houston) to police (Chicago) and then back again. In the Bronx, jurisdiction changed hands roughly half a dozen times throughout the decade. One police functionary complained in 1977 that "what has surfaced is an uncoordinated mish-mash of agencies working opposite each other, some bordering on compartmentalization, working in their own cocoon, isolated from the rest, and alienating the others from the investigative picture."[24]

Until 1975, responsibility for arson investigation in New York City lay exclusively with the fire marshals of the FDNY. Between the arson wave and the fiscal crisis, the marshals office was increasingly overburdened and understaffed in the 1970s, with only thirty-five fire marshals working citywide at one point in 1975. Staffing issues created major disruptions in their operations, which required delicate and time-consuming labor. "Arson is a most difficult crime to prove," Merola explained to the Senate Committee on Governmental Affairs. For an indictment to hold up in court, the fire must be shown to have been lit intentionally, a difficult task, given that the flames tend to destroy evidence of their own ignition. Arson, the stuff of historians' nightmares, often erases its own archive.[25]

Precisely because of this predicament, fire marshals trained for years to build up, as Frank Logue described it, their "ability to read a fire and make the critical judgment as to the cause and origin." Since fires usually burn up, not down, marshals searched for the lowest and deepest point of charring, which was often where the blaze began. The surest way to identify arson was to locate multiple and distinct points of origin. Other obvious clues included the presence of "trailers," such as kerosene-soaked rags, or the absence of furniture, goods, or other trappings of habitation or use. When fires resisted easy readings, marshals would draw on forensic equipment and techniques, including portable gas chromatographs called sniffers that would test for accelerants like gasoline.[26]

Even when a fire was deemed incendiary, however, the investigation usually hit a dead end after the marshals filed their report. For much of the 1970s, arrests for arson were extremely rare, and successful prosecutions were almost unheard of. A national study by the Stanford Research Institute found that only 1 percent of those charged with arson were convicted. The National Fire Protection Association put the number closer to 0.1 percent, finding in 1975 that "fewer than 200 firebugs nationwide may have been successfully prosecuted and convicted for arson from a potential universe of 144,000." Most of those convicted were likely torches caught in the act; it was exceedingly difficult to indict landlords who had commissioned the blaze. "It is almost impossible to prosecute an arson case," investigators told the *New York Times*, "without the help of an informer—preferably the person hired to light the fire." As we've seen, the arson rings that were prosecuted in the late 1970s were brought down by torches who had been caught or wanted to clear their conscience.[27]

While municipal underfunding during the fiscal crisis played a major role in the poor conviction rates of fire marshal investigations, many in the city's law enforcement orbit also blamed marshal misconduct. Barry Kluger, an assistant DA under Merola, privately called "the vast majority of the marshals cases . . . 'bullshit' arrests." Kluger went on to describe cases in which fire marshals tampered with dead bodies, planted evidence, and allowed active investigations to go cold. Even one of their own, Deputy Chief Fire Marshal John Barracato, admitted that the Division of Fire Investigation was "isolationist." He reported being told by FDNY leadership that marshals should not "converse or interact with any community-based organizations," whose members were seen as "outsiders."[28]

Merola decided to empower the NYPD in the anti-arson task force of 1975, a decision following from his dissatisfaction with fire marshal performance, and one that was hastened by pressure from Reverend Connolly and other community advocates. Around the same time, the NYPD's Arson and Explosion Division was established in response to the bombing of Fraunces Tavern near Wall Street by Fuerzas Armadas de Liberación Nacional, a Puerto Rican independence group. The entry of the Arson and Explosion Division into the city's official arson response did little to ease the administrative disarray, as the untimely demise of the 1975 task force made clear. The resulting bureaucratic soap opera—what Merola called an "internecine struggle" between police and fire marshals—carried on for at least the next five years. "Each department accuses the other of incompetence, and the lack of cooperation brings both scant success," observed the *Times*, which marveled that "a majority of the investigations into fires in which arson is suspected are abandoned *within two hours*."[29]

Merola was a shrewd statesman, and soon after his meeting with the Bronx clergy he grasped that "declaring war on these arsonists," as he put it in June 1975, would require more assistance than the local emergency services could provide. On June 6, two days after his task force fell apart, Merola and Borough President Robert Abrams appealed for aid from Clarence Kelley, the director of the Federal Bureau of Investigation. "The fire problem reached a new high," they wrote to Washington, "and we are hereby requesting that the FBI immediately assign personnel to join with our local Police and Fire Departments." This was at least the third time the DA's office had solicited federal help, and the FBI was unwavering in its lack of concern. "There did not appear to be any violations of Federal law at this particular point in time," its assistant director had replied to an earlier request.[30]

Federal aid was withheld for two more years, but Merola's entreaty may have found an audience in the New York FAIR plan. His 1975 letter was perhaps the first documented instance of a public official linking the NYPIUA to the high rates of arson in the Bronx. In attempting to convince the FBI that there were legal grounds for federal involvement, Merola pointed out that "many of these destroyed buildings are insured through the FAIR Insurance Plan, which is mandated by federal law." Although the FBI was unmoved, there are signs that the NYPIUA got wind of Merola's claims. In November 1975, the NYPIUA expressed a willingness to collaborate with the Vera Institute of Justice on a proposed program that would train laid-off firefighters to develop "a salvage/repair program . . . to maintain high occupancy rates and thereby minimize the threat of arson." Though the program did not pan out, the NYPIUA would continue to demonstrate a commitment to curbing arson.[31]

In response to both its soaring cumulative losses and the pressure coming from Merola's office, the NYPIUA situated itself, beginning in 1976, as the insurance industry's "advance guard in the fight against arson." Precisely because its establishment had been a condition of possibility for the arson wave, the NYPIUA was in a prime position to intervene. As of November 1975, the NYPIUA had suffered a net underwriting loss of over $16 million in that fiscal year alone, which increased its cumulative deficit by about 73 percent, to over $38 million. Losses that high forced a reckoning. In April 1976, the NYPIUA adopted "more stringent standards of insurability" in its underwriting guidelines. Later that year, it resolutely "stopped insuring properties that are substantially unoccupied or vacant." The NYPIUA spearheaded a host of other anti-arson initiatives over the next few years, including field patrols, public education campaigns, in-house investigators, and advanced recordkeeping of the fire history for each of its buildings. As one researcher noted, "Because they had to cover the very worst risks, the so-called residual market, New York Property responded with innovative underwriting and claims techniques which have made them far and away the leader in the fight against arson."[32]

Although these measures were long overdue, the NYPIUA's crackdown proved to be pivotal in slowing the arson wave. Rates of arson began declining after 1976, and the NYPIUA's anti-arson initiatives were a major reason why. The NYPIUA, which had helped spark the arson wave, was uniquely positioned to help stamp out the flames, and other insurers would follow a similar course later in the decade.

+++

IN 1977, WITH the borough's tenants feverishly organizing their buildings and blocks, the Bronx DA loudly declaring war on arson, and its chief insurer adopting a robust set of anti-fraud initiatives, the tide was turning. But it took the collective reckoning of the July 13 blackout that summer to draw the media spotlight to the arson problem and drum up the political will for more far-reaching change. The spectacle of some 168 fires in the Bronx during the blackout—together with hundreds more across the other boroughs—jolted lawmakers into action. The New Yorkers who took to the streets during the blackout had—intentionally or not—forced the problem of arson onto the legislative agenda, and two immediate developments followed the restoration of power on July 14. Soon after the blackout, Mayor Abe Beame revived and scaled up the task force model; the Mayor's Arson Task Force included representatives from the FDNY, the NYPD, the Human Resources Administration, and the Department of Housing Preservation and Development. The Mayor's Arson Task Force survived longer than its predecessors, operating for about a year before being reorganized into the Arson Strike Force. Then in August, the Division of Fire Investigation and the Department of Social Services implemented new measures to curb welfare arson, including a required interview of welfare recipients suspected of firesetting.[33]

More consequential was the passage of tax lien legislation, which marked Albany's first concerted effort to take the profit out of arson. The Fire Insurance Proceeds Law of 1977 aimed to simultaneously disincentivize arson and increase municipal tax revenue by allowing unpaid property taxes to be deducted from insurance payouts before they reached landlords. The law required property insurers to notify local tax districts of all fire loss claims before paying the insured parties. "Local tax districts have the authority to file a lien on fire insurance proceeds if the property has tax arrears of one year or more," explained the Arson Strike Force.[34]

Tax lien legislation materialized out of the conviction that any attempt to slow the wave of arson would have to take on the prevailing winds of profit. Although Genevieve Brooks and Reverend Connolly had made this point years earlier, legislative action was inconceivable until the blackout brought things to a boiling point. Even then, however, state intervention took its cues from tenant mobilization on the ground.

The origins of New York's tax lien legislation can be traced to early 1977 and the work of tenant activists in Boston's Fenway neighborhood, where landlord arson had been terrorizing the residents of the Symphony Road area since 1973. Some thirty suspicious fires had killed five tenants and displaced hundreds of others. "People were afraid to lie down and go to sleep," recalled one tenant. When a fire on September 12, 1976, killed four-year-old Jesse Oliver—charring him so badly that his godfather could identify him only because "the body appeared to be the right size"—it roused the neighborhood to action. That night, neighbors gathered in grief and resolved to band together in their own defense. Their collective effort was dubbed STOP, for Symphony Tenants Organizing Project, and they "started by tracing the histories of burned buildings—who owned them, their value, what they were insured for."[35]

Unlike the South Bronx, which was deep in a cycle of disinvestment, the Fenway and Back Bay neighborhoods were undergoing the initial stages of gentrification. A stone's throw from the Prudential Center, the Museum of Fine Arts, and Northeastern University, the Symphony Road area drew the rapacious gaze of speculators seeking to cash in on what was prime real estate. But their ambitions for the neighborhood were tempered by a city statute requiring landlords to give two years of notice to tenants before they could convert apartments to condominiums and thereby get out from under rent-control regulations. Arson enabled a just-in-time eviction, with an insurance payout to boot. "The problem with Symphony road," noted STOP's David Scondras, "is not that it's poverty stricken. The problem with Symphony road is that it's a very valuable piece of property."[36]

Grasping the economic incentives behind the fires, STOP spoke of "arson for profit," a term that it would help popularize over the coming years. After collecting data on their buildings, the tenant organizers of STOP isolated certain variables that seemed to predict which buildings would fall prey to arson. Scondras, one of the group's lead organizers, had recently earned a graduate degree in economics from Northeastern University, and in 1977 he helped develop algorithms that evaluated dozens of data points, including "the number of ownership changes in a short period, the number of mortgages on a property, the proportion of cash invested, and the fire experience, if any, of the current owners." His algorithms were institutionalized nationwide as early as 1979, when the United States Fire Administration and the Law Enforcement Assistance Administration bankrolled STOP and its offshoot, Urban Educational Systems, to train community groups and arson investigators in developing computerized early warning systems in their own cities. So groundbreaking was STOP's system that the Law Enforcement Assistance Administration was apparently willing to overlook the group's socialist bent. "Capitalism is the root of arson," the organizers wrote in 1977, positing that "as long as ownership and profit work side by side, deplorable housing and arson will be a fact of life."[37]

Its revolutionary goals notwithstanding, STOP lobbied for immediate reforms, such as tax lien legislation, that could decrease the profitability of arson. On February 10, 1977, the group held a press conference at the Massachusetts State House, pressuring lawmakers to see to it "that any insurance settlements be applied to back taxes or to settle negligence suits brought by tenants." Two weeks later, Mayor Kevin White reluctantly came out in favor of the proposal, defying his chief fire marshal, who had assured him and the press that the fires were the work of "vandals or drunks" and "arson-for-revenge." That same fire marshal was later arrested alongside thirty-two other conspirators—including landlords, insurance brokers, and police officers—in an arson ring that was brought down by STOP's algorithmic sleuthing. Despite the scope of the bust, Scondras maintained, "Catching the crook and putting him behind bars is not going to solve the problem of arson." Instead, he predicted at a Senate hearing a few months after the arrests that "arson will be solved by people who use pencils instead of guns for weapons because it is a problem that has to do with profit and with money."[38]

STOP's approach traveled down I-95 from Boston to the Bronx, where it was embraced by Mario Merola. "We began to treat arson as an economic crime," remembers Barry Kluger, who helmed the new arson bureau in Merola's office. STOP's framework of arson for profit found new converts in post-blackout Gotham, and soon enough Merola helped push through tax lien legislation. "That was my law, sir," Merola boasted to Senator John Glenn a few months after its passage. He added, with some regret, "The law didn't quite come out exactly the way we had hoped it would."[39]

Originally, a cash-strapped city hall had wanted to "get first crack at fire insurance money to satisfy back taxes," reported the *Daily News*. But after the bill passed through a state assembly that was dominated by real estate interests, that role was usurped by banks and mortgage lenders, who claimed first dibs on unpaid mortgage debt before the city would be able to collect tax arrears. "The city's plan to pick up millions of dollars in unpaid real-estate taxes could turn into a windfall for local banks instead," noted an upstate newspaper. Far from a meaningful revenue boost to the debt-ridden city government, the law thus amounted to a lateral transfer of wealth from insurers to the mortgage-financing industry. Capital would remain within the privatized ecosystem of the FIRE industries. What's more, in some cases of straw ownership, as the *Times* pointed out, the mortgage lender was "the very person who has arranged for the fire," meaning that the withheld payment would just shift from the owner's right pocket to the left. Like the FAIR plan itself, tax lien legislation put property rights ahead of the public good.[40]

In its compromised form, the Fire Insurance Proceeds Law of 1977 still worked to curb arson, cutting into landlords' profit margins. Since an estimated 50 percent of all torched buildings were in tax arrears, Merola's law did manage to appreciably diminish the rate of return on a large swath of arson-for-profit schemes. But its impact was felt more in terms of its deterrent effects than its ability to filter out and intercept fraudulent claims for the city. The program netted less than $1 million a year for the city during the first five years after its passage, just a fraction of the tens of millions of insurance payouts linked to arson. This was not only the result of mortgage lenders having first crack at the insurance settlements but also a function of insurer noncompliance. The Arson Strike Force blamed companies for "not complying as well as they should be," in part "because we have no system in New York to determine who is the insurer of a building."[41]

As arson investigations grew in profile throughout the 1970s, the insurance industry acquired a reputation for noncooperation and even obstruction. Until 1970, the National Board of Fire Underwriters had a hundred-person "arson squad," which lent expertise to local investigations across the country. The squad was unceremoniously dissolved just as the arson wave was starting, and any industry-wide commitment to deterring incendiarism went with it. In New York, investigators reported experiencing "frequent antagonism and disagreements between law enforcement agencies and the insurance industry." Merola himself, when building his case against Joe Bald, Harry Rosen, and Luis Ayala, "angrily denounced the insurance industry," claiming it "balked at cooperating with local authorities in the arson investigation."[42]

The insurance industry finally began to warm to anti-arson initiatives in 1977, when the media spotlight on the fires was growing brighter by the day. A number of factors figured into the about-face. First, the NYPIUA's revelations about the urgency of combating insurance fraud began to percolate into other firms. Since the NYPIUA was the "arson expert" of an insurance industry heavily concentrated in New York, its anti-arson measures—including tighter underwriting, scrupulous investigation of claims, and a computerized directory of the fire history for each insured property—were later adopted industrywide. Moreover, the industry was to some extent simply unable to continue ignoring the soaring cumulative toll of the arson wave. Ten years in, insurers were shelling out astronomical sums, with the Arson Strike Force estimating that in 1977 alone, the "insurance industry paid out $1.6 billion in claims for fires classified as arson." No matter how intricate or extensive the reinsurance network had become, losses that high would eventually come home to roost.[43]

But the most significant factor behind insurers' newfound concern for incendiary fires was the increasing risk of carrying the blame for what was becoming the scandal of the season. As arson for profit made headlines in the months following the 1977 blackout and President Carter's visit, the industry grew nervous that culpability would be laid at its door. In 1967, the Hughes Panel had shown that broad public scrutiny attracted the roving eye of lawmakers, and what kept industry leaders up at night was the threat of falling under federal regulation. A flurry of congressional hearings on arson for profit followed the blackout, and insurance representatives were called to testify on the Senate floor. As James E. Jones of the Alliance of American Insurers remarked, "Once, smoke on the horizon signified industry, progress and jobs. Now it often means a burned out shell in an increasingly desolate urban environment."[44]

To a degree that had not been true since the advent of the FAIR plans a decade earlier, property insurers felt they had an optics problem. When industry executives opened their Sunday *New York Times* on the morning of September 11, 1977, and saw the headline "Upsurge in Arson Calls for Insurance Reform" on the front page of the Real Estate section, they likely began to think twice about rejecting the most basic anti-arson initiatives. That editorial, written by an economist in the Bronx, went far beyond the muted approach of tax lien legislation. Insurers must have recoiled against a line like "the fundamental problem of the industry in approaching the arson-for-profit problem lies in the nature of property insurance in the United States. It insures the financial interest and not the physical structure."[45]

Such sweeping statements threatened to rouse federal policymak-

> # THE PROFIT MOTIVE BUILT THIS BUILDING. IT ALSO BURNED IT DOWN.
>
> Arson is our fastest growing crime. Its most significant motivation: the dollar, of course.

This 1977 advertisement by the Travelers Insurance Company minced no words in conceding the economic roots of the arson wave. The copy accompanied a photo of a building at full blaze.

ers from the laissez-faire slumber they had been lulled into by the McCarran-Ferguson Act of 1945, which had exempted the insurance industry from federal regulation. According to James Brady, a sociologist and the director of Boston's Arson Strike Force, "The worst industry nightmare would be the repeal of the McCarran-Ferguson Act of 1945. . . . This is precisely what has been demanded by some anti-arson activists." Fearing federal encroachment, the industry sought to wrest control of the narrative. In December 1977, the Travelers Insurance Company ran an advertisement that announced in startlingly candid terms the financial origins of the arson wave: "THE PROFIT MOTIVE BUILT THIS BUILDING. IT ALSO BURNED IT DOWN." The ad conceded the violent effects of FIRE capitalism ("the profit motive . . . burned it down") even as it promised that "the profit motive" could somehow be tamed and reoined in by industry vigilance. Travelers presumably hoped to harness the rhetorical force of a blunt mea culpa to lend credibility to its assurance that it would change its approach. The company introduced readers of several national outlets to the Property Insurance Loss Register, a computerized data-sharing service that identified suspicious patterns in loss claims across companies. Member companies, including the various state FAIR plans, subscribed and contributed data to the service.[46]

Just a mile away from Travelers, in the insurance hub of Hartford, Connecticut, Aetna rolled out its own public relations strategy, with a former deputy chief fire marshal of the FDNY, John Barracato, as its mouthpiece. A few weeks before poaching Barracato from the city,

Aetna had been humiliated by an NBC special on arson. A seasoned arsonist sat hooded before the camera and told a national audience, "Aetna was the patsy of the business" because it was "the easiest to swindle." Mortified, the insurer turned to Barracato, the author of *Arson!*, a recently published account of his adventures in the city's arson wars, and likely the highest-profile fire marshal in the nation at the time. Barracato could be counted on for dishing out bombastic quotes to the press. "The fire tells you whether a male set it, a female, a juvenile," he babbled to the *Hartford Courant*. The media ate it up. In one six-week stretch, he appeared on no fewer than twenty-five television and radio shows. Aetna featured him in its own advertising campaign, touting Barracato as America's fire marshal in national magazines from *Newsweek* to *Ebony*.[47]

Although property insurers were pulled into the anti-arson effort in an attempt to stop the bad publicity, their involvement was more than cosmetic. In 1978, an all-industry council representing 85 percent of the nation's property and casualty business banded together as the Insurance Committee for Arson Control. The ICAC was principally an attempt to repair the industry's reputation (its public relations committee was twice the size of any other), but nevertheless it did help shift insurers' anti-arson strategy away from the adjustment side (arson detection) and toward underwriting (arson prevention). The all-industry committee helped standardize a two-tier insurance application that subjected especially arson-prone properties to more searching review. It also worked to push through immunity legislation that smoothed the transfer of information between insurers and law enforcement by shielding insurance companies from libel lawsuits. Insurers who had unearthed evidence of arson could now pass it along to fire marshals, police, or other law enforcement agencies without fear of legal reprisal. The first such bill was enacted by the Ohio legislature in 1976. New York passed similar legislation shortly thereafter, and by the mid-1980s, all fifty states had immunity laws on the books.[48]

Between the tightened underwriting endorsed by the ICAC and the enhanced adjustment enabled by the Property Insurance Loss Register, the industry's conspicuous, if performative, embrace of anti-fraud measures proved decisive. Because the insurance gap was the precondition for the fire wave, an effective anti-arson effort required addressing the gaping disparity between a property's valuation by mortgage markets on the one hand and its valuation by insurance companies on the other. When insurers added anti-arson protections to the underwriting and the adjustment stages of the insurance process, they created friction within a supply chain that landlords had experienced for years as seamless.

By the end of the decade, property owners in the Bronx were finding it more difficult to procure overinflated insurance policies and collect on the fraudulent policies they already had. These restrictions did not bring about a return to yesterday's redlining, though insurers continued to devise ways to base underwriting decisions on race. Instead, the principal effect of these policies was the closing of the insurance gap. Rates of arson fell dramatically after 1977 and kept falling through the early 1980s, fulfilling the 1977 prediction of an executive with the American Mutual Insurance Alliance: "Only when we take the profit out of arson can we reduce it." Nonetheless, the arson industry that had evolved over the course of the decade did not disappear overnight. As the large-scale arson schemes demonstrated, insurance cancellations and adjuster investigations were not enough to halt

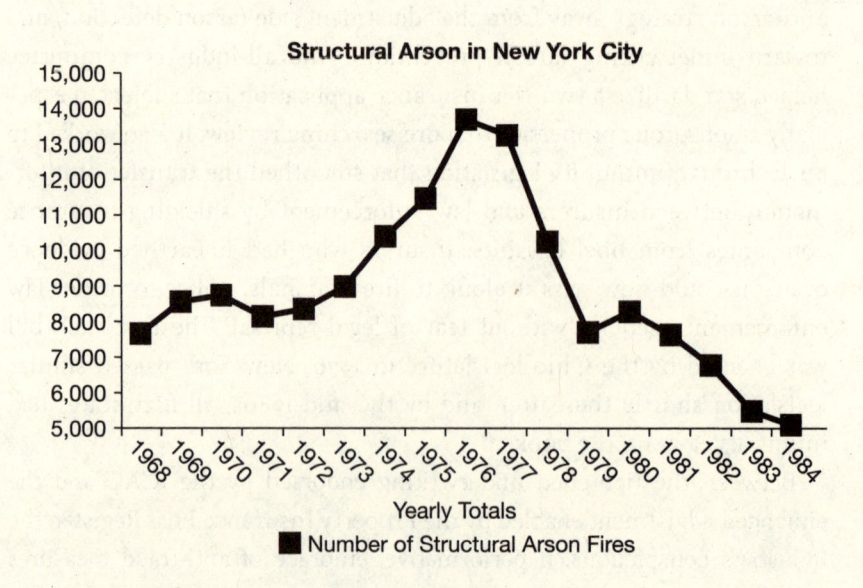

Structural Arson in New York City

■ Number of Structural Arson Fires
Yearly Totals

Data from the Arson Strike Force revealed 1976 to be the height of arson in New York City, with dramatic declines in structural arson fires after 1977.

an arson ring once it had gathered momentum. Far from spelling doom for these rings, being dropped by the NYPIUA in 1976 or 1977 simply meant that landlords were pushed toward an unregulated excess line market then being flooded with policies linked to Lloyd's of London's Sasse syndicate. The crackdown by insurers removed a great deal of kindling, but only state intervention could douse the flames.[49]

+++

UNTIL 1978, THE most significant battles of the war on arson in the Bronx were waged in three distinct theaters: tenant and block associations, the office of DA Mario Merola, and the boardrooms of the NYPIUA and private insurance companies. Beginning in August 1978, the campaign acquired a new command post. Named in Cold War lingo, the New York Arson Strike Force (ASF) played a central role by coordinating the struggle to take the profit out of arson.

If you had entered the offices of the Arson Strike Force shortly after its founding, you would have come upon fourteen elderly researchers operating million-dollar IBM 370 terminals. The improbable research team had been recruited from the city's Department for the Aging and various local nursing homes. The ASF leadership sought out these workers after recognizing that arson "has a devastating effect on elderly people" because it "most often occurs in declining neighborhoods where some of the last tenants to leave are the elderly." Such concerns translated into an organic investment in the work. The "anti-arson zealots" staffed the ASF's Arson-for-Profit Information Center, which provided "arson investigators and prosecutors with computerized information including ownership, building condition, previous arson history and financial background of buildings that have had arson fires." Gathering this information electronically meant the workers could glean in a single afternoon what might have previously required weeks of investigation.[50]

The working conditions were far from optimal. The researchers endured several New York winters without heat in their offices, and because of the poor ventilation in the computer room, the terminals were frequently inoperative. For an agency whose name had a special forces luster, the Arson Strike Force was incongruously headquartered in the crumbling Beaux Arts remains of what had been the city's largest bank building when it was built, at the height of the Progressive Era. By 1978, the Emigrant Industrial

Savings Bank Building, with its cracked ceilings and peeling paint, had been acquired by the city. Its stained-glass windows read "MANUFACTURE" in tribute to a bygone industrial age. It now housed various operations generating municipal revenue in a post-Fordist manner: the New York City Parking Violations Bureau and a booth for off-track betting, recently legalized. As members of the Arson Strike Force ascended to their offices on the fifth floor, they passed a betting parlor that may well have been placing wagers on the same horses as London's Tim Sasse, who had a habit of gambling away the insurance profits he made at Lloyd's.[51]

While the Arson-for-Profit Information Center was the most idiosyncratic division of the Arson Strike Force, the agency was unorthodox across the board. Compared to prior, short-lived task forces, it had been given a clearer mandate and more discretionary power by the city council and the newly elected mayor, Ed Koch. Some saw Koch's formation of the ASF as nothing more than an attempt to fix the city's "image crisis." To be sure, the optics of the imperial city aflame were not good—for the city or the empire. The same year the ASF was established, members of the Soviet Union's Bolshoi Ballet left Lincoln Center and toured the South Bronx to "witness the other side of capitalism." "In Moscow," said one dancer, "everything is not perfect, but we provide housing for everyone. There is no such thing as an abandoned house." Two years later, city councilman Gilberto Gerena Valentín invited a nine-member Soviet delegation to the Bronx and asked for $5 billion in foreign aid to reconstruct the borough. One of the visiting delegates was overheard saying, "It seems like it was bombed." No such aid was forthcoming.[52]

Optics mattered, of course, but the ASF was not just for show. It was a bona fide white-collar crime squad, coordinating action across the entire municipal bureaucracy. In conjunction with Mario Merola's office, the ASF implemented a new division of labor between police and fire officials, limiting the role of Bronx fire marshals to the investigation of a fire's cause and origin. In turn, the ASF granted all the remaining investigative authority to the Bronx police, a ruling that ruffled more than few feathers in the FDNY. "I would get death threats at home from fire marshals," recalled Michael Jacobson. Nevertheless, the decision held, having received the blessing of Mayor Koch.[53]

The ASF's ramshackle quarters were fitting for an agency that leaned into its renegade status within the city bureaucracy. Jacobson, who helped lead the ASF from 1978 to 1983, called it a "start-up." "There was no road map," he said. "We had a big problem. We were basically told: 'Do something about it. Here's a bunch of money.'" Having secured early and ample funding from the federal Law Enforcement Assistance Administration, the ASF staff doubled, then tripled. Aside from the septuagenarians who worked the computers, the office was staffed by workers in their twenties and thirties. "Socially, it was a wild place," Jacobson remembered. He showed no surprise when I reported that during my archival research, I'd found multiple empty vodka bottles mixed in with the ASF papers, which had sat untouched for decades in offsite storage, unknown even to the veteran archivists of the New York Municipal Archives.[54]

From the start, the ASF's priority was halting arson for profit. The success of that effort hinged on the strike force's ability to identify arson-prone buildings before they burned. Using the algorithmic models developed by STOP in Boston, ASF researchers undertook a two-year study of twenty thousand buildings, evaluating data from the FDNY, the NYPIUA, the Department of Housing Preservation and Development, the Department of Finance, the Department of City Planning, Consolidated Edison, and the Human Resources Administration. The result was the Arson Risk Prediction Index, which was able to predict with 80 percent accuracy whether a building would be torched. Once a high-risk building was identified, ASF agents contacted its owners directly, alerting them that their building was under surveillance.[55]

Take 3204 Holland Avenue, a large building in the East Bronx owned by Ernest Milchman, who held or managed some four thousand apartment units across the city. After the tenants of 3204 Holland notified the ASF that their building had suffered two small fires on back-to-back days, an ASF staffer put Milchman on notice. The tenants "have expressed fear that another fire may occur," she told him, demanding that Milchman account for the fires and the building's other code violations. Milchman responded with hostility. "He was abusive," the staffer recorded in his file. As a result of his noncompliance, the ASF dispatched an inspector from the Office of Code Enforcement, and fines and enhanced oversight likely followed.[56]

For all the sophistication of the early warning systems, they were worthless without the intel and groundwork offered by tenant and block associations. The ASF's collaborations with community anti-arson efforts across the city were the central pillar of its operations. In the Bronx, the ASF worked with and offered funding to the Northwest Bronx Community and Clergy Coalition, whose earlier mobilizations against arson had helped spur the city to action. The mid-1970s campaigns of an NWBCCC affiliate, the Morris Heights Neighborhood Improvement Association, had fallen short of stemming arson in the Northwest Bronx, but by 1980, the ASF had established the infrastructure for effective community action. As the fires pushed north of Morris Heights, the ASF and the NWBCCC facilitated a series of large community meetings in 1980 and 1981. Turnout was good and spirits high. Out of these town halls came more advanced block patrols, which used Arson Risk Prediction Index scores to surveil high-risk buildings. With institutional funding from Aetna and technical support from the ASF, most other chapters of the NWBCCC—all to the north of Morris Heights—enjoyed considerably greater success than the MHNIA in holding the fire line.[57]

In the summer of 1981, the partnership between the ASF and the NWBCCC was formalized and deepened with the advent of the Northwest Bronx Fire and Arson Prevention Project (FAPP), which used proprietary data to identify arson-prone buildings that could benefit from reinvestment. When the buildings' owners were willing, FAPP helped them procure government loans and launched initiatives like weatherization programs, resulting in "an upgraded, fuel-efficient property with greatly reduced arson risk." For "uncooperative owners" or vacant buildings, FAPP assisted tenant associations in initiating foreclosure actions, housing court suits, rent strikes, seal-ups, and court receivership. With funding and support from the ASF, insurers like Aetna and Allstate, and the Ford Foundation's Local Initiatives Support Corporation, FAPP targeted fifty-two large apartment buildings in its first year and successfully intervened in 80 percent of them. A year later, after a four-month pressure campaign, the NWBCCC scored a major victory when the FDNY brass acceded to its demand that the department's specialized anti-arson program be implemented in the Northwest Bronx. Named after the red baseball hats donned by its fire marshals, the Red Cap program stationed dozens of highly visible arson investigators within a bounded neighborhood for months at a time. Red Caps had achieved a dramatic reduction of arson in areas of Manhattan, Brooklyn, and Queens, but they had been barred from the Bronx because of the long-standing jurisdictional beef between the police and

Neighborhood chapters of the Northwest Bronx Community and Clergy Coalition, in partnership with the Arson Strike Force, organized town halls and block patrols to combat arson.

fire departments. Frustrated over the bureaucratic red tape, thirty NWB-CCC members "threatened to chain themselves to the Red Cap van in protest." That did the trick, and the FDNY hurriedly deployed the Red Caps to saturate University Heights, South Fordham, and Morris Heights, where they effected a 21 percent drop in suspicious fires within five months.[58]

The ASF further supported community groups like the NWBCCC by serving as a liaison between them and the NYPIUA, creating an ASF-endorsed form that tenant associations could send directly to the insurer when a building fell into disrepair. The form enabled tenants to "request that NYPIUA cancel the fire insurance policy" if landlords failed to furnish heat, hot water, or building security or if other indicators of arson-proneness were present. For the tenants whose lives had been shaped by the brownlining of the Bronx, this linking of insurance access to the well-being of a building's residents was a significant shift. The NYPIUA was easily the most cooperative insurer when it came to supporting these and other initiatives. Usually it took the NYPIUA no more than twenty-four hours after receiving a tip-off from a community group to inspect a building and take the necessary action.[59]

Yet for all its emphasis on the financial aspects of arson, the ASF was a law enforcement agency, and its white-collar focus could drift off course. ASF staffers did at times flatten the various causes of arson, downplaying the threat of arson for profit within a one-among-many framework that drew a false equivalency between landlord arson and pyromania or revenge arson. In the early 1980s, the ASF initiated youth-oriented programs aiming to intervene in juvenile firesetting. Such programs reflected the ASF's own findings that hired torches tended to be young; naturally, the ASF hoped to stop their involvement. But although the ultimate objective of such programs was deterring landlord arson, the ASF pursued that goal using the racialized paradigm of juvenile delinquency. In Park Slope, Brooklyn, the ASF—with funding from Aetna and Citibank—organized a youth anti-arson patrol called the "Brown Berets" (with no affiliation with the West Coast–based Chicano revolutionary organization). Echoing the emergent rhetoric of at-risk youth, one ASF organizer told the *Daily News* that the patrol's fifteen teenaged members "are street-smart kids who might otherwise get into trouble." A co-sponsor of the patrol framed it in more coded terms, assuring neighbors that these Brown Berets were not to be confused with any similarly named groups on the West Coast or the Young Lords, closer to home: "Don't be alarmed if you see youths on your block in beige berets and khaki shirts carrying walkie-talkies."[60]

Other youth-targeted programming attempted to achieve a more delicate balance. In 1982, the strike force waged a campaign to pull from the shelves an arson-themed video game called *Firebug*. Released for Apple II by Baltimore-based Muse Software, best known for the *Wolfenstein* first-person shooter series, *Firebug* casts the player in the role of arsonist. Set in a five-story apartment building, the torch is tasked with gathering gas cans and selecting a fuse length that will leave them enough time to escape. Although the game is devoid of plot, the reward structure perfectly mirrors the motivations of a landlord seeking to defraud an insurance company. "Points are scored depending on how much of each floor is burned," and "bonus points [are] awarded for burning down every wall on a given floor." As in the 1970s Bronx, "you lose only if you are caught in the flames"; to wit, there is no risk of getting apprehended by police officers or fire marshals. Instead of arrest, losing is marked by the message "YOU MADE AN ASH OF YOURSELF" popping up on the screen. Arson investigators the nation over were aghast that a game "designed primarily for youth" would "encourage firesetting by explaining how to set fires." In New York, the Arson Strike Force joined the statewide Office of Fire Prevention and Control to pressure Muse Software to cease production of the game, and "after several discussions with the MUSE Company, on November 4, 1982, we were informed by a representative that the production of the game had been discontinued."[61]

Through its mixed record battling youth arson, the ASF demonstrated that even an investigative body organized to combat white-collar crime was liable to reproduce the criminalization of the Black and Brown poor. Although it took a stand against incendiary and negligent landlords, the Arson Strike Force was far from mounting a confrontation with the property regime. A less volatile stage of the business cycle would do.

The ASF complemented its campaign against arson-curious media like *Firebug* with its own public education initiatives. In a series of early-1980s radio PSAs that ran on the new wave and disco station WKTU-FM (among others), the ASF transmitted frequencies that had a droll, rhythmic resemblance to the music of the band Talking Heads, with whom they shared the air. Targeting the city's eighteen-to-thirty-year-old demographic, the ASF counseled listeners to "make a note" of where they saw a fire: "Which floor, which window, which side of the building?" Meanwhile, Talking Heads front man David Byrne had sputtered a few years earlier, "Which is my face / which is a building / which is on fire." The ASF continued, "Watch out for people making arson threats," while the following year Byrne launched into "Burning Down the House" with "Watch out, you might get what you're after." In the end, though, the PSAs closed with a more unironic—and possibly more melodic—final verse than Byrne's "Fighting fire with fire." The ASF assured listeners, "America is burning—and arson is the cause . . . America is burning—but you can put out the fire."[62]

The ASF translated these publicity campaigns into public policy. In the summer of 1981, ASF leadership traveled to Albany alongside members of the NWBCCC to lobby lawmakers in support of statewide anti-arson legislation. In July, the passage of the New York State Omnibus Anti-Arson Law introduced a number of measures designed to throw a wrench into arson-for-profit schemes. The law, noted an ASF newsletter, "requires applicants

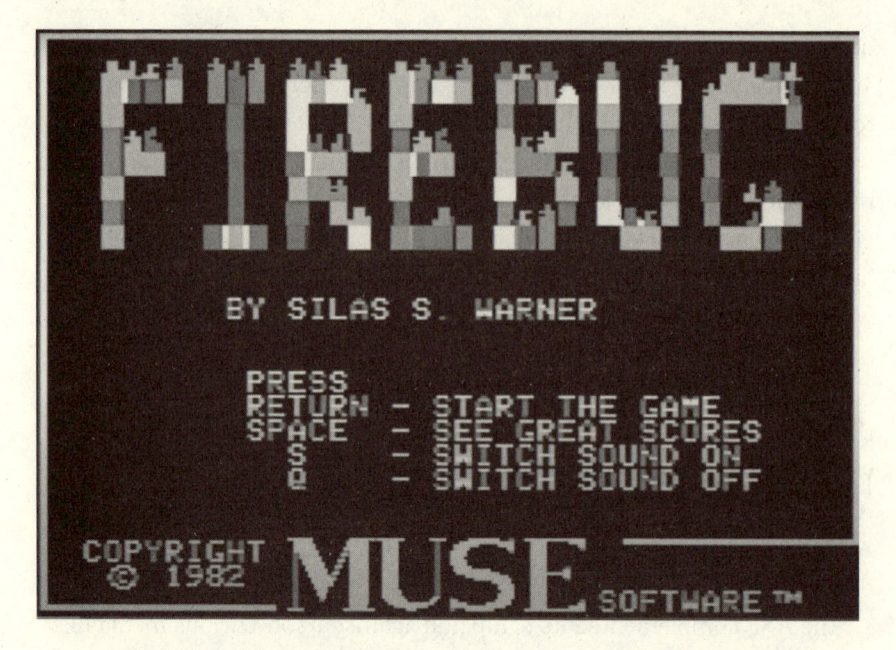

"Can you succeed at a test of fire?" asked the makers of *Firebug*, an arson-themed video game released in 1982 for Apple II. When members of the Arson Strike Force learned that the game instructed players how to set fires, they lobbied successfully for its discontinuation.

for fire insurance to disclose far more information to potential insurers than ever before." That included the names and addresses of all corporate owners and beneficiaries, the property's sales history, the applicant's loss history, all unpaid taxes, and all current building violations. It also strengthened the enforcement and reach of the state's tax lien legislation, incentivized insurance companies to more thoroughly investigate claims, and required all fire losses to be reported to the state. In line with other criminal justice reforms of the era, the legislation heightened the penalties for arson and bumped insurance fraud offenses from misdemeanors to felonies. More forward-looking was the law's creation of financial incentives for owners to rebuild on-site with the insurance proceeds.[63]

A year later, on October 12, 1982, the federal Anti-Arson Act of 1982 was signed into law by Ronald Reagan. The law extended federal jurisdiction over arson and made permanent its classification as a Part I crime, a designation that required the FBI to begin keeping arson statistics. The push to reclassify arson so that it would be included in the FBI's Uniform Crime Reports had been in motion since 1977. It struck many as an uncontroversial proposal; at the time, as a Part II crime, arson was on par with public drunkenness or illegal gambling. Nevertheless, the FBI, continuing its streak of sitting out the fight against arson, repeatedly testified in opposition to the reclassification.[64]

The Anti-Arson Act authorized the continuous collection of arson statistics for the first time, but by that point, the blazes were already declining sharply across New York City and the nation. In the final analysis, the war on arson in the Bronx was won only after successive waves of community mobilization, which, in turn, spurred the necessary governmental and insurer action. It took the triangulated response of these three groups of actors—community organizations, government agencies, and insurance companies—to turn back the tide. Tax lien legislation, the ASF's early warning system, and insurer crackdowns were all essential elements in the long campaign to "take the profit out of arson." But they came to pass only because of pressure from the tenant movement, and likewise it was a network of tenant and block associations that actually did the work of holding landlords in check. As the wave of arson receded, the tenant movement would have to grapple with both the devastated built environment and the warped financial landscape it left in its wake. What would come after brownlining?

EIGHT

Corrective Capitalism

We can't depend on anyone but ourselves. The laws of private ownership, the court system, HDA, HUD are a farce.

—PEOPLE'S DEVELOPMENT CORPORATION, C. 1976[1]

One can't very well hurl his body into the path of an oncoming bulldozer when he (or she) is the developer.

—NEAL PEIRCE AND CAROL STEINBACH,
CORRECTIVE CAPITALISM, 1987[2]

Volunteers cleaning up Charlotte Street during the 1980 People's Convention—organized in protest of the Democratic National Convention, being held in Madison Square Garden.

"Is arson a necessary evil to provide insurance to the inner city?" The question, posed by industry speakers at a 1977 anti-arson conference in New York City, revealed much about the actuarial worldview. From the perspective of many in the insurance industry, American cities faced a binary choice: redlining or arson. This framework presumed that insurance access and insurance fraud went hand in hand, at least in urban neighborhoods of color. In the words of the Federal Insurance Administration director, "The dilemma of how to keep vital insurance available without encouraging fraud is an agonizing one." Her predecessor at the FIA had testified a few years earlier that "we have been concerned lest this [arson] problem be used as an excuse to justify invidious redlining in urban areas." The National Association of Insurance Commissioners admitted as much, announcing its support for efforts to stop underwriting areas "which are particularly arson-prone," but fretting that this would "sustain attack as being discriminatory or as being 'redlining.'"[3]

The notion that neighborhoods of color in U.S. cities were consigned to suffer either insurance redlining *or* insurance arson was undercut by the fact that anti-redlining measures ended up being integral to the city's successful campaign against arson. In 1980, the NYPIUA deepened its partnership with the ASF, agreeing to "jointly undertake an anti-arson pilot project involving the selection of fire insurance applicants in New York City's high fire risk neighborhoods. *Increasing the availability of fire insurance in these areas is an important component of the city's anti-arson policy*" (emphasis mine). In a marked departure from the brownlining era, the initiative furnished insurance policies at reasonable rates, underwriting buildings only after careful vetting. As predicted, the program's implementation corresponded with ongoing and dramatic reductions to the city's arson rate. And it was not an anomaly. After a series of pitched congressional battles in the late 1970s, FAIR plans nationwide were forced to dramatically lower their rates in order for insurance companies to remain eligible for federal riot reinsurance. Ever wary of federal encroachment, the New York insurance world rejected the new regulations, but the NYPIUA still ended up reducing its rates drastically, thereby making its insurance policies significantly more affordable. Those changes coincided with the continued decline in arson rates. Ultimately, the end of the arson wave did not correlate with the return to redlining and a rise in race-based insurance denials but, rather, with the reining in of brownlining.[4]

The end of brownlining quelled the arson wave, but this more equitable era of property insurance availability was of limited impact for the tenants who had been most affected by the fires. Insurers themselves admitted that property insurance coverage was far from a panacea for the volatility of urban real estate at a moment when the nation was in full transition toward post-Fordism. These were the years of the Volcker shock—a period of prolonged high interest rates—the second oil crisis, and the corresponding explosion in the unemployment rolls, evictions, and utility bills. As one industry insider put it: "The alleviation of poverty should not be a function for the private insurance mechanism." Another industry official struck a similar note: "The insurance mechanism is being made the dumping ground for difficult, perplexing and unsolved social problems." Without a doubt, such disavowals sprang from rank self-interest, obfuscating how the "insurance mechanism" itself produced and reproduced those very problems. But in the case of the Bronx and its tenants, these assessments were largely correct, though for the wrong reasons. Property insurance would never rectify the violence of racial capitalism; insurance serves only one master, and that master is property itself. Although renters feel acutely its absence or deficiency, the presence of insurance does not in turn guarantee better housing conditions.[5]

Housing conditions in the Bronx would only improve as a result of the labor, sacrifice, and endurance of the borough's renters. The tenant movement that had been so pivotal in turning back the tide of the arson wave created the organizational infrastructure that would eventually enable one of the largest-scale rebuilding efforts in the history of American cities. Yet it was one thing to stamp out arson, and quite another to envision the future of the Bronx's built environment. With scorched expanses lying before them, Bronxites were faced with the herculean task of reconstructing what had been lost to the burning years. Two overlapping models materialized. The first was called sweat equity, and it was rooted in self-help, urban homesteading, and a vision of a Bronx without landlords. The second, community development corporations (CDCs), shared many of these values but moved toward a distinct political horizon. In contrast to sweat equity organizations, community development corporations enshrined private property, and though they took form in response to the political economy of landlordism, many CDCs grew to become the largest landlords in their neighborhoods.

The contest between these varying approaches, chronicled in this chapter via two representative organizations, held the fate of the borough—and, indeed, many American cities—in the balance. When community development corporations eclipsed sweat equity in the late 1970s, funded in no small part by insurance companies, they became the primary agents of affordable housing construction nationwide. The story of their ascendance is the story of financialization percolating into the community-based housing organization. Long before the subprime lending of the 1990s and 2000s, the world of finance courted the affordable housing sector in search of tax shelters and good PR. The CDC was a crucial conduit in that process.

+++

AT THE START of the 1970s, Ramón Rueda was a draft resister living underground. By the end of the decade, he was the national face of sweat equity and the movement to create common ground. Rueda's political biography is the story of the New York Left over the course of the 1970s. Having grown up in the South Bronx and East Harlem, Rueda was almost twenty years old in 1968 when the assassination of Martin Luther King Jr. politicized him, pushing him into the orbit of the Young Lords and Black Panther Party. He followed the movement to Connecticut and the end of the Metro-North line during the 1970 trials of the "New Haven Nine," a flashpoint in the FBI's war on the Black Panther Party. He was especially drawn to the culture of collective dissent: "There was a sense of camaraderie—it was such a charge! The scene reminded me of what I'd read about the French revolution."[6]

By that point, Rueda was a student at Long Island University, and upon his return from New Haven, he led the effort to shut down all local campuses in protest of the Kent State shootings. The press singled him out when he helped organize a six-week free-breakfast program for children in nearby Glen Cove, modeling it on the practices of the Panthers and the Lords. But in 1971, he and his pregnant wife, Leslie, decided to go underground to resist the draft, and he vanished from the public eye. The family remained incognito until his cover was blown in late 1973, when three FBI agents, with guns drawn, arrested him in the Manhattan shoe store where he was working. Sentenced to three years of probation, Rueda emerged from the ordeal indignant and adrift. Eager to plug back into political work, he visited East Harlem to meet the Renigades, an early sweat equity organization whose members were renovating an abandoned apartment building in exchange for an ownership stake in a unit. Curious about housing issues in his old stomping grounds of Morrisania, he visited the South Bronx neighborhood of his youth and was aghast at what he encountered. In 1974, one-third of Morrisania's buildings were abandoned and another third were on their way. Blocks away from Charlotte Street and the 41st Precinct (of *Fort Apache* notoriety), this was the epicenter of the arson wave at mid-decade.[7]

Rueda wanted to bring the fledgling sweat equity movement to the Bronx, and he found his proving ground at 1186 Washington Avenue, an abandoned six-story tenement in the heart of Morrisania. The building's owner appeared to have walked away, but several apartments were occupied by a handful of squatters living without heat or electricity. Rueda knew that without immediate intervention, the building was likely to fall prey to arson: "It was just sitting there waiting to be burned out and demolished." Yet although the building was falling apart, its bones were intact, and on the whole, it was in better shape than most of the neighborhood's structures. In Rueda's eyes, the block itself had a lot going in its favor, despite its many ravaged buildings. At one corner, apartment houses had recently been converted to public housing, which meant they were immune to arson and could help anchor the block. Rueda figured that "1186 would take care of the opposite end, and then we could do the buildings in between and thus stabilize the entire block."[8]

Rueda tapped friend and family networks, pulling together in late 1974 the ten founding members of what would become the People's Development Corporation, or PDC (despite its name, the PDC was not a community development corporation of the sort discussed later in this chapter). Like Rueda, most were Puerto Rican men in their twenties, with a few women and Black resident-workers among them. Eladio Velez, a friend of Rueda's, credited his participation to Rueda's vision and leadership: "From the beginning I didn't believe we could do this.... There were no resources, there was no guarantee. But I trusted Ramon." Jane Benitez, another founding member, had also written off the project as a fool's errand. "After seeing the building and all the holes," she said, "I started cracking up." But her comrades softened her cynicism, and within weeks, she was helping with security: "I was guarding the building at night, me, can you believe that?"[9]

The work was arduous and, for a time, thankless. Gathering most nights and weekends, the group began renovations in December 1974 and spent the cold winter months gutting the building. "It took weeks just to clean the ice-cold mud, filth, and dead animals from the cellar," stressed Rueda. Many of the resident-workers squeezed in the rehab work between full-time jobs, school, or other hustles, all without funding or the promise of a payoff at a later point. They labored for seven months before receiving any resources or recognition from the city. Untrained and under-resourced, the group "did three times the work we should have," Velez noted with exasperation. On top of the physical risks of the work, there were legal worries, too. The group was "breaking the law that winter," pointed out one journalist. "They were tearing apart a building they didn't own," and there was little recent precedent indicating whether the city would refrain from giving them trouble, let alone honor their equity in the building. But this was the Bronx in 1974, and the very same process of disinvestment that had led to the building's abandonment offered the PDC effective license to "liberate" the property. Rueda soon found that "nobody gave a damn about 1186—not the landlord, certainly not the city."[10]

Given the hazardous conditions, grueling work schedule, and uncertainty surrounding outside funding or legal recognition, what kept the resident-workers of the PDC committed to 1186 Washington? Rueda's conviction certainly helped win converts, but just as important were the PDC's non-hierarchical structure and its early commitment to governing by consensus. For one member, "If the point of urban homesteading was to build and own an apartment through cooperative self-help, then that was also PDC's point as a whole. If the building belonged to the homesteaders, then so did PDC."[11]

Still, what held the group together went beyond its governance structure. The People's Development Corporation was an exercise in rethinking property rights and creating a new model of housing. With sweat equity, property was made commensurate with toil. The down payment—which has long served as a racially discriminatory barrier to the federally backed mortgage—was de-financialized and yoked directly to the labor of the building's residents. The down payment was, in other words, transformed into an embodied form, the non-monetary currency of sweat. The PDC's reconceptualization of property was an explicit rejection of the private housing market and the limited public and subsidized options available: "We can't depend on anyone but ourselves. The laws of private ownership, the court system, HDA, HUD are a farce. They were never set up to serve our housing needs." In the words of one member, the PDC would succeed precisely "'cause there won't be no landlords."[12]

In its challenge to landlordism, the PDC drew on the Bronx radical tradition. The Bronx had been a hotbed of tenant activism since the Progressive Era, when the borough's Socialist Women's Consumers League, Bronx Tenant League, and scores of other groups made it "the best organized borough" in the city—no small feat. That distinction persisted into the Depression years, when the borough's socialist and Communist tenants kicked off the Great Rent Strike War of 1932, which helped bring about the modern housing reform movement and, eventually, the city's rent-control apparatus.[13]

But more than any other antecedent, it was the Young Lords Party that laid the groundwork for the PDC, and not only because of Rueda's early association with the group. The Lords, who opened their Bronx office in early 1970, had gained prominence with highly visible occupations of underutilized or mismanaged institutions like the borough's own Lincoln Hospital. The group had come to see landlordism as a form of structural violence inflicted upon Black and Brown New Yorkers. Member Richie Perez (later a founder of the Committee Against Fort Apache) described landlords as a primary antagonist of the movement: "Our feeling is that nationalism is important . . . but pride alone is not gonna free us, the ability to play congas . . . [and] speak Spanish fluently is not gonna stop landlords." Rueda cited the Young Lords and Black Panthers as the PDC's formative influences. But as its name suggested, the People's Development Corporation integrated the Lords' doctrine with the vernacular of self-help and a burgeoning faith in market-based remedies to racial and economic inequality. Alongside the Lords and the Panthers, Rueda credited two other sources for inspiring the PDC: Mao Zedong's principle of self-reliance and E. F. Schumacher, the neo-Keynesian economist responsible for the "small is beautiful" philosophy.[14]

Across these influences, the politics of self-determination figured centrally. As one of the PDC's resident-workers described it: "This project has loosened the noose around our neck, now we have a chance to breathe. The community has a chance to visualize reconstruction and that is generating hope and further reaction in the neighborhood." Rueda likewise framed the PDC's efforts as a countermovement against state disinvestment: "What we are saying is that this is our piece of land, this is our stake in our future, and this represents our last hope." Strikingly, the PDC's vision of self-determination found value in that which had been discarded by racial capitalism. Member Steve Katz described this act of reclamation as having the power "to literally turn the world upside down." He went on: "So it was that a group of abandoned buildings up by the Cross-Bronx Expressway became the 'Fulton Mines,' filled with a wealth of lumber, tiles, BX cable, marble stair treads, doors and the last remnants of copper pipe." Instead of extracting a commodity from nature, the PDC's mining found worth in precisely that which the human world rendered disposable.[15]

To win support from the city government, the PDC relied on political theater in ways reminiscent of the Young Lords. In February 1975, as it was gaining steam, the group began to search for a loan to finance the mounting costs of the renovation. When they were rebuffed by the city's Housing and Development Administration (HDA)—then under the direction of Roger Starr, of planned shrinkage fame—they decided to hold a sit-in at HDA headquarters. As Katz described it, the PDC "'Mau-Maued' its way into the funding pipeline for 1186 Washington Avenue by coming down to a meeting with city officials intentionally filthy in plaster, carrying crowbars and hammers." Thirty-one PDC members were arrested, but the theatrics succeeded in getting the recently launched Urban Homesteading Assistance Board (UHAB) to advocate on their behalf. With UHAB's help, they secured the first sweat equity municipal loan in the Bronx, a city construction loan for $311,000, which they supplemented with job-training contracts from the Criminal Justice Coordinating Council. Thus began the PDC's fraught dependency on strings-attached government support, which Rueda dubbed "plantationism." The group made huge strides on 1186 Washington once the municipal loan was secured, in late 1975, and as the resident-workers gained skills in crafts like carpentry and plumbing, the building became a showcase for the potentialities of sweat equity. Its roof was outfitted with solar panels, and one resident-worker, Raoul Reyes, equipped his new apartment with track lighting and "the only sunken bathroom in the Bronx." In early 1977, the first tenants moved in, leading one to predict, "Wait till you see the politicians who show up . . . trying to take credit for what we've done."[16]

At this point, President Carter's trip to the Bronx was only a few months away, an event that, among its other effects, transformed the PDC into the national face of sweat equity overnight. Though Carter's itinerary had been planned well ahead of time, the White House did not give the PDC (or other Bronxites) the courtesy of advance notice, and Rueda had to be roused hurriedly from his bed for the nine a.m. visit. "Suddenly, in the wake of Carter's 15-minute tour of 1186 Washington Avenue, we were all stars," remembered Katz. The trickle of funding that began before Carter's visit became a flood, and the organization's budget and membership increased tenfold in just one year. Before long, the PDC had been transformed into an

President Jimmy Carter made an unannounced stop at the People's Development Corporation's renovated building at 1186 Washington Avenue on October 5, 1977. Overnight, the PDC became the national face of sweat equity.

organization with a $4 million budget and 250 staff members. "Ramon was Carterized," another Bronx activist observed. "It changed his whole life."[17]

After Carter's tour, the PDC's ambitions expanded far beyond housing, eventually encompassing nearly every aspect of community life. The group drew up a detailed plan for a nine-block area surrounding 1168 Washington, complete with a host of new social services and economic development projects. The catchment area was to house some forty-five hundred residents, and the PDC envisioned a network of interconnected institutions serving the community's needs, including a food cooperative, a day-care center, a senior citizens program, and a series of small parks. The proposed economic projects were equally ambitious, involving conventional businesses such as a carpentry shop, coin laundry, vegetarian restaurant and bakery, and pharmacy, along with more experimental projects like a youth-led photography enterprise and a vermiculture waste-management initiative.[18]

By 1978, the PDC had stretched the sweat equity concept into a utopian experiment in urban communal living. As the nine-block blueprint swelled into a forty-block plan, Ramón Rueda crystallized his vision of an "urban village," a bastion within the larger city: "We want to be as self-sufficient as we can. We even want to grow some of our own food on vacant lots. We'll be an extended family of 10,000 people." Rueda, who was known to sport a blue Mao cap, modeled his vision on Dazhai, the Chinese village that served as Mao Zedong's prototype for collective, self-sufficient living during the Cultural Revolution. The PDC succeeded in implementing many of its plans, including multiple head-to-toe renovations, a community garden and park, an aquaculture project, and a solar-powered water-heating system. According to one study, by the end of the decade, the PDC had "completed the largest sweat equity rehabilitation program in New York." It became one of the first two organizations to receive a pilot grant from the national Urban Homesteading Demonstration Program, administered by HUD.[19]

But despite the PDC's extraordinary success securing funding for sweat equity, its relationship with the state and funders was riven by contradictions. The PDC was born out of conditions of state failure and dispossession, and it positioned itself as an alternative to state-led redevelopment. As Rueda explained, "The people of Morrisania—long used to the unfulfilled promises of successive governments and agency administrators and

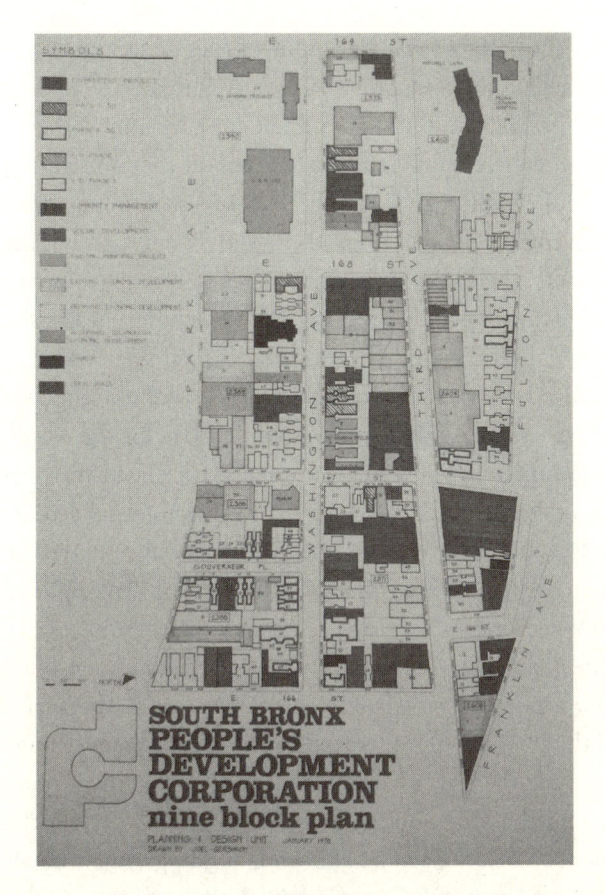

The People's Development Corporation sought to transform Morrisania into an urban village founded on Maoist political thought. Its plans went far beyond housing, including a food cooperative, a day-care center, a youth-led photography enterprise, a pharmacy, and a waste-to-energy vermiculture operation.

tired of being the square pegs for Washington's round holes—decided to generate their own programs." But as one critic cautioned, "approval of the sweat [equity] efforts is facile because they get the government off the hook." What was intended as a repudiation of state paternalism could double as permission for the state not to do anything at all.[20]

When the PDC did coax funding from the government, it could create unwanted vulnerabilities for the organization. "Twice in PDC's history, government-imposed delays seriously damaged the group's cohesion and strength," Steve Katz recalled. In one of these instances, the resident-workers who had sunk so much sweat equity into 1186 Washington Avenue moved into the building and immediately assumed the burden of paying maintenance fees and real estate taxes "at the same time that they faced months of unemployment," due to delays in funding. Those financial pressures coincided with a flood of publicity, a disorienting confluence that strained the PDC. Meanwhile, Rueda began to tour the country on the emergent sweat equity speaking circuit, leaving a leadership void at the exact moment that the organization was exploding in size. By 1979, the PDC had hundreds on the payroll, making it one of the larger employers in the Bronx. Scaling up so rapidly proved to be toxic for the organizational culture. According to Katz, Rueda, who was "truly exhausted by this time, seemed to have decided that PDC's experiment in internal democracy was a failure. . . . It would have to be replaced with clear lines of vertical authority." Landlords may have been evicted by the People's Development Corporation, but bosses were still around.[21]

PDC homesteaders and staffers bristled at Rueda's turn toward executive control, and racial and gender tensions rose to the surface. Black members of the PDC felt marginalized by the predominantly Puerto Rican leadership, a dynamic that was exacerbated by antagonisms between the community and the PDC. Because of the group's spotty efforts to align with the tenant associations of neighboring buildings, many of which were led by Black women, the PDC seemed, in the eyes of its neighbors, to be "just another community organization, like so many that had come their way before." The disconnect was compounded by the absence of women in leadership positions. One former member blamed the resulting masculinist style of leadership for the ultimate downfall of the organization: "The bluff-and-threat that worked so well when it came to outfoxing government agencies was supremely destructive when it was used against co-workers."[22]

In a supreme irony, the bad blood between the rank and file and the PDC leadership led to an act of arson in early 1979. Managers had fired a group of outspoken workers, and a few days later the main offices of the PDC were mysteriously torched. The damage from the fire was not cataclysmic, and Rueda responded with a series of community meetings that he hoped would de-escalate the situation. But the organization had grown so quickly that there was no foundation to be rebuilt. A few months later, a second arson job obliterated the PDC headquarters, incinerating its records and bringing the organization "to a grinding halt." The White House circulated an internal memo that reported, "The damage is extensive, and Ramon is having a hard time." Presidential adviser and soon-to-be chief of staff Jack Watson tried to give Rueda a call to express his condolences, but the phone line was dead.[23]

And with that, an organization that had emerged to reimagine an urban area decimated by arson itself fell prey to the decade's firestorm. The PDC never recovered from the second fire, and Rueda soon left the organization and began a contracting business. The PDC was in many ways a victim of its own success. It had lost touch with its small-scale, non-hierarchical roots. Even its founding achievement, 1186 Washington Avenue, came to a dismal end. As one member recalled with anguish, "Ultimately, 1186, the object of so much love and the source of much inspiration, was seized by the city for nonpayment of real estate taxes."[24]

Years later, reflecting on the collapse of the group, Rueda reframed its demise as a refusal to be incorporated into the existing power structure: "Was I successful at instituting an organization, no. I did not believe in the system. I was not willing to let PDC become a part of the system." True enough: the fall of the PDC meant that sweat equity did evade institutionalization. Though instead of vanishing from the Bronx, the PDC approach was incorporated in another sense—by the broader push for community development.[25]

+++

THE BANANA KELLY Community Improvement Association germinated in the same ashen soil as the neighboring People's Development Corporation. "Ramon was our inspiration, he was always there for us," remembered Banana Kelly's co-founder Harry DeRienzo. Through the twists and turns of the 1980s, Banana Kelly morphed from a sweat equity collective in the PDC mold into one of the nation's foremost community development corporations. In this way, its organizational arc demonstrated the promises and pitfalls of community development, the primary engine for affordable housing construction and rehabilitation in the post-1960s United States.[26]

In 1976 and 1977, Harry DeRienzo, a white college-educated organizer, was employed doing youth outreach for the Casita Maria Settlement House, at the edge of the Hunts Point neighborhood. As he wrote in his memoir, "I remember a brother and a sister who were doing very poorly in school. I arranged for tutoring help in English and Math, as well as daily homework help. But when I made a home visit, I learned that their family had been burned out of separate homes no less than three times in the past year! No wonder the children were having trouble in school." Disgusted with the "band-aid" solutions he had been tasked with applying for the settlement house, he began "working with residents on the issue that seemed most relevant to them: saving their homes." Unknowingly, he was replicating the trajectory of Mid-Bronx Desperadoes' Genevieve Brooks, who had also launched her anti-arson crusade after witnessing the effects of fire on the young people in her neighborhood.[27]

As part of his work with Casita Maria, DeRienzo opened the gym for late-night games of basketball. It was on the court that he met Leon Potts and his neighbors on Kelly Street, which was rapidly succumbing to arson. Known as "Banana Kelly" because of the crescent-shaped curve of the street, the block in question had recently lost six of its fifteen buildings to fire. Leon Potts's parents, Frank and Nancy, owned a couple of the remaining apartment houses, and as Black landlords in a redlined neighborhood, they were feeling the sting of state and capital disinvestment. "They are trying to run all the blacks out," Frank Potts said. Unlike most of the other landlords chronicled in this book, the Potts family was firmly invested in the well-being of the block. They were still landlords, though, and this investment did not necessarily extend to the well-being of the renters, as was evident when Nancy Potts blamed tenants on welfare for "ruining everything." Despite, and perhaps because of, such contradictions, the Potts family was singularly positioned to prevent what was left of Kelly Street from going up in flames.[28]

One night after a game of basketball, Leon Potts told DeRienzo that the city planned to demolish three of Kelly Street's burned-out buildings and expressed his fear that the resulting rubble-strewn lots could accelerate the abandonment of the block. There and then, Potts and DeRienzo "decided to make a stand on Kelly Street," looking to neighboring organizations for inspiration on how to stop the fires. In the summer of 1977, they paid a visit to 1186 Washington, and after talking with the PDC's Ramón Rueda and the South East Bronx Community Organization's Father Gigante, they announced the launch of the Banana Kelly Community Improvement Association, a new sweat equity initiative. The goal was to take "control of buildings from landlords before they had the opportunity to torch." By the end of the year, thirty neighbors had enlisted as core members of the group, and together they "liberated" the three condemned buildings. As with 1186 Washington, the first priority was gutting the buildings, an onerous task that asked a lot of volunteers, who were promised apartments in return for their labor. For better and worse, President Carter's visit to the Bronx that October passed over Banana Kelly, sparing it from both the spotlight and the funding streams received by the PDC. It was not until 1979 that the group raised the necessary financing to fully renovate the three buildings, a pace that allowed for slower but more sustainable growth. Four years after its formation, twenty-one families moved into the three rehabbed buildings.[29]

Whereas the PDC's approach to sweat equity rejected the private real estate market in favor of de-financialized housing, Banana Kelly put forward a more modest vision. The group's slogan, "Don't move, improve!" encapsulated the core mission, and though Harry DeRienzo claims coinage, the mantra was associated with a number of Bronx organizations and organizers, most notably the NWBCCC's Anne Devenney. It reflected not only the group's core ethos but the principal demand emanating out of the borough's community development movement: a refusal to leave and a right to remain. As Banana Kelly stated in a funding proposal:

> While landlords rob tenants of one service after another, allow tenements to run down and finally burn, collecting fire insurance and after all blaming the prevailing conditions on those who occupy their buildings, there are those in this community still who refuse to be driven out. *We refuse to leave* not because we have no choice but because this area holds a special value, a commitment which comes from growing up in a neighborhood and calling it your own. We refuse to leave because we prefer to rebuild that which has been destroyed through neglect and profit motive rather than move to similar circumstances, one stage removed, in another area of this city.

"Don't move, improve!" was a direct challenge to the disinvestment and brownlining that had made displacement a simple fact of life in the Bronx and beyond.[30]

Inasmuch as Potts and DeRienzo launched Banana Kelly to "make a stand" against these systemic forces, the group's brand of sweat equity tended more toward aspirational than adversarial politics. Mildred Velez, one of its original members, explained, "We don't condemn landlords. We're here to help them." Similarly, in answer to the question "Should Banana Kelly fight against some faceless landlord, dysfunctional government agency or uncaring bank or insurance company?" DeRienzo was adamant: "This seemed pointless." Distrust of the state's ability or willingness to meet the needs of Bronxites ran deep, and it was well earned: "We urged people to stop hoping for public housing when the waiting list was more than ten thousand—and instead reclaim vacant buildings." Rather than "organizing for redress from some third party," Banana Kelly turned toward "self-help," a shift that DeRienzo pinpoints as "the true beginning of the community development movement in the South Bronx and similar inner city areas." As a predominantly Black organization, the group's emphasis on self-help invoked an old strain of bootstraps-centered Black politics.[31]

"Don't move, improve! Improve our minds, health, children and standard of living. Improve the way we feel about our neighborhood and ourselves."
–Leon Potts of Banana Kelly.

"Don't move, improve!" was the rallying cry of community development in the Bronx. Leon Potts, a co-founder of the Banana Kelly Community Improvement Association, articulated the mission of the organization within the terms of community uplift.

At the tail end of the 1970s, Banana Kelly's pragmatic politics led it to reorganize as a community development corporation (CDC), the ascendant model of urban revitalization across the Bronx and the United States. While Banana Kelly was not the first Bronx CDC—Mid-Bronx Desperadoes and the South East Bronx Community Organization (SEBCO), among others, preceded it—it may have been the only group to successfully transition from sweat equity to community development. Its trajectory can thus illustrate the differences between the two approaches, and why those differences matter.

Once funding started to stream into Banana Kelly, much of it through the Comprehensive Employment and Training Act (CETA), the group registered as a nonprofit CDC. With DeRienzo as its executive director, Banana Kelly transitioned from a volunteer organization to a nonprofit corporation that owned and managed a number of Kelly Street properties. By 1981, the group had evolved into a full-service CDC, supplementing its work in housing with a food co-op, a park, a solar-power program, and employment training.[32]

As DeRienzo later reflected, "our leaders became managers, our organizers became employees, and our members became clients." The overhaul created significant rifts within the organization, and at the end of 1981, DeRienzo stepped down as director. The new leader clashed with and eventually terminated Leon Potts, the other co-founder, and before long Banana Kelly was unrecognizable. In the early 1980s, it managed about a hundred housing units, employed a dozen staff members, and had an operating budget of less than $1 million. A decade later, the organization was overseeing a thousand housing units with a budget of $60 million and one hundred workers on staff. Although some might have viewed this transformation as an "unqualified success," DeRienzo lamented the fact that amid its meteoric growth, Banana Kelly's relationship with its tenants and the surrounding community had degenerated. The organization had begun to "treat [its tenants and neighbors] more like asset-deficient, service-dependent clients, than active stakeholders in their own institution."[33]

By the end of the 1990s, Banana Kelly, which had emerged two decades earlier to neutralize delinquent landlords, was itself accused of being "no better than a slumlord." Its tenants complained of scores of code violations, including "an army of rats that look like puppies." This moment proved to be the nadir of Banana Kelly's history, and the organization's reputation and performance in the Bronx eventually—and emphatically—recovered. But its evolution from squatter to slumlord raises a number of questions about the role of CDCs in the late-twentieth-century city.[34]

+++

AN ACCIDENTAL OUTGROWTH of the federal War on Poverty, launched in 1964 by President Lyndon Johnson, the CDC model first emerged in reaction to the more radical and democratic currents within the federal anti-poverty program. The nation's earliest CDC, the Bedford Stuyvesant Restoration Corporation, took form in 1967 when Central Brooklyn's War on Poverty apparatus was subsumed by a neighborhood revitalization movement aligned with and shaped by Senator Robert F. Kennedy. Unlike the federally funded Community Action Program, which fanned the flames of radical protest, the Bedford Stuyvesant Restoration Corporation offered something more politically palatable: a bricks-and-mortar solution to the problem of urban disinvestment. Early CDCs were notable for synthesizing the Black power movement's emphasis on self-determination with the promises of Black capitalism, a term that was already in ascendance when President Richard Nixon made it a plank of his 1968 campaign. "The essential purpose" of CDCs, wrote Robert L. Allen in his seminal book *Black Awakening in Capitalist America*, was "putting black power into business." If CDCs promised a form of "collective capitalism," they delivered something more akin to "corrective capitalism," as their primary funder, the Ford Foundation, called it. By offering tax shelters to investors, CDCs helped draw capital back into neighborhoods scarred by decades of disinvestment. In this way, they played a key role in the financialization of affordable housing development.[35]

Much ideological diversity existed within the umbrella category of the community development corporation, but by the late 1970s, nearly all CDCs would distance themselves from the more radical mobilizations of the 1960s. Banana Kelly, for its part, defined its mission as a rejection of the War on Poverty paradigm. DeRienzo set Banana Kelly against groups that were "stuck in the past funded glory of the 'War on Poverty' programs" and "still funded through varied though diminishing government programs." CDCs, in contrast, thrived in an era of retrenchment. By the mid-1970s, the CDC model had proven that it could grow well in the arid soil of austerity, and it branched out far beyond its Brooklyn roots. The national urban landscape was aflower with CDCs in the 1980s; between 1981 and 1987, as Reaganomics and federal cutbacks took their toll on municipal and state budgets, at least one thousand CDCs incorporated across the country. A report by the Ford Foundation observed, "In a decade of contracting federal domestic activity, CDCs along with their allies in churches and other nonprofit organizations, have become the principal suppliers of low-income housing in the United States." This was a revolution in national housing policy, but a quiet one, and its effects have gone relatively unnoticed.[36]

What was it about CDCs that allowed them to blossom in such a barren budgetary landscape? CDCs thrived because they cross-fertilized the neighborhood-based, community-control impulses of the War on Poverty with market-oriented economic development. The CDC model advanced along the well-worn grooves of community control that had underpinned the Community Action Program in the 1960s. But it departed from its forebears by replacing poverty with property as its center of gravity. CDCs routed community action through the property relation, offering a lift-all-boats vision of economic development via affordable housing.

As the foremost institutional funder of community development in its early years, the Ford Foundation helped introduce the concept to skeptical urban leaders across the nation. "For many Americans the mention of 'community organization' conjures up 1960s images of radicals storming city hall, of civil rights marches, anti-Vietnam protests, lettuce boycotts, and distrust of anyone in a business suit," acknowledged the authors of a Ford Foundation report on CDCs. "But with rare exceptions, the 1960s are now as much history for them as for the rest of American society. One can't very well hurl his body into the path of an oncoming bulldozer when he (or she) is the developer." For Ford, CDCs promised to rehabilitate not just housing but also the very concept of the community organization. *Corrective Capitalism*, the foundation's 1987 report, argued that CDCs had shed the sins of the 1960s and were able to thread the needle between social spending and state atrophy: "Neither heavy government spending on the one hand, nor supply-side economics on the other, has 'solved' problems that lie deep in community and social disorganization."[37]

Community development offered a third way, defined by its ability to adapt to the funding constraints of the post–War on Poverty era. Although they exhibited significant heterogeneity, practically all CDCs were nonprofit organizations, usually with 501(c)(3) status. As such, CDCs made ideal partners for private investors and developers seeking tax abatements. The Ford Foundation reported in 1987 that "it is nearly impossible to find one CDC among the thousands that does not now feature some form of partnership financing." These partnerships were compelled by government cutbacks: as the federal funding pool shrank, CDCs proved especially adept at cobbling together financing from private sources and foundations, on top of what they could extract from the state.[38]

The public-private partnership model was premised upon a simple quid pro quo: partnering with CDCs rewarded private investors with immediate and sweeping tax abatements. As an institutional form, the CDC triangulated between the state and private equity, catalyzing development via tax relief. Community development bankrolled the construction of affordable housing by transforming it into a tax shelter; in the process, the nonprofit housing industry became "essentially a manufacturer of depreciation," in the words of one banker. In the Hunts Point neighborhood, the Ford Foundation found in 1979 that SEBCO's Father Gigante "stands at the center of a small galaxy of developers," a neighborhood-scale power broker for the post–Robert Moses era. By 1981, SEBCO had pocketed $1 million by selling interest in its development projects to investors, who could take advantage of this tax shelter because of SEBCO's nonprofit status. Upon the priest's death in 2022, it was revealed that this strategy had amassed him $7 million in personal wealth.[39]

Reagan's 1986 Tax Reform Act formalized the arrangement, creating the Low-Income Housing Tax Credit (LIHTC), which enabled developers of "affordable" rental housing to earn federal tax credits. Nonprofit CDCs had no need for these credits since they did not pay taxes; instead, they sold the credits to corporate investors for large sums. Such "back-door funds" were routed through the Internal Revenue Service rather than the official agency presiding over affordable housing, the Department of Housing and Urban Development. IRS jurisdiction kept the LIHTC from the political spotlight, and the program became the principal mechanism for producing affordable housing in the United States, generating 2.5 million units by 2012.[40]

Among the private investors backing affordable housing construction, no sector was more instrumental than the insurance industry. This was not the first instance of the insurance industry throwing its weight behind subsidized housing. In 1967, as the property insurance industry was lobbying for the FAIR plan, the nation's major life insurers convened to form the Joint Committee on Urban Problems, which pledged $2 billion to stimulate the housing market in once-redlined areas. A decade later, insurers became the largest backers of the Local Initiatives Support Corporation (LISC), a Ford Foundation offshoot designed as an intermediary between CDCs and investors. In 1979, Aetna and Prudential alone contributed two-thirds of the initial capitalization of LISC, which would quickly become the "largest private, nonprofit community development organization in the country." LISC sought to smooth the transfer of capital between CDCs and corporate investors; perhaps its most critical service was processing the complex financial transactions involved when selling tax credits to investors.[41]

LISC quickly designated the Bronx as a laboratory, citing the borough's history of sweat equity as one of its virtues. Ed Logue, the president of the South Bronx Development Organization, credited the People's Development Corporation as "one small reason why LISC was created." The national attention the PDC drew after Carter's visit unleashed a torrent of philanthropic capital that had been unthinkable just a few months earlier. In November 1979, a month after launching LISC, the Ford Foundation confessed that it was "about to propose what we once were sure we would not propose—a program to help the restoration of the South Bronx." The foundation described how it was disabused of its cynicism: "The more and the longer we looked gave us an increasing conviction that the TV image of the Bronx—burnt-out Dresden and Fort Apache—was wrong."[42]

With the aid of LISC, the Bronx entered the 1980s with an intricate and expanding network of CDCs that was prepared to ratchet up housing construction once state funding started to flow again. The Ford Foundation counted no fewer than seven hundred nonprofit organizations within the South Bronx. From the mid-1970s to the mid-1980s, the CDCs of the Bronx worked in a small-scale, piecemeal fashion to rehabilitate the borough's housing, a majority of which was owned by the city. Following the 1976 passage of Local Law 45, the city had begun seizing *in rem* buildings—that is, buildings whose owners were at least a year behind on property taxes. Management of these properties was taken over by the newly established Department of Housing Preservation and Development, which was soon overwhelmed by its burgeoning portfolio. The Carter administration estimated at the end of the 1970s that two-thirds of South Bronx buildings had been seized and were now owned by the city. For a beleaguered HPD, CDCs were an indispensable vehicle for offloading ownership onto the private sector.[43]

In 1985, Mayor Ed Koch unveiled a housing program that supercharged the process, vastly expanding the rehabilitation, construction, and privatization of city-owned property. What was known as the Koch Housing Plan was a ten-year, nearly $10 billion initiative that, as one scholar notes, "became perhaps the largest municipal investment in housing in U.S. history." For the first time since the fiscal crisis, Albany had permitted the city government to borrow for capital expenditures, and Koch surprised even his own aides by patching together the funds for the monumental project. A full 36 percent of the housing that was rehabbed or constructed was in the Bronx, a far higher proportion than in any other borough. The reconstruction coincided with the crack years and the HIV/AIDS epidemic, which splintered the borough's social fabric to such an extent that its physical overhaul went mostly unnoticed by those outside the Bronx. But by the year 2000, 57,361 new or renovated apartment units had been added to its housing stock, with another 9,557 units in small one-, two-, or three-family houses. The scale of what has been called the "Bronx miracle" was truly breathtaking. In the two decades after 1980, 15 percent of the borough's housing stock—almost as much as had been lost to arson and abandonment in the preceding years—was redeveloped or rebuilt, largely by CDCs.[44]

+++

IN THE AGE of financialization, even miracles need insurance. Without adequate and affordable property insurance in the post-1978 period, the reconstruction of the borough never would have happened. Indeed, insurance inaccessibility had ranked among the obstacles confronting the PDC during the high tide of sweat equity in the Bronx. "The availability and cost of property insurance have become major stumbling blocks in the way of self-help efforts to revitalize decaying urban neighborhoods," one study of the PDC and twenty-three other sweat equity groups concluded. Throughout the mid-1970s, most sweat equity groups across New York City had been forced to purchase insurance from the exorbitantly priced NYPIUA or the unregulated excess and surplus line market. In either case, the high cost and low value of these policies could be so burdensome, the study added, as to "threaten the financial viability" of the projects. Brownlining, in other words, had a hand in the demise of sweat equity. Naturally, the fortunes of community development in the Bronx would also rest on the insurance question. Would CDCs be able to procure sufficient property insurance for all the housing they were churning out?[45]

No death knell was sounded when the age of brownlining came to an end; its fall was too partial, its excision from the landscape too jagged. But end it did, beginning with the insurance industry's embrace of anti-arson protocols in the years after 1976. The closing of the insurance gap went a long way toward curbing the arson wave, yet it could not guarantee insurance access for the first generation of Bronx CDCs. For that, Bronxites would have to come to grips with the question of affordability, and in April 1977 Representative Elizabeth Holtzman of Brooklyn entered the fray. The youngest woman elected to Congress (until 2014), Holtzman introduced legislation that would prohibit the NYPIUA from charging such high rates. "Although New York State's FAIR PLAN is supposed to provide insurance for property owners victimized by insurance company redlining," she charged in a press release, "the FAIR PLAN itself further victimizes these people by charging them as much as five times what they were paying privately."[46]

Forcing insurance redlining back onto the legislative agenda, Holtzman took aim at the self-rated structure of the NYPIUA, unique among the nation's FAIR plans, and inveighed against the practice of setting insurance rates based solely on the NYPIUA's loss experience, as opposed to the losses on all properties throughout the state (the standard rate-setting practice in the industry). Holtzman's bill would desegregate the pool of customers on which the NYPIUA determined its rates, and it earned support from Shirley Chisholm, Herman Badillo, Charles Rangel, and fourteen other members of the New York congressional delegation. The insurance industry fought tooth and nail against these proposals, preventing their passage during the 1977 session.[47]

But Holtzman and her allies regrouped the next year, thrusting the debate around insurance redlining into the public discourse in the most prominent manner since the Hughes Panel, a decade earlier. In 1978, she introduced another congressional bill, this one mandating that FAIR rates be commensurate with the voluntary market (with prices capped at 30 percent above conventional market rates) and that one-third of the FAIR plan governing board be "public members" without connections to the insurance industry. The Holtzman Amendment, as it became known, targeted the NYPIUA (whose thirteen-member governing board was made up entirely of industry representatives), but it would apply to all FAIR plans nationwide. Holtzman gave the bill teeth: it required compliance in order for insurers to be eligible for the riot reinsurance program that had first induced the industry to embrace the FAIR plan in 1968.[48]

Both planks of the Holtzman Amendment were anathema to the insurance industry, but insurers focused their energy on muddying the waters of the redlining issue. The insurance lobby dispatched George Bernstein, the former head of the FIA who had overseen the rollout of the FAIR plans, to testify before Congress. "Redlining," Bernstein scoffed, "is merely the catch phrase used by proponents of the amendment to generate anti-industry sentiment." Another industry spokesperson conceded the existence of insurance discrimination but justified its centrality to the underwriting prerogative. Defending the "pivotal role of discrimination in differentiating between different types of risks," he advanced an as-American-as-apple-pie view of underwriting discrimination. The South Bronx was invoked as the self-evidently uninsurable landscape. "Any insurer who writes in the South Bronx in New York City should have his license revoked for endangering the surplus and the welfare of all its policyholders and stockholders," Bernstein insisted, obscuring the fact that the NYPIUA's anti-arson procedures prioritized ongoing coverage in the Bronx. "That is not redlining, that is sound underwriting judgment."[49]

Ultimately, insurers knew full well that their freedom to discriminate was inviolable, a birthright of the insurance function that Congress dare not disturb. The industry's objections to the Holtzman Amendment had more to do with the precedent it might set for federal incursion into the state regulatory system. As had been true during the Hughes proceedings, the federal boogeyman loomed large for industry executives. Bernstein himself acknowledged that the industry's "main opposition" to the Holtzman Amendment was the "precedent of the Federal Government... inserting itself in the State ratemaking procedures."[50]

When the Holtzman Amendment was signed into law by Jimmy Carter as part of the 1978 Housing and Community Development Act, its tame half step toward federal regulation was met with unbridled anger from the New York insurance world. In the New York State Legislature, regulators and insurers locked horns over whether to adopt the Holtzman Amendment or brave banishment to the private market for riot reinsurance. As a measure of how much the insurance marketplace had shifted since 1968, when the industry had lobbied aggressively for federal riot reinsurance, the Alliance of American Insurers publicly admitted, "We're advising our companies that we'd be better off not complying and not buying the Federal riot reinsurance." Driving those shifts was not only a waning fear of urban uprisings (the reinsurance fund had gone largely untapped) but also the fact that Lloyd's of London had in recent years returned to the U.S. property insurance market. Representative Holtzman had underestimated insurers' hostility to the measure, dismissing industry protests as "a bad case of sour grapes." As it turned out, Holtzman herself was left with the bitter fruit in March 1979 when New York State refused to ratify her bill, opting to forfeit federal reinsurance rather than yield to Washington's will.[51]

A mere three months after that jurisdictional drama, the New York State Legislature passed a bill similar to the Holtzman Amendment, though exempting the state from both federal regulation and the mandate to include consumers on the NYPIUA board. Enacted without fanfare in July 1979, the law drastically reduced what the NYPIUA was permitted to charge its customers. Rates that had surged to 300 to 500 percent above the voluntary market were suddenly capped at 20 to 40 percent above conventional prices, a reduction so drastic that the New York State insurance superintendent called the law the "most important and least publicized bill of the year." Almost overnight, the exorbitant rates of the brownlining era were brought in line with the voluntary market. The gross imbalances of the racially stratified insurance market were, to some degree, mitigated. A number of other states followed New York's lead, forgoing federal riot reinsurance. In 1983, the Reagan administration pulled the plug on the reinsurance program. Without the specter of civil unrest and with a revived private reinsurance market, the federal government had been made redundant.[52]

+++

THE PUSH FOR the Holtzman Amendment was one strand of a broader reinvestment movement that was seeking to force a range of financial institutions to suspend and remedy redlining policies that had been in place for decades. Rooted in National People's Action (NPA), a nationwide Alinskyite network founded in Chicago in 1972, the reinvestment movement is most recognized for its role in pushing for the passage of the Home Mortgage Disclosure Act in 1975 and the Community Reinvestment Act in 1977. The bills forced banks and mortgage lenders to open their books and adopt more proactive measures for extending credit to redlined neighborhoods. In the Bronx, the local affiliate of NPA was the Northwest Bronx Community and Clergy Coalition. In the prior chapter, we saw how the coalition made its name working to build tenant power and hold the line against encroaching arson, but it was not until its staffers attended a 1977 NPA conference in Washington, D.C., that it doubled down on anti-redlining work. Using data accrued through the Home Mortgage Disclosure Act, the NWBCCC accused local banks of mortgage redlining in early 1977. They first targeted Eastern Savings (formerly Bronx Savings), which had not granted a single new mortgage in the Northwest Bronx during the entire calendar year of 1976, despite the fact that Bronxites made up the lion's share of the bank's depositors. Even more troubling were findings that Eastern was trying to liquidate its portfolio of Bronx holdings, selling off mortgages to shady landlords at huge discounts and potentially setting the stage for arson. (The bank denied the charges.) On April 1, 1977, clergy and lay members of the NWBCCC gathered in front of Eastern's branch on Pelham Parkway, next to a pornographic theater. "Many of the people thought we were picketing the theater," organizer Anne Devenney recalled. "We had to tell them, no, no, no, it's not dirty pictures we're picketing, it's dirty money."[53]

The NWBCCC pressured Eastern to grant new mortgages and to enforce the "good repair clause" on mortgages it already held. This provision of the mortgage contract empowered the mortgagee to foreclose on a property if the owner or landlord refused to fix building violations. When the Community Reinvestment Act passed, in 1977, the NWBCCC acquired new leverage to force reinvestment from Eastern and other local banks. The NWBCCC was one of the first organizations to wield the new powers provided by the act in challenging the mergers, acquisitions, and branching requests of banks that continued to disinvest from urban neighborhoods.[54]

These were important victories, but mortgage-centric ones, of little use to community organizations facing off against property insurers. In the period between the passage of the Community Reinvestment Act in 1977 and the Holtzman Amendment (and associated legislation) in 1978–79, property insurance popped up as the next major obstacle thwarting reinvestment. As NPA co-founder Gale Cincotta put it, "After we had been dealing with the banks for a long time, and after we were starting to get some more money rolling into the neighborhoods, we suddenly started getting a lot of complaints again about insurance unavailability."[55]

In 1978, the reinvestment movement zeroed in on property insurance as a significant source of friction in urban housing markets. Around the same time, the NWBCCC pivoted toward the problem of property insurance, declaring redlining by insurers to be a "key issue" besetting the Bronx. The local struggle took off after one of the NWBCCC's constituents received an insurance cancellation. Rita Campbell owned a ten-unit apartment building at 2679 Briggs Avenue and lived in a smaller building next door. A number of blocks north of East Fordham Road, Campbell's building was not considered part of the South Bronx, which helps explain why a voluntary market insurer had been covering it until 1978. When her insurance was canceled without cause, Campbell went, seething, to her neighborhood office of the NWBCCC, where she registered her complaint.[56]

There was something novel about a landlord coming to the NWBCCC for help. Up to that point, the work of the NWBCCC had been mostly focused on organizing tenant and block associations, and accordingly, owners "looked at the Coalition from its origin as an anti-landlord type of operation." Its Reinvestment Committee aimed to draw owners of property into the coalition by making common cause against the financial institutions that shaped housing conditions for both renters and landlords. The goal was to smooth the functioning of the real estate market, and property insurance was a crucial lubricant. Making plain the aims of the reinvestment movement during one congressional hearing, a coalition member dryly observed, "We are attempting to compel a private institution to make a profit from our community."[57]

Soon after Campbell brought her insurance predicament to light, the Reinvestment Committee jumped on the issue. It conducted a survey, asking owners if they were experiencing trouble with their coverage, and test-calling insurance brokers to assess availability issues. Their findings confirmed that the borough had been brownlined: "the patterned response was that they had either gotten Lloyd's of London or Fair Plan coverage." The NWBCCC objected not only to the residual market's higher premiums and shoddier coverage—no theft or liability protection—but to the stigma of being "marked as a bad risk." Declaring "full insurance coverage (fire, extended, theft, liability) is a right," the NWBCCC disputed the very legitimacy of the residual market as an actuarial designation. Its Reinvestment Committee was determined to look beyond FAIR and bring the voluntary market to the Bronx.[58]

The NWBCCC set its sights on Aetna, which had recently made a big show of its newfound commitment to curbing arson rates in U.S. cities. Perhaps for that reason, Aetna had been the first insurer targeted by NPA activists in Chicago, prompting a meeting between Gale Cincotta and Aetna president William O. Bailey in 1978. In turn, NPA connected the NWBCCC with Bailey's office, and the coalition's Reinvestment Committee sat down with Aetna's president in January 1979. After "a number of heated meetings and confrontations," Bailey pledged to begin underwriting properties in the Northwest Bronx. "There was a substantial turn around" after that meeting, committee member Bill Frey remembers. By June 1980, Aetna had underwritten 194 apartment buildings and 352 homes in the area. Offering better coverage than the NYPIUA or Lloyd's—including liability insurance—for a third or even a fourth of the price, Aetna's entry into the Bronx market brought substantial savings to policyholders. Travelers, Allstate, and State Farm were not far behind. All four companies launched marketing campaigns for the aging housing stock of U.S. cities, taking out monthly ads in the NWBCCC bulletin, *Action*. To the movement's calls for a "right" to property insurance, insurers responded by promoting the "choice" newly available to urban consumers.[59]

In the Northwest Bronx, the era of "back of the bus" insurance had passed. As we've seen, the introduction of comprehensive, voluntary market insurance not only failed to exacerbate the arson wave—as insurers had warned it would a few years earlier—but was part and parcel of a robust anti-arson program. In 1981, Aetna, Allstate, and Travelers signed a statement of commitment to combat the twin problems of "arson and redlining" in the Bronx. The NWBCCC's Insurance Committee (an offshoot of the Reinvestment Committee) framed "re-investment and anti-arson programs" as mutually reinforcing and equally vital for their neighborhoods. Brownlining and the arson wave had to be extinguished side by side, doused by the same hose.[60]

The property insurance industry did not put up much of a fight against the reinvestment movement. There were a few contentious meetings, even a picket outside State Farm's headquarters in Bloomington, Illinois, by two busloads of Chicago NPA members, but on the whole, insurers were quicker to comply with activists' demands than their counterparts in the savings and loan sector. For the organizers of the NWBCCC, the industry's willingness to reverse course was understood as an effort to ward off the type of legislative victories claimed by NPA in the fight against mortgage redlining. As Bill Frey put it, "They were trying to prove to everybody that they didn't have to be regulated, that they would do something on their own without Congress or federal kind of regulations."[61]

The industry was not about to countenance its own version of the Community Reinvestment Act, and it had reason to be worried. After NPA's successful advocacy for the Holtzman Amendment in 1978, the group began pushing for the repeal of the McCarran-Ferguson Act, which had long delegated insurance regulation to the states. Since the act had exempted the industry from federal regulation since 1945, its nullification would be a necessary prerequisite to federal anti-redlining legislation. As we've seen, nothing spooked insurers more than the prospect of losing McCarran-Ferguson. By acquiescing to NPA demands in areas where its affiliates wielded real power, like the Bronx, the industry was able to defuse such legislative momentum.[62]

+++

AS OF THIS writing, the McCarran-Ferguson Act remains the law of the land, preserving a state-based regulatory system that gives insurers wide latitude in exercising their underwriting prerogative. Since 1968, the industry has consistently used its participation in the FAIR plans—which remain massive in scope—to argue that the redlining problem has been resolved. Nonetheless, grassroots and legal charges of redlining have been leveled repeatedly over the past six decades. These claims reached a crescendo amid heavy losses from the 1992 Los Angeles uprising, after the acquittal of four police officers in the beating of Rodney King, then again during the 1995 settlement of an NAACP anti-discrimination suit brought on behalf of Black homeowners in Milwaukee. Such periodic bursts of activism and visibility notwithstanding, the long campaign against insurance redlining has remained, in the words of one scholar and activist, "the ugly duckling of the fair housing movement."[63]

After the killing of George Floyd by Minneapolis police in the late spring of 2020, calls to end redlining practices again echoed—however faintly—across the insurance world. Lloyd's of London, for its part, took the occasion to officially apologize for its "shameful" role underwriting the transatlantic slave trade. The insurance behemoth made no mention of reparations, or of its more recent triangular trade in risk brought to light by the Sasse scandal. Though long absent from public discourse, the related issue of riot reinsurance—now available from the private market, rather than a federal fund—appears likely to become salient again.[64]

The age of brownlining may have passed, but the conditions that brought it into being—the inviolable rights of property, the actuarial discretion of insurers, the political power of the FIRE industries, the state sanction of anti-Black violence, and the mass uprisings that insistently follow—still prevail. The lessons of the arson wave have yet to be learned.

EPILOGUE

The Ashes of History

What shall we build on the ashes of a nightmare?
—ROBIN D. G. KELLEY, 2002[1]

A 2011 mural of Evelina López Antonetty in the South Bronx by the legendary graffiti artists Tats Cru.

If you find yourself shopping for property insurance in Sarasota, Santa Rosa, or on Long Island, chances are you will come across a FAIR plan. Long after the anti-arson and reinvestment movements turned back the tide of insurance brownlining, FAIR plans—and the "high-risk" residual markets they represent—continue to thrive. As of this writing, FAIR plans are the largest providers of property insurance in numerous states, and their share of policyholders is expanding at a rapid clip, rising 29 percent nationally between 2018 and 2021. What drives their recent growth? It would be easy, though mistaken, to point to the 2020 George Floyd uprisings. Though the rebellion resulted in an unprecedented $2 billion in insurable losses in the U.S.—far higher than the cumulative damages from the 1960s uprisings—the property insurance industry did not lean heavily on the FAIR plans to manage the financial fallout, as it had decades earlier. Insurers instead relied upon standard mechanisms like reinsurance and rate increases to cope with the losses, and unlike in 1968, few fretted publicly that the industry would abandon the U.S. urban market.[2]

Climate shocks, not mass uprisings, are behind the present expansion of FAIR plans. Born amid insurrectionary risk, the plans now specialize in the ecological sort. The transition comes as private insurers in fire-prone and coastal areas tremble before the scorched and waterlogged landscapes of our looming and already-here catastrophes. In May 2023, State Farm, the largest property insurer in California, announced that it would cease issuing new policies in one of the world's largest property markets, citing the state's "rapidly growing catastrophe exposure." When Allstate followed suit a few days later, the *New York Times* reported that an ever-growing share of property owners are being forced to "lean on the [California] FAIR plan," which more than doubled in size between 2018 and 2022. Florida's FAIR plan, meanwhile, reported "growth rates approaching 500%" in 2022 after six insurance companies were declared insolvent. Louisiana trailed close behind, with its FAIR plan expanding from 35,000 to 128,000 policyholders between 2021 and 2023, a period that saw twelve of the state's insurance companies descend into insolvency. In New York, the NYPIUA has become heavily concentrated on the coastal areas along Long Island, far from the "riot-affected areas" it was created to serve. As it had in 1967, volatility in the reinsurance market accounted for much of this FAIR plan growth nationally, with reinsurance rates skyrocketing by as much as 40 percent on January 1, 2023.[3]

The feverish growth of the FAIR plans in the early 1970s revealed the extent of insurance redlining's colossal toll over the preceding decades. In the twenty-first century, it signals a novel dysfunction within the insurance economy. As Eric Andersen, the president of Aon, a mammoth global insurance firm, told the Senate Budget Committee in 2023, climate change has triggered "a crisis of confidence around the ability to predict loss." These words should sound familiar; the 1960s uprisings were likewise deemed uninsurable because of their "unpredictability." One thing the late 1960s Hughes Panel makes clear is that when insurance moguls testify about a "crisis of confidence" in underwriting, they are teeing up a policy agenda. Sure enough, in his next breath, Andersen presented his congressional audience with "two choices" for adapting to the economy's overexposure to climate risk: "We can shrink the amount of carbon emitted by shrinking the amount of economic activity—we can make less steel, build fewer buildings, travel fewer places—or we can make new markets." As though taking a swig of actuarial truth serum, he continued: "Obviously the first choice is no choice at all." Warning that "capital will not go where it is not protected," he counseled, "this is why *public-private partnerships* are so important." What is being negotiated is how the risks and rewards of climate disaster will be distributed between government and private enterprise.[4]

The FAIR plan model beckons. Spurred by Hurricane Andrew in 1992 and Hurricane Katrina in 2005, "these plans shifted away from their original purpose as predominantly urban property insurers," according to the Insurance Information Institute. In the twenty-first century, they evolved "from their traditional role as markets of last resort into much larger insurance providers, in some cases even becoming the largest property insurer in a state." This shift has occurred even though, as "insurers of last resort," FAIR plans are statutorily discouraged from eating up a large slice of a state's property and casualty business. Nevertheless, when private firms balk at the infinite perils of the present crisis, public-private FAIR plans pick up the slack. In racial capitalism's turbulent encounter with climate change, insurers are the shock absorbers.[5]

What does it mean that the climate crisis is being fought with the same tools invented a half century earlier to confront the urban crisis? For one, it shows that protecting private property will rank as the foremost policy goal in the face of a systemic crisis. But more specifically, it indicates a broadening of the residual market, where property insurers discard their hard-to-place risks. To be the insurance industry's dustbin is to record its suspicions and fears. At the start of the history recounted in this book, the "last resort" residual market was a clear euphemism for redlined areas. What it has morphed into is a more discordant entity, in which a "high-risk" property could just as likely be a Malibu mansion as a poorly maintained Bronx building. In the process of insuring an extensive share of the nation's coasts, the FAIR plans have come to count among their policyholders the second-home set. This new tendency raises some questions: As the ranks of those on the front lines of climate change inexorably expands, will a growing swath of property holders get swallowed up by the residual market? When vulnerability to disaster becomes a more generalized condition, will insurers and the state continue to depend on the FAIR plan and the residual market, or will they opt for a more radical redistribution of risk?

The stubborn persistence of the residual insurance market well into the twenty-first century is telling. No indemnity without inequality: this is the essential truth of property insurance. There is only one type of financial protection recognized by private property, and it is conditioned on discrimination and differentiation.

That unlearned lesson was on full display in the foreclosure maps of 2007 and 2008, when racially targeted subprime mortgages—the home loan equivalent of the residual market—blew up the global economy. It is no coincidence that in New York City, the highest concentration of subprime loans was issued in the Bronx: over 34 percent of all citywide subprime lending activity in 2005 took place in the borough. Even more striking, neighborhoods that were hit hardest by the 1970s arson wave, including Morrisania and University Heights, topped the list of districts with the highest rates of subprime lending. Redlining, brownlining, subprime lending—each successive wave has carved even deeper into the old racial grooves of maps that profess to depict only risk.[6]

+++

WHILE THE SAME historical forces that burned the Bronx made it vulnerable to subprime lending, for many years those forces proved to be an unlikely defense against that other epochal urban threat, gentrification. Though situated within one of the hottest real estate markets in the world, the Bronx had long managed to dodge the waves of gentrification that have hit much of New York City over the last half century. Although the community development movement had brought extraordinary reinvestment to the Bronx, it did so without precipitating the massive displacement of poor tenants and residents of color that routinely went hand in hand with urban revitalization in those years. As late as 2013, one of the borough's leading critics of unchecked development could still claim that "there has not been widespread gentrification," and media coverage of the subject clung to the conditional or future tense. A number of factors had coalesced to shield the Bronx from the onslaught of gentrification, including its muscular tenant movement, dense network of nonprofits and CDCs, and readiness to mobilize against development projects that ran counter to the will of a given neighborhood. But the Bronx was hardly unique in these respects; the Lower East Side and Park Slope fell prey to gentrification despite organized opposition.[7]

If there was a bulwark against gentrification in the Bronx until the early 2010s, it was the still-luminous afterimage of the burning years. Long after the rubble was cleared, the fires persisted as a symbol of—or even shorthand for—the Bronx. For decades, these associations endured, to the chagrin of developers and boosters, who, as the *New York Times* reported in 2013, have been "trying to remove the scorch marks from its name since the 1970s." The article added, "Even today, a Bronx leader in charge of economic development said she had to beg Bronx officials not to mention 'the Bronx' and 'burning' in the same sentence." That the alliterative phrase was singled out and censored by a Bronx booster in 2013—nearly four decades after it was supposedly (and apocryphally) uttered by Howard Cosell during the 1977 World Series—is perhaps the best sign of the enduring potency of the image.[8]

The slender Harlem River did more than delineate the Bronx from upper Manhattan; it dammed the borough against the surging real estate market to its south and west. By the same token, however, these tidal straits have damned the Bronx to its social inheritances: second-rate city services, high concentrations of environmental hazards, and, as of 2024, its southern end's status as the poorest congressional district in the United States. And though gentrification-related displacement spared the borough until recently, the Bronx now has the highest eviction rates in New York City. The borough's history may have insulated it from gentrification, but that was just one struggle among many.[9]

Over the past decade, even that bulwark proved vulnerable. In December 2013, the *Daily News* ran a story on the "anticipated gentrification" of the Bronx, hypothesizing that "it may not be so far-fetched." By April 2015, the same paper could declare, "If someone says the Bronx is burning, it's because the real estate market is on fire." Sales of multifamily buildings and development sites had soared 67 percent and 85 percent in a single year, respectively—figures that recalled the fabled redevelopment of Manhattan's SoHo and Brooklyn's Dumbo neighborhoods in the 1980s and 1990s. Gentrification had swept into the Bronx after all. "It took nearly 20 years to prime the pump to get it going," the president of SoBro (the South Bronx Overall Economic Development Corporation) noted proudly.[10]

Real estate interests that had spent decades trying to shake off the stigma of the burning Bronx suddenly found value in it. The classic agent's gimmick is to bake cookies before showing a home, but in the 2015 Bronx, the borough's leading developer instead whipped up a curated display of burned-out cars and trash can fires to spark interest in his new project. On October 29, Manhattan-based developer Keith Rubenstein of Somerset Partners threw a lavish, A-list party titled Macabre Suite to promote his planned residential and commercial complex on the industrial waterfront of Port Morris. The event showcased the work of artist Lucien Smith and drew the likes of Kendall Jenner, Naomi Campbell, and Adrien Brody. Carpeting one room was an expanse of fallen bricks—a disquieting, if accidental, echo of 1982's *Bricks* series by the Kids of Survival. Partygoers, bused in on private charters from Manhattan and Brooklyn, tweeted out the hashtag #thebronxisburning and #thenextbestthing. "It's got character," Rubenstein rhapsodized as he pitched investment in the Bronx. "It's authentic. It's edgy."[11]

The blazes had become the brand. Against the backdrop of the sanitized glass-scape that had overtaken much of New York, the Bronx's fiery past—stripped of any mention of landlords or insurers—morphed from a liability into an asset. Just two blocks away, at a new sushi restaurant, partygoers could order "Bronx Is Burning" salmon rolls for $12.95. In the same register but at a steeper price point, the Macabre Suite party dressed the $400 million redevelopment project in the now-marketable wounds of the past: the ashes of this painful history rendered into ornamentation as value added. From those cinders would rise the new Bronx, and Rubenstein shared his ambitions freely. "This will be the most transformative project in the last 50 years," he boasted, promising that SoBro will be the next SoHo.[12]

When Bronxites voiced their outrage at the gala's "sad caricature of urban blight," Rubenstein appeared to be caught unawares, telling the *Times*, "I apologize for that and will try to do a better job expressing our message in the future—which is only that the Bronx is a great place." What Rubenstein *had* anticipated, however, was being condemned as an interloping gentrifier. To preempt such charges, he booked the borough's own DJ Kool Herc, the hip-hop trailblazer we met in chapter 7, to perform and rubber-stamp the project. In monetizing the burning Bronx, the developers were to some extent hitching their wagons to one of the world's preeminent cultural forms. In this they were greatly aided by fellow traveler and filmmaker Baz Luhrmann, a guest at the Macabre Suite who was then in the process of making *The Get Down*, the (far less exploitative) Netflix series about the birth of hip-hop in the 1970s Bronx. The Macabre Suite betrayed a palpable nostalgia for a grittier era in New York history—an era before broken windows policing. Ironically, such nostalgia is now being marshaled to sell real estate, even though Bronx boosters and developers themselves credit broken windows policing as a central factor boosting property values.[13]

Drowning out Somerset Partners' perverse deployment of Bronx history was the collective outcry of Bronx residents, who by and large saw right through the marketing scheme. As the Committee Against Fort Apache had done three decades earlier, Bronxites protested the reduction of their borough's history to a set of sensational, decontextualized images of urban ruin. Ed García Conde, the founder of a popular blog about the Bronx, told the *New York Times*, "What person in their right mind would say this is a good idea for the South Bronx? Can you imagine the response if we held a party themed with vestiges of the Holocaust? For people in the South Bronx, this was our Holocaust."[14]

One answer to Conde's questions came from visual artist and activist Shellyne Rodriguez, an organizer with Take Back the Bronx, who explained that in lieu of "erasing the cultural history of the Bronx," real estate interests and the city's power brokers have "worked to appropriate it in the service of rebranding." The organization, committed to "taking back our hoods from police, landlords and politicians," picketed numerous events and spaces associated with Somerset Partners, connecting its redevelopment project to racialized police violence in the borough. The group inherited and reinvigorated a Bronx radical tradition of taking on both landlords and police—property and the state—that stretches back to the Young Lords. This genealogy includes the "Don't move, improve!" formations of the 1970s and the campaign launched in 1993 by Nos Quedamos (We Stay) to ensure that the redevelopment of the Melrose neighborhood did not displace existing residents. "The Bronx is not for sale," Take Back the Bronx proclaimed in a broadside against gentrification from early 2016, reminding neighbors, "We made it through the 'Bronx is burning' years of the 1970s and 80s. We are a borough of resistance fighters." Instead of accepting the prevailing rhetorical contrast between urban disinvestment and its supposed remedy, redevelopment, Take Back the Bronx reframed these two processes as mutually reinforcing movements within an ongoing cycle of dispossession. The group thereby identified chronic displacement and housing precarity as inherent—not aberrant—effects of a system designed to extract maximum value from land.[15]

When Bronx anti-gentrification activists summon the arson years, they not only call attention to the continuities between the 1970s and the 2010s, but they stake a claim to the neighborhood grounded in their collective survivorship (or that of their forebears). The fight against gentrification has taken on a localized form of what I would call *threat equity*: a sense of community ownership and belonging made stronger by past hardship and struggle. Like the sweat equity movement, which reimagined ownership claims via the labor and embodied experiences of its resident-workers, threat equity insists that belonging is determined not by financial relationships but by history, community, and the struggle for housing justice. Two historical truths uphold this argument: first, the tremendous physical and psychic injuries inflicted on a generation of Bronx residents by the arson wave; and second, the herculean efforts required to stem its tide, then rebuild in its wake. "For over 40 years, no one wanted us," explains Ed García Conde. "But now that my community who stayed and rebuilt from the literal ashes through blood, sweat, tears and people's lives are facing displacement. There is something deeply immoral about that."[16]

In the documentary *Decade of Fire*, Vivian Vázquez Irizarry identifies the struggle against gentrification as the heir to the anti-arson organizing chronicled by the film. "I'm clear that I stand on the struggle and the blood sweat and tears of people who fought," she emphasizes. What she demonstrates is that the fight for the future of the Bronx is in part over how the burning years will be remembered and what lessons they hold. We must see these histories not as jarring contrasts to the gentrified city but, rather, as continuous with the urban order today. The words of Evelina López Antonetty of United Bronx Parents are instructive. From her mural in the Bronx's Longwood neighborhood, her voice resounds:

> We will never stop struggling here in the Bronx, even though they've destroyed it around us. We would pitch tents if we have to rather than move from here. We would fight back, there is nothing we would not do. They will never take us away from here. I feel very much a part of this and I'm never going to leave. And, after me, my children will be here to carry on.[17]

Antonetty's words carry new meanings as climate change—a form of state- and corporate-led mass arson—threatens not just the American city but all of us, and as housing becomes an ever more precarious proposition for so many people in this country. Can we imagine protections against future harms that go beyond the established model of property insurance, which does little to address underlying causes and, in fact, often exacerbates them through discrimination? What shape would a city take were it to actively confront and redress its violent past and immiserating present? And if the actuarial stranglehold on the future were slackened or even broken, what freedom dreams might be realized?[18]

For now, property insurance remains the principal tool for mitigating the many hazards that beset the metropolis. Just as it had during the 1970s conflagrations, insurance continues to offer little security to the most vulnerable residents of American cities. The wave of landlord arson has receded, yet its source—the lethal alchemy of race and capitalism—endures.

ACKNOWLEDGMENTS

In 2014, I began researching a book about how risks get distributed across society. I should have known better, but I assumed the risk of such an undertaking was, more or less, mine alone to bear. When I fell ill with a health condition that forced me to put down the pen for nearly four years, I was fully disabused of the fiction of writerly autonomy. As I learned to cope with the limitations of my now disabled body, I came to appreciate in a new way that the weight of knowledge production is necessarily shouldered by a multitude: loved ones, mentors, colleagues, friends, sources, historical subjects, and health-care providers. Any errors are mine alone. But without the unflagging support of those named below, these words would never have made it to the page.

The first conversations I had about this project were with Joanne Meyerowitz and Michael Denning, and they received my initial half-baked theories of fire and disco with a healthy mix of encouragement and skepticism. Joanne saw the historian in me before I did, and she taught me the way of the craft with her characteristic subtlety, rigor, and wit. Upon reading an earlier draft of this book, she warned of too many stylistic "pirouettes." Few others could have convinced me to twirl less, but Joanne is always right. Michael made sure I never lost sight of the political stakes of the project. He has long modeled a life of the mind that finds sustenance as much from picket lines as seminar rooms. His refusal to turn away from contradiction and his commitment to liberation on the page and in the streets have been world-opening. Daniel Martinez HoSang pushed my thinking on racial formation and political economy, demanding the precision and clarity that the moment requires. Mary Lui nurtured this project from its inception, and I am grateful to have had her as a guide to the world of urban history. And Robin D. G. Kelley's generosity with his genius rekindled my faith in the project amid the pandemic lockdown and job market collapse. A Post-it note reading "Believe Robin" remains affixed to the wall overlooking my desk.

The book was sharpened by an impossibly luminous group of readers who gathered at the New School's Heilbroner Center for Capitalism Studies for the manuscript workshop of my dreams. Over seven hours, the project was taken apart and put back together by Bethany Moreton, Destin Jenkins, Keeanga-Yamahtta Taylor, Julia Ott, and Salonee Bhaman. It was one of the most meaningful experiences of my career.

My steadfast agent, Elise Capron, gave me a crash course in the publishing industry and made sure this book found its ideal home. I was overjoyed when she placed the book in the deft hands of Dan Gerstle, then at Liveright. Even after he was named editor in chief of W. W. Norton, Dan's keen editorial eye never wavered from the project. For his patience, exactitude, and vision, I am deeply grateful. Zeba Arora efficiently shepherded the book through the publication process. Thank you also to Steve Attardo and Janice Ackerman for the powerful cover, Louise Mattarelliano for production management, and Bonnie Thompson for the excellent copyediting.

At Yale, I was fortunate to learn from and with a phenomenal community of scholars. I couldn't have asked for a better guide to the history of capitalism than Jean-Christophe Agnew, whose intricate, braided mode of storytelling has indelibly shaped my approach to scholarship and pedagogy. Elizabeth Hinton and I were ships in the institutional night, but still I have learned so much from her, and this book owes much to her support and counsel. Lisa Lowe taught me what it means to stand by your students. In and out of the classroom, I benefited from conversations with Vanessa Agard-Jones, Jafari Allen, Laura Barraclough, Daphne Brooks, George Chauncey, Kathryn Dudley, Crystal Feimster, Glenda Gilmore, Inderpal Grewal, Matt Jacobson, Greta LaFleur, Stephen Pitti, Alicia Schmidt Camacho, and Jenifer Van Vleck. Departmental life would have been pure chaos without the logistical savvy of Susan Shand, Jean Cherniavsky, and the late Jen Fleischer. Kate Redburn, Pedro Regalado, and Sylvia Ryerson were lifelines through some difficult years; cheering each other on since then has been a steady source of joy. Salonee Bhaman has been a dazzling thought partner in all things housing and insurance. I've also been fortunate to think with Josh Aiken, Hamzah Baig, B. Alex Beasley, Karla Cornejo Villavicencio, Gavriel Cutipa-Zorn, Lena Eckert-Erdheim, Lucero Estrella, Kelly Goodman, Molly Greene, Kelsey Henry, Lucia Hulsether, Ashley James, Ryan Cecil Jobson, LiLi Johnson, Anne Lessy, Jessie Modi, Devin McGeehan Muchmore, Nichole Nelson, Ever Osorio Ruiz, Maru Pabón, Kaneesha Parsard, Héctor Peralta, Sebastián Perez, Danya Pilgrim, Olivia Polk, Tina Post, Peter Raccuglia, Justin Randolph, Aanchal Saraf, Courtney Sato, Randa Tawil, Simon Torracinta, Jacinda Tran, Viet Trinh, Monique Ulysses, Beans Velocci, Damian Vergara Bracamontes, Stephen Vider, Yuhe Faye Wang, and Talya Zemach-Bersin. Various constellations of these bright lights have convened in the working groups that hold together intellectual life at Yale: Racial Capitalism and the Carceral State, the Urban History Working Group, and the Black Marxism Reading Group. The Working Group on Globalization and Culture deserves a special shout-out because it managed to cobble together a brilliant and earnest intellectual community even in the days of impending Zoom. When I entered graduate school, this was the space I had hoped to find.

At Harvard's Charles Warren Center for Studies in American History, Walter Johnson and Tiya Miles created a refuge from the ravages of the pandemic. I was fortunate to collaborate with Kyera Singleton and DeAnza Cook during my time there—boundless thanks to Mariame Kaba, Dara Kwayera Imani Bayer, Camila Pelsinger, and Sofia Meadows for joining us for a conversation about transformative justice and the university. Thanks, too, to Sara Awartani, Kris Klein Hernandez, Evan Taparata, and Ida Yalzadeh for the camaraderie and commiseration. And thanks to Lizabeth Cohen and those in the Twentieth-Century U.S. History Workshop, including Ken Alyass, Jake Anbinder, Erik Baker, Tim Barker, Ione Barrows, Ryan Fontanilla, Jonathan Karp, Erica Sterling, and Tina Wei.

I entered the Dartmouth Society of Fellows hoping for a neurological reset after a few rough seasons on the academic job market. Those years in the Vermont hills provided that, and much more. "Let's make some good trouble," Bethany Moreton wrote to me when I received the offer. She and Pamela Voekel rolled out the (muddy) red carpet and taught me how to hold on to your soul in the imperial university. Thanks to all the members of the Society of Fellows, WGSS, and the Departments of History and Geography, especially Erin Collins, Jorge Cuéllar, Mona Domosh, Laura Edmondson, Curt Gambetta, rl Goldberg, Jane Henderson, Mingwei Huang, Tory Jeffay,

Jodi Kim, John Kulvicki, Eng-Beng Lim, tish Lopez, Abby Neely, Golnar Nikpour, Annelise Orleck, Julia Rabig, Miriam Rich, Aanchal Saraf, Amy Schiller, Patricia Stuelke, Monique Ulysses, Emily Walton, Robby Zeinstra, and Yiren Zheng. Laura McDaniel and Bruch Lehmann went above and beyond, ensuring that everything ran smoothly. Endless gratitude to all the members of FSJP, who kept me afloat in the bleakest of times. Solidarity with the Upper Valley Tenants Union, who showed me that rural tenant organizing in the United States is not a thing of the past. Karla Bourland and Allen Swartz began these years as landlords and ended them as adoptive parents—no easy feat, considering this book's subject matter. And to the students in Histories of the Carceral State: you make it all worthwhile.

I am writing these words just a few weeks into my time at Temple University, and yet colleagues and students have somehow already made me feel at home. I wake up each day in disbelief. Thank you to the entire History Department for the warm reception. For going out of their way to support my transition, I'm especially thankful for Bryant Simon and Petra Goedde, along with Lila Berman, Seth Bruggeman, Matthias Fuelling, Travis Glasson, Hilary Iris Lowe, Jay Lockenour, Alan McPherson, Katya Motyl, Harvey Neptune, Danya Pilgrim, Mónica Ricketts, Jess Roney, Eileen Ryan, and Jake Wolff. And enormous thanks goes to TJ Cusack and Annette Vega for helping me get my feet on the ground at Temple.

The book greatly benefited from conversations with a multitude of colleagues and comrades at other institutions, many of whom have commented on this work at various stages of the research. I'm grateful for the support of Arielle Angel, George Aumoithe, Minju Bae, Brian Balogh, Ari Brostoff, Rachel Bunker, Brent Cebul, Marcia Chatelain, N.D.B. Connolly, Daniel Cumming, Andrew Delbanco, Demetrius Eudell, Jared Farmer, Johanna Fernández, Lily Geismer, Ruth Wilson Gilmore, Michael Glass, Dylan Gottlieb, Matt Guariglia, LaShawn Harris, Andrew Hartman, Rachel Herzing, Ben Holtzman, Daniel Immerwahr, Alison Isenberg, Khalil Anthony Johnson, Andrew Kahrl, Julilly Kohler-Hausmann, Susan Koshy, Jessica Levy, Jonathan Levy, Peter L'Official, Becky Marchiel, Eileen Markey, Katherine McKittrick, Stephen Mihm, Donna Murch, Mark Naison, Sarah Nelson, Gayle Pemberton, Kim Phillips-Fein, Brian Purnell, Michael Ralph, Akira Drake Rodriguez, Ashraf Rushdy, Robert Self, Anu Sharma, Ellie Shermer, Brad Simpson, Sarah Sklaw, Dean Spade, David Stein, Tom Sugrue, Andie Tucher, Jackie Wang, Mason Williams, Gabriel Winant, and Noel

K. Wolfe. Dan Berger didn't ask for this title, but he has been my shadow adviser since I first considered applying to graduate school.

This book was made possible by a host of fellowships and grants, many of which have since been discontinued—a sad and telling indication of the state of the humanities. An American Council of Learned Societies Fellowship was crucial to its completion. The Society of American Historians' Allan Nevins Prize provided the infrastructure and network to place this book with the most fitting publisher. The support of a Mellon/American Council of Learned Societies (ACLS) Dissertation Completion Fellowship and the Jefferson Scholars National Fellowship aided in the completion of my dissertation. I am also grateful for the Social Science Research Council's (SSRC) Dissertation Proposal Development Fellowship, the Council on Library and Information Resources' (CLIR) Mellon Fellowship for Dissertation Research in Original Sources, the Harvard-Mellon Urban Initiative, the LBJ Foundation's Moody Research Grant, Yale's John F. Enders Research Grant, and the Yale Center for the Study of Race, Indigeneity, and Transnational Migration (RITM) for enabling extensive travel to various archives.

The assistance of archivists and librarians has been essential to piecing together this story. Steven Payne has been an indispensable resource for Bronx history since he joined the Bronx County Historical Society. Allen Fisher at the LBJ Library, Janet Munch at the Leonard Lief Library, Juber Ayala at Centro de Estudios Puertorriqueños, Ken Cobb and Dwight Johnson at the New York City Municipal Archives, Tab Lewis at the National Archives Records and Administration II, Youlanda Logan at the Jimmy Carter Library, David Gary at Yale, and Richard Waller at the Davis Library together helped me locate hundreds of boxes of material. Special thanks to Molly Roy, Jonathan Tarleton, Rebecca Solnit, and Joshua Jelly-Schapiro for sharing the beautiful map featured in the introduction. And enormous gratitude to the Bronx African American History Project (and its offshoots), especially the efforts of Mark Naison. This book would be virtually inconceivable without the hundreds of oral histories conducted by the BAAHP.

No one has played a larger role in making these histories known than Vivian Vázquez Irizarry. *Decade of Fire*, the film she made in 2019 with Gretchen Hildebran and Julia Steele Allen, has been a gift to the Bronx and to housing justice movements everywhere. It was an honor to work on the project as a researcher, though I'm sure I learned more from the film's makers than they from me.

In order to capture those stories that have evaded the archival record, I have been incredibly fortunate to speak with many of those who witnessed, survived, and played leading roles in the histories told here. My gratitude goes to Ron Cassesso, John Engel, Ron Hine, Michael Jacobson, Jill Jonnes, Barry Kluger, Sara Morales, Gelvin Stevenson, Greg Tate, Lynn Tierney, Eric Warner, and those who wish to remain anonymous, for speaking with me about experiences decades old and often painful to recall.

Much of this history is only on record because of the efforts of the community organizations who fought to end the fires. To those chronicled here—the Northwest Bronx Community and Clergy Coalition, the People's Development Corporation, the Committee Against Fort Apache, the Banana Kelly Community Improvement Association, the Mid-Bronx Desperadoes, the Symphony Tenants Organizing Project, and Take Back the Bronx—and to all those who endured the arson wave in the Bronx and elsewhere, I hope this telling has captured even a fragment of the fierceness, commitment, and vision you brought and bring to these struggles. Special thanks to Edward Garcia at NWBCCC and Cea Weaver at Housing Justice for All, who shared their deep expertise of housing justice with all of us in the backwoods of Vermont and New Hampshire.

I'll say once more that none of this would have been possible without the abundant and enduring support of the family I was born into and the one I've chosen. Dear friends in Philly, New Haven, Vermont, and beyond have been a constant ballast. I am so grateful to Julia Allen, Leslie Allison, Dana Barnett, Talia Barrett, Dan Berger, Beth Blum, Sara Bohnsack, Chris Bolden-Newsome, Roan Boucher, Timothy Colman, Damon Constantinides, Jason David, Justin Denis, Chrysanthemum Desir, Molly Fischer, Annie Frazier, Hilary Glass, Cayden Halligan, Mingwei Huang, Aaron Jafferis, Esteban Kelly, Eira Lipkin, Nina Macintosh, Kelly McCarthy, Nova McGiffert, Wazhmah Osman, Yasmeen Perez, Jenna Peters-Golden, Mendal Polish, Beth Pulse, Kate Redburn, Pedro Regalado, Dexter Rose, Sylvia Ryerson, Aanchal Saraf, Camille Seaberry, River Seidelman, David Stein, L. Suze, Owen Taylor, Sarah Tracy-Wanck, Maggie Von Vogt, Dillon Vrana, Jade Walker, Wren Warner, Francis Weiss Rabkin, and Laura Winnick, who have collectively held me through hell and high water. It has been my immense fortune to organize with Philly Stands Up, which has taught me again and again that safety is forged from struggle, not reprisal. To be writing these words back in Philadelphia, where community just hits different, is a dream from which I hope to never wake.

As this book was nearing its completion, I lost two of the four people on my phone's speed dial: my father, James Ansfield, and grandmother Shirley Langer. I'm heartbroken that they are not here to witness the birth of the book they cheered on for so long. My deepest appreciation goes to Lena and Dima Braginsky, Marci Masur, and the entire Langer and Ansfield families for their tireless support in good times and bad. To Amy and Jonathan Ansfield, who brought Mirah, Rivah, and impossible joy into my life. And to my parents, Julie and Barry Karp and James and Joni Ansfield, who have always believed in my voice and have done everything they could to ensure that I can continue to use it. For their love I am endlessly grateful.

To Sal and her immaculate paws, thank you for reminding me about the sun. And finally to Bruce, the heart home who sustained this decade-long study of housing, whose influence is felt in every footnote and each new formulation, and whose love points me forever toward justice, toward the fabulous, and toward myself.

NEW YORK FAIR PLAN LOSS EXPERIENCE

New York City Fire Experience on Properties Purchased Since 1974
Insurance Experience Period June 1977 to June 1979

Ratio of Amount of Insurance to Purchase Price	Number of Properties	Average Purchase Price (Estimate)	Average Amount of Insurance	No. of Claims	Paid Losses	2 Yr. Claim Frequency (Per 100 Properties)	Average Claim Cost	Average 2 Yr. Loss Cost (Per Property)
Greater than 6	1,455	$8,193	$57,350	241	$1,222,139	16.6	$5,071	$840
5.1 to 6.0	330	9,132	50,226	53	256,744	16.1	4,844	778
4.1 to 5.0	632	10,450	47,025	128	623,685	20.3	4,873	987
3.1 to 4.0	1,066	13,492	47,222	175	851,294	16.4	4,865	799
2.1 to 3.0	2,174	17,779	44,448	317	1,293,844	14.6	4,082	595
Subtotal	5,657	13,182	48,914	914	4,247,706	16.2	4,648	751
1.1 to 2.0	6,860	26,630	39,945	663	2,684,917	9.7	4,050	391
Less than 1.1	7,645	27,627	20,720	388	1,390,559	5.1	3,584	182
Total	20,162	23,235	35,172	1,965	8,323,182	9.7	4,236	413

The insurance gap as revealed by a mandatory 1980 filing of the Federal Insurance Administration before the Senate Subcommittee on Insurance. The first two columns show that 62 percent of NYPIUA properties were affected by the insurance gap—that is, properties where the ratio of insurance coverage to purchase price exceeds 1.1. The seventh and eighth columns show a correlation between the size of the insurance gap and the frequency and extent of the loss. (From: *Flood Insurance and Crime and Riot Reinsurance: Hearing Before the Subcommittee on Insurance of the Committee on Banking, Housing, and Urban Affairs, U.S. Senate* [Washington, DC: U.S. Government Printing Office, 1980], February 28, 1980, 181.)

A NOTE ON ARSON STATISTICS

Arson statistics were notoriously unreliable and inconsistent throughout the 1970s. A fire was officially recorded as arson only if it could be legally proven that it was set intentionally. This was a difficult undertaking, since evidence of incendiarism was often "consumed by the fire itself."[1] If sufficient proof did not exist, a fire was classified as "suspicious" and not recorded in arson data, despite the national consensus among arson investigators that almost all suspicious fires were indeed incendiary.[2]

A second and more damning issue with arson data was how it tracked fire marshal staffing in an era of fiscal crisis and municipal layoffs. For much of the 1970s, when arson investigation was under the jurisdiction of the fire service, a fire could be classified as incendiary only by a trained fire marshal; one was called to the scene for forensic analysis if the fire battalion chief marked a blaze as suspicious.[3] Until the late 1970s, the fire marshal's office was hopelessly understaffed and unable to investigate a large number of fires. In 1976, amid New York City's fiscal crisis, a mere sixty-five marshals were charged with investigating every fire in the city, meaning each marshal carried an impossible caseload of nearly 160 suspicious fires.[4] As a result, only 59 percent of suspicious fires were investigated that year.[5] Moreover, in order to prioritize investigations of occupied buildings, battalion chiefs almost never classified fires in vacant buildings as suspicious during these years, despite knowing full well that "fires do not start accidentally in buildings where no one lives."[6]

In 1979, the city added 135 fire marshals, dramatically expanding its investigative capabilities.[7] As marshals' ability to respond to suspicious fires exceeded 90 percent in the following years, a significantly larger number of fires were classified as arson.[8] In short: more fire marshals, higher arson numbers. In the words of Arson Strike Force administrator Michael Jacobson, "If we got rid of fire marshals, would there be no arson? And yes, that's kind of true. There'd be no arson because you wouldn't have a government agency to tell you it was arson. And so in places that had very few of these [fire marshals]—there are other cities that might have had huge arson waves. Do they even know about it?"[9]

The final issue with arson data was that the method of data collection changed dramatically over the course of the 1970s due to (a) the advent of computerized arson databases and (b) the piecemeal reclassification of arson as a Part I federal crime between 1978 and 1982 (thus involving the FBI in arson statistics for the first time).[10]

As a result of these variables in staffing and recordkeeping, Jacobson discerns "two distinct periods" in citywide data collection. During the first period, from 1970 through 1977, suspicious fires "rose phenomenally" through 1976. "The first major rise in suspicious fires occurred in 1971–1972," which tracked with the growth of the NYPIUA. In the second period, from 1977–78 to 1982, the FDNY had upgraded its recordkeeping and tripled the number of fire marshals. In these years, the total number of structural fires decreased quite dramatically, even as the number of suspicious fires increased moderately.[11] In other words, suspicious fires as a percent of all structural fires grew after 1977. This suggests that New York City arson data prior to 1977 was artificially low, and that its levels after 1977 were likely inflated by improved recordkeeping, not escalating arson.

Although the 1970s FDNY data was particularly unreliable, statistical inconsistency afflicted fire departments across the country. Reviewing arson losses in large Texas cities, an insurance firm noted,

"It is entirely possible that a city with an apparently 'bad' track record where arson is concerned, may simply be doing a better job than others in arson detection."[12] The general rule, though, was that municipalities underreported their rates of arson. A group of Stanford researchers concluded in 1972 that "arson actually occurs three times more often than published statistics indicate."[13] Another study found that arson was "the most underestimated ... of all crimes."[14]

That most arson statistics missed a great deal of actual arson helps make sense of a recent revisionist misreading of the 1970s arson wave. The best-known historical monograph on the New York City fire wave of the 1970s is journalist Joe Flood's *The Fires: How a Computer Formula, Big Ideas, and the Best of Intentions Burned Down New York City—and Determined the Future of Cities*. Flood controversially downplays the extent of the arson wave, claiming that "for all its ubiquity, the arson story is ultimately fiction."[15] Contending that "at its peak in the late 1970s, arson made up less than 7 percent of fires," Flood instead speculates that "what killed those neighborhoods was an earlier wave of conventional fires, which spread over the poorer quarters of the city like a contagion."[16]

The archival record is unequivocal in its refutation of this argument. As one community-based anti-arson organization put it,

> The great increase in fires is no accident. All the electrical systems in the Bronx didn't start short-circuiting while those in Queens remained safe. We aren't smoking twice as much or twice as carelessly as we were in 1970. All the furnaces in cities did not begin failing at once while suburban furnaces continued to heat safely. The fires are being set, usually for money.[17]

According to the office of the New York City fire marshals, 6,100 of the Bronx's 13,948 fires in 1976 were suspicious—a rate of 44 percent—and even that figure is thought to be low.[18]

The Bronx's rate of arson (as a percentage of all fires) was in line with the national figure: the American Insurance Association estimated in 1976 that arson produced 40 to 50 percent of all fire losses nationwide.[19] The toll of all types of arson—including wildfires and non-structural arsons like car fires—was an estimated $2 billion in direct losses and $10 to $15 billion in total losses (including secondary damages like loss of employment) during that year alone.[20]

That said, as this book has striven to show, arson's true toll cannot be captured in numbers. In the words of Saidiya Hartman, such statistics are but "murderous abstractions."[21]

SOURCES CONSULTED

Archival Collections

Atlanta, Georgia
Jimmy Carter Presidential Library (JC)
    Frontier Development Corporation Records
    National Commission on Neighborhoods, Insurance Redlining Reports
    Records of the Cabinet Secretary, Arson Records
    People's Development Corporation Files
    Presidential Correspondence with the South Bronx Development Organization
    Urban Crisis Task Force Records

Austin, Texas
Lyndon Baines Johnson Presidential Library (LBJ)
    Records of the National Advisory Commission on Civil Disorders
    Records of the President's National Advisory Panel on Insurance in Riot-Affected Areas (Hughes Panel)
    White House Subject File on Insurance, Fire Insurance

College Park, Maryland
National Archives Records and Administration II (NARA)
    Records of the National Fire Administration, Arson Records
    Records of the National Fire Prevention and Control Administration (NFPCA)

New Haven, Connecticut
Yale Beinecke Library
Yale University Arts Library Repository
Yale Manuscripts and Archives, Yale University (YMA)
    Edward J. Logue Papers

New York City, New York
Bronx County Historical Society (BCHS)
    Bronx Council on the Arts Records
    Gelvin Stevenson Collection
    Gil Fagiani Papers
    Mel Rosenthal Collection
    NWBCCC Collection

Bronx Institute Archives, Leonard Lief Library at Lehman College (LLL)
    Bronx Chamber of Commerce Collection
    Bronx Regional and Community History Oral Collection
    Northwest Bronx Community and Clergy Coalition Papers (NWBCCC)
    Papers of Jill Jonnes (JJ)
Centro de Estudios Puertorriqueños, Hunter College (CEP)
    Carlos Ortiz Papers
    Diana Caballero Papers
    Lourdes Torres Papers
    Richie Perez Papers
    Robert Garcia Papers
    United Bronx Parents Papers
Davis Library and Insurance Archives, St. John's University (DLIA)
    New York Insurance Department Annual Reports
    New York Property Insurance Underwriting Association Records
Fales Library, New York University (FL)
    Downtown Collection, Fashion Moda Gallery Archive
Mand Library, Fire Department of the City of New York (ML)
    FDNY Annual Reports
New York Municipal Archives (NYMA)
    Mayor Ed Koch Papers & Departmental Records
    New York Arson Strike Force Records (ASF)
Tamiment Library and Robert F. Wagner Labor Archives, New York University (TL)
    Ronald Lawson Papers

Personal Archives
Papers of John Engel
Papers of Michael Jacobson
Papers of Clifford Karchmer
Papers of Barry Kluger
Papers of Gelvin Stevenson

Interviews and Oral Histories

Conducted by Author
Ron Cassesso. Tape Recording. New Haven, Connecticut. August 8, 2018.
John Engel. Tape Recording. New York, New York. July 24, 2018.
Ron Hine. Tape Recording. New Haven, Connecticut. February 27, 2019.
Michael Jacobson. Tape Recording. New Haven, Connecticut. September 18, 2017.
Barry Kluger. New York, New York. July 24, 2018.
Sara Morales. New Haven, Connecticut. May 6, 2016.
Gelvin Stevenson. Tape Recording. New Haven, Connecticut. July 5, 2018.
Greg Tate. New York, New York. July 24, 2015.
Lynn Tierney. Tape Recording. New Haven, Connecticut. June 18, 2018.
Eric Warner. New York, New York. July 24, 2018.

The Bronx African American History Project, Fordham University
Genevieve Brown (formerly Brooks). Oral History by Brian Purnell. April 19, 2008.
John Byas. Oral History by Mark Naison. March 19, 2009.
Samuel Christian. Oral History by Mark Naison et al. February 15, 2006.
Hetty Fox. Oral History by Mark Naison et al. October 1, 2015.
Robert Gumbs. Oral History by Mark Naison et al. October 1, 2015.

Christopher Hayes. Oral History. October 29, 2015.
James Henderson. Oral History by Mark Naison. January 13, 2004.
Paula Morris. Oral History by Mark Naison et al. February 3, 2005.
Joseph Orange. Oral History by Mark Naison. September 28, 2015.
Darney "K-Born" Rivers. Oral History by Mark Naison and Lisa Betty. October 18, 2016.
Anthony Rivieccio. Oral History by Mark Naison. December 4, 2015.
Ivan Sanchez. Oral History by Mark Naison. May 2, 2008.
Shelley Sanderson. Oral History by Mark Naison. April 18, 2006.
Chrystal Wade. Oral History by Mark Naison. September 17, 2015.

The Bronx Institute Oral History Project, Leonard Lief Library at Lehman College
Irving Bick. Oral History by Emita Hill. May 18, 1983.
John Comisky. Oral History by Bertha Battle. February 21, 1983.
William Frey. Oral History by Davis Ross. April 22, 1982.
Thomas Washington. Oral History by Katie W. Bukofzer. March 6, 1982.

Newspapers, Periodicals, and News Sites

The Aetna-izer
Artforum
The Asbury Park Press
Associated Press (AP)
The Atlanta Constitution
Atlanta Daily World
Austin American-Statesman
Best's Weekly
The Boston Globe
Boston Review
Bronx Press Review
Business Week
The Catholic News
Chicago Tribune
The Christian Science Monitor
City Limits
The Cleveland Press
Colorlines
Computerworld
El Coquí
Curbed
Detroit Free Press
El Diario
Ebony
The Fader
Financial Guardian
Financial Times
Firehouse
The Forward
Gannett Today
Gay Community News
The Gazette (Montreal)
The Globe and Mail
GQ
The Guardian
Hartford Courant
The Hollywood Reporter
Independent Agent
The Institutional Investor
Insurance Advocate
Insurance Journal
The Intercept
International Firefighter
The Irish Times
Los Angeles Times
Michigan Chronicle
The Nation
The National Underwriter
Nation's Cities
Newark Star-Ledger
Newsday
Newsweek
New York
New York Amsterdam News
New York Daily News
The New Yorker
New York Post
New York Sunday News
The New York Times
The New York Times Magazine
Northwest Bronx Neighborhood Action
The Observer
On Location
Parade
Paterson Morning Call
Philadelphia Daily News
The Philadelphia Inquirer
The Philadelphia Tribune
The Real Deal
Real Estate Forum

Real Estate Record and Builders' Guide
Risk & Insurance
Risk Market News
The Riverdale Press
Saturday Review
Sentinel Star (Orlando)
The Spectator
The Sun
Sunday Pennsylvanian
Sunday Times Advertiser (Trenton)
Time

The Times (London)
Times Union
United Press International (UPI)
U.S. News & World Report
Variety
The Village Voice
The Wall Street Journal
The Washington Post
The Washington Star
Welcome2TheBronx

NOTES

Abbreviations

ASF	New York Arson Strike Force Records
BAAHP	Bronx African American History Project
BCHS	Bronx County Historical Society
CEP	Centro de Estudios Puertorriqueños, Hunter College
DLIA	Davis Library and Insurance Archives, St. John's University
FL	Fales Library, New York University
JC	Jimmy Carter Presidential Library
JJ	Papers of Jill Jonnes
LBJ	Lyndon Baines Johnson Presidential Library
LLL	Bronx Institute Archives, Leonard Lief Library at Lehman College
ML	Mand Library, Fire Department of the City of New York
NARA	National Archives Records and Administration II
NFPCA	Records of the National Fire Prevention and Control Administration
NWBCCC	Northwest Bronx Community and Clergy Coalition Papers
NYMA	New York Municipal Archives
TL	Tamiment Library and Robert F. Wagner Labor Archives
YMA	Yale Manuscripts and Archives, Yale University

Introduction: Race and Risk in the Burning Years

1 Fanon is quoting an unnamed friend. Frantz Fanon, *Black Skin, White Masks*, trans. Richard Philcox (1952; repr., New York: Grove Press, 2008), 108.
2 James Romaine, "Making History," in *Tim Rollins and K.O.S.: A History*, ed. Ian Berry (Cambridge, MA: MIT Press, 2009), 41; Lara Mimosa Montes, *Thresholes* (Minneapolis: Coffee House Press, 2020), 54; and Wesley Pearman, "The War Years Engine 82–85 and Ladder 31 Untold Stories," Facebook, July 5, 2020, https://www.facebook.com/groups/359533454878619/permalink/731689750996319.
3 On the Mendoza family, see Romaine, "Making History," 44. Quotations from Tim Rollins, "Who's Teaching What to Whom and Why," *Upfront*, 1983, reprinted on the website 98 Bowery: 1969–89, emphasis mine.
4 Romaine, "Making History," 41.
5 Albert Davila, "8 Indicted in Insurance Blazes in South Bronx," New York *Daily News*, June 12, 1975, and Joseph B. Treaster, "8 Landlords and Associates Are Indicted in Bronx Fires," *New York Times*, June 12, 1975, 44. See also Mario Merola, *Big City D.A.* (New York: Random House, 1988), 77–78.

6 See Treaster, "8 Landlords," for "epidemic" quotation. On Soviet suspicion, see Merola, *Big City D.A.*, 77–78. For insurance figures, see Treaster, "8 Landlords," and Patrick McDonnell, "Arson: Trying to Douse the 'Torches,'" New York *Daily News*, June 19, 1977, 64.

7 Elizabeth Hinton, *America on Fire: The Untold History of Police Violence and Black Rebellion* (New York: Liveright, 2021); Janet Abu-Lughod, *Race, Space, and Riots in Chicago, New York, and Los Angeles* (New York: Oxford University Press, 2007); Peter B. Levy, *The Great Uprising: Race Riots in Urban America During the 1960s* (Cambridge: Cambridge University Press, 2018); Pedro Regalado, "Urban Uprisings, 1960s–1970s," in *50 Events That Shaped Latino History: An Encyclopedia of the American Mosaic*, ed. Lilia Fernández (Santa Barbara: ABC-CLIO, 2018), 556–72; Clay Risen, *A Nation on Fire: America in the Wake of the King Assassination* (Hoboken, NJ: John Wiley & Sons, 2009); and Diane McWhorter, *Carry Me Home: Birmingham, Alabama: The Climactic Battle of the Civil Rights Revolution* (New York: Simon & Schuster, 2001).

8 The 1967 figures are from Levy, *The Great Uprising*, 17, and Hughes Panel (President's National Advisory Panel on Insurance in Riot-Affected Areas), *Meeting the Insurance Crisis of Our Cities* (Washington, DC: U.S. Government Printing Office, 1968), 4. The arson figures are from Frank Logue, "Combating Arson," *New York Times*, June 26, 1980. See "New York FAIR Plan Loss Experience" (on page 273) for an extended discussion about arson data. On historical memory, Daniel Kerr raises a similar question in the context of Cleveland's history of "controlled burns." Daniel Kerr, "Who Burned Cleveland, Ohio? The Forgotten Fires of the 1970s," in *Flammable Cities: Urban Conflagration and the Making of the Modern World*, ed. Greg Bankoff, Uwe Lübken, and Jordan Sand (Madison: University of Wisconsin Press, 2012), 332–52.

9 Quotation is from Arthur Unger, "'Fire Next Door': Bill Moyers in Smouldering South Bronx," *Christian Science Monitor*, March 21, 1977, 22. The data is from Michael A. Stegman, *The Dynamics of Rental Housing in New York City* (New Brunswick, NJ: Rutgers University, 1982), 50, 177; see also "New York FAIR Plan Loss Experience."

10 Fanon, *Black Skin, White Masks*, 108.

11 Oberlander and Webber's actions echoed a longer history of sidestepping anti-Semitism by performing Blackness. In *The Jazz Singer* (1927), the first talkie, Al Jolson's character, Jakie Rabinowitz, dons blackface as a means to transform himself into the Americanized Jack Robin. "In playing black, the Jew becomes white," writes Matthew Frye Jacobson of a racial transfiguration that is accompanied by a geographic one: Rabinowitz pledges to move his family from the Lower East Side up to the Bronx. Matthew Frye Jacobson, *Whiteness of a Different Color: European Immigrants and the Alchemy of Race* (Cambridge, MA: Harvard University Press, 1998), 120, and Eric Lott, *Love and Theft: Blackface Minstrelsy & the American Working Class* (1993; repr., New York: Oxford University Press, 2013), 21. See also Simon Balto, "Racial Framing: Blackface Criminals in America," *Journal of American History* 111, no. 2 (2024): 290–308. For more on Black-Jewish relational racialization, see Jeffrey Melnick, *A Right to Sing the Blues: African Americans, Jews, and American Popular Song* (Cambridge, MA: Harvard University Press, 1999).

On "Jew risks" and "Jewish lightning," see Jeffrey A. Marx, "Moral Hazard: The 'Jew Risks' Affair of 1867," *American Jewish History* 106, no. 3 (2022): 255–81. See also Earl Ganz, "Jewish Lightning," *Iowa Review* 6, no. 1 (1975): 20, and Aviya Kushner, "Why Do People Call Arson 'Jewish Lightning'—and Is It Anti-Semitic?" *The Forward*, May 18, 2017. On Jewish landlords and Black-Jewish relations, see Beryl Satter, *Family Properties: How the Struggle over Race and Real Estate Transformed Chicago and Urban America* (New York: Picador, 2010), especially 17–19, 261–64; Lila Corwin Berman, *Metropolitan Jews: Politics, Race, and Religion in Postwar Detroit* (Chicago: University of Chicago Press, 2015), 96–105, 145; and Jeffrey Melnick, *Black-Jewish Relations on Trial: Leo Frank and Jim Conley in the New South* (Jackson: University Press of Mississippi, 2000).

12 On the contemporary housing crisis and the rebirth of the tenant movement, see Tara Raghuveer and John Washington, "The Case for the Tenant Union," *Poverty & Race Research Action Council* 32, no. 1 (2023); Tracy Rosenthal, "Inside LA's Homeless Industrial Complex," *New Republic*, May 19, 2022; Cea Weaver, "From Universal Rent Control to Cancel Rent: Tenant Organizing in New York State," *New Labor Forum* 30, no. 1 (2021): 93–98; Matthew Desmond, *Evicted: Poverty and*

Profit in the American City (New York: Broadway Books, 2016); After Echo Park Lake Research Collective, *(Dis)Placement: The Fight for Housing and Community After Echo Park Lake* (Los Angeles: UCLA Luskin Institute on Inequality and Democracy, 2022); and Erin McElroy, "Countermapping Displacement and Resistance in Alameda County with the Anti-Eviction Mapping Project," *American Quarterly* 70, no. 3 (2018): 601–4. On the expansion of private equity and fintech firms into the rental real estate market, see especially Heather Vogell with Haru Coryne and Ryan Little, "Rent Going Up? One Company's Algorithm Could Be Why," *ProPublica*, October 15, 2022, and Heather Vogell, "When Private Equity Becomes Your Landlord," *ProPublica*, February 7, 2022.

13 Saidiya Hartman, *Scenes of Subjection: Terror, Slavery, and Self-Making in Nineteenth-Century America* (New York: Oxford University Press, 1997), 22, 42.

14 This periodization is indebted to Giovanni Arrighi, *The Long Twentieth Century: Money, Power and the Origins of Our Times* (New York: Verso, 1994), 118, 127–28, 310. Recent work has suggested that financialization actually began earlier, during the postwar period, when multinational conglomerates internalized a host of financial functions—an inadvertent product of the New Deal state's separation of industrial firms from banks. Stephen Maher and Scott Aquanno, *The Fall and Rise of American Finance: From J. P. Morgan to Blackrock* (Brooklyn: Verso, 2024). See also Fernand Braudel, *Civilization and Capitalism, 15th–18th Century*, vol. 3, *The Perspective of the World* (New York: Harper & Row, 1984), 246, and Greta Krippner, "The Financialization of the American Economy," *Socio-Economic Review* 3 (2005): 174.

15 On financialization and industrial relocation, see Greta Krippner, *Capitalizing on Crisis: The Political Origins of the Rise of Finance* (Cambridge, MA: Harvard University Press, 2012); Randy Martin, *Financialization of Daily Life* (Philadelphia: Temple University Press, 2002); David Harvey, *A Brief History of Neoliberalism* (New York: Oxford University Press, 2005); Kim Phillips-Fein, *Fear City: New York's Fiscal Crisis and the Rise of Austerity Politics* (New York: Metropolitan Books, 2017); Gerald Davis, *Managed by the Market: How Finance Re-Shaped America* (Oxford: Oxford University Press, 2009); Jefferson Cowie, *Stayin' Alive: The 1970s and the Last Days of the Working Class* (New York: New Press, 2010); Judith Stein, *Running Steel, Running America: Race, Economic Policy, and the Decline of Liberalism* (Chapel Hill: University of North Carolina Press, 1998); and *Pivotal Decade: How the United States Traded Factories for Finance in the Seventies* (New Haven, CT: Yale University Press, 2010). On the nation's trade balance over time, see Brian Reinbold and Yi Wen, "How Industrialization Shaped America's Trade Balance," *Regional Economist* (Federal Reserve Bank of St. Louis), February 6, 2020. The U.S. Steel quotation and the corresponding analysis are from Jonathan Levy, *Ages of American Capitalism: A History of the United States* (New York: Random House, 2021), 599–605. See also Karen Ho, *Liquidated: An Ethnography of Wall Street* (Durham, NC: Duke University Press, 2009), 183–88.

16 For Schneiderman quotation and background on Triangle Shirtwaist, see Mike Wallace, *Greater Gotham: A History of New York City from 1898 to 1919* (New York: Oxford University Press, 2017), 723. Wallace writes that "there were plenty of eyebrows raised" after the factory owners collected more than $60,000 in insurance claims from the fire (724). For a study of fire and its relationship to Fordism and post-Fordism in a different context, see Bryant Simon, *The Hamlet Fire: A Tragic Story of Cheap Food, Cheap Government, and Cheap Lives* (Chapel Hill: University of North Carolina Press, 2017).

17 Though the symbolism of the Triangle Shirtwaist fire was tied to the rise of Fordism, it is important to note that New York City was never a capital of American Fordism in the same manner as Detroit or Milwaukee. Joshua Freeman memorably calls it a "non-Fordist city in the age of Ford." Joshua B. Freeman, *Working-Class New York: Life and Labor Since World War II* (New York: New Press, 2000), 3–22. See also Mason B. Williams, *City of Ambition: FDR, La Guardia, and the Making of Modern New York* (New York: W. W. Norton, 2013).

18 It is no coincidence that the term "racial capitalism" was developed in the 1970s by activists and scholars in apartheid South Africa. In the early 1980s United States, the concept found a home in certain intellectual circles, but it was not until the 2010s that it achieved significant currency

outside the academy. The 2007–08 subprime loan crisis, triggered by massive defaults on racially targeted, adjustable-rate mortgage loans, had elicited questions that existing paradigms, mired in a zero-sum debate between race and class, were unable to answer. In its long aftermath, as Black and Brown mortgagors and government programs to expand homeownership became easy scapegoats for the crisis, racial capitalism offered a beacon of clarity. When the Movement for Black Lives emerged in 2014, it further propelled the concept into the public sphere.

The postwar financialization literature is almost always written as a process distinct from the racial upheavals of the second half of the twentieth century. A new generation of scholarship promises to rethink that bifurcation. Keeanga-Yamahtta Taylor, Pedro Regalado, Destin Jenkins, David Stein, and others are leading the way. In addition to Taylor's work, see the contributions in Destin Jenkins and Justin Leroy, eds., *Histories of Racial Capitalism* (New York: Columbia University Press, 2021). See also David Stein, "Containing Keynesianism in an Age of Civil Rights: Jim Crow Monetary Policy and the Struggle for Guaranteed Jobs, 1956–1979," in *Beyond the New Deal Order: U.S. Politics from the Great Depression to the Great Recession*, ed. Gary Gerstle et al. (Philadelphia: University of Pennsylvania Press, 2019), 124–40; Ho, *Liquidated*; Louis Hyman, *Debtor Nation: The History of America in Red Ink* (Princeton, NJ: Princeton University Press, 2011), chapter 6; and Phillips-Fein, *Fear City*.

For elaborations on racial capitalism, see Cedric Robinson, *Black Marxism: The Making of the Black Radical Tradition* (Chapel Hill: University of North Carolina Press, 2000); Stuart Hall, "Race, Articulation, and Societies Structured in Dominance," in *Stuart Hall Essential Essays*, vol. 1, ed. David Morley (1980; repr., Durham, NC: Duke University Press, 2019); W.E.B. Du Bois, *Black Reconstruction in America* (New York: Harcourt, 1935); C.L.R. James, *The Black Jacobins: Toussaint L'Ouverture and the San Domingo Revolution* (New York: Dial Press, 1938); Walter Johnson, *River of Dark Dreams: Slavery and Empire in the Cotton Kingdom* (Cambridge, MA: Harvard University Press, 2013); Ruth Wilson Gilmore, *Golden Gulag: Prisons, Surplus, Crisis, and Opposition in Globalizing California* (Berkeley: University of California Press, 2007); Robin D. G. Kelley, *Race Rebels: Culture, Politics, and the Black Working Class* (New York: Free Press, 1994); Jenkins and Leroy, *Histories of Racial Capitalism*; Peter James Hudson, *Bankers and Empire: How Wall Street Colonized the Caribbean* (Chicago: University of Chicago Press, 2017); N.D.B. Connolly, *A World More Concrete: Real Estate and the Remaking of Jim Crow South Florida* (Chicago: University of Chicago Press, 2014); David McNally, *Blood and Money: War, Slavery, Finance, and Empire* (Chicago: Haymarket Books, 2020); Walter Johnson and Robin D. G. Kelley, eds., "Race, Capitalism, Justice," special issue, *Boston Review* 1 (2017); Jodi A. Byrd, Alyosha Goldstein, Jodi Melamed, and Chandan Reddy, "Predatory Value: Economies of Dispossession and Disturbed Relationalities," *Social Text* 36, no. 2 (June 2018): 1–18; Donna Murch, *Assata Taught Me: State Violence, Racial Capitalism, and the Movement for Black Lives* (Chicago: Haymarket Books, 2022); Jodi Melamed, *Represent and Destroy: Rationalizing Violence in the New Racial Capitalism* (Minneapolis: University of Minnesota Press, 2011); and Susan Koshy, Lisa Marie Cacho, Jodi A. Byrd, and Brian Jordan Jefferson, eds., *Colonial Racial Capitalism* (Durham, NC: Duke University Press, 2022). For Gilmore quotation, see Ruth Wilson Gilmore, *Abolition Geography: Essays Towards Liberation* (2015; repr., Brooklyn: Verso, 2022), 451. Racial capitalism emerged in South African anti-apartheid contexts in the mid-1970s, and it was later introduced to U.S. readers by Cedric Robinson's *Black Marxism* in 1983. Robin D. G. Kelley, "Why *Black Marxism*? Why Now?" foreword to Cedric Robinson, *Black Marxism: The Making of the Black Radical Tradition* (Chapel Hill: University of North Carolina Press, 2020). For connections to the subprime loan crisis, see Destin Jenkins and Justin Leroy, "Introduction: The Old History of Capitalism," in *Histories of Racial Capitalism*, 2. The Movement for Black Lives (M4BL), "Vision for Black Lives," 2015–16, accessed August 18, 2023.

19 Testimony of Michael Smith (an alias) in *Arson-for-Hire: Hearings Before the Permanent Subcommittee on Investigations of the Committee on Governmental Affairs, U.S. Senate* (Washington, DC: U.S. Government Printing Office, 1978), 11. Zenia Kish and Justin Leroy, "Bonded Life:

Technologies of Racial Finance from Slave Insurance to Philanthrocapital," *Cultural Studies* 29, no. 5–6 (2015): 630–51.
20 The Red Krayola and Lora Logic, "Born in Flames," by Art & Language and Mayo Thompson, Rough Trade Records, 1980.

One: The Crisis of Insurance and the Insuring of the Crisis

1 John Bainbridge, *Biography of an Idea: The Story of Mutual Fire and Casualty Insurance* (Garden City, NY: Doubleday, 1952), 16.
2 Quoted in *Take This Hammer*, directed by Richard O. Moore, first broadcast February 4, 1964, by KQED for National Educational Television, https://www.youtube.com/watch?v=J9UG9nJ2E9U (accessed June 23, 2024).
3 "GAB in Watts," Folder: General Adjustment Bureau, Box 3, Series 5: Correspondence with Insurance Agencies, Hughes Panel, RG220, LBJ.
4 For the GAB quotation, see "GAB in Watts." The Scranton quotation can be found in Robert B. Semple Jr., "Study Is Started on Riot Insurance," *New York Times*, August 23, 1967. The interview tally is from Hughes Panel, *Meeting the Insurance Crisis of Our Cities*, 161.
5 "Hailed" is from Janet Abu-Lughod, *Race, Space, and Riots in Chicago, New York, and Los Angeles* (New York: Oxford University Press, 2007), 4. Otto Kerner et al., *Report of the National Advisory Commission on Civil Disorders* (New York: Bantam Books, 1968), 1. The characterization of LBJ's response is from Elizabeth Hinton, *From the War on Poverty to the War on Crime: The Making of Mass Incarceration in America* (Cambridge, MA: Harvard University Press, 2016), 127. See also Julian E. Zelizer, "Introduction to the 2016 Edition," *The Kerner Report: The National Advisory Commission on Civil Disorders*, new ed. (1968; Princeton, NJ: Princeton University Press, 2016), xiii–xxxvi.

Recent studies of the War on Crime have found in Johnson's law-and-order liberalism— including the Kerner recommendations that he did ultimately support—an origin point for mass incarceration. Naomi Murakawa, *The First Civil Right: How Liberals Built Prison America* (New York: Oxford University Press, 2014); Steven M. Gillon, *Separate and Unequal: The Kerner Commission and the Unraveling of American Liberalism* (New York: Basic Books, 2018); Stuart Schrader, *Badges Without Borders: How Global Counterinsurgency Transformed American Policing* (Oakland: University of California Press, 2019), 4–5; and Hinton, *From the War on Poverty to the War on Crime*.
6 As panel staffer Herbert Denenberg slyly noted, "You may wish to speculate on the reasons for the contrast between the near-record speed in implementing the Hughes Panel Report and the fate of the Kerner Commission proposals." Herbert S. Denenberg, "Meeting the Insurance Crisis of Our Cities: An Industry in Revolution," *Insurance Law Journal* 4 (1970): 207.

The quotation describing the formation of the separate panel is from Hughes Panel, *Meeting the Insurance Crisis of Our Cities*, ii. The quote from Richard Hughes can be found in Mark Krasovic, *The Newark Frontier: Community Action in the Great Society* (Chicago: University of Chicago Press, 2016), 153.
7 "City's Riot Insurance Canceled, Councilman Wants Investigation," *Philadelphia Inquirer*, August 19, 1967, 1; Lawrence H. Geller, "Fear of Riots Causes Insurance Firms to Cancel Many Policies," *Philadelphia Tribune*, August 22, 1967, 1; "Riot-Area Insurance Costs Doubled," *Philadelphia Inquirer*, August 23, 1967, 6; Harvey D. Shapiro, *Fire Insurance and the Inner City* (New York: New York City Rand Institute, 1971), 14.
8 Kenneth Jackson, *Crabgrass Frontier: The Suburbanization of the United States* (New York: Oxford University Press, 1985), Arnold Hirsch, *Making the Second Ghetto: Race and Housing in Chicago, 1940–1960* (Chicago: University of Chicago Press, 1998); Thomas Sugrue, *Origins of the Urban Crisis: Race and Inequality in Postwar Detroit* (Princeton, NJ: Princeton University Press, 2005).

9 "Too Many Expensive Fires Cause School Board to Lose Insurance," *Philadelphia Tribune*, December 13, 1969, 36.
10 The quote is from the Merritt Committee in 1910–11 and can be found in Mark Tebeau, *Eating Smoke: Fire in Urban America, 1800–1950* (Baltimore: Johns Hopkins University Press, 2003), 248. On fire and indemnity more generally, see, in addition to the Tebeau study, Daniel Immerwahr, "All That Is Solid Bursts into Flame: Capitalism and Fire in the Nineteenth-Century United States," *Past & Present* (2024); Stephen J. Pyne, *Fire in America: A Cultural History of Wildland and Rural Fire* (Princeton, NJ: Princeton University Press, 1982); and *Between Two Fires: A Fire History of Contemporary America* (Tucson: University of Arizona Press, 2015).
11 For the HUD quotation, see Henry B. Schechter, Statement Before the Hughes Panel, September 14, 1967, p. 2, Folder: Panel Meeting – Sept. 14, 1967, Box 1, Series 1: Program Planning Records, Records of the National Advisory Commission on Civil Disorders, Insurance Panel (Hughes Panel), RG220, LBJ. See also Richard F. Syron, *An Analysis of the Collapse of the Normal Market for Fire Insurance in Substandard Urban Core Areas* (Boston: Federal Reserve Bank of Boston, 1972), 18. George R. Smith, "Documents for FHA Loans," *Bankers' Magazine*, May 1936, 418.
12 For the "pit states" quotation, see Caley Horan, *Insurance Era: Risk, Governance, and the Privatization of Security in Postwar America* (Chicago: University of Chicago Press, 2021), 7–8, and Horan's "Actuarial Age: Insurance and the Emergence of Neoliberalism in the Postwar United States" (PhD diss., University of Minnesota, 2011), 163.

    Single-line insurance companies became the norm in the U.S. market for a number of reasons. Specialized companies were easier for state insurance departments to regulate and tax. They also reflected a belief that keeping companies specialized would increase their chances of solvency. See John D. Long and Davis W. Gregg, *Property and Liability Insurance Handbook* (Homewood, IL: Irwin, 1965), 734–36, 985, and Kenneth J. Meier, *The Political Economy of Regulation: The Case of Insurance* (Albany: State University of New York Press, 1988), 9. On the growth of multi-line policies, along with insurers' claims to be exempt from the Fair Housing Act, see Stephen M. Dane, "Application of the Federal Fair Housing Act to Homeowners Insurance," in *Insurance Redlining: Disinvestment, Reinvestment, and the Evolving Role of Financial Institutions*, ed. Gregory D. Squires (Washington, DC: Urban Institute Press, 1997), 27–35. For "shackles" quotation, see Federal Insurance Administration, "Full Insurance Availability: Report of the Federal Insurance Administration" (1974), 22.
13 Gelvin Stevenson, *Fire Insurance: Its Nature and Dynamics* (National Fire Prevention and Control Administration, 1978), 14.
14 Bainbridge, *Biography of an Idea*, 314; Stevenson, *Fire Insurance: Its Nature and Dynamics*, 14–15; FIA, "Full Insurance Availability," 22–23. The figures are from Long and Gregg, *Property and Liability Insurance Handbook*, 732.
15 FIA, "Full Insurance Availability," 23.
16 The racially stratified insurance market was one constitutive element of a broader "infrastructural investment of whiteness" that defined the postwar metropolis. See Destin Jenkins, *The Bonds of Inequality: Debt and the Making of the American City* (Chicago: University of Chicago Press, 2021). For the "market of last resort" quote, see Federal Insurance Administration, *Insurance Crisis in Urban America* (Washington, DC: U.S. Government Printing Office, 1978), 3. The 400 percent figure can be found in agent and broker responses to questionnaires: Folder: Agents and Brokers, Box 1, Series 12: Responses to Questionnaires, Hughes Panel, RG220, LBJ.
17 "Wholesale" quotation is from FIA, "Full Insurance Availability," 24. Aetna Bulletin No. 103, 1964, Folder: 10/29/67 – 11/4/67, Box 3, Series 3: Chronological Correspondence File, Hughes Panel, RG220, LBJ (emphasis mine). Travelers Interoffice Memorandum, August 10, 1964, Box 7, Series 12: Responses to Questionnaires, Hughes Panel, RG220, LBJ.
18 New York Urban Coalition, "Fire Insurance: A Crisis for New York's Neighborhoods" (1978), 5. Sylvia Downer, in *Hearings Before the President's National Advisory Panel on Insurance in Riot-Affected Areas* [Hughes Panel], November 8, 1967 (Washington, DC: U.S. Government Printing Office, 1968), 3.

19 FIA, "Full Insurance Availability," 24. James Tate to David O. Maxwell, April 8, 1967, Folder: Questionnaires—City Officials Mayors, Box 2, Series 12: Responses to Questionnaires, Hughes Panel, RG220, LBJ. The Newark agent: Stephen S. Thomas, statement in *Hearings Before the President's National Advisory Panel on Insurance in Riot-Affected Areas*, November 8, 1967, 35. New York Urban Coalition, "Fire Insurance: A Crisis," 37.

20 Renter's insurance was developed in its modern, standardized form in the 1970s. "Cutting the Redline: Insurance Progress," *Northwest Bronx Neighborhood Action* 4, no. 1 (1977). On race and rent, see N.D.B. Connolly, *A World More Concrete: Real Estate and the Remaking of Jim Crow South Florida* (Chicago: University of Chicago Press, 2014), 7, 98.

21 My approach to the literature on the urban crisis—and the title of this chapter—is deeply indebted to Stuart Hall et al., *Policing the Crisis: Mugging, the State, and Law and Order* (New York: Palgrave Macmillan, 1978). Beryl Satter makes a similar observation about the uprisings and urban crisis: see *Family Properties: How the Struggle over Race and Real Estate Transformed Chicago and Urban America* (New York: Picador, 2010), 459. See also Sugrue, *Origins of the Urban Crisis*; Scott Kurashige, *The Shifting Grounds of Race: Black and Japanese Americans in the Making of Multiethnic Los Angeles* (Princeton, NJ: Princeton University Press, 2008); Amanda Seligman, *Block by Block: Neighborhoods and Public Policy on Chicago's West Side* (Chicago: University of Chicago Press, 2005); and David Freund, *Colored Property: State Policy and White Racial Politics in Suburban America* (Chicago: University of Chicago Press, 2007).

22 "Text of the Moynihan Memorandum on the Status of Negroes," *New York Times*, printed March 1, 1970 (first publicized in January 1970), 69. The Law Enforcement Assistance Administration report: Kendall Moll, *Arson, Vandalism and Violence: Law Enforcement Problems Affecting Fire Departments* (Washington, DC: United States Department of Justice, 1974), 14. On this conflation within the historiography, see Satter, *Family Properties*, 459, and Barry Goetz, *On the Frontlines of the Welfare State: How the Fire Service and Police Shape Social Problems* (New York: Routledge, 2017), 9. Harold DeRienzo, *The Concept of Community: Lessons from the Bronx* (Milan: IPOC, 2008), 208; also Jacobson, interview by author, September 18, 2017, New Haven, CT.

23 Stanford Sesser, "Complaints of Bias in Granting Insurance Spur Congressional, State Investigations," *Wall Street Journal*, October 10, 1967, 34.

24 Seymour E. Smith, statement in *Hearings Before the President's National Advisory Panel on Insurance in Riot-Affected Areas*, November 9, 1967, 221–22.

25 Ibid. T. L. Wenck to Herbert Denenberg, October 31, 1967, Folder: 10/29/67–11/4/67, Box 3, Series 3: Chronological Correspondence File, Hughes Panel, RG220, LBJ.

26 Long and Gregg, *Property and Liability Insurance Handbook*, 985; Andrew Tobias, *The Invisible Bankers: Everything the Insurance Industry Never Wanted You to Know* (New York: Linden Press, 1982), 17; James Brady, "Arson, Urban Economy, and Organized Crime: The Case of Boston," *Social Problems* 31, no. 1 (1983): 13.

27 Harlow Unger, "Insurance Industry Faces $715m Bill from US Race Riots," London *Times*, July 30, 1967. As Clyde Woods has written, Hurricane Betsy was nicknamed "Billion-Dollar Betsy" and was thought to be the most damaging natural disaster in U.S. history up to that point. Clyde Woods with Jordan T. Camp and Laura Pulido, eds., *Development Drowned and Reborn: The Blues and Bourbon Restorations in Post-Katrina New Orleans* (Athens: University of Georgia Press, 2017), 181–87. "Official Transcript of Proceedings Before the National Advisory Commission on Civil Disorders: The Advisory Panel on Insurance in Riot-Affected Areas," September 14, 1967, 46, Folder: Transcripts, Sept. 14, Box 1, Series 2: Minutes of Meetings, Aug.–Nov. 1967, Hughes Panel, RG220, LBJ. National Association of Insurance Commissioners, Minutes from Meeting of September 6, 1967, p. 5, Folder: NAIC, Box 1, Series 1: Program Planning Records, Hughes Panel, RG220, LBJ.

28 Herb Jaffe, "No Insurance . . . Ghetto Stores Quit," Newark *Star-Ledger*, October 29, 1967, 12.

29 "Official Transcript of Proceedings Before the National Advisory Commission on Civil Disorders," September 14, 1967, pp. 87–88, Folder: Transcripts, Sept. 14, Box 1, Series 2: Minutes of

Meetings, Aug.–Nov. 1967, Hughes Panel, RG220, LBJ. The aerial photography quotation is from Insurance Information Institute, "GAB Releases Aerial Photographic Maps of Areas Damaged in Detroit Disorders," August 10, 1967, Folder: Insurance Information Institute, Box 3, Series 5: Correspondence with Insurance Agencies, Hughes Panel, RG220, LBJ. See also General Adjustment Bureau, "Report No. Four," July 28, 1967, Folder: General Adjustment Bureau, Box 3, Series 5: Correspondence with Insurance Agencies, Hughes Panel, RG220, LBJ. James C. Scott, *Seeing Like a State: How Certain Schemes to Improve the Human Condition Have Failed* (New Haven, CT: Yale University Press, 1998). Thanks to Joanne Meyerowitz for illuminating this connection.

30 Hughes Panel, "Meeting the Insurance Crisis of Our Cities," 4. Quotation is from Dykhouse, statement in *Hearings Before the President's National Advisory Panel on Insurance in Riot-Affected Areas*, November 8, 1967, 72.

31 Robert Works, "Whatever's *FAIR*—Adequacy, Equity, and the Underwriting Prerogative in Property Insurance Markets," *National Insurance Law Review Service* (1977): 260.48.

32 On insurance, history, and futurity, see Jonathan Levy, *Freaks of Fortune: The Emerging World of Capitalism and Risk* (Cambridge, MA: Harvard University Press, 2012); Dan Bouk, *How Our Days Became Numbered: Risk and the Rise of the Statistical Individual* (Chicago: University of Chicago Press, 2015); Horan, *Insurance Era*; Ian Baucom, *Spectres of the Atlantic: Finance Capital, Slavery, and the Philosophy of History* (Durham, NC: Duke University Press, 2005); Nikolas Rose, "A Risk of Madness," in *Embracing Risk: The Changing Culture of Insurance and Responsibility*, ed. Tom Baker and Jonathan Simon (Chicago: University of Chicago Press, 2002), 209–37. For more on the history of insurance in American capitalism, see Hannah Farber, *Underwriters of the United States: How Insurance Shaped the American Founding* (Chapel Hill: University of North Carolina Press, 2021), and Nate Holdren, *Injury Impoverished: Workplace Accidents, Capitalism, and Law in the Progressive Era* (New York: Cambridge University Press, 2020); Melinda Cooper, *Family Values: Between Neoliberalism and the New Social Conservatism* (Brooklyn: Zone Books, 2017), chapter 5.

Note that this book's focus is the property insurance industry, rather than the life insurance industry. Whereas African American life insurance companies like North Carolina Mutual Life Insurance Company thrived during the twentieth century, there was no Black-owned analogue in the property insurance sector.

It is noteworthy that the anti-war movement was not a concern of the Hughes Panel, even though it was reaching its heyday in 1967. The Travelers quotation is from Smith, statement in *Hearings Before the President's National Advisory Panel on Insurance in Riot-Affected Areas*, November 8, 1967, 221. Bentley quotation: "Insurers Expecting New Riots," *Atlanta Constitution*, September 3, 1967.

The questions posed here build upon the work of Destin Jenkins and Keeanga-Yamahtta Taylor. Jenkins, *The Bonds of Inequality*; Taylor, *Race for Profit: How Banks and the Real Estate Industry Undermined Black Homeownership* (Chapel Hill: University of North Carolina Press, 2019).

33 Although the Hughes Panel (like the Kerner Commission) was solely concerned with Black uprisings, Puerto Rican and other Latinx uprisings were also erupting across U.S. cities in the 1960s and later decades. Pedro Regalado, "Urban Uprisings, 1960s–1970s," in *50 Events That Shaped Latino History: An Encyclopedia of the American Mosaic*, ed. Lilia Fernández (Santa Barbara: ABC-CLIO, 2018).

34 National Association of Insurance Commissioners, Minutes from Meeting of September 6, 1967, p. 4, Folder: NAIC, Box 1, Series 1: Program Planning Records, Hughes Panel, RG220, LBJ. "Companies Meet over Riot Losses," *Best's Weekly*, July 31, 1967. California Commissioner Richard Roddis, statement in *Hearings Before the President's National Advisory Panel on Insurance in Riot-Affected Areas*, November 8, 1967, 52.

35 "Riots and Civil Commotion: Insurance Developments Since 1914," *The Spectator*, October 1967, 82; Sam Roberts, "100 Years Later, Scar Remains from a Strike's Fatal Legacy in Manhattan," *New York Times*, July 3, 2014. "Riot, Insurrection, Civil Commotion and Explosion Insurance," *The Aetna-izer*, November 1919. Wenck to Denenberg, October 31, 1967, LBJ.

36 Interview with Carrie B. Johnson by David Bliss, November 30, 1967, p. 71, Folder: Commission Interviews, Nebraska, Omaha, Box 4, Series 14: Field Interviews, Oct.–Dec. 1967, Hughes Panel, RG220, LBJ.

37 "Riot Insurance Subsidy Urged," *Sunday Times Advertiser*, August 13, 1967; H. J. Maidenberg, "Insurers Urge US Cooperation on 'Riot-Prone Area' Coverage," *New York Times*, August 15, 1967.
38 On Hughes: Krasovic, *The Newark Frontier*, 153; Michael J. Birkner, Donald Linky, and Peter Mickulas, eds., *The Governors of New Jersey: Biographical Essays* (New Brunswick, NJ: Rutgers University Press, 2014), 293–97. On the panel's tenant lacuna: Hughes Panel, *Meeting the Insurance Crisis of Our Cities*, 162. For the reinsurance quotation, see William B. Ross, "Friend or Foe—Federal Riot Reinsurance in Perspective," address given on January 23, 1969, DLIA.
39 John R. Lewis, "A Critical Review of the Federal Riot Reinsurance System," *Journal of Risk and Insurance* 38, no. 1 (1971): 30. Staffer quotation is from Denenberg, "Meeting the Insurance Crisis of Our Cities: An Industry in Revolution," 207. For Wozencraft quotation, see "Official Transcript of Proceedings Before the National Advisory Commission on Civil Disorders," September 14, 1967, p. 103, Folder: Transcripts, Sept. 14, Box 1, Series 2: Minutes of Meetings, Aug.–Nov. 1967, Hughes Panel, RG220, LBJ.
40 "Inquiry Suspects Sabotage," *Michigan Chronicle*, November 4, 1967, 1.
41 Richard Hughes, Press Release, October 26, 1967, p. 6, Folder: 10/21/67–10/28/67, Box 3, Series 3: Chronological Correspondence File, Hughes Panel, RG220, LBJ.
42 A. A. Roberts, "A. A. Roberts, Reliance Head, Eyes Turmoil of Today, Tomorrow's Tempo," *National Underwriter*, 47.
43 The analyst quotation is from Works, "Whatever's *FAIR*," 260.3. See also Hughes Panel, "Meeting the Insurance Crisis of Our Cities." For the new underwriting prohibitions, see "The Central City Insurance Crisis: Experience Under the Urban Property Protection and Reinsurance Act of 1968," *University of Chicago Law Review* 38, no. 3 (1971): 672. Insurance Information Institute, "Residual Market Property Plans: From Markets of Last Resort to Markets of First Choice," 2014.
44 "Cornerstone" quotation: Hughes Panel, *Meeting the Insurance Crisis of Our Cities*, 1. For the LBJ quote, see Paul Hathaway, "Panel Reports to Johnson: Riot-Area Insurance Urged," *Washington Star*, January 28, 1968, A2. Betty Furness, statement in *Hearings Before the President's National Advisory Panel on Insurance in Riot-Affected Areas*, November 8, 1967, 31.
45 "Insurance in the Ghetto," *Newsday*, January 30, 1968, 1.
    Conversations with Daniel Martinez HoSang helped me articulate the counterinsurgent aspects of the program. See also Taylor, *Race for Profit*, and Robert L. Allen, *Black Awakening in Capitalist America: An Analytic History* (New York: Doubleday, 1969).
46 "The Central City Insurance Crisis," 673. Works, "Whatever's *FAIR*," 260.52, 260.9.
47 As a public-private hybrid, the program lends support to recent studies of neoliberalism that buck against its easy equation with privatization and instead foreground the ways the state was mobilized to the benefit of market interests since the 1970s. See Quinn Slobodian, *Globalists: The End of Empire and the Birth of Neoliberalism* (Cambridge, MA: Harvard University Press, 2018), 6, and Brent Cebul, Lily Geismer, and Mason B. Williams, eds., *Shaped by the State: Toward a New Political History of the Twentieth Century* (Chicago: University of Chicago Press, 2019). For more on the deep history of the public-private partnership, see Brent Cebul, *Illusions of Progress: Business, Poverty, and Liberalism in the American Century* (Philadelphia: University of Pennsylvania Press, 2023). Works, "Whatever's *FAIR*," 260.84–85.
48 It should be noted that the Urban Property Protection and Reinsurance Act did not fulfill all of the ambitions of the insurance lobby. Tax deferrals on insurers' surplus funds, though recommended by the Hughes Panel's report, never made it into the legislation. John Thornton, "The Impact of the FAIR Plans on the Urban Core Insurance Problem in the United States" (PhD diss., Georgia State University, 1974), 348. Roberts, "A. A. Roberts, Reliance Head, Eyes Turmoil of Today," 46–47. New York Urban Coalition, "Fire Insurance: A Crisis," 12–20.
49 For the "boon" quotation, see "The Central City Insurance Crisis," 678. Federal Insurance Administration, "Insurance Crisis in Urban America," 6. For GAO quote, see Deborah Orin, "Insurance Plan May Spur Arson," *New York Post*, June 13, 1978.
50 As this book went to press, the Federal Reserve of Chicago published a longitudinal study confirming the FAIR plans' deleterious effects. Ingrid Gould Ellen, et al., "The Bronx Is Burning:

Urban Disinvestment Effects of the Fair Access to Insurance Requirements," Federal Reserve Bank of Chicago, December 16, 2024. Federal Insurance Administration, "Insurance Crisis in Urban America," 18. See also Michael Jacobson, "The Enigmatic Crime: A Study of Arson in New York City" (PhD diss., City University of New York, 1985), 131. Juanita Gear, Statement Before the Subcommittee on Insurance, *Flood Insurance and Crime and Riot Reinsurance: Hearing Before the Subcommittee on Insurance of the Committee on Banking, Housing, and Urban Affairs, U.S. Senate* (Washington, DC: U.S. Government Printing Office, 1980), February 28, 1980, 317.

51 Robin D. G. Kelley describes public transportation in 1940s Birmingham as having "no fixed dividing line" with "black and white riders . . . continually contesting adjustments to what was a fluid boundary," in *Race Rebels: Culture, Politics, and the Black Working Class* (New York: Free Press, 1994), 60. For Chicago data, see Gear, Statement Before the Senate Subcommittee on Insurance, 316. FIA, *Insurance Crisis*, 36. "Riot-prone," like "inner city," signifies race while disavowing it. Bench Ansfield, "Unsettling 'Inner City': Liberal Protestantism and the Postwar Origins of a Keyword in Urban Studies," *Antipode* 50, no. 5 (2018): 1166–85.

52 On insurance and race, see Benjamin Wiggins, *Calculating Race: Racial Discrimination in Risk Assessment* (New York: Oxford University Press, 2020); Horan, *Insurance Era*; and Khalil Gibran Muhammad, *The Condemnation of Blackness: Race, Crime, and the Making of Modern Urban America* (Cambridge, MA: Harvard University Press, 2010).

Building on Taylor's work on "predatory inclusion," which she describes as "the hope . . . that property ownership could tame the Black rebellion coursing through cities across the country," this book shifts from her focus on homeownership to the rental real estate market and the race-based vicissitudes of insurability. It's important to note that *predation* was not the governing logic of the insurance programs chronicled herein. Their purpose was not profit, per se, but rather the protection of property assets. As do the programs highlighted in Taylor's work, the FAIR plan shows how even after the formal renunciation of redlining practices, race continued to structure the market as a material force. Importantly, both sets of programs originated in the same omnibus legislation, the HUD Act of 1968. It is also worth noting that the insurance industry long considered itself exempt from the Fair Housing Act of 1968, though activist and legal attempts to apply the law to the industry met with more success during the Obama and Biden presidencies. Taylor, *Race for Profit*, 17. Squires, *Insurance Redlining*.

53 New York Property Insurance Underwriting Association, "FAIRFacts," Folder: NYPIUA Lists, Box 7, General Subject Files, 1978–1984, ASF, NYMA.

54 Emphasis mine. Charles P. Russ Jr., "Taking the Profit Out of Arson-for-Profit," Folder: NYPIUA, Box 5, General Subject Files, 1978–1984, ASF, NYMA.

55 "Official Transcript of Proceedings Before the National Advisory Commission on Civil Disorders: The Advisory Panel on Insurance in Riot-Affected Areas," September 14, 1967, 95, 70, Folder: Transcripts, Sept. 14, Box 1, Series 2: Minutes of Meetings, Aug.–Nov. 1967, Hughes Panel, RG220, LBJ.

56 For Illinois AFL-CIO quotation, see R. G. Soderstrom to Stanford Ross, November 14, 1967, Folder: Questionnaires Community Leaders and Civil Rights Organizations, Box 2, Series 12: Responses to Questionnaires, Hughes Panel, RG220, LBJ.

Absent a broader policy response to the uprisings, it is unclear whether a publicly operated insurance program would have incentivized arson. Thomas Policastro and Edwin Brown to Stanford Ross, November 3, 1967, Folder: Questionnaires Unions, Box 11, Series 12: Responses to Questionnaires, Hughes Panel, RG220, LBJ.

57 George Bernstein to Donald Stewart, March 21, 1980, submitted to the Senate Subcommittee on Insurance, Committee on Banking, Housing, and Urban Affairs, *Flood Insurance and Crime and Riot Reinsurance: Hearing Before the Subcommittee on Insurance of the Committee on Banking, Housing, and Urban Affairs, U.S. Senate* (Washington, DC: U.S. Government Printing Office, 1980), February 28, 1980, 276. For "the nation's fastest-growing counties" quotation, see Andrew W. Kahrl, *The Land Was Ours: African American Beaches from Jim Crow to the Sunbelt South* (Cambridge, MA: Harvard University Press, 2012), 213. The FIA finding was reported by George Bernstein, Statement Before the Senate Subcommittee on Insurance, Committee on Banking,

Housing, and Urban Affairs, *Flood Insurance and Crime and Riot Reinsurance: Hearing Before the Subcommittee on Insurance of the Committee on Banking, Housing, and Urban Affairs, U.S. Senate* (Washington, DC: U.S. Government Printing Office, 1980), February 28, 1980, 261, 267. Gilbert M. Gaul, *The Geography of Risk: Epic Storms, Rising Seas, and the Cost of America's Coasts* (New York: Sarah Crichton Books, 2019), 136.

58 Bernstein quote appears in Gaul, *The Geography of Risk*, 127–28; see also 136. Congressional Research Service, "Introduction to the National Flood Insurance Program," June 30, 2022, https://sgp.fas.org/crs/homesec/R44593.pdf.

59 Rebecca Elliott, *Underwater: Loss, Flood Insurance, and the Moral Economy of Climate Change in the United States* (New York: Columbia University Press, 2021), 15.

60 "The Best Insurance," Paterson *Morning Call*, August 28, 1967.

61 Tebeau, *Eating Smoke*. "Riot Insurance Company Formed," *Atlanta Daily World*, July 8, 1943, 1.

62 Insurance Information Institute, "Survival of P/C Insurance as Free Enterprise Keyed to Residual Market," May 26, 1977, Folder: FAIR Plans, DLIA.

Two: The Brownlining of the Bronx

1 Sonia Sanchez, "The Bronx Is Next," *Drama Review: TDR* 12, no. 4 (1968): 78–84.

2 Testimony and exhibits of Hedy Byrd in *Arson-for-Hire: Hearings Before the Permanent Subcommittee on Investigations of the Committee on Governmental Affairs, U.S. Senate* (Washington, DC: U.S. Government Printing Office, 1978), September 13, 1978, 156–64.

3 Ibid.

4 "Bronx Realty Protest Snuffed Out," *New York Times*, September 14, 1973, 43.

5 Ibid.

6 The question of articulation builds from Saidiya Hartman's influential query, "How does one revisit the scene of subjection without replicating the grammar of violence?" posed in "Venus in Two Acts," *Small Axe* 12, no. 2 (2008): 4. Evelyn Gonzalez, *The Bronx* (New York: Columbia University Press, 2004), chapter 3; Lloyd Ultan, *The Northern Borough: A History of the Bronx* (Bronx: Bronx County Historical Society, 2009). *Real Estate Record and Guide*, June 19, 1915, quoted in Gonzalez, *The Bronx*, 84.

7 One scholar claims that the Bronx boasts "one of the most vibrant nostalgia industries of any city in the United States." Ray Bromley, preface to *Bronx Faces and Voices: Sixteen Stories of Courage and Community*, ed. Emita Brady Hill and Janet Butler Munch (Lubbock: Texas Tech University Press, 2014), xxi; see the same source for the "egg creams" quotation. On the ghetto pastoral, see Michael Denning, *The Cultural Front: The Laboring of American Culture in the Twentieth Century* (Brooklyn: Verso, 1997), chapter 6. Lloyd Ultan and Gary Hermalyn, *The Bronx in the Innocent Years, 1890–1925* (Bronx: Bronx County Historical Society, 1991); Constance Rosenblum, *Boulevard of Dreams: Heady Times, Heartbreak, and Hope Along the Grand Concourse in the Bronx* (New York: New York University Press, 2009). For more recent histories that explicitly resist this impulse, see Peter L'Official, *Urban Legends: The South Bronx in Representation and Ruin* (Cambridge, MA: Harvard University Press, 2020); Vivian Vázquez Irizarry and Gretchen Hildebran, *Decade of Fire* (Red Nut Films, 2019); Eric Tang, *Unsettled: Cambodian Refugees in the New York City Hyperghetto* (Philadelphia: Temple University Press, 2015), 59–60; Johanna Fernández, *The Young Lords: A Radical History* (Chapel Hill: University of North Carolina Press, 2020). "Staging ground" is from Jill Jonnes, *South Bronx Rising: The Rise, Fall, and Resurrection of an American City* (New York: Fordham University Press, 2002), 4. See also Ed García Conde, "Bronx Jewish Hall of Fame Inducts 2017's Honorees," Welcome2TheBronx, December 1, 2017.

8 Demographic data is from Gonzales, *The Bronx*, 99–102. "Closed to black residents" is found in Mark Naison and Bob Gumbs, *Before the Fires: An Oral History of African American Life in the Bronx from the 1930s to the 1960s* (New York: Fordham University Press, 2016), xiii. See also Brian Purnell, "Desegregating the Jim Crow North: Racial Discrimination in the Postwar Bronx and the Fight to Integrate the Castle Hill Beach Club (1953–1973)," *Afro-Americans in New York Life and History* 33,

no. 2 (2009): 47–78. Maria Newman, "Fond Memories of the Bronx of Yore; Many of Its Natives Are Long Gone, but the Old Borough Is Not Forgotten," *New York Times*, September 15, 1992.
9 "Ravaged hulks" is found in Robert Caro, *The Power Broker: Robert Moses and the Fall of New York* (New York: Alfred A. Knopf, 1974), 893. "Largest concentration" is from Jonnes, *South Bronx Rising*, 118. Gonzalez, *The Bronx*, 109–15.
10 For Tancl quotation, see Thomas Glynn, "The South Bronx: What Went Down Should Come Up," *Neighborhood: The Journal for City Preservation* 5, no. 2 (August 1982): 12. Robert Gumbs, transcript of an oral history conducted by Mark Naison et al. on October 1, 2015, Bronx African American History Project. Naison and Gumbs, *Before the Fires*, xii; Gonzalez, *The Bronx*, 114–15.
11 Office of the New York State Comptroller, "An Economic Snapshot of the Bronx," July 2018, 2. Annemarie Sammartino, *Freedomland: Co-op City and the Story of New York* (Ithaca, NY: Cornell University Press, 2022), chapter 2. "Vacuum cleaner" line is from Paul Brant in 1971, quoted in Gonzalez, *The Bronx*, 149. On Moses's support, see Caro, *The Power Broker*, 1151.
12 Marshall Berman, *All That Is Solid Melts into Air: The Experience of Modernity* (New York: Penguin Books, 1982), 325–26. Robert Fitch, *The Assassination of New York* (New York: Verso, 1993), 106–7; Joe Flood, *The Fires: How a Computer Formula, Big Ideas, and the Best of Intentions Burned Down New York City—and Determined the Future of Cities* (New York: Riverhead Books, 2010), 156; Miriam Greenberg, *Branding New York: How a City in Crisis Was Sold to the World* (New York: Routledge, 2008), 100. See also Joshua B. Freeman, *Working-Class New York: Life and Labor Since World War II* (New York: New Press, 2000), chapter 9. Richard J. Devine et al., "Where the Lender Looks First: A Case Study of Mortgage Disinvestment in Bronx County, 1960–1970," National Urban League, 1973; Carolyn McLaughlin, *South Bronx Battles: Stories of Resistance, Resilience, and Renewal* (Oakland: University of California Press, 2019), 66–7; Gonzalez, *The Bronx*, 111.
13 Kim Phillips-Fein, *Fear City: New York's Fiscal Crisis and the Rise of Austerity Politics* (New York: Metropolitan Books, 2017), 228; see also 73–88, 206–7. Freeman, *Working-Class New York*, 99–287; David Harvey, *A Brief History of Neoliberalism* (New York: Oxford University Press, 2005); Flood, *The Fires*, chapters 14–15; Jonnes, *South Bronx Rising*, 286–87, 298–99, 304–5; Deborah Wallace and Rodrick Wallace, *A Plague on Your Houses: How New York Was Burned Down and National Public Health Crumbled* (New York: Verso, 1998), 7.
14 See Roger Starr, "Making New York Smaller," *New York Times Magazine*, November 14, 1976. See also Tang, *Unsettled*, 59–60; Greenberg, *Branding New York*, 143. As the urban epidemiologists Deborah Wallace and Rodrick Wallace write in their oft-cited book on the fire cuts, "Roger Starr's ideology of sick communities did not become policy until 1976.... Eventually, the outcry from black communities forced him from office, but by that time planned shrinkage had long been implemented and made part of municipal government culture." Wallace and Wallace, *A Plague on Your Houses*, 25. The salience of this explanatory framework is enduring, as evidenced, for example, by a related subplot in Garth Risk Hallberg's novel *City on Fire* (New York: Vintage, 2015).
15 David Harvey, "Neoliberalism as Creative Destruction," *Annals of the American Academy of Political and Social Science* 610, no. 1 (2007): 21–44. The Section 8 figure is from Ford Foundation, untitled internal report, April 23, 1980, Folder: Ford Foundation 1978–Jun 80, Box 47, Edward Joseph Logue Papers, Accession 1985-M-009, YMA. The quotation can be found in Nicholas Dagen Bloom and Matthew Gordon Lasner, "The Decentralized Network," in *Affordable Housing in New York: The People, Places, and Policies That Transformed a City*, ed. Nicholas Dagen Bloom and Matthew Gordon Lasner (Princeton, NJ: Princeton University Press, 2016), 248.
16 Quoted in David Black, "Free-Fire Zone," *New Times*, July 11, 1975.
17 Robert B. Cooper to the Hughes Panel, October 27, 1967, Folder: 10/21/67–10/28/67, Box 3, Series 3: Chronological Correspondence File, Records of the National Advisory Commission on Civil Disorders, Insurance Panel (Hughes Panel), RG220, LBJ.

Unlike fire insurance, problems of auto insurance unavailability are managed in some states through assigned-risk plans, which require that insurers offer insurance for *all* high-risk drivers. State of New York Insurance Department, "Fire Insurance in Congested Areas: A Report to Governor Nelson A. Rockefeller," March 7, 1967, 18–20.

18 Harvey D. Shapiro, *Fire Insurance and the Inner City* (New York City Rand Institute, 1971), 18–20.
19 Judith Stein, *Pivotal Decade: How the United States Traded Factories for Finance in the Seventies* (New Haven, CT: Yale University Press, 2010); Benjamin Holtzman, *The Long Crisis: New York City and the Path to Neoliberalism* (New York: Oxford University Press, 2021); Julilly Kohler-Hausmann, *Getting Tough: Welfare and Imprisonment in 1970s America* (Princeton, NJ: Princeton University Press, 2017); Gary Gerstle, *The Rise and Fall of the Neoliberal Order: America and the World in the Free Market Era* (New York: Oxford University Press, 2022); Annelise Orleck, *Storming Caesar's Palace: How Black Mothers Fought Their Own War on Poverty* (Boston: Beacon Press, 2005); Bethany Moreton, *To Serve God and Wal-Mart: The Making of Christian Free Enterprise* (Cambridge, MA: Harvard University Press, 2010); Alice O'Connor, *Poverty Knowledge: Social Science, Social Policy, and the Poor in Twentieth-Century U.S. History* (Princeton, NJ: Princeton University Press, 2001). Michael Denning, "Wageless Life," *New Left Review* 66 (2010): 79–97; Ruth Wilson Gilmore, *Golden Gulag: Prisons, Surplus, Crisis, and Opposition in Globalizing California* (Berkeley: University of California Press, 2007); Elizabeth Hinton, *From the War on Poverty to the War on Crime: The Making of Mass Incarceration in America* (Cambridge, MA: Harvard University Press, 2016).
20 As Jenkins, Klein, and Winant have all shown, such tendencies within the welfare state have been visible since the dawn of the New Deal. What distinguishes the 1970s is the disappearance of any pretense of redistributive intent. On security and the welfare state, see Jennifer Klein, *For All These Rights: Business, Labor, and the Shaping of America's Public-Private Welfare State* (Princeton, NJ: Princeton University Press, 2003); Destin Jenkins, *The Bonds of Inequality: Debt and the Making of the American City* (Chicago: University of Chicago Press, 2021); and Gabriel Winant, *The Next Shift: The Fall of Industry and the Rise of Health Care in Rust Belt America* (Cambridge, MA: Harvard University Press, 2021). On safety and the carceral state, see Christina B. Hanhardt, *Safe Space: Gay Neighborhood History and the Politics of Violence* (Durham, NC: Duke University Press, 2013), and Gilmore, *Golden Gulag*, 178.
21 For the Massachusetts FAIR plan quotation, see Insurance Information Institute, "Government Retreat from Urban Areas Draws Rebuke at FAIR Plan Meeting," February 25, 1976, Folder: FAIR Plans, DLIA. Hughes Panel, "Meeting the Insurance Crisis of Our Cities," 1.
22 "N.Y. Pool to Begin 17-Day Binder System Jan. 25," *Insurance Advocate*, January 25, 1969, 5; Frank Hatfield, memorandum, April 23, 1971, in "Reports on FAIR Plan Operations 1971," DLIA; New York Property Insurance Underwriting Association, "About NYPIUA," accessed June 6, 2019, http://www.nypiua.com/history.html; Shapiro, *Fire Insurance and the Inner City*, 2, 18, 21; New York Insurance Department, *1968 Annual Report*, 33. The 25 percent figure reflects the NYPIUA's share of fire and extended coverage policies, not homeowners insurance. Federal Insurance Administration, "Full Insurance Availability: Report of the Federal Insurance Administration" (1974), 30.
23 Gelvin Stevenson, *Fire Insurance: Its Nature and Dynamics* (National Fire Prevention and Control Administration, 1978), 129. For 1976 data: General Accounting Office, *Arson-for-Profit: More Could Be Done to Reduce It* (Washington, DC: U.S. Government Printing Office, 1978), Appendix I, 3. The 1979 data and the following quotation are from Gloria Jimenez, Statement Before the Senate Subcommittee on Insurance, Committee on Banking, Housing, and Urban Affairs, *Flood Insurance and Crime and Riot Reinsurance: Hearing Before the Subcommittee on Insurance of the Committee on Banking, Housing, and Urban Affairs, U.S. Senate* (Washington, DC: U.S. Government Printing Office, 1980), February 28, 1980, 23.
24 Although the Bronx became a prime market for insurance policies designed for "riot-prone" neighborhoods, the borough did not experience much unrest during New York's 1964 uprising, the decade's largest in the city. And the New York City uprising in the wake of the assassination of Martin Luther King Jr. was muted compared to those in other cities, with the Bronx left largely undamaged. Michael W. Flamm, *In the Heat of the Summer: The New York Riots of 1964 and the War on Crime* (Philadelphia: University of Pennsylvania Press, 2017); Clay Risen, *A Nation on Fire: America in the Wake of the King Assassination* (Hoboken, NJ: John Wiley & Sons, 2009), 58–63; Martin Gansberg, "Damage Here Since Slaying of Dr. King Is Near '64 Riot Level," *New

York Times, April 10, 1968, 35; and Martin Gansberg, "More Blazes Set in Brownsville," New York Times, April 11, 1968, 36.

The NYPIUA was the largest property insurer in New York City as a whole, and its greatest losses were concentrated in the Bronx. Bronx District Attorney Arson Unit, Quarterly Report, October 1, 1977–December 31, 1977, p. 2, Folder: Arson Strike Force, August 28, 1978–December 31, 1978, Box 12, General Subject Files, 1978–1984, ASF, NYMA; Robert Abrams to Clarence Kelley, June 6, 1975, Folder: Fr. Neil A. Connolly, Box 1, JJ, Harry T. Johnson Collection, LLL; Shapiro, *Fire Insurance and the Inner City*, 18–22. Juanita Gear, Statement Before the Senate Subcommittee on Insurance, *Flood Insurance and Crime and Riot Reinsurance: Hearing Before the Subcommittee on Insurance of the Committee on Banking, Housing, and Urban Affairs, U.S. Senate* (Washington, DC: U.S. Government Printing Office, 1980), February 28, 1980, 316. "Brokers reported" is from Shapiro, *Fire Insurance and the Inner City*, 8; see also New York Insurance Department, *Annual Report of the Superintendent of Insurance to the New York Legislature Covering the Calendar Year 1967* (New York, 1968), 245.

25 Hetty Fox, transcript of an oral history conducted by Mark Naison et al., October 1, 2015, Bronx African American History Project. For redline "fever" quotation, see New York Urban Coalition, "Fire Insurance: A Crisis for New York's Neighborhoods" (1978), 6.

The "voluntary market" was made up of companies "at liberty to choose with whom they will do business," while the FAIR plan was forbidden from considering locational or environmental factors when determining whether to cover a given risk. See New York Urban Coalition, "Fire Insurance: A Crisis," 3. Juanita Gear to Donald Stewart, March 3, 1980, submitted to the Senate Subcommittee on Insurance, Committee on Banking, Housing, and Urban Affairs, *Flood Insurance and Crime and Riot Reinsurance: Hearing Before the Subcommittee on Insurance of the Committee on Banking, Housing, and Urban Affairs, U.S. Senate* (Washington, DC: U.S. Government Printing Office, 1980), February 28, 1980, 304. For Bronx data, see Alan S. Oser, "Fire Risk Pool for Slum Aid Now Citywide," *New York Times*, October 25, 1970, R1. Robert Abrams, borough president of the Bronx, "The Insurance Industry: It Redlines Too," January 9, 1978, 2.

26 Abrams, "The Insurance Industry," 8. For the NWBCCC quotation, see "Insurance Redlining: Eight Danger Signs," *Northwest Bronx Neighborhood Action*, August 31, 1978, 4. Greenberg, *Branding New York*, chapters 2 and 5; Phillips-Fein, *Fear City*, 55–56; Bench Ansfield, "The Broken Windows of the Bronx: Putting the Theory in Its Place," *American Quarterly* 72, no. 1 (2020): 103–27. Fordham University Institute for Urban Studies, "Industrial Activity in the Inner City: A Case Study of the South Bronx," April 1981, p. 47, Box 14, JJ, Harry T. Johnson Collection, LLL.

27 Michael Javen Fortner, *Black Silent Majority: The Rockefeller Drug Laws and the Politics of Punishment* (Cambridge, MA: Harvard University Press, 2015). The Federal Insurance Administration, which nominally oversaw the FAIR plans at the federal level, also offered a crime insurance program, but it was remarkably unpopular and was eventually phased out. Its failure was likely a result of the exorbitant expense its target customers were already incurring for basic fire insurance. Kenneth J. Meier, *The Political Economy of Regulation: The Case of Insurance* (Albany: State University of New York Press, 1988), 42.

28 The 40 percent figure is from Fordham University Institute for Urban Studies, "Industrial Activity in the Inner City," 73. For the Lederman quotations, see Abrams, "The Insurance Industry," Appendix F. People's Development Corporation, "Neighborhood Revitalization Strategy," 29–30, Folder: People's Development Corporation, Box 50, Edward Joseph Logue Papers, Accession 1985-M-009, YMA.

29 Michael Stern, "Coalition of Bronx Leaders Drafts Job-Creation Program to Revivify Borough," *New York Times*, March 11, 1974, 31. For data on depopulation, see Gonzalez, *The Bronx*, 137.

30 Figure is from Freeman, *Working-Class New York*, 274.

31 Peter Marcuse, "Why the Housing Loss in the Bronx?" (paper presented at the Bronx Institute Conference on Housing and the Homeless, Lehman College, November 18, 1988). Devine et al., "Where the Lender Looks First," chapter 4. Homefront Abandonment Committee, *Housing Abandonment in New York City* (New York: Homefront, 1977), 17.

32 For the abandonment study, see Women's City Club of New York, *With Love and Affection: A Study of Building Abandonment* (New York: Women's City Club, 1977), 29. On the offensive against rent control, see Benjamin Holtzman, "'I Am Not Co-op!': The Struggle over Middle-Class Housing in 1970s New York," *Journal of Urban History* 43, no. 6 (2017): 867; Holtzman, *The Long Crisis*, chapters 1–2; Joel Schwartz, "Tenant Power in the Liberal City, 1943–1971," in *The Tenant Movement in New York City, 1904–1984*, ed. Ronald Lawson and Mark Naison (New Brunswick, NJ: Rutgers University Press, 1986), 134–208. For the Sterling quotations, see Ava Plakins, "The Landlords' Lament," *New York*, January 31, 1983, 39.

33 Homefront, *Housing Abandonment in New York City*, 17–18; Peter Marcuse, "Why the Housing Loss in the Bronx?" Women's City Club of New York, *With Love and Affection*, 43.

34 L'Official, *Urban Legends*, 26; Ann Meyerson and Tony Schuman, "From Disinvestment (Abandonment) to Reinvestment (Gentrification): Homefront's Abandonment Analysis Thirty Years Later," Planners Network, July 24, 2004.

35 Homefront, *Housing Abandonment in New York City*, 20, 23, 27.

36 Ibid., 29. Devine et al., "Where the Lender Looks First," xi, iv. In 1960, the bank wrote 352 mortgages inside the Bronx and 46 outside it. In 1970, the bank wrote only 187 mortgages in the Bronx, while writing 838 mortgages outside the borough. See chapter 5 of the report for the full data set. Freeman, *Working-Class New York*, 275; Letter from Northwest Bronx Community and Clergy Coalition to Muriel Siebert, January 17, 1978, Folder: Correspondence, 1975–1981, Box: 7, JJ, Harry T. Johnson Collection, LLL. Robert Scheer, "Bronx—Landscape of Urban Cancer," *Los Angeles Times*, August 6, 1978, 32.

37 Ann T. Meyerson, "The Determinants of Institutional Mortgage Investment in Bronx County" (PhD diss., New York University, 1979), 20–21; Homefront, *Housing Abandonment in New York City*, 38–39; Freeman, *Working-Class New York*, 275; Devine et al., "Where the Lender Looks First," 20.

38 Homefront, *Housing Abandonment in New York City*, 33. Letter from Tenants Committee 3836–3844 Bailey Ave., May 10, 1974, Folder: 3836–44 Bailey Ave., Box: 78, NWBCCC Records, BCHS. For the quote about Davidson Ave., see *CBS Reports*, "The Fire Next Door," first broadcast March 22, 1977, by CBS. For the description of Teichner, see Robert Magnuson, "Redevelopment and the Community in the South Bronx" (master's thesis, Columbia University, 1977), 7.

39 Abrams, "The Insurance Industry," 10. New York Urban Coalition, "Fire Insurance: A Crisis," 1, 14.

40 For the Newark survey, see George Sternlieb and Robert W. Burchell, *Residential Abandonment: The Tenement Landlord Revisited* (New Brunswick, NJ: Center for Urban Policy Research at Rutgers University, 1973), 302. *Hearings Before the President's National Advisory Panel on Insurance in Riot-Affected Areas* [Hughes Panel] (Washington, DC: U.S. Government Printing Office, 1968), November 8, 1967, especially 81–85. For the Fortunato quote, see Abrams, "The Insurance Industry," Appendix E-1.

41 New York Urban Coalition, "Fire Insurance: A Crisis," 12. Shapiro, *Fire Insurance and the Inner City*, 19. The NYPIUA was the only FAIR plan in the nation to use an entirely self-rated system for much of the 1970s, and its policies were thus the highest in the country (though inflated rates were common for FAIR plans nationwide). Juanita Gear, Statement Before the Senate Subcommittee on Insurance, Committee on Banking, Housing, and Urban Affairs, in *Problem of Property Insurance in Urban America: Hearing Before the Subcommittee on Housing and Urban Affairs, U.S. Senate* (Washington, DC: U.S. Government Printing Office, 1978), August 7, 1978, 40.

The Brueckner quote is in Gelvin Stevenson and Robert Magnuson, "High-Risk Urban Insurance Is Under Attack in State," *New York Times*, April 24, 1977, R1 (emphasis mine). The development of this racially segmented market for property insurance in the 1970s was especially baleful in light of the decade's victories against bank and mortgage lender redlining, embodied by the Home Mortgage Disclosure Act (1975) and the Community Reinvestment Act (1977). See chapter 8 of this book, along with Rebecca Marchiel, *After Redlining: The Urban Reinvestment Movement in the Era of Financial Deregulation* (Chicago: University of Chicago Press, 2020).

42 Bernard Melewski and Mollie Lampi, *Where Do You Draw the Line? Insurance Redlining in New York* (Albany: New York Public Interest Research Group, 1978), 28.
43 Property insurance was structured to be a "disciplinary device" in the same sense that Michel Foucault theorized: it enlisted property owners in their own self-governance. Insurance Information Institute, "Survival of P/C Insurance as Free Enterprise Keyed to Residual Market Solutions, Says I.I.I. Leader," May 26, 1977, Folder: FAIR Plans, DLIA (emphasis mine); Michel Foucault, *Discipline and Punish: The Birth of the Prison* (New York: Random House, 1977).
44 For the Bateman quotation, see Insurance Information Institute, "Survival of P/C Insurance as Free Enterprise." PIPSO, "Underwriting Losses for State FAIR Plans Exceed $42 Million in First Half of 1977," January 4, 1978, Folder: FAIR Plans, DLIA. For the Illinois FAIR quotation, see Candace P. Davis, "Arson-for-Profit: Is It a FAIR Plan Problem?" *Federation of Insurance Counsel Quarterly* 31, no. 2 (1981): 181. New York Urban Coalition, "Fire Insurance: A Crisis for New York's Neighborhoods" (1978), 25.
45 Analyzing the insurance industry's valuation of enslaved Black lives through a study of the 1781 *Zong* massacre, Ian Baucom asserts that insurance "utterly detach[es] value from the material existence of objects." Baucom, *Spectres of the Atlantic: Finance Capital, Slavery, and the Philosophy of History* (Durham, NC: Duke University Press, 2005), 96. Bronx insurance watchdog: Gelvin Stevenson, "Upsurge in Arson Calls for Insurance Reform," *New York Times*, September 11, 1977, 8.
46 Richard A. Ryan, "The Arson Triangle," *The Forum* (Section of Insurance, Negligence, and Compensation Law, American Bar Association) 14, no. 2 (1978): 187.

Three: To Torch a Fireproof Building

1 Talking Heads, "Burning Down the House," by David Byrne, Chris Frantz, Jerry Harrison, and Tina Weymouth, Sire Records, 1983.
2 Rock Master Scott & the Dynamic Three, "The Roof Is on Fire," by Celita Evans, Charles Pettiford, Gregory Wigfall, Jerry Bloodrock, and Richard Fowler, Reality Records, 1984.
3 "'Arsonlords' Arrested," *Northwest Bronx Neighborhood Action*, April 1977, 1; Tony Burton, "The Big Burn Boom," New York *Daily News*, July 14, 1981, 15.
4 Peter McLaughlin, "Landlord Gets 15 Yrs. in Arson," New York *Daily News*, December 13, 1978, 67. Due to privacy laws in place until the late 1970s, it was exceedingly difficult to ascertain which insurance company covered a given building. Most Bronx property holders were insured through the NYPIUA, but this is difficult to verify on a building-to-building level. In Lanni's case, this link was authenticated by an op-ed written by an executive at the NYPIUA. Charles P. Russ, "Revenge and Vandalism Are Sparks for Arson," New York *Daily News*, August 1, 1981. Burton, "The Big Burn Boom."
5 Northwest Bronx Community and Clergy Coalition (NWBCCC), "North Side Savings Bank and the Northwest Bronx!!" Folder: North Side Savings Bank, Box 7, JJ, Harry T. Johnson Collection, LLL. NWBCCC, "Mortgages Sold by North Side Savings Bank," Folder: North Side Savings Bank, Box 7, JJ, Harry T. Johnson Collection, LLL.
6 Arthur Miller, *Death of a Salesman* (1949; repr., New York: Penguin, 1977), 98. On New York and the FIRE industries, see Saskia Sassen, *The Global City: New York, London, Tokyo* (1991; repr., Princeton, NJ: Princeton University Press, 2001).
7 Burton, "The Big Burn Boom."
8 Ibid. The arson figure is from New York Arson Strike Force, "Arson in New York: 1984," September 1985, 32, accessed October 7, 2023, https://www.ncjrs.gov/pdffiles1/Digitization/99975NCJRS.pdf.
9 Burton, "The Big Burn Boom"; McLaughlin, "Landlord Gets 15 Yrs. in Arson." Richard Edmonds, "Cops Nab 6 Landlords on Arson-for-Hire Rap," New York *Daily News*, March 10, 1977, 8. "Common knowledge" quotation is from "'Arsonlords' Arrested," *Northwest Bronx Neighborhood Action*.

On "finishers," see Gelvin Stevenson, "The Abandonment of Roosevelt Gardens," in *Devastation/Resurrection: The South Bronx*, ed. Robert Jensen (New York: Bronx Museum of Art, 1979), 72–80.
10 Edmonds, "Cops Nab 6 Landlords."
11 For Merola testimony, see *Arson-for-Profit: Its Impact on States and Localities; Hearings Before the Subcommittee on Intergovernmental Relations of the Committee on Governmental Affairs, U.S. Senate* (Washington, DC: U.S. Government Printing Office, 1978), December 15, 1977, 189. Herman Weisman, *Arson Resource Directory* (Washington, DC: Arson Resource Center of the U.S. Fire Administration, 1982), 103.
12 Nina Glick Schiller and Michael Jacobson (New York City's Arson Strike Force), "The Crime of Stress-Induced Arson," 1983, p. 21, Folder: Arson Literature, Box: 11, General Subject Files, 1978–1984, ASF, NYMA.
13 Michael Jacobson, "The Enigmatic Crime: A Study of Arson in New York City" (PhD diss., City University of New York, 1985), 202. See also Mercer Sullivan, "Crime and the Social Fabric," in *Dual City: Restructuring New York*, ed. John Mollenkopf and Manuel Castells (New York: Russell Sage, 1992), 225–44. For arrest data, see New York Arson Strike Force, "Arson in New York: 1984," 75; Frank Logue, "Arson in the South Bronx," 1980, General Subject Files, 1978–1984, Box 2, ASF, NYMA, 8. "2 14-Year-Old Youths Held in Bronx Fire That Killed 6," *Messenger-Inquirer*, November 11, 1978, 18. Note that Vega was an anomaly in being promised half the insurance proceeds, though he never received that large sum.
14 Unemployment data is from the New York City Office of the Mayor, "The South Bronx: A Plan for Revitalization," 1977, 1–2. Padilla quoted in Vivian Vázquez Irizarry and Gretchen Hildebran, *Decade of Fire* (Red Nut Films, 2019).
15 Bronx D.A. Work Sheet, Bronx Arson Scrapbook, Box 4, JJ, Harry T. Johnson Collection, LLL; Albert Davila, "8 Indicted in Insurance Blazes in South Bronx," New York *Daily News*, June 12, 1975; "Arson Arranger Pleads Guilty to Hiring 'Torch,'" *Bronx Press Review*, July 10, 1975.
16 Joseph Treaster, "Bronx Boy Says He Set 40 to 50 Fires for $3 Up," *New York Times*, July 16, 1975. Padilla quoted in Vázquez and Hildebran, *Decade of Fire*. Testimony of Joe Willis (an alias) in *Arson-for-Hire: Hearings Before the Permanent Subcommittee on Investigations of the Committee on Governmental Affairs, U.S. Senate* (Washington, DC: U.S. Government Printing Office, 1978), August 24, 1978, 73. For more instances of torches refusing to set fires in occupied buildings, see the complete hearing transcripts.
17 Robert Pesner et al., "Arson Analysis and Prevention Project Final Report," September 1981, p. 12, Box 2, General Subject Files, 1978–1984, ASF, NYMA. "Verdict: Guilty of Burning: What Prosecutors Should Know About Arson," p. 6, Box 8, General Subject Files, 1978–1984, ASF, NYMA. Rita Ann Reimer, "Arson for Profit: Techniques, Scope, and Impact," Congressional Research Service, Library of Congress, 1986, 3.
18 Alan Saly, "Red Caps," *Firehouse*, August 1983, 50.
19 Vera Institute of Justice, "A Proposal for a Neighborhood Arson Prevention Program," October 21, 1977, p. 15, Folder: Vera Report, Box 3, General Subject Files, 1978–1984, ASF, NYMA. On "organized abandonment," see Ruth Wilson Gilmore, *Abolition Geography: Essays Towards Liberation* (Brooklyn: Verso, 2022), 303–8. For more on arson and the emergence of Bronx hip-hop, see especially Jeff Chang, *Can't Stop Won't Stop: A History of the Hip-Hop Generation* (New York: Picador, 2005), chapters 1–4. Mario Merola, *Big City D.A.* (New York: Random House, 1988), 88. Urban Educational Systems, "Profiles: A Handbook on Community Arson Prevention," 1981, p. 9, Box 3, General Subject Files, 1978–1984, ASF, NYMA. "Natural flue" is from John Barracato with Peter Michelmore, *Arson!* (New York: W. W. Norton, 1976), 17. National Fire Protection Association, "The Fire Fighter's Responsibility in Arson Detection," 1972, p. 4, Folder: Arson/Crime, Box 5, Office of the Administrator Subject File 1974–77, Records of the National Fire Control and Prevention Administration, RG 437, NARA.
20 Pesner et al., "Arson Analysis and Prevention Project Final Report," 11.
21 Emphasis in original. *Arson-for-Profit: Its Impact on States and Localities*, 186.

22 Ibid., 187–89. Jim Rooney, *Organizing the South Bronx* (Albany: State University of New York Press, 1995), 200–201; James Harney, "Arson Report Points at HUD," New York *Daily News*, July 22, 1982. On the Section 8 program's proclivity for arson, see Michael Goodwin, "City Housing Programs Tied to Arson in Report," *New York Times*, July 21, 1982.

23 The quotation from the rent control official is taken from Stevenson, "The Abandonment of Roosevelt Gardens," 80. Joe Conason and Jack Newfield, "Arson for Hire," *Village Voice*, June 2, 1980. Michael Magner, "Suspicious Blazes: Arson Problem Raging Through U.S. Cities," Newark *Star-Ledger*, November 1, 1976. Gelvin Stevenson, "Upsurge in Arson Calls for Insurance Reform," *New York Times*, September 11, 1977.

24 I am borrowing here from Neil Smith's rent gap theory of gentrification. In a paradigm-shifting 1979 essay, Smith defined the rent gap as "the disparity between the potential ground rent level and the actual ground rent capitalized under present land use" (545). "Once the rent gap is wide enough," he argued, "gentrification may be initiated." Neil Smith, "Toward a Theory of Gentrification: A Back to the City Movement by Capital, Not People," *Journal of the American Planning Association* 45, no. 4 (1979): 538–48.

25 Deborah Stone, "Beyond Moral Hazard: Insurance as Moral Opportunity," in *Embracing Risk: The Changing Culture of Insurance and Responsibility*, ed. Tom Baker and Jonathan Simon (Chicago: University of Chicago Press, 2002), 52–79; John D. Long and Davis W. Gregg, *Property and Liability Insurance Handbook* (Homewood, IL: Irwin, 1965), chapter 14.

26 Michael N. Dobkowski, "American Anti-Semitism: A Reinterpretation," *American Quarterly* 29, no. 2 (1977): 174; Victor Jew, "The Meanest Man in the World: Arson in the United States; A History of Legal and Social Responses to Incendiarism, 1870–1920" (PhD diss., University of Wisconsin, 1994); Aviya Kushner, "Why Do People Call Arson 'Jewish Lightning'—and Is It Anti-Semitic?" *The Forward*, May 18, 2017; Daniel Immerwahr, "All That Is Solid Bursts into Flame: Capitalism and Fire in the Nineteenth-Century United States," *Past & Present* (2024); Moishe Postone, "Anti-Semitism and National Socialism: Notes on the German Reaction to 'Holocaust,'" *New German Critique* 19, no. 1 (1980): 97–115. See also Francesca Trivellato, *The Promise and Peril of Credit: What a Forgotten Legend About Jews and Finance Tells Us About the Making of European Commercial Society* (Princeton, NJ: Princeton University Press, 2019); Jeffrey A. Marx, "Moral Hazard: The 'Jew Risks' Affair of 1867," *American Jewish History* 106, no. 3 (2022): 270.

27 A. Stoddart, "To the Editor of the New York Herald," *New York Herald* (March 23, 1867), 5. Quoted in Marx, "Moral Hazard."

28 Jonathan Levy, *Freaks of Fortune: The Emerging World of Capitalism and Risk* (Cambridge, MA: Harvard University Press, 2012), 87. This discussion is informed by Deborah Stone's critique of the "moral hazard argument." Stone, "Beyond Moral Hazard," 52–54.

29 It should be noted that rental income, a critical determinant of a landlord's bottom line, is factored into the calculation of the insurance gap in that a property's market value is heavily shaped by its projected rental income.

30 In the 1960s, *replacement cost* became the standard coverage within the voluntary (or non-FAIR) property insurance market. Replacement cost often far surpasses a building's market value, especially in the case of older properties, which would be more expensive to replace than to purchase. In this sense, an insurance gap may be considered a systemic issue. Crucially, though, many FAIR plans, including the NYPIUA, were only permitted to issue coverage based on market value, *not* replacement value. "HUD Reports on Insurance Crisis in Inner Cities," *Los Angeles Times*, June 18, 1978, k19; see also Jeffrey E. Thomas and Brad M. Wilson, "The Indemnity Principle: Evolution from a Financial to a Functional Paradigm," *Journal of Risk Management and Insurance* 10, no. 30 (2005).

The average property damage in buildings with an insurance gap greater than two was four times larger than the damage in properties without a gap.

31 Landlord arson, of course, long predates the 1970s, but it is safe to say that this decade was historically distinct in the scale and prevalence of incendiarism. See Jew, "The Meanest Man in the World"; David Huyssen, *Progressive Inequality: Rich and Poor in New York, 1890–1920*

(Cambridge, MA: Harvard University Press, 2014), 57–62. General Accounting Office, *Arson-for-Profit: More Could Be Done to Reduce It* (Washington, DC: U.S. Government Printing Office, 1978), Appendix I, 3. Joseph R. Biden, Statement Before the Senate Subcommittee on Criminal Justice, Senate Committee on the Judiciary, September 10, 1980, 3.

32 Mark Tebeau, *Eating Smoke: Fire in Urban America, 1800–1950* (Baltimore: Johns Hopkins University Press, 2003), 199.

33 Howard Tipton, "The Fire Service and the Fire Insurance Industry: Creating Incentives for Local Fire Service Improvement," July 12, 1972, p. 1, Folder: Historical File, Box 12, Office of the Administrator Subject File 1974–77, Records of the National Fire Control and Prevention Administration, RG 437, NARA. Tebeau, *Eating Smoke*, 269; Immerwahr, "All That Is Solid Bursts into Flame."

34 Tipton, "The Fire Service and the Fire Insurance Industry," 2–3. Porter W. Homer, John W. Lawton, and Costis Toregas, "Challenging the ISO Fire Rating System," *Public Management* 59, no. 7 (1977): 4.

35 The National Commission on Fire Prevention and Control, *America Burning* (Washington, DC: U.S. Government Printing Office, 1973), 1, 18. Bill Webb, "Restoring the Flame at the U.S. Fire Administration," *Firehouse*, October 23, 2012.

36 "Fire Safety Education Programs Demonstrated at NFPCA Conference," press release, November 12, 1975, Folder: News Release 6-74, Box 1, Public Information Office, Press Release Files, 1974–76, Records of the National Fire Control and Prevention Administration, RG 437, NARA. "Fire Prevention Week, 1976: A Proclamation by the President," Folder: Fire Prevention Week, Box 11, Office of the Administrator Subject File 1974–77, Records of the National Fire Control and Prevention Administration, RG 437, NARA. Chief Edwin Jennings to Ed Koch, November 29, 1977, p. 3, Folder: Arson Grant Proposals 12/31/77, Box 12, General Subject Files, 1978–1984, ASF, NYMA. Thomas A. Martin, Statement Before the Senate Subcommittee on Criminal Justice, Committee on the Judiciary, September 10, 1980, 109.

37 "Six Bold New Public Safety Ideas in Search of a City," *Nation's Cities*, September 1977, 21.

38 For fire marshal quotation, see John R. Dunne, "Getting Fire Insurance the FAIR Way," *New York Daily News*, April 2, 1979. For NYPIUA quote, see Howard Blum and Leslie Maitland, "Arson Destroying New York Housing at a Record Rate," *New York Times*, November 10, 1980, B4. For "windshield" quotation, see New York Urban Coalition, "Fire Insurance: A Crisis for New York's Neighborhoods" (1978), 27.

39 The FIA's defense of the FAIR plans was fundamentally a defense of brownlining, and Jimenez rightly feared that any admission to the program's susceptibility to fraud would be used to jettison it completely—and thus force a return to the redlining of the pre-1968 period. The FIA claimed that up to 95 percent of FAIR policyholders nationwide did not file a claim in a given year, though its arguments were challenged by the Senate Committee on Governmental Affairs. It is also worth noting that because the FIA had only two staff members overseeing all the statewide FAIR plans, it did not keep its own records of arson rates. Gloria Jimenez, Statement Before the Senate Subcommittee on Insurance, Committee on Banking, Housing, and Urban Affairs, *Flood Insurance and Crime and Riot Reinsurance: Hearing Before the Subcommittee on Insurance of the Committee on Banking, Housing, and Urban Affairs, U.S. Senate* (Washington, DC: U.S. Government Printing Office, 1980), February 28, 1980, 41; Testimony of Gloria Jimenez in *Arson-for-Hire: Hearings Before the Permanent Subcommittee*, September 14, 1978, 215, 262, 280. For the NYPIUA and Bronx DA quotes, see Blum and Maitland, "Arson Destroying New York Housing," B4. For the Illinois data, see Candace P. Davis, "Arson-for-Profit: Is It a FAIR Plan Problem?" *Federation of Insurance Counsel Quarterly* 31, no. 2 (1981): 181. The federal inquiry: General Accounting Office, *Arson-for-Profit: More Could Be Done to Reduce It*, 3–4.

40 Pesner et al., "Arson Analysis and Prevention Project Final Report," 17; Fred Shapiro, "Raking the Ashes of the Epidemic of Flame," *New York Times*, July 13, 1975; Robert Abrams to Clarence Kelley, June 6, 1975, Folder: Fr. Neil A. Connolly, Box 1, JJ, Harry T. Johnson Collection, LLL. General Accounting Office, *Arson-for-Profit: More Could Be Done to Reduce It*, Appendix I, 4; James Brady, "The Social Economy of Arson: Vandals, Gangsters, Bankers, and Officials in the

Making of an Urban Problem," in *Crime and Capitalism*, ed. David F. Greenberg (Philadelphia: Temple University Press, 1993), 231.

41 Jacobson, "The Enigmatic Crime," 132–33.

42 For the GAO quotation, see Deborah Orin, "Insurance Plan May Spur Arson," *New York Post*, June 13, 1978. For the Merola quotation, see *Arson-for-Profit: Its Impact on States and Localities*, 177. The ASF official: Jacobson, "The Enigmatic Crime," 114–15. The fire marshal: "The Hottest New Crime," *Newsweek*, January 8, 1979. The 1977 data was reported by the International Association of Fire Chiefs. *Arson-for-Profit: Its Impact on States and Localities*, 302. "How the Arson Evil Spreads," *New York Times*, July 5, 1980, 18.

43 Jacobson, "The Enigmatic Crime," 122. For the anti-arson organization quote, see Urban Educational Systems, *Fire Insurance: What It Is and How It Works*, 1983, Box 2, General Subject Files, 1978–1984, ASF, NYMA. See also James Brady, "Arson, Urban Economy, and Organized Crime: The Case of Boston," *Social Problems* 31, no. 1 (1983): 13. For the Oakar testimony, see *The Anti-Arson Act of 1979: Hearings Before the Subcommittee on Intergovernmental Relations of the Committee on Governmental Affairs, U.S. Senate* (Washington, DC: U.S. Government Printing Office, 1979), April 26, 1979, 11.

44 Logue, "Arson in the South Bronx," 4. Harvey D. Shapiro, *Fire Insurance and the Inner City* (New York City Rand Institute, 1971), 10. In 1972, 25 percent of first mortgages in New York City were held by insurance companies. Homefront Abandonment Committee, *Housing Abandonment in New York City* (New York: Homefront, 1977), 30. See also Gelvin Stevenson, *Fire Insurance: Its Nature and Dynamics* (National Fire Prevention and Control Administration, 1978), chapter 7. New York Insurance Department, *Annual Report of the Superintendent of Insurance to the New York Legislature Covering the Calendar Year 1976* (New York, 1977), 41. For the quotation by the insurance VPs, see G. Buddy Nichols and Kenneth W. Smith, "Who's Really to Blame for the Current Insurance Crisis?" *Risk Management* 32, no. 7 (1985): 45.

45 "Significant investment" is from Kenneth J. Meier, *The Political Economy of Regulation: The Case of Insurance* (Albany: State University of New York Press, 1988), 90. Greta Krippner, *Capitalizing on Crisis: The Political Origins of the Rise of Finance* (Cambridge, MA: Harvard University Press, 2012). Michael Jacobson and Philip Kasinitz, "Burning the Bronx for Profit: Why Arson Pays," *The Nation*, November 15, 1986, 512.

46 The quotation about money markets is from Meier, *The Political Economy of Regulation*, 90. American investment in money market funds jumped from $1.7 billion in 1974 to over $200 billion in 1982. Bruce J. Schulman, *The Seventies: The Great Shift in American Culture, Society, and Politics* (Cambridge, MA: Da Capo, 2001), 138. Kenneth T. Rosen and Larry Katz, "Money Market Mutual Funds: An Experiment in Ad Hoc Deregulation: A Note," *Journal of Finance* 38, no. 5 (1983): 1011.

As explored in chapter 5, these shifting priorities sometimes led the voluntary market to reabsorb risks previously written only by the NYPIUA. This process was called the depopulation of the FAIR plan. Urban Educational Systems, *Fire Insurance: What It Is and How It Works*, 1983, Box 2, General Subject Files, 1978–1984, ASF, NYMA. "Sacrificed underwriting profit" is from Johnny C. Finch, "Profitability of the Property/Casualty Insurance Industry," Statement Before the Senate Consumer Subcommittee, Committee on Commerce, Science, and Transportation, May 20, 1986, 1.

47 The premiums collected by the NYPIUA were likewise invested, but the pool's underwriting losses in the 1970s tended to exceed investment income, generating net losses that were absorbed by individual companies. Jacobson, "The Enigmatic Crime," 115 (emphasis mine). Michael Jacobson, interview by author, September 18, 2017, New Haven, CT.

48 Industry data is from Meier, *The Political Economy of Regulation*, 12. See also Barbara D. Stewart, "Profit Cycles in Property-Liability Insurance," in *Issues in Insurance*, vol. 1, ed. John D. Long and Everett D. Randall (Malvern, PA: American Institute for Property and Liability Underwriters, 1984), 332.

49 Even when social scientists address the uneven geographies of financialization, it is seldom associated with a place like the Bronx. In her seminal book *The Global City: New York, London, Tokyo*, sociologist Saskia Sassen notes, "Today we see increased asymmetry: The conditions promoting growth in global cities contain as significant components the decline of other areas of the United States." But this "asymmetry" sprang up not only between New York and Detroit, between the financial services metropole and the industrial Carthage; it materialized within the metropole itself. Saskia Sassen, *The Global City: New York, London, Tokyo* (1991; repr., Princeton, NJ: Princeton University Press, 2001), 13.

50 For NWBCCC quotation, see NWBCCC, unsigned memorandum, March 16, 1977, Folder: Correspondence 1975–1981, Box 7, JJ, Harry T. Johnson Collection, LLL. "New Homeowners Recall Three Years of Struggle," New York *Daily News*, August 31, 1981. The $93,000 figure was calculated using the $7,000 purchase price versus the $100,000 valuation. Burton, "The Big Burn Boom."

51 For NWBCCC quotation, see NWBCCC, unsigned memorandum, March 16, 1977, Folder: Correspondence 1975–1981, Box 7, JJ, Harry T. Johnson Collection, LLL; "'Arsonlords' Arrested," *Northwest Bronx Neighborhood Action*. Burton, "The Big Burn Boom."

52 "New Homeowners Recall Three Years of Struggle."

Four: "We Went to Bed with Our Shoes on Every Night"

1 From Walker's journals, written in New York on December 21, 1977. Alice Walker, *Gathering Blossoms Under Fire: The Journals of Alice Walker, 1965–2000*, ed. Valerie Boyd (New York: Simon & Schuster, 2022), 92.

2 Anthony Rivieccio, transcript of an oral history conducted by Mark Naison on December 4, 2015, Bronx African American History Project.

3 Ibid.

4 "Fire" was on the set list at Liquid Smoke on December 14, 1974. Vince Aletti, *The Disco Files 1973–78: New York's Underground, Week by Week* (New York: D.A.P., 2018), 59; Mark Jacobson, "Hollyw-o-o-o-d! The Return of the New York Disco," *New York*, July 1, 1974, 51; Ohio Players, "Fire," by Billy Beck et al., Mercury Records, 1974. An inventory of disco's fire songs would also include Dan Hartman's "Relight My Fire" (1979), Eddie Kendricks's "Goin' Up in Smoke" (1976), Sylvester's "Dance (Disco Heat)" (1978), and Arabesque's "In the Heat of a Disco Night" (1979), to name a few. Bill Higgins, "Hollywood Flashback: The Biggest Stars Battled a 'Towering Inferno' in 1974," *Hollywood Reporter*, July 12, 2018. Audre Lorde, "New York City 1970," in *New York Head Shop and Museum* (Detroit: Broadside Press, 1974). On *Prairie Fire*, see Dan Berger, *Outlaws of America: The Weather Underground and the Politics of Solidarity* (Oakland: AK Press, 2006), 183–96.

5 Rivieccio, BAAHP.

6 Herbert E. Meyer, "The War Zone Is South Bronx," *Newsday*, December 2, 1975.

7 This analysis and method were informed by discussions with Crystal Feimster, LaShawn Harris, and Kathryn Dudley, along with Nell Irvin Painter, *Soul Murder and Slavery: Toward a Fully Loaded Cost Accounting* (Waco, TX: Baylor University Press, 1995), and Kidada E. Williams, "The Wounds That Cried Out: Reckoning with African Americans' Testimonies of Trauma and Suffering from Night Riding," in *The World the Civil War Made*, ed. Gregory Downs and Kate Masur (Chapel Hill: University of North Carolina Press, 2015), 159–82. In her research on Bronxite Eleanor Gray Bumpurs, historian LaShawn Harris has called attention to the interior fallout that could result from a fire. "Beyond the Shooting: Eleanor Gray Bumpurs, Identity Erasure, and Family Activism Against Police Violence," *Souls* 20, no. 1 (2018): 97.

8 Ivan Sanchez, transcript of an oral history conducted by Mark Naison on May 2, 2008, Bronx African American History Project. Shelley Sanderson, transcript of an oral history conducted by Mark Naison on April 18, 2006, Bronx African American History Project.

9 Samuel Christian, transcript of an oral history conducted by Mark Naison et al. on February 15, 2006, Bronx African American History Project. Mario Merola, *Big City D.A.* (New York: Ran-

dom House, 1988), 80. Genevieve Brown, transcript of an oral history conducted by Brian Purnell on April 19, 2008, Bronx African American History Project.

10 "Statement by His Eminence, Terence Cardinal Cooke," May 20, 1975, Bronx Arson Scrapbook, Box 4, JJ, Harry T. Johnson Collection, LLL. Louis Gigante, interview with Jill Jonnes, September 8, 1983, p. 7, Folder: Fr. Louis Gigante, Box 1, JJ, Harry T. Johnson Collection, LLL. Merola, *Big City D.A.*, 80, 94.

11 "Arson Problems in New York City," Hearings Before the Subcommittee of the Committee on Appropriations, U.S. House of Representatives, April 28, 1979, 18. For the second study, see Urban Educational Systems, "Profiles: A Handbook on Community Arson Prevention," 1981, p. 1, Box 3, General Subject Files, 1978–1984, ASF, NYMA. The third cited study is Women's City Club of New York, *With Love and Affection: A Study of Building Abandonment* (New York: Women's City Club, 1977), 10.

12 David W. Dunlap, "A Scavenged Building Reflects Bronx Decay," *New York Times*, February 22, 1982, B1. Thomas Glynn, "The South Bronx: What Went Down Should Come Up," *Neighborhood: The Journal for City Preservation* 5, no. 2 (August 1982): 10.

13 Patrick W. Sullivan, "S. Bronx: A Line of Fire," *New York Post*, April 27, 1977, 41. Robert Scheer, "Bronx—Landscape of Urban Cancer," *Los Angeles Times*, August 6, 1978, A1. It is worth noting that arson research is itself conducted in the language of epidemiology, with researchers commonly using "etiology" to describe motives for firesetting. Bench Ansfield, "Unsettling 'Inner City': Liberal Protestantism and the Postwar Origins of a Keyword in Urban Studies," *Antipode* 50, no. 5 (2018): 1166–85. For "social cancer" quotation, see "Urban Cancer," *New York Times*, January 18, 1973, 40.

14 Harold DeRienzo, *The Concept of Community: Lessons from the Bronx* (Milan: IPOC, 2008), 14–15. Genevieve Brown, BAAHP. Joseph Orange, transcript of an oral history conducted by Mark Naison on September 28, 2015, Bronx African American History Project.

15 DeRienzo, *The Concept of Community*, 14. The Ortiz and Ruiz accounts are found in David Vidal, "Bronx Fires Leave Trail of Homelessness and Fear," *New York Times*, June 23, 1975, 30. The renter quoted was a tenant of Roosevelt Gardens, a large apartment building on the Grand Concourse. Gelvin Stevenson, "The Abandonment of Roosevelt Gardens," in *Devastation/Resurrection: The South Bronx*, ed. Robert Jensen (New York: Bronx Museum of Art, 1979), 80.

16 "Fear, panic" quotation is from Brent Owens, *The Bronx: A Cry for Help* (Brent Owens Productions, 1987). Darney "K-Born" Rivers, transcript of an oral history conducted by Mark Naison and Lisa Betty on October 18, 2016, Bronx African American History Project.

17 Vidal, "Bronx Fires Leave Trail of Homelessness."

18 About a thousand Americans were estimated to die annually in arson fires. Committee on Governmental Affairs of the U.S. Senate, *Arson in America* (Washington, DC: U.S. Government Printing Office, 1979), 43; The New York City statistic is from Michael Jacobson, "The Enigmatic Crime: A Study of Arson in New York City" (PhD diss., City University of New York, 1985), 13. National Fire Prevention and Control Administration, "Highlights of Fire in the United States," June 1978, p. 3, Folder: Insurance Co. (AIA & Aetna), Box 12, General Subject Files, 1978–1984, ASF, NYMA. Robin Herman, "Cabby Chases and Seizes Suspect in Fire Fatal to 2," *New York Times*, June 25, 1979. "Man Killed in Leap from Fire in Bronx," *New York Times*, July 7, 1980, B3. James Brady, "The Social Economy of Arson: Vandals, Gangsters, Bankers, and Officials in the Making of an Urban Problem," in *Crime and Capitalism*, ed. David F. Greenberg (Philadelphia: Temple University Press, 1993), 214.

19 Vera Institute of Justice, "A Proposal for a Neighborhood Arson Prevention Program," October 21, 1977, p. 3, Folder: Vera Report, Box 3, General Subject Files, 1978–1984, ASF, NYMA. "Fire Exacts Heavy Psychological Toll on Young Survivors, Victims," *Sentinel Star*, January 30, 1977. Hetty Fox, transcript of an oral history conducted by Mark Naison et al. on October 1, 2015, Bronx African American History Project. The Byrd and Boyd quotations can be found in Committee on Governmental Affairs of the U.S. Senate, *Arson in America*, 43–44.

20 "Fire Exacts Heavy Psychological Toll." Quote about sleep can be found in Committee on Gov-

ernmental Affairs of the U.S. Senate, *Arson in America*, 44. Robert Gumbs, transcript of an oral history conducted by Mark Naison et al. on October 1, 2015, Bronx African American History Project. James Henderson, transcript of an oral history conducted by Mark Naison on January 13, 2004, Bronx African American History Project.

21 For a brilliant discussion on "institutional mourning," see Eve L. Ewing, *Ghosts in the Schoolyard: Racism and School Closings on Chicago's South Side* (Chicago: University of Chicago Press, 2018), chapter 4. Fernando Ferrer, foreword to *Bronx Faces & Voices: Sixteen Stories of Courage and Community*, ed. Emita Brady Hill and Janet Butler Munch (Lubbock: Texas Tech University Press, 2014), xiv. Poem printed in "Conclusion," *Bulletin of Science, Technology & Society* 3, no. 3 (June 1983): 245. For the Rodriguez quotations, see Daniel O'Grady, "Fire Robs Family of Home—and Dignity," New York *Daily News*, June 6, 1975, 31.

22 Chrystal Wade, transcript of an oral history conducted by Mark Naison on September 17, 2015, Bronx African American History Project.

23 Donald Singleton, "Shelter's an Oasis in the Midst of Arson City," New York *Daily News*, June 19, 1975, 5.

24 Committee on Governmental Affairs of the U.S. Senate, *Arson in America*, 44. For the Murphy quotation and New York Urban Coalition study, see Glynn, "The South Bronx," 10, 12.

25 Charlotte Street described by Genevieve Brown, BAAHP. Darney "K-Born" Rivers, BAAHP.

26 DeRienzo, *The Concept of Community*, 15. Chrystal Wade, BAAHP. For Morrisania data, see Mark Naison and Bob Gumbs, *Before the Fires: An Oral History of African American Life in the Bronx from the 1930s to the 1960s* (New York: Fordham University Press, 2016), 176. For boroughwide data and "burn index" quote, see Rodrick Wallace, "Urban Desertification, Public Health and Public Order: 'Planned Shrinkage,' Violent Death, Substance Abuse and AIDS in the Bronx," *Social Science & Medicine* 31, no. 7 (1990): 801–2. According to the *Journal of American Insurance*, between ten thousand and twenty thousand New Yorkers were not just displaced but "made homeless by these arson-for-insurance fires," as of 1978. "Urban Decay: A Real World Perspective," *Journal of American Insurance*, 1978, reprinted in *Problem of Property Insurance in Urban America: Hearing Before the Subcommittee on Housing and Urban Affairs, U.S. Senate* (Washington, DC: U.S. Government Printing Office, 1978), August 7, 1978, 62.

27 Herbert J. Freudenberger with Geraldine Richelson, *Burn Out: How to Beat the High Cost of Success* (originally published in 1980 as *Burn-Out: The High Cost of High Achievement*; repr., New York: Bantam Books, 1981), xv. For the details on Freudenberger's burnout and his work in the clinic, see Freudenberger with Richelson, *Burn Out*, xv–xxi; Matthew J. Hoffarth, "The Making of Burnout: From Social Change to Self-Awareness in the Postwar United States, 1970–82," *History of the Human Sciences* 30, no. 5 (2017); Wilmar B. Schaufeli, "Burnout: A Short Socio-Cultural History," in *Burnout, Fatigue, Exhaustion: An Interdisciplinary Perspective on a Modern Affliction*, ed. Sighard Neckel et al. (Cham, Switzerland: Palgrave Macmillan, 2017); Jonathan Malesic, *The End of Burnout: Why Work Drains Us and How to Build Better Lives* (Oakland: University of California Press, 2021), chapter 2. For the details on the East Village, see Christopher Mele, *Selling the Lower East Side: Culture, Real Estate, and Resistance in New York City* (Minneapolis: University of Minnesota Press, 2000), 196.

28 Herbert J. Freudenberger, "The Staff Burn-Out Syndrome in Alternative Institutions," *Psychotherapy: Theory, Research, and Practice* (1975): 161. Freudenberger with Richelson, *Burn Out*, xv. Elizabeth Mehren, "Societal Burnout Pandemic in the Era of Automation," *Los Angeles Times*, October 26, 1982, 5.

29 Freudenberger with Richelson, *Burn Out*, xvi–xvii, 18. For a deeper exploration of this history, see Bench Ansfield, "Edifice Complex," *Jewish Currents* (Winter 2022).

30 As critic Pete L'Official notes, "By becoming the nation's shorthand for urban American ruin, the South Bronx simultaneously made that ruin more difficult to see everywhere but in the Bronx." *Urban Legends: The South Bronx in Representation and Ruin* (Cambridge, MA: Harvard University Press, 2020), 23. Phillip Fisher testimony in *Arson-for-Profit: Its Impact on States and Localities; Hearings Before the Subcommittee on Intergovernmental Relations of the Committee*

on *Governmental Affairs, U.S. Senate* (Washington, DC: U.S. Government Printing Office, 1978), December 15, 1977, 16.

31 Herman Weisman, *Arson Resource Directory*, U.S. Fire Administration, 1980, Box 12, General Subject Files, 1978–1984, ASF, NYMA.

32 New York Insurance Department, *1975 Annual Report of the Superintendent of Insurance* (New York, 1976), 48–49; Harvey D. Shapiro, *Fire Insurance and the Inner City* (New York City Rand Institute, 1971), 19; "FAIR Plans Hit by $58.8 Million Operating Loss; Arson Epidemic Cited," *Insurance Advocate*, July 24, 1976, 8. James P. Brady, "Arson, Fiscal Crisis, and Community Action: Dialectics of an Urban Crime and Popular Response," *Crime & Delinquency* 28 (April 1982): 252. Randy Revelle, "Combating Arson in Seattle," in *Arson-for-Profit: Its Impact on States and Localities*, 35. "Why Is Worcester Burning?" Folder: Outreach Work Outside NYC, Box 3, General Subject Files, 1978–1984, ASF, NYMA.

33 General Accounting Office, *Arson-for-Profit: More Could Be Done to Reduce It* (Washington, DC: U.S. Government Printing Office, 1978), 7. For the Paul quotation, see "Bolling Predicts Action Within Week," *Boston Globe*, October 20, 1977, 3. For the "sitting ducks" quotation, see William Greider, Warren Brown, and Harold Logan, "Landlord Arson: Cut-Rate Type of Urban Renewal," *Washington Post*, May 8, 1978, A1. Michael Graham and Jim Neubacher, "Insurers Sloppy About Arson," *Detroit Free Press*, July 16, 1974. David Barrett, "Plans to Reduce Arson Drawn Up," *Hartford Courant*, February 16, 1977. Insurance Committee for Arson Control, "Arson Fact Sheet," 1983, Folder: Activity Report, Box 11, General Subject Files, 1978–1984, ASF, NYMA.

34 Alexander Kiorpes, "The Depopulation Task Force," GEICO, 1980, Folder: FAIR Plans, DLIA. John Glenn, Statement Before the Senate Subcommittee on Criminal Justice, Senate Committee on the Judiciary, September 10, 1980, 5.

35 "Statements of National Significance to the Fire Problem in the United States," in *Arson-for-Profit: Its Impact on States and Localities*, 327.

Though a suspect source in general, Nathan Glazer is helpful on this point: "One sees nothing like it [arson] in England's declining midland cities, even though their populations and employment opportunities have been more radically reduced, and much of the housing stock has been demolished or is in bad repair. One sees nothing like it in the great cities of the Continent, or the developing world." Glazer, "The South-Bronx Story: An Extreme Case of Neighborhood Decline," *Policy Studies Journal* 16, no. 2 (Winter 1987): 271. The National Commission on Fire Prevention and Control, *America Burning* (Washington, DC: U.S. Government Printing Office, 1973), 1.

36 Jacobson, "The Enigmatic Crime," 13. Steven R. Weisman, "Moynihan Urges Priority for Jobs in South Bronx," *New York Times*, December 20, 1978, B1. Marshall Berman, "Views from the Burning Bridge," *Dissent* (Summer 1999): 78 (emphasis in original).

37 Ann F. Barker, *Arson: A Review of the Psychiatric Literature* (Oxford: Oxford University Press, 1994), 3, 5, 24, 32, 36. Joan W. Scott and Louise A. Tilly, "Women's Work and the Family in Nineteenth-Century Europe," *Comparative Studies in Society and History* 17, no. 1 (January 1975): 36–64. Sigmund Freud, "The Acquisition of Power over Fire," *International Journal of Psychoanalysis* 13 (1932): 405.

38 W. Hurley and T. M. Monahan, "Arson: The Criminal and the Crime," *British Journal of Criminology* 9, no. 1 (1969): 15. Barker, *Arson*, 32–34. Massachusetts lieutenant quoted in Barry Goetz, *On the Frontlines of the Welfare State: How the Fire Service and Police Shape Social Problems* (New York: Routledge, 2017), 10. New York City fire marshal quoted in Barker, *Arson*, 33. Michael Magner, "Suspicious Blazes: Arson Problem Raging Through U.S. Cities," Newark *Star-Ledger*, November 1, 1976.

39 Robert W. Fieseler, *Tinderbox: The Untold Story of the Up Stairs Lounge Fire and the Rise of Gay Liberation* (New York: Liveright, 2018).

40 Laurie Johnston, "Arson Destroys Gay Activist Site," *New York Times*, October 16, 1974, 19; Tim Lawrence, *Loves Saves the Day: A History of American Dance Music Culture, 1970–1979* (Durham, NC: Duke University Press, 2003), 343–44 and chapter 10. Sylvester, "Dance (Disco Heat)," by Eric Robinson and Victor Osborn, Fantasy Records, 1978.

41 "South of the Border," *Gay Community News* 7, no. 42 (May 17, 1980): 2.

42 David Goldberg, *Black Firefighters and the FDNY: The Struggle for Jobs, Justice, and Equity in New York City* (Chapel Hill: University of North Carolina Press, 2017), 26. See also Daniel Immerwahr, "Burning Down the House: Slavery and Arson in America," *Journal of American History* 110, no. 3 (2023): 449–73, and Jill Lepore, *New York Burning: Liberty, Slavery, and Conspiracy in Eighteenth-Century Manhattan* (New York: Alfred A. Knopf, 2005). Edwin G. Burrows and Mike Wallace, *Gotham: A History of New York City to 1898* (Oxford: Oxford University Press, 1999), 887–99, and Carla L. Peterson, "African Americans and the New York Draft Riots: Memory and Reconciliation in America's Civil War," *Nanzan Review of American Studies* 27 (2005): 5.

43 Khalil Gibran Muhammad, *The Condemnation of Blackness* (Cambridge, MA: Harvard University Press, 2010), chapter 2. Frederick L. Hoffman, *Race Traits and Tendencies of the American Negro* (New York: American Economic Association, 1896), 220–21. Sarah Haley, *No Mercy Here: Gender, Punishment, and the Making of Jim Crow Modernity* (Chapel Hill: University of North Carolina Press, 2016). Manning Marable, *How Capitalism Underdeveloped Black America* (1983; repr., Cambridge, MA: South End, 2011), 117.

44 "Text of the Moynihan Memorandum on the Status of Negroes," *New York Times*, printed March 1, 1970 (first publicized in January 1970), 69. This is an instance of what Daniel Martinez HoSang and Joseph E. Lowndes call "racial transposition," wherein social meanings transfer from one racialized group to another. If Glazer is transposing the "culture of poverty" framework from Black to Puerto Rican communities, it is worth noting the framework's origins in Oscar Lewis's research in Mexico. Oscar Lewis, *Five Families: Mexican Case Studies in the Culture of Poverty* (New York: Basic Books, 1959). Daniel Martinez HoSang and Joseph E. Lowndes, *Producers, Parasites, Patriots: Race and the New Right-Wing Politics of Precarity* (Minneapolis: University of Minnesota Press, 2019), 12–15, and Nathan Glazer, "The Puerto Ricans in New York," in *Poverty in the Affluent Society*, ed. Hanna H. Meissner (New York: Harper & Row, 1966), 110.

45 Richard Higgins, "NYC Trying to Snuff Out Arson," *Boston Globe*, October 18, 1979, 3. Of course, some fires were in fact set out of jealousy and revenge. In the Bronx, the most famous of these was the Puerto Rican Social Club Fire of 1976, which killed twenty-five and was allegedly motivated by jealousy. I am not denying that this type of arson did occur but, rather, arguing that it was overrepresented in popular and legal discourses. Dena Kleiman, "Youth Guilty of Causing 25 Deaths in Bronx Social Club Fire in 1976," *New York Times*, February 11, 1978, 1. For the NYPIUA quotation, see Charles P. Russ, "Revenge and Vandalism Are Sparks for Arson," New York *Daily News*, August 1, 1981. FDNY chief quoted in Vivian Vázquez Irizarry and Gretchen Hildebran, *Decade of Fire* (Red Nut Films, 2019). Smith is quoted in Carol Oppenheim and Joseph Egelhof, "Even Before the Blackout, N.Y. Had Arson Epidemic," *Chicago Tribune*, July 31, 1977, 6.

46 Berman, "Views from the Burning Bridge," 78–79. Vázquez Irizarry and Hildebran, *Decade of Fire*.

47 Jacobson, interview by author. Jacobson, "The Enigmatic Crime," 57–58. "We know the most" quotation is by Bernard Levin of the Center for Fire Research, quoted in Harvey French, *The Anatomy of Arson* (New York: Arco, 1979), 13. "Beame Signs Laws to Curb Arson," *New York Times*, November 15, 1977. See also the notes from the insurance industry's Property Insurance Loss Register, Folder: Various Conferences, Box 12, General Subject Files, 1978–1984, ASF, NYMA. Frank Logue, "Arson in the South Bronx," 1980, p. 8, Box 2, General Subject Files, 1978–1984, ASF, NYMA.

48 Quoted in New York Arson Strike Force, "New York Arson Resource Center," p. 4, Folder: NY Arson Resource Ctr., Box 9, General Subject Files, 1978–1984, ASF, NYMA. NFPCA quotation is from General Accounting Office, *Arson-for-Profit: More Could Be Done to Reduce It*, 11. Joseph Biden, *Arson for Profit: Hearing Before the Subcommittee on Criminal Justice of the Committee on the Judiciary, U.S. Senate* (Washington, DC: U.S. Government Printing Office, 1981), September 10, 1980, 3. For Biden's role in the drug war, see David Stein, "The Untold Story: Joe Biden Pushed Ronald Reagan to Ramp Up Incarceration—Not the Other Way Around," *The Intercept*, September 17, 2019.

49 Dylan Gottlieb, "Hoboken Is Burning: Yuppies, Arson, and Displacement in the Postindustrial City," *Journal of American History* 106, no. 2 (2019): 390–416; Brady, "Arson, Fiscal Crisis, and Community Action," 260. Jon Ronson, "San Francisco Is Burning," *GQ*, June 22, 2017; Anti-Eviction Mapping Project, "San Francisco Fires and Evictions," February 3, 2017, accessed February 7, 2020, https://www.antievictionmap.com/blog/2017/2/3/sf-fires?rq=fire.

50 David W. Dunlap, "A Scavenged Building Reflects Bronx Decay," *New York Times*, February 22, 1982, B1. "The 'Stripper' Makes Profits from Salvage," *New York Times*, February 22, 1982, B3.

51 "The 'Stripper' Makes Profits from Salvage." Nicholas Borg and Leonard David, "Arson: A Multi-Dimensional Problem," April 29, 1976, p. 1, Folder: Society of Fire Protection Engineers, Box 3, General Subject Files, 1978–1984, ASF, NYMA.

52 The figure of the "welfare queen" originated in the mid-1970s, and its resonance would grow in later decades. Julilly Kohler-Hausmann, "'The Crime of Survival': Fraud Prosecutions, Community Surveillance, and the Original 'Welfare Queen,'" *Journal of Social History* 41, no. 2 (2007): 329–54. See also Robert O. Self, *All in the Family: The Realignment of American Democracy Since the 1960s* (New York: Hill and Wang, 2012), especially 38–45; Alice O'Connor, *Poverty Knowledge: Social Science, Social Policy, and the Poor in Twentieth-Century U.S. History* (Princeton, NJ: Princeton University Press, 2001), chapter 8; and Michael B. Katz, *The Undeserving Poor: From the War on Poverty to the War on Welfare* (New York: Pantheon Books, 1989), 102–5. Kay Gardella, "The Fire and the Decay," New York *Daily News*, March 22, 1977, 88. Mike Nuñez, oral history in *Bronx Faces and Voices*, 124. Peter D. Salins, *The Ecology of Housing Destruction: Economic Effects of Public Intervention in the Housing Market* (New York: New York University Press, 1980), 11. One report found that landlords "sought out" welfare tenants because the "Dept. of Social Services pays generous rent for substandard accommodations." Peter Freiberg, "The Bronx: Forgotten Borough?" *New York Post*, November 30, 1971, 47.

53 "Real need" quotation appears in Vidal, "Bronx Fires Leave Trail of Homelessness." For Barracato quote, see Joseph B. Treaster, "20% Rise in Fires Is Adding to Decline of South Bronx," *New York Times*, May 18, 1975, 50. Dollar Savings president: Henry G. Waltemade, "Political Expediency Stymies New York Housing," *Real Estate Forum* 32nd Annual Review, February 1977. Office of Welfare Inspector General Press Release, February 22, 1977, Folder: Newsletters-Brochures, Box 26, Office of the Administrator Subject File 1974–77, Records of the National Fire Control and Prevention Administration, RG 437, NARA.

Jill Jonnes's *South Bronx Rising*, which remains a definitive history of the borough's crisis years, emphasized welfare arson over its other etiologies, devoting eight lines to welfare arson, with only three lines for landlord-brokered fires. Even Elizabeth Hinton's otherwise magisterial monograph *From the War on Poverty to the War on Crime: The Making of Mass Incarceration in America* arrives at this same unsound verdict. Describing the New York arson wave, she writes, "Businesses set some of the fires, reasoning that the prospect of collecting insurance money offered more promise than maintaining a business in an area of extreme poverty. Despairing residents, however, set most of the fires themselves, seeking thrills, relocation, and metal to sell." Jill Jonnes, *South Bronx Rising: The Rise, Fall, and Resurrection of an American City* (New York: Fordham University Press, 2002), 232; Elizabeth Hinton, *From the War on Poverty to the War on Crime: The Making of Mass Incarceration in America* (Cambridge, MA: Harvard University Press, 2016), 300.

54 New York City Arson Strike Force Community Outreach Unit, "Anti-Arson Strategies: A Guide for Community Organizations," April 1981, p. 13, Box 7, General Subject Files, 1978–1984, ASF, NYMA. On the J-51 program, see Michael Goodwin, "City Housing Programs Tied to Arson in Report," *New York Times*, July 21, 1982. Vidal, "Bronx Fires Leave Trail of Homelessness."

55 The bracketed phrase appeared in parentheses in the original. Nina Glick Schiller and Michael Jacobson (New York City Arson Strike Force), "The Crime of Stress-Induced Arson," 1983, p. 21, Folder: Arson Literature, Box 11, General Subject Files, 1978–1984, ASF, NYMA.

56 New York Penal Law § 150.00–150.20 (1973).

57 David Medina, "Visit to Scorched Bronx Starts Legislative Push," New York *Daily News*, April 19, 1977.

58 Testimony of Hedy Byrd in *Arson-for-Hire: Hearings Before the Permanent Subcommittee on Investigations of the Committee on Governmental Affairs, U.S. Senate* (Washington, DC: U.S. Government Printing Office, 1978), September 13, 1978, 159. John Byas [Jazzy Jay], transcript of an oral history conducted by Mark Naison on March 19, 2009, Bronx African American History Project. Jonnes, *South Bronx Rising*, 232. On public housing, see Edward G. Goetz, *Clearing the Way: Deconcentrating the Poor in Urban America* (Washington, DC: Urban Institute Press, 2003); Katherine L. Shester, "The Local Economic Effects of Public Housing in the United States, 1940–1970," *Journal of Economic History* 73, no. 4 (2013): 978–1016.

59 "Widespread feeling" is from Jonathan B. Bingham to Carla A. Hills, April 25, 1975, Bronx Arson Scrapbook, Box 4, JJ, Harry T. Johnson Collection, LLL. People's Development Corporation, "Statement of Purpose," n.d., Folder: People's Development Corporation, Box 50, Edward Joseph Logue Papers, Accession 1985-M-009, YMA.

60 Vázquez Irizarry and Hildebran, *Decade of Fire*.

Five: A Triangular Trade in Risk

1 Emphasis in original. Tom Wolfe, *The Bonfire of the Vanities* (New York: Picador, 1987), 5.

2 David Harvey, *The Limits to Capital* (1982; repr., Brooklyn: Verso, 2018), 266.

3 Murray Schumach, "Fireworks Emblazon Sky Around Statue of Liberty," *New York Times*, July 5, 1976; Miriam Greenberg, *Branding New York: How a City in Crisis Was Sold to the World* (New York: Routledge, 2008), 167. Joan Cook, "Bicentennial Fever Is Gripping State," *New York Times*, December 7, 1975.

4 Gil Scott-Heron, "Bicentennial Blues," Arista Records, 1976. Scott-Heron spent his adolescence in the Bronx. Marcus Baram, *Gil Scott-Heron: Pieces of a Man* (New York: St. Martin's, 2014), chapter 4. This analysis is indebted to Katherine McKittrick, "Mathematics Black Life," *Black Scholar* 44, no. 2 (Summer 2014): 16–28. On the blues epistemology and its global circulation, see Clyde Woods, "'Sittin' on Top of the World': The Challenges of Blues and Hip Hop Geography," in *Black Geographies and the Politics of Place*, ed. Katherine McKittrick and Clyde Woods (Cambridge, MA: South End, 2007), 66; Michael Denning, *Noise Uprising: The Audiopolitics of a Musical Revolution* (Brooklyn: Verso, 2015); and Gerhard Kubik, *Africa and the Blues* (Jackson: University Press of Mississippi, 1999). Saidiya Hartman, *Lose Your Mother: A Journey Along the Atlantic Slave Route* (New York: Farrar, Straus and Giroux, 2007), 6.

5 As Zenia Kish and Justin Leroy have argued, the *Zong* case "formed the basis for a relationship between race and finance that would survive slavery." Kish and Leroy, "Bonded Life: Technologies of Racial Finance from Slave Insurance to Philanthrocapital," *Cultural Studies* 29, nos. 5–6 (2015): 630–51. Jane Webster, "The *Zong* in the Context of the Eighteenth-Century Slave Trade," *Journal of Legal History* 28, no. 3 (2007): 285–98; James Walvin, *The Zong: A Massacre, the Law and the End of Slavery* (New Haven, CT: Yale University Press, 2011), xii.

6 Juanita Gear, Statement Before the Senate Subcommittee on Insurance, *Flood Insurance and Crime and Riot Reinsurance: Hearing Before the Subcommittee on Insurance of the Committee on Banking, Housing, and Urban Affairs, U.S. Senate* (Washington, DC: U.S. Government Printing Office, 1980), February 28, 1980, 317. "Keeping the market elastic" is from Michael Jacobson, "The Enigmatic Crime: A Study of Arson in New York City" (PhD diss., City University of New York, 1985), 131.

7 Note that 1971 was well before the arson wave had reached its height. New York Insurance Department, *Annual Report of the Superintendent of Insurance to the New York Legislature for 1972* (New York, 1973), 90. Insurance Information Institute, "'Depopulation' Is the Key Word in PIPSO Report on FAIR Plans," June 12, 1974, Folder: FAIR Plans, DLIA. New York Urban Coalition, "Fire Insurance: A Crisis for New York's Neighborhoods" (1978), 17. On Hartford, see Gelvin Stevenson, *Fire Insurance: Its Nature and Dynamics* (National Fire Prevention and Control Administration, 1978), 132; Gelvin Stevenson and Robert Magnuson, "High-Risk Urban Insurance Is Under Attack in State," *New York Times*, April 24, 1977, R8.

8 Federal Insurance Administration, "Insurance Crisis in Urban America," (1978), 3–4; James Brady, "A Different Kind of Insurer Helps Fan the Arson Flames," *Boston Globe*, August 31, 1982.

9 Note that excess line companies were also called alien or non-admitted insurers. Bernard Melewski and Mollie Lampi, *Where Do You Draw the Line? Insurance Redlining in New York* (Albany: New York Public Interest Research Group, 1978), 33; Michael Jacobson and Philip Kasinitz, "Burning the Bronx for Profit: Why Arson Pays," *The Nation*, November 15, 1986, 512; Jacobson, "The Enigmatic Crime," 135; and Richard F. Syron, *An Analysis of the Collapse of the Normal Market for Fire Insurance in Substandard Urban Core Areas* (Boston: Federal Reserve Bank of Boston, 1972), 85. New York City Arson Strike Force, *NYC Anti-Arson Update* 2, no. 1 (1983): 3, Folder: Community Publications, Box 2, General Subject Files, 1978–1984, ASF, NYMA.

10 New York Insurance Department, *Annual Report of 1972*, 83–84. Jacobson and Kasinitz, "Burning the Bronx for Profit," 513. For the quotation by the broker, see Melewski and Lampi, *Where Do You Draw the Line?*, 33. New York Insurance Department, *Annual Report of the Superintendent of Insurance: A Preliminary Report to the Legislature for the Year Ending December 31, 1979* (New York, 1980), 42, 62; Jacobson, "The Enigmatic Crime," 135.

11 Eric Williams, *Capitalism and Slavery* (1944; repr., Chapel Hill: University of North Carolina Press, 1994), 104. For histories of Lloyd's of London, see Godfrey Hodgson, *Lloyd's of London: A Reputation at Risk* (New York: Penguin Books, 1986); Adam Raphael, *Ultimate Risk* (New York: Bantam Press, 1994); Andrew Duguid, *On the Brink: How a Crisis Transformed Lloyd's of London* (New York: Palgrave Macmillan, 2014); and Elizabeth Luessenhop and Martin Mayer, *Risky Business: An Insider's Account of the Disaster at Lloyd's of London* (New York: Scribner, 1995). Durante and Grable quotation appears in Jacobson, "The Enigmatic Crime," 136.

12 Robin Pearson, "The Development of Reinsurance Markets in Europe During the Nineteenth Century," *Journal of European Economic History* 24, no. 3 (1995): 557–72. Quotation is from Jacobson and Kasinitz, "Burning the Bronx for Profit," 513.

13 Jonathan Levy, *Ages of American Capitalism: A History of the United States* (New York: Random House, 2021), 539–58; Judith Stein, *Pivotal Decade: How the United States Traded Factories for Finance in the Seventies* (New Haven, CT: Yale University Press, 2010), chapter 2; Saskia Sassen, *The Global City: New York, London, Tokyo* (1991; repr., Princeton, NJ: Princeton University Press, 2001), 33, 66–67; Benjamin Braun et al., "Financial Globalization as Positive Integration: Monetary Technocrats and the Eurodollar Market in the 1970s," *Review of International Political Economy* 28, no. 4 (2020): 794–819.

14 David Harvey, *The Enigma of Capital and the Crises of Capitalism* (New York: Oxford University Press, 2011), 33. Sassen, *The Global City*, 66. See also Levy, *Ages of American Capitalism*, 539–58; Stein, *Pivotal Decade*, chapter 2; and Braun et al., "Financial Globalization as Positive Integration."

15 Quotation is from Lynn Brenner, "Why the World Reinsurance Market Has the Jitters," *Institutional Investor* (January 1980): 176. Kenneth J. Meier, *The Political Economy of Regulation: The Case of Insurance* (Albany: State University of New York Press, 1988), 8.

16 Quoted in Jacobson, "The Enigmatic Crime," 150–52.

17 Ibid., 152. Brenner, "Why the World Reinsurance Market Has the Jitters," 177.

18 For "high returns" quotation, see Raphael, *Ultimate Risk*, 58–59, 70. Murray Seeger, "Heavy Losses Put Lloyd's Tradition to Test," *Los Angeles Times*, February 11, 1980. Hodgson, *Lloyd's of London*, 35.

19 Grandmaster Melle Mel and the Furious Five, "Beat Street Breakdown," by Melvin Glover and Reggie Griffin, Atlantic Records, 1984; Joseph C. Ewoodzie Jr., *Break Beats in the Bronx: Rediscovering Hip-Hop's Early Years* (Chapel Hill: University of North Carolina Press, 2017), 103–8. The precise date of this fire is impossible to pinpoint. Jacobson and Kasinitz, "Burning the Bronx for Profit," 513. See "New York FAIR Plan Loss Experience" for a discussion of how arson statistics were underreported. "Howell Resident Indicted in Insurance Fraud Case," *Asbury Park Press*, April 19, 1984, 13.

20 "Howell Resident Indicted in Insurance Fraud Case." See also Jacobson and Kasinitz, "Burning the Bronx for Profit," 513.
21 Jacobson and Kasinitz, "Burning the Bronx for Profit," 515. Arnold H. Lubasch, "3 Accused of Setting Fire to 19 Buildings to Collect Insurance," *New York Times*, November 30, 1983, B3. "Man, 82, Is Sentenced to 10 Years in Prison," *New York Times*, January 16, 1985, B4. "Bribes, gratuities" quote is from the federal indictment.
22 "Greatest centre" line is from Hodgson, *Lloyd's of London*, 9. Jacobson and Kasinitz, "Burning the Bronx for Profit," 512, 514.
23 Alfred J. Lima, "Insurance Fraud, Organized Crime, and Arson-for-Profit: An Example of Abuse in the Non-Admitted Insurance Market," United States Fire Administration, June 16, 1980, Folder: 11, Box 13, JJ, Harry T. Johnson Collection, LLL.
24 Ibid.
25 The Lima memo meets the genre conventions of both an amicus brief and the 1970s spate of financial fiction. Its interest in the collision of disparate geographies makes it a kindred text to Tom Wolfe's sprawling 1987 novel *Bonfire of the Vanities*. For the role of "master of the universe," the memo cast Tim Sasse, who traded not in bonds, like *Bonfire*'s Sherman McCoy, but instead trafficked in the dealing of risks. Wolfe, *Bonfire of the Vanities*; Leigh Claire La Berge, *Scandals and Abstraction: Financial Fiction of the Long 1980s* (New York: Oxford University Press, 2015). Hodgson, *Lloyd's of London*, 246–51. Patrick Bishop, "Low Notes for the Tenor of Lloyd's," *The Observer*, February 10, 1980, 3. Luessenhop and Mayer, *Risky Business*, 22; Tom Tickell, "Liable to Trouble," *The Guardian*, September 20, 1979, 15.
26 "Easy money" quoted in Hodgson, *Lloyd's of London*, 251. F. H. Sasse, *Theme on a Pipe Dream: A Formula for Buying, Breeding, and Backing the Derby Winner* (London: J. A. Allen, 1969), 4.
27 "Hands-off style" is from Raphael, *Ultimate Risk*, 65. Hodgson, *Lloyd's of London*, 251–52. Lima, "Insurance Fraud," 30.
28 Lima, "Insurance Fraud," 1–4, 31, 33; Hodgson, *Lloyd's of London*, 262.
29 Hodgson, *Lloyd's of London*, 258. Lima, "Insurance Fraud," 4–5.
30 Lima, "Insurance Fraud," 4–5.
31 Ibid. Jacobson and Kasinitz, "Burning the Bronx for Profit," 514.
32 "Lloyd's Syndicate Sues Reinsurers," *Financial Guardian*, March 22, 1978. Jacobson and Kasinitz, "Burning the Bronx for Profit," 513.
33 Lima, "Insurance Fraud," 2; Jacobson and Kasinitz, "Burning the Bronx for Profit," 514. On IRB, see Claudio R. Contador, "Reinsurance in Brazil: Challenges and Opportunities of the Opening of the Market," *Revista Brasileira de Risco e Seguro* 10, no. 18 (2014–2015): 1–48; Marcelo de Paiva Abreu and Felipe Tâmega Fernandez, "The Insurance Industry in Brazil: A Long-Term View," working paper for Harvard Business School, 2010, accessed December 25, 2020, https://www.hbs.edu/faculty/Publication%20Files/10-109_0f4bd05f-0f64-4817-b64a-df83080cbf6f.pdf.
34 Lima, "Insurance Fraud," 7. I am drawing here on scholar David Harvey's question, posed in the epigraph, "With such profound speculative dangers, why does capitalism tolerate fictitious capital in the first place?" Reading Marx's third volume of *Capital*, Harvey rejects the facile tendency to draw absolute distinctions between real and fictitious capital, concluding that "fictitious capital is contained in the very concept of capital." In other words, Harvey contends that even abstract, financialized forms of capital have some basis in—or material effects on—reality. Harvey, *The Limits to Capital*, 265–69.
35 Tom Shales, "The Great Cliches of 1978," *Washington Post*, December 31, 1978, F1. The media's treatment of the arson wave is detailed at length in the following chapter. Lima, "Insurance Fraud," 11; Jacobson and Kasinitz, "Burning the Bronx for Profit," 514.
36 Lima, "Insurance Fraud," 11. Bishop, "Low Notes for the Tenor of Lloyd's."
37 Lima, "Insurance Fraud," 11. Tom Tickell, "Lloyd's Pick Up Sasse Bill," *Financial Guardian*, July 25, 1980, 17.
38 Leslie Maitland and Howard Blum, "Arson in New York: The Landlords and Their 'Torches,'" *New York Times*, November 11, 1980, A1, B4.

39 Ibid., A1. Joe Conason and Jack Newfield, "Arson for Hire," *Village Voice*, June 2, 1980.
40 Maitland and Blum, "Arson in New York," A1, B4.
41 Barry Kluger, interview by author, July 24, 2018, New York City; Maitland and Blum, "Arson in New York," B4.
42 Kluger, interview. Conason and Newfield, "Arson for Hire." Maitland and Blum, "Arson in New York," B4.
43 Kluger, interview. Office of the District Attorney of Kings County press release, "DA's Torch Fire-for-Hire Ring," June 30, 1980, private records of Barry Kluger; Maitland and Blum, "Arson in New York," B4.
44 Kluger, interview. Office of the District Attorney of Kings County press release, "DA's Torch Fire-for-Hire Ring"; Maitland and Blum, "Arson in New York," B4.
45 Maitland and Blum, "Arson in New York," B4.
46 Ibid. Conason and Newfield, "Arson for Hire."
47 Office of the District Attorney of Kings County press release, "DA's Torch Fire-for-Hire Ring"; "Suspicious Fires Found to Have Patterns in City," *New York Times*, November 12, 1980. For more on straw ownerships in 1970s New York City, see conceptual artist Hans Haacke's piece *Shapolsky et al. Manhattan Real Estate Holdings, a Real-Time Social System, as of May 1, 1971*. Quotation is from Urban Educational Systems, *Neighborhood Arson Control Systems: A Manual for Community Organizations* (excerpts), 1983, p. 4.3, Box 2, General Subject Files, 1978–1984, ASF, NYMA.
48 *Arson-for-Profit: Its Impact on States and Localities; Hearings Before the Subcommittee on Intergovernmental Relations of the Committee on Governmental Affairs*, U.S. Senate (Washington, DC: U.S. Government Printing Office, 1978), December 15, 1977, 112. Office of the District Attorney of Kings County press release, "DA's Torch Fire-for-Hire Ring." Conason and Newfield, "Arson for Hire."
49 Conason and Newfield, "Arson for Hire." Statement by Mario Merola before the New York State Senate Committee on Insurance, September 24, 1980, p. 3, Bronx Arson Scrapbook, Box 4, JJ, Harry T. Johnson Collection, LLL. For a partial list of members of the Bald ring, see Office of the District Attorney of Kings County press release, "DA's Torch Fire-for-Hire Ring."
50 Maitland and Blum, "Arson in New York," B4. Daniel Hays and Stephen McFarland, "Arraign 7 in 37 Housing Torchings," New York *Daily News*, July 13, 1983. "Suspicious Fires Found to Have Patterns in City," *New York Times*, November 12, 1980; Lima, "Insurance Fraud," 5.
51 Lima, "Insurance Fraud," 12, 14. Tickell, "Liable to Trouble." Reprinted in the *Irish Times*: "Lloyds Updates Its Rules of Operation," *Irish Times*, March 14, 1980, 12.
52 La Berge, *Scandals and Abstraction*. Hodgson, *Lloyd's of London*, 246. Williams, *Capitalism and Slavery*; Lisa Lowe, *The Intimacies of Four Continents* (Durham, NC: Duke University Press, 2015); Cedric Robinson, *Black Marxism: The Making of the Black Radical Tradition* (Chapel Hill: University of North Carolina Press, 2000), especially chapters 2 and 5; and Paige Glotzer, *How the Suburbs Were Segregated: Developers and the Business of Exclusionary Housing, 1890–1960* (New York: Columbia University Press, 2020).
53 Tom Tickell, "Some 'Sasse Names' Put the Heat on Lloyd's," *The Guardian*, February 7, 1980, 19. The one exception to this tendency was written not by a journalist but by two social scientists (one a former member of New York City's Arson Strike Force), and it was not published until 1986. Jacobson and Kasinitz, "Burning the Bronx for Profit."
54 Luessenhop and Mayer, *Risky Business*, 138. Hodgson, *Lloyd's of London*, 107–8. "Sasse Amends IRB Claim," *The Guardian*, June 29, 1978; Tom Tickell, "Why Lloyd's Has Got That Sinking Feeling," *The Guardian*, July 24, 1979, 23; Murray Seeger, "Heavy Losses Put Lloyd's Tradition to Test," *Los Angeles Times*, February 11, 1980. Bishop, "Low Notes for the Tenor of Lloyd's."
55 "Mutiny" quote is from Hodgson, *Lloyd's of London*, 248. Tickell, "Liable to Trouble." "Just isn't done" is taken from Gregory Jensen, "300-Year Tradition Falls by Wayside: The Rich Are Suing Lloyd's of London," UPI (in *Fort Lauderdale News and Sun-Sentinel*), February 10, 1980. "Not a monolithic" is from Robert McDonald, "Lloyd's Financial Backers Rebel," *The Gazette*, March 18, 1980, 32. Lima, "Insurance Fraud," 12–14.

56 Jensen, "300-Year Tradition Falls by Wayside"; Hodgson, *Lloyd's of London*, 247.
57 Quotations are from Raphael, *Ultimate Risk*, 66. Gregory Jensen, "Lloyd's of London Hurting," *Sunday Pennsylvanian*, May 11, 1980, 12B. Luessenhop and Mayer, *Risky Business*, 138–39, 146–47.
58 Meier, *The Political Economy of Regulation*, 92. Lloyd's relationship to the American market was highly sensitive to the larger market cycles of the reinsurance sector. See Paula Jarzabkowski, Rebecca Bednarek, and Paul Spee, *Making a Market for Acts of God: The Practice of Risk-Trading in the Global Reinsurance Industry* (Oxford: Oxford University Press, 2015).
59 Hodgson, *Lloyd's of London*, 263. Brenner, "Why the World Reinsurance Market Has the Jitters," 177.
60 Rob Nixon, *Slow Violence and the Environmentalism of the Poor* (Cambridge, MA: Harvard University Press, 2013). On the dialectic between "slow death" and state-sanctioned violence, see Robin D. G. Kelley, "Thug Nation: On State Violence and Disposability," in *Policing the Planet: Why the Policing Crisis Led to Black Lives Matter*, ed. Jordan T. Camp and Christina Heatherton (Brooklyn: Verso, 2016), 32.

Six: Out of the Shadows and into the Streets

1 William Wolf, "Paul Newman Breaks the Mold," *New York*, February 9, 1981.
2 Grandmaster Flash and the Furious Five, "The Message," by Duke Bootee, Melle Mel, and Sylvia Robinson, Sugar Hill Records, 1982.
3 Lee Dembart, "Carter Takes 'Sobering' Trip to South Bronx," *New York Times*, October 6, 1977, 1; "Carter Takes Unscheduled Tour of Blighted Bronx Area," *Los Angeles Times*, October 5, 1977, A2. White House Press Secretary Release, October 5, 1977, p. 6, Folder: South Bronx: Announcement, April 12, 1978, Box 411, Jack Watson Subject Files, JC. Patricia Roberts Harris to Jimmy Carter, October 1, 1977, Folder: South Bronx [1], Box 411, Jack Watson Subject Files, JC. John Shanahan, quoted in Paul Grogan and Tony Proscio, *Comeback Cities: A Blueprint for Urban Neighborhood Revival* (Boulder: Westview, 2000), 19.
4 Harris to Carter. Peter Kihss, "'Benign Neglect' on Race Is Proposed by Moynihan," *New York Times*, March 1, 1970. Dembart, "Carter Takes 'Sobering' Trip to South Bronx."
5 "Statement by Jack H. Watson, Jr. at Bronx County Building," October 10, 1978, Folder: South Bronx: Announcement, October 10, 1978, Box 411, Jack Watson Subject Files, JC. Lizabeth Cohen, *Saving America's Cities: Ed Logue and the Struggle to Renew Urban America in the Suburban Age* (New York: Farrar, Straus and Giroux, 2019), chapter 9.
6 "Shocking" is from "Carter's Visit Elicits Reactions from Local Leaders," *El Coqui*, December 1977, 3. "Symbol" is from Richard Severo, "Bronx a Symbol of America's Woes," *New York Times*, October 6, 1977, 46. David Gonzalez, "Of Cameras and Community," in *Urban Mythologies: The Bronx Represented Since the 1960s*, ed. Lydia Yee and Betti-Sue Hertz (New York: Bronx Museum of Art, 1999), 102; David K. Shipler, "Councilmen Angered by Hunts Point Decay," *New York Times*, March 3, 1970. "Psychologists, sociologists" is a Ricky Flores quote, in Mel Rosenthal, *In the South Bronx of America* (Willimantic, CT: Curbstone, 2000), 100. Manny Fernandez, "When Presidents Visited the South Bronx," *New York Times*, October 5, 2007. "Worst ghetto" is taken from Austrian artist Stefan Eins, quoted in the *New Yorker*; cited in Betti-Sue Hertz, "Artistic Interventions in the Bronx," in *Urban Mythologies: The Bronx Represented Since the 1960s*, ed. Yee and Hertz, 18; David Gonzalez, "Faces in the Rubble," *New York Times*, August 21, 2009. The Auschwitz quote can be found in "The Trip to the Bronx," *New York Times*, October 6, 1977, 26.
7 As Emily Brooks's study of 1930s vice policing demonstrates, law-and-order liberalism had been ascendant in Gotham since the mayoralty of Fiorello La Guardia. But it was not until the post–fiscal crisis conjuncture of the late 1970s and early 1980s that revanchist liberalism became the defining political impulse of New York's liberal center. By placing the blame for the city's plight on the racialized figure of the criminal, liberal pundits and policymakers could offer punitive policies as a supposed remedy for the mounting crises of the city. Emily Brooks, *Gotham's War*

Within a War: Policing and the Birth of Law-and-Order Liberalism in World War II–Era New York City (Chapel Hill: University of North Carolina Press, 2023). Jonathan Soffer, *Ed Koch and the Rebuilding of New York City* (New York: Columbia University Press, 2010), 317. Julilly Kohler-Hausmann, *Getting Tough: Welfare and Imprisonment in 1970s America* (Princeton, NJ: Princeton University Press, 2017). Elizabeth Hinton, *From the War on Poverty to the War on Crime: The Making of Mass Incarceration in America* (Cambridge, MA: Harvard University Press, 2016), 254. See also Naomi Murakawa, *The First Civil Right: How Liberals Built Prison America* (New York: Oxford University Press, 2014). Bench Ansfield, "The Broken Windows of the Bronx: Putting the Theory in Its Place," *American Quarterly* 72, no. 1 (March 2020): 103–27.

8 John Glenn, *The Anti-Arson Act of 1979: Hearings Before the Subcommittee on Intergovernmental Relations of the Committee on Governmental Affairs, U.S. Senate* (Washington, DC: U.S. Government Printing Office, 1979), April 26, 1979, 1.

9 CBS Reports, "The Fire Next Door," first broadcast March 22, 1977, by CBS, https://www.youtube.com/watch?v=3zDvsS8JsnY (accessed May 30, 2020). On the blackout, see John J. Goldman and Philip Hager, "N.Y. Buildings and Citizens Smoldering," *Los Angeles Times*, July 16, 1977, A1, 16–17; "In the Bronx, Fires and Tempers Raged on Blackout Night," *New York Amsterdam News*, July 23, 1977, B5. Kim Phillips-Fein, *Fear City: New York's Fiscal Crisis and the Rise of Austerity Politics* (New York: Metropolitan Books, 2017), chapter 17; Miriam Greenberg, *Branding New York: How a City in Crisis Was Sold to the World* (New York: Routledge, 2008), 185–95; Jonathan Mahler, *Ladies and Gentlemen, the Bronx Is Burning: 1977, Baseball, Politics, and the Battle for the Soul of a City* (New York: Picador, 2005). NYPIUA data is from *Flood Insurance and Crime and Riot Reinsurance: Hearing Before the Senate Subcommittee on Insurance of the Committee on Banking, Housing, and Urban Affairs, U.S. Senate* (Washington, DC: U.S. Government Printing Office, 1980), February 28, 1980, 188. Caz and Wiz quoted in Jim Fricke and Charlie Ahearn, *Yes Yes Y'All: The Experience Music Project Oral History of Hip-Hop's First Decade* (Oxford: Perseus, 2002), 133.

10 Robert Curvin and Bruce Porter for the Ford Foundation, *Blackout Looting!* (New York: Gardner, 1979), xv, 21–22. "The Myth of Blackout Looters," *New York Times*, July 13, 1978. Phillips-Fein, *Fear City*, 278.

11 Phillips-Fein, *Fear City*, 272. Curvin and Porter, *Blackout Looting!*, 12–13, 47, 87.

12 "Until that blackout" is from Michael Jacobson, "The Enigmatic Crime: A Study of Arson in New York City" (PhD diss., City University of New York, 1985), 5, 76. Glenn, *The Anti-Arson Act of 1979*, 1.

13 Jordan quotation is found in Warren Brown, "President Is Taken to Task," *Washington Post*, July 25, 1977. Cohen, *Saving America's Cities*, 350. Joe Flood, *The Fires: How a Computer Formula, Big Ideas, and the Best of Intentions Burned Down New York City—and Determined the Future of Cities* (New York: Penguin Group, 2010), 13–14; Mahler, *Ladies and Gentlemen, the Bronx Is Burning*; Sports Media Watch, "World Series Ratings Chart (1972–Present)."

14 Director quoted in Greenberg, *Branding New York*, 150–51. James Sanders, *Celluloid Skyline: New York and the Movies* (New York: Alfred A. Knopf, 2001), 422.

15 The origins of the screenplay were somewhat contested. Many alleged that the screenplay was, at least in part, an adaptation of officer Tom Walker's 1976 memoir *Fort Apache*, chronicling his experiences in the 41st Precinct. Mia Amato, "Fort Apache: The Bronx," *On Location*, October 1980, 56; Peter L'Official, *Urban Legends: The South Bronx in Representation and Ruin* (Cambridge, MA: Harvard University Press, 2020), 216, 235–36. David Susskind deposition, *Rodriguez and Robinson v. Susskind and Time-Life Films*, 05918/80 (NY 1980), 2.

16 "By his own admission" and Newman quotation are from Clarke Taylor, "Newman: The Movie Star vs. the Actor," *Los Angeles Times*, February 1, 1981. Joe Nicholson, "Switch Averts 'Ft. Apache' War," *New York Post*, March 25, 1980. Aljean Harmetz, "Paul Newman, a Magnetic Titan of Hollywood, Is Dead at 83," *New York Times*, September 27, 2008; "Actor Paul Newman Dies at 83," *Los Angeles Times*, September 28, 2008. The critics' quotations are from Wolf, "Paul Newman Breaks the Mold," 48, and Richard Natale, "Film Icon Paul Newman Dies at 83," *Variety*, September 27, 2008.

17 See Neil Smith, *The New Urban Frontier: Gentrification and the Revanchist City* (New York: Routledge, 1996). For Newman quotation, see Wolf, "Paul Newman Breaks the Mold," 48.
18 On the precinct nickname, see "New York Illustrated: Saturday Night at Fort Apache," National Broadcasting Company, March 4, 1973, https://www.youtube.com/watch?v=ICLcal7nNOk (accessed June 26, 2020). Film marketing found in Committee Against Fort Apache (CAFA), "The Selling of 'Fort Apache,'" 1981, p. 3, Folder: 6, Box 12, Diana Caballero Papers, CEP. L'Official, *Urban Legends*, 200.
19 Richard Slotkin, *Gunfighter Nation: The Myth of the Frontier in Twentieth-Century America* (Norman: University of Oklahoma Press, 1998). Office location is from Johanna Fernández, *The Young Lords: A Radical History* (Chapel Hill: University of North Carolina Press, 2020), 274. "Analysis of the Screenplay 'Fort Apache-The Bronx,'" p. 6, Folder: 3, Box 34, Diana Caballero Papers, CEP.
20 Peter Hackes, "Working with the News Media," October 18, 1976, Folder: Speeches, Box 2, Office of the Administrator Subject File 1974–77, Records of the National Fire Control and Prevention Administration, RG 437, NARA.
21 David Susskind deposition, *Rodriguez and Robinson v. Susskind and Time-Life Films*, 05918/80 (NY 1980), 2. Producer quoted in Amato, "Fort Apache: The Bronx," 89. Newman quoted in Jack Kroll, "Battleground," *Newsweek*, February 16, 1981, 81.
22 On *Dirty Harry*, see Pauline Kael, "Dirty Harry: Saint Cop," *New Yorker*, January 15, 1972. For Newman quotation: "Angry Newman Blasts Opponents of 'Fort Apache,'" New York *Daily News*, April 8, 1980. Andrew Sarris, "Liberalism's Last Stand," *Village Voice*, February 10, 1981, 45. Jerry Kearns and Lucy R. Lippard, "Cashing In a Wolf Ticket (Activist Art and *Fort Apache: The Bronx*)," *Artforum*, October 1981.
23 Quotes from Richie Perez, "Committee Against Fort Apache: The Bronx Mobilizes Against Multinational Media," in *Cultures of Contention*, eds. Douglas Kahn and Diane Neumaier (Seattle: Real Comet, 1985), 186. Eli Teiber, "Uprising at Fort Apache," *New York Post*, March 22, 1980.
24 Perez, "Committee Against Fort Apache," 182–83. For more on the coalitional politics of Black and Brown organizing in this era, see Sonia Song-Ha Lee, *Building a Latino Civil Rights Movement: Puerto Ricans, African Americans, and the Pursuit of Racial Justice in New York City* (Chapel Hill: University of North Carolina Press, 2014).
25 "Educate the community" is from "Chronological History of the Committee Against Fort Apache," 1981, Folder: 5, Box 12, Diana Caballero Papers, CEP; Fernández, *The Young Lords: A Radical History*, chapter 9.
26 CAFA goals appear in "Chronological History of the Committee Against Fort Apache." On the declension narratives of 1970s social movements, see Dan Berger, ed., *The Hidden 1970s: Histories of Radicalism* (New Brunswick, NJ: Rutgers University Press, 2010).
27 "Adopted the position" is from Richie Perez, "Richie Perez Watches 'Fort Apache: The Bronx,'" Paper Tiger Television on YouTube, December 16, 2015 (1983), https://www.youtube.com/watch?v=1HRA3oHhSuw&t=166s. "Analysis of the Screenplay 'Fort Apache-The Bronx,'" 1, 4. Orlando Patterson, *Slavery and Social Death* (Cambridge, MA: Harvard University Press, 1982); Sylvia Wynter, "Novel and History, Plot and Plantation," *Savacou* 5 (1971): 95–102.
28 Quoted in Pablo Guzman, "A Director's Defense, a Community's Anger," New York *Daily News*, February 1, 1981. "Analysis of the Screenplay 'Fort Apache-The Bronx,'" 4, 6.
29 CAFA Press Release, March 22, 1980, Folder: South Bronx, Gelvin Stevenson Collection, BCHS. For "budgets" quotation, see Unión Patriótica Puertorriqueña, "The Movie Fort Apache Is a Racist Attack on Puerto Ricans and Blacks," February 26, 1980, p. 6, Folder: 6, Box 12, Diana Caballero Papers, CEP.
30 CAFA, "Questions & Answers About the Movie 'Fort Apache,'" Folder: 6, Box 12, Diana Caballero Papers, CEP. "Editorial: 'Fort Apache, the Bronx,'" *El Diario*, April 11, 1980.
31 "Report on Meeting with Time-Life Corp.," 1980, Folder: 5, Box 12, Diana Caballero Papers, CEP.
32 Perez, "Committee Against Fort Apache," 186. Nicholson, "Switch Averts 'Ft. Apache' War."
33 Kearns and Lippard, "Cashing In a Wolf Ticket." Perez, "Committee Against Fort Apache," 187.

34 Letter from Dan Petrie, n.d., Folder: 7, Box 8, Lourdes Torres Papers, CEP; Susskind deposition. Lorraine Hansberry Literary Trust, "The Private Life of Lorraine Hansberry: Letters, Lists, and Conversations," https://www.lhlt.org/news/private-life-lorraine-hansberry-letters-lists-and-conversations.

35 Perez, "Committee Against Fort Apache," 189. For Newman quotation, see Bob Herbert, "Author-Cop Opens Fire on 'Fort,'" New York *Daily News*, April 21, 1980, 18. Phil Roura and Tom Poster, "Susskind Apologizes to Cops," New York *Sunday News*, April 27, 1980.

36 "Analysis of the Screenplay 'Fort Apache-The Bronx,'" 2. For Newman quotation, see Taylor, "Newman: The Movie Star vs. the Actor," 6 (emphasis in original).

37 Juan Gonzalez, "Review of the Movie 'Fort Apache, the Bronx,'" Folder: South Bronx, Gelvin Stevenson Collection, BCHS. For Petrie quotation, see CAFA Bulletin, April 13, 1981, p. 3, Folder: 6, Box 12, Diana Caballero Papers, CEP. CAFA, "The Selling of 'Fort Apache.'"

38 Perez, "Committee Against Fort Apache," 193. Nat Hentoff, "New York City Council Cavalry Rides on 'Fort Apache,'" *Village Voice*, February 25, 1981. Linn Washington, "Council Protests 'Apache,'" *Philadelphia Daily News*, February 6, 1981. CAFA Bulletin, April 13, 1981, p. 1.

39 *Variety* quoted in CAFA Bulletin, April 13, 1981, 4–5; Perez, "Committee Against Fort Apache," 196.

40 Juan González, "Latinos, Race, and Empire" (lecture, CUNY Graduate Center, New York, December 12, 2022).

41 On the politics of early hip-hop, critic Greg Tate remembers, "the major concern was survival." Interview by author, July 24, 2015, New York City: Jeff Chang, *Can't Stop Won't Stop: A History of the Hip-Hop Generation* (New York: Picador, 2005), 131. CAFA, "The Fort Apache Bop," January 15, 1981, Folder: 6, Box 12, Diana Caballero Papers, CEP. CAFA Bulletin, April 13, 1981, p. 7.

42 See L'Official, *Urban Legends*, chapter 1. Charles Mohr, "Udall, Campaigning in the South Bronx, Keeps a Watchful Eye on Wisconsin," *New York Times*, March 20, 1976, 12. Aline Amon Goodrich, "And What Is the Bad News?" *New York Times*, June 17, 1978, 21. Robert Caro, *The Power Broker: Robert Moses and the Fall of New York* (New York: Alfred A. Knopf, 1974), 893. "Excerpts from the Carter-Reagan Debate," *Boston Globe*, October 29, 1980, 17.

43 Anthony Yudis, "Ed Logue Faces His Biggest Challenge," *Boston Globe*, January 7, 1979, A1.

44 Paul L. Montgomery, "Neat Apartments with a Park Envisioned at Site of Bronx Ruin," *New York Times*, February 5, 1973, 17. Nicholas King, "Charlotte Street: Notes from the South Bronx," *The Sun*, June 15, 1983, A15. Jack Smith, "Vinylly We're Vindicated, as New York Decal-ifornializes Our Image of Self-Nowhereness," *Los Angeles Times*, December 26, 1983, D1.

45 Jill Jonnes, *South Bronx Rising: The Rise, Fall, and Resurrection of an American City* (New York: Fordham University Press, 2002), 4. See also: Robert Scheer, "Bronx—Landscape of Urban Cancer," *Los Angeles Times*, August 6, 1978, A1, and Richard Severo, "Bronx a Symbol of America's Woes," *New York Times*, October 6, 1977, 46. On the nexus of space, race, and matter, see especially Katherine McKittrick, *Demonic Grounds: Black Women and the Cartographies of Struggle* (Minneapolis: University of Minnesota Press, 2006); Mel Chen, *Animacies: Biopolitics, Racial Mattering, and Queer Affect* (Durham, NC: Duke University Press, 2012); Katherine McKittrick and Clyde Woods, eds., *Black Geographies and the Politics of Place* (Cambridge, MA: South End, 2007); and Bench Ansfield, "Still Submerged: The Uninhabitability of Urban Redevelopment," in *Sylvia Wynter: On Being Human as Praxis*, ed. Katherine McKittrick (Durham, NC: Duke University Press, 2015), 124–41.

46 W. R. Messenger, "The Growth of the Bronx in 1911," *Real Estate Record and Builders' Guide*, January 13, 1912. For the quotation about landlord ROI, see Evelyn Gonzalez, *The Bronx* (New York: Columbia University Press, 2004), 85. Robert M. Fogelson, *The Great Rent Wars: New York, 1917–1929* (New Haven, CT: Yale University Press, 2013), 82; Ronald Lawson and Mark Naison, *The Tenant Movement in New York City, 1904–1984* (New Brunswick, NJ: Rutgers University Press, 1986).

47 Ella Baker and Marvel Cooke, "The Bronx Slave Market," *Crisis* 43 (1935): 330–31, 340; Barbara Ransby, *Ella Baker and the Black Freedom Movement: A Radical Democratic Vision* (Chapel Hill: University of North Carolina Press, 2002), 76–78.

48 Baker and Cooke, "The Bronx Slave Market," 331; Matthew Frye Jacobson, *Whiteness of a Different Color: European Immigrants and the Alchemy of Race* (Cambridge, MA: Harvard University Press, 1998). Gonzalez, *The Bronx*, chapters 4–6; Constance Rosenblum, *Boulevard of Dreams: Heady Times, Heartbreak, and Hope Along the Grand Concourse in the Bronx* (New York: New York University Press, 2009), chapters 2–3.

49 Vytenis Babrauskas, "Glass Breakage in Fires," Fire, Science, and Technology Inc. (2009), https://www.interfire.org/features/glass_breakage.asp (accessed November 21, 2024). David Goldberg, *Black Firefighters and the FDNY: The Struggle for Jobs, Justice, and Equity in New York City* (Chapel Hill: University of North Carolina Press, 2017), 175–76; Flood, *The Fires*, 4. Fergus M. Bordewich, "Clearance Work Stirs Objections," *New York Times*, February 10, 1980, R1, 6; Joanne Lipman, "Manhattan Towers Rest on Foundation of Nerve and Timing," *Wall Street Journal*, February 16, 1984, 1, 18.

50 Roger Starr, "Seals of Approval," *New York Times*, June 7, 1982, A18. Lee Lescaze, "Mott Haven: Special Place in Sad History of Public Housing," *Washington Post*, March 14, 1980, A2. Joseph P. Fried, "Housing Project a Fiscal Victim," *New York Times*, November 2, 1975, 1.

51 James Q. Wilson and George L. Kelling, "Broken Windows: The Police and Neighborhood Safety," *Atlantic Monthly*, March 1982; Jordan T. Camp and Christina Heatherton, eds., *Policing the Planet: Why the Policing Crisis Led to Black Lives Matter* (New York: Verso, 2016); Bernard E. Harcourt, *Illusion of Order: The False Promise of Broken Windows Policing* (Cambridge, MA: Harvard University Press, 2001), chapter 1; Tanya Erzen, "Turnstile Jumpers and Broken Windows: Policing Disorder in New York City," in *Zero Tolerance: Quality of Life and the New Police Brutality in New York City*, ed. Andrea McArdle and Tanya Erzen (New York: New York University Press, 2001), 19–49; and Jonathan Soffer, *Ed Koch and the Rebuilding of New York City* (New York: Columbia University Press, 2010), 327–28.

52 Wilson and Kelling cite one other study in addition to the Zimbardo experiment in establishing these connections, but they use this citation solely to support their argument about the role of police in maintaining order, not the relationship between disorder and crime. In substantiating the link between one broken window and many, Zimbardo's experiment alone is cited. For a published account of the second experiment, see Police Foundation, *The Newark Foot Patrol Experiment* (Washington, DC: Police Foundation, 1981).

53 Philip Zimbardo, *The Lucifer Effect: Understanding How Good People Turn Evil* (New York: Random House, 2007), 24. "Crime: Diary of a Vandalized Car," *Time*, February 28, 1969.

54 Philip Zimbardo, "The Human Choice: Individuation, Reason, and Order Versus Deindividuation, Impulse, and Chaos," in *Nebraska Symposium on Motivation*, ed. William J. Arnold and David Levine (Lincoln: University of Nebraska Press, 1969), 290. Philip G. Zimbardo, "Vandalism: An Act in Search of a Cause," *Bell Telephone Magazine* 51, no. 4 (1972): 17.

55 Wilson and Kelling, "Broken Windows." For more on this signifying work, see Bench Ansfield, "The Broken Windows of the Bronx: Putting the Theory in Its Place," *American Quarterly* 72, no. 1 (March 2020): 103–27.

56 This line of argumentation was not new for Wilson—he had been dismissing charges of racism within the criminal legal system since at least the 1970s. Wilson and Kelling, "Broken Windows." Hinton, *From the War on Poverty to the War on Crime*, 270–71; Robin D. G. Kelley, "Thug Nation: On State Violence and Disposability," in Camp and Heatherton, *Policing the Planet: Why the Policing Crisis Led to Black Lives Matter*; Ruth Wilson Gilmore and Craig Gilmore, "Restating the Obvious," in *Indefensible Space: The Architecture of the National Insecurity State*, ed. Michael Sorkin (New York: Routledge, 2008), 141–62; Robert J. Sampson and Stephen W. Raudenbush, "Seeing Disorder: Neighborhood Stigma and the Social Construction of 'Broken Windows,'" *Social Psychology Quarterly* 67, no. 4 (2004); Nikhil Pal Singh, "The Whiteness of Police," *American Quarterly* 66, no. 4 (2014): 1091–99.

57 Janice Simpson and Derek Reveron, "Ghetto Landscape: On Gutted Kelly Street, Vandalism and Arson Aren't Anything New," *Wall Street Journal*, July 20, 1977, 19. Morris Justice Project, "A Summary of Our Findings," accessed January 2, 2021, https://morrisjustice.org/reports. Jorge

Rivas, "NYPD Breaks Down 'Stop-Frisk' Data by Precinct and Race," Colorlines, February 8, 2013. Jennifer Kelley et al., "Lawsuits Show the High-Cost of NYPD Abuse in the Bronx," *The Intercept*, August 19, 2020. Brenden Beck, "Policing Gentrification: Stops and Low-Level Arrests During Demographic Change and Real Estate Reinvestment," *City & Community* 19, no. 1 (2020): 245–72.

58 Soffer, *Ed Koch and the Rebuilding of New York City*, 327. "New York City Tries to Cover-Up on Vandalism," *Hartford Courant*, October 10, 1980, B11. For a brilliant discussion of Occupied Look, see L'Official, *Urban Legends*, chapter 2. Robert D. McFadden, "Derelict Tenements in the Bronx to Get Fake Lived-In Look," *New York Times*, November 7, 1983, A1.

59 McFadden, "Derelict Tenements, B5.

60 John J. Goldman, "City Officials Stung by Criticism of Cosmetic Efforts," *Los Angeles Times*, December 18, 1983, B1. Marshall Berman, "Views from the Burning Bridge," *Dissent* (Summer 1999): 79. George F. Will, "Dressing Up New York: Not as Crazy as It Seems," *Hartford Courant*, December 4, 1983, B3. David W. Dunlap, "Fake Window Decals Pulled in Favor of Real Occupants," *New York Times*, July 12, 1989, B1–2. Soffer, *Ed Koch and the Rebuilding of New York City*, chapter 19.

61 Hetty Fox, transcript of an oral history conducted by Mark Naison et al. on October 1, 2015, Bronx African American History Project. Gonzalez, "Of Cameras and Community," 102.

Seven: Fighting Fire with FIRE

1 David Scondras testimony in *Arson-for-Profit: Its Impact on States and Localities; Hearings Before the Subcommittee on Intergovernmental Relations of the Committee on Governmental Affairs, U.S. Senate* (Washington, DC: U.S. Government Printing Office, 1978), December 15, 1977, 203.

2 Genevieve Brown, transcript of an oral history conducted by Brian Purnell on April 19, 2008, Bronx African American History Project.

3 Ibid.

4 Ibid. Emphasis mine. Genevieve Brooks, "Community Initiatives" (paper presented at the Bronx Institute Conference on Housing and the Homeless, Lehman College, November 18, 1988). Jill Jonnes, *South Bronx Rising: The Rise, Fall, and Resurrection of an American City* (New York: Fordham University Press, 2002), 251–52.

5 Kathleen Teltsch, "Once Desperate, a Bronx Housing Group Earns Praise," *New York Times*, October 30, 1987.

6 Joseph B. Treaster, "Suspicious Fires Up in Slums Here; Buildings Looted," *New York Times*, September 2, 1974, 16. Bronx Arson Task Force, "Fires in Vacant Buildings," 1974, Folder: Fr. Neil A. Connolly, Box 1, JJ, Harry T. Johnson Collection, LLL.

7 Jonnes, *South Bronx Rising*, 258.

8 Testimony of Hedy Byrd in *Arson-for-Hire: Hearings Before the Permanent Subcommittee on Investigations of the Committee on Governmental Affairs, U.S. Senate* (Washington, DC: U.S. Government Printing Office, 1978), September 13, 1978, 170.

9 Ken Auletta, "The Greening of the South Bronx," WNET Reports, March 23, 1978, Folder: South Bronx News Clips, Box 418, Jack Watson Subject Files, JC. The epidemiological study is Deborah Wallace and Rodrick Wallace, *A Plague on Your Houses: How New York Was Burned Down and National Public Health Crumbled* (New York: Verso, 1998), 55. The 108,000 figure is from Michael A. Stegman, *The Dynamics of Rental Housing in New York City* (New York: Routledge, 1982), 50, 177.

10 A parallel argument, albeit one with a slightly different periodization, is advanced by Eric Tang, who points to the 1980s influx of Southeast Asian refugees as one reason the Northwest Bronx did not burn. See Eric Tang, "How the Refugees Stopped the Bronx from Burning," *Race & Class* 54, no. 4 (2013): 48–66, along with Tang, *Unsettled: Cambodian Refugees in the New York City Hyperghetto* (Philadelphia: Temple University Press, 2015).

11 Morris Heights Neighborhood Improvement Association (MHNIA), "Annual Report—1976," March 1, 1977, p. 1, Folder: South Bronx: Morris Heights, Box 417, Jack Watson Subject Files, JC.
12 Alice Kemp-Habib, "How Bad Urban Planning Led to the Birth of a Billion-Dollar Genre," *The Fader*, August 18, 2016. Curtis Stephen, "A Herculean Task: Keeping Mitchell-Lamas Affordable," *City Limits*, January 21, 2008. Herc quotation can be found in Jeff Chang, *Can't Stop Won't Stop: A History of the Hip-Hop Generation* (New York: Picador, 2005), 79. Joseph C. Ewoodzie Jr., *Break Beats in the Bronx: Rediscovering Hip-Hop's Early Years* (Chapel Hill: University of North Carolina Press, 2017), 41–42.
13 The area was further destabilized by the withdrawal of New York University from nearby University Heights in 1973. See Themis Chronopoulos, "Urban Decline and the Withdrawal of New York University from University Heights, the Bronx," *Bronx County Historical Society Journal* 46, nos. 1–2 (2009): 5–24.
14 MHNIA, "Annual Report—1976," 1. "Digging a trench" is from Christopher Hayes, transcript of an oral history conducted by the Bronx African American History Project on October 29, 2015. Brant quoted in Jonnes, *South Bronx Rising*, 347.
15 "Firebrand" is from Jonnes, *South Bronx Rising*, 348. "More stable landlords" is from MHNIA, "Organizational Background," p. 2, Folder: South Bronx: Morris Heights, Box 417, Jack Watson Subject Files, JC. "Tired of moving" is from MHNIA, "Annual Report—1976," 2–3.
16 Murray Schumach, "A Harsh Winter Lashes Elderly and Poor," *New York Times*, February 7, 1977, 20. MHNIA, "Annual Report—1976, 5, 7, 14.
17 Priest quoted in Jonnes, *South Bronx Rising*, 347. Patrick V. Ahern, "The Bronx: Can Anything Good Come Out of That Place?" homily delivered at Fordham University Church, October 6, 1974, Folder: Testimony & Statements, Box 7, JJ, Harry T. Johnson Collection, LLL. Peter Freiberg, "Their Aim: To Stem Slums," *New York Post*, February 8, 1975, 45. See also testimony of Patrick V. Ahern before the Board of Estimate and City Council Hearings, February 18, 1975, Folder: Testimony & Statements, Box 7, JJ, Harry T. Johnson Collection, LLL. "Most extensive" is from Albert Davila, "161st St. Line Drawn Against Decay," New York *Sunday News*, July 20, 1975. Chris Sheridan, "Bronx Coalition Petitions the Elusive Mayor Koch," *Catholic News*, March 1978. For more on church involvement in urban affairs, see John T. McGreevy, *Parish Boundaries: The Catholic Encounter with Race in the Twentieth-Century Urban North* (Chicago: University of Chicago Press, 1998), and Bench Ansfield, "Unsettling 'Inner City': Liberal Protestantism and the Postwar Origins of a Keyword in Urban Studies," *Antipode* 50, no. 5 (2018): 1166–85.
18 "There's no hope" is from Davila, "161st St. Line Drawn Against Decay." Harold DeRienzo, *The Concept of Community: Lessons from the South Bronx* (Milan: IPOC, 2008), 24. "The NWBCCC Community Organization Project," 1974–5, p. 2, Folder: What Is the NWBCCC, Box 7, JJ, Harry T. Johnson Collection, LLL. Reverend Carol Matteson Cox and Reverend Juan W. Sosa to John Keenan, October 25, 1982, Folder: Office Correspondence, Box 8, General Subject Files, 1978–1984, ASF, NYMA.
19 MHNIA, "Annual Report—1976," i. New York Arson Strike Force (ASF), "Arson Activity Report November-December, 1980," p. 3, Folder: Arson Activity Report, Box 17, General Subject Files, 1978–1984, ASF, NYMA.
20 Alexander von Hoffman, *House by House, Block by Block: The Rebirth of America's Urban Neighborhoods* (Oxford: Oxford University Press, 2003), 1.
21 Neil A. Connolly to Jill Jonnes, May 25, 1983, Folder: Fr. Neil A. Connolly, Box 1, JJ, Harry T. Johnson Collection, LLL. Connolly quoted in Thomas Glynn, "The South Bronx: What Went Down Should Come Up," *Neighborhood: The Journal for City Preservation* 5, no. 2 (August 1982): 12. U.S. attorney quotation: Paul Curran to Neil A. Connolly, February 13, 1975, Folder: Fr. Neil A. Connolly, Box 1, JJ, Harry T. Johnson Collection, LLL. Jonnes, *South Bronx Rising*, 259.
22 Meeting details can be found in Minutes to March 13, 1975, Meeting, Folder: Fr. Neil A. Connolly, Box 1, JJ, Harry T. Johnson Collection, LLL. Jill Jonnes points out the noted discrepancy, asking,

"Why did the [clerical] coalition succeed where Gennie Brooks had failed?" Jonnes, *South Bronx Rising*, 260.
23 "Deceased DA Merola Wins Re-Election," Associated Press, November 3, 1987.
24 Mario Merola and Robert Abrams, "Arson Task Force Formed in Bronx," draft press release, March 29, 1975, Bronx Arson Scrapbook, Box 4, JJ, Harry T. Johnson Collection, LLL. Donald Singleton, "Blazes Hit After Cops & Firemen Stopped Patrols," New York *Daily News*, June 4, 1975. National Fire Prevention and Control Administration, *Arson: America's Malignant Crime* (Columbus, OH: Battelle, 1976), 9. "Mish-mash" quote is from Lieutenant George Porette, memorandum, April 13, 1977, Box 2, General Subject Files, 1978–1984, ASF, NYMA.
25 Division of Fire Investigation, "The New York City Fire Marshal's Office," Box 4, General Subject Files, 1978–1984, ASF, NYMA. Testimony of Mario Merola, *Arson-for-Profit: Its Impact on States and Localities; Hearings Before the Subcommittee on Intergovernmental Relations of the Committee on Governmental Affairs, U.S. Senate* (Washington, DC: U.S. Government Printing Office, 1978), December 15, 1977, 190.
26 For quotation, see Frank Logue, "Arson in the South Bronx," 1980, p. 13, Box 2, General Subject Files, 1978–1984, ASF, NYMA. "Verdict: Guilty of Burning, What Prosecutors Should Know About Arson," pp. 4–5, Folder: Battelle, Box 8, General Subject Files, 1978–1984, ASF, NYMA. Herman Weisman, "Arson Resource Directory," U.S. Fire Administration, 1980, pp. 87–9, Box 12, General Subject Files, 1978–1984, ASF, NYMA.
27 For NFPA data, see Testimony of James E. Jones Jr., *Arson for Profit: Hearing Before the Subcommittee on Criminal Justice of the Committee on the Judiciary, U.S. Senate* (Washington, DC: U.S. Government Printing Office, 1981), September 10, 1980, 59. Howard Blum and Leslie Maitland, "Arson Destroying New York Housing at a Record Rate," *New York Times*, November 10, 1980, B4.
28 For Kluger quotations, see John Engel, memorandum re: "Arson Strike Force," September 22, 1978, Folder: Arson Strike Force, August 28, 1978–December 31, 1978, Box 12, General Subject Files, 1978–1984, ASF, NYMA. Barracato quoted in Barry Goetz, *On the Frontlines of the Welfare State: How the Fire Service and Police Shape Social Problems* (New York: Routledge, 2017), 66.
29 Michael Jacobson, "The Enigmatic Crime: A Study of Arson in New York City" (PhD diss., City University of New York, 1985), 70–71. Mario Merola to Herbert Sturz, February 15, 1978, Bronx Arson Scrapbook, Box 4, JJ, Harry T. Johnson Collection, LLL. Blum and Maitland, "Arson Destroying New York Housing" (emphasis mine).
30 Joseph B. Treaster, "8 Landlords and Associates Are Indicted in Bronx Fires," *New York Times*, June 12, 1975, A1. Robert Abrams to Clarence Kelley, June 6, 1975, Folder: Fr. Neil A. Connolly, Box 1, JJ, Harry T. Johnson Collection, LLL. J. Wallace La Prade (FBI) to Mario Merola, May 1975, Bronx Arson Scrapbook, Box 4, JJ, Harry T. Johnson Collection, LLL.
31 Merola and Abrams to Clarence Kelley. Treaster, "8 Landlords and Associates Are Indicted." For "salvage/repair" quotation, see Claire Cooney to Nick Borg, November 12, 1975, Folder: Arson-Grant Proposals-12/31/77, Box 12, General Subject Files, 1978–1984, ASF, NYMA.
32 For "advance guard" quotation, see Charles P. Russ Jr., "Taking the Profit Out of Arson-for-Profit," Folder: NYPIUA, Box 5, General Subject Files, 1978–1984, ASF, NYMA. New York Insurance Department, *1975 Annual Report of the Superintendent of Insurance* (New York, 1976), 48–49. For "more stringent" quotation, see Statement by Richard G. Brueckner (NYPIUA), New York Insurance Department Public Hearing, June 30, 1977, Folder: News, Gelvin Stevenson Collection, BCHS. For "stopped insuring" quote, see New York Urban Coalition, "Property Insurance Workshop," April 21, 1977, Folder: FAIR Plan, Gelvin Stevenson Collection, BCHS. Researcher's quotation: Jacobson, "The Enigmatic Crime," 127.
33 Jacobson, "The Enigmatic Crime," 76. Michael Jacobson memorandum, December 5, 1978, Folder: August 28, 1978–December 31, 1978, Box 12, General Subject Files, 1978–1984, ASF, NYMA.
34 ASF, "Semi-Annual Report to the City Council #9," July 1, 1982–December 31, 1982, p. 8, Folder: Semi-Annual, Box 1, General Subject Files, 1978–1984, ASF, NYMA.
35 For "People were afraid" quote, see Jack Canavan, "How One Neighborhood Foils Arsonists," *Parade*, October 1, 1978. For "body appeared" quotation, see "Body of Boy in Back Bay Fire Iden-

tified," *Boston Globe*, September 14, 1976, 6. For "started by tracing" quote, see Law Enforcement Assistance Administration, "We Are All Victims of Arson," pamphlet (Washington, DC: Department of Justice, 1979).

36 Alexander Hawes, "An Area Complains," *Boston Globe*, November 15, 1976. This same dynamic played out in other cities, including Hoboken, New Jersey. James P. Brady, "Arson, Fiscal Crisis, and Community Action: Dialectics of an Urban Crime and Popular Response," *Crime & Delinquency* 28 (1982): 260; Dylan Gottlieb, "Hoboken Is Burning: Yuppies, Arson, and Displacement in the Postindustrial City," *Journal of American History* 106, no. 2 (2019): 390–416.

37 Goetz, *On the Frontlines of the Welfare State*, 56. Quote about Scondras from Peter Miller, "Preventing Arson," *Washington Post*, November 5, 1977, E33. Urban Educational Systems, "Arson Prevention Seminar," April 9, 1983, Box 2, General Subject Files, 1978–1984, ASF, NYMA; Kirk Scharfenberg, "Stopping the Fires Next Time," *Boston Globe*, December 22, 1979, 13. "Capitalism is the root" can be found in Brady, "Arson, Fiscal Crisis, and Community Action," 268.

38 Michael Kenney, "Curbs Asked on Fire Loss Payments," *Boston Globe*, February 11, 1977, 3. Michael Kenney, "Fire Help Pledged to Symphony Area," *Boston Globe*, February 24, 1977, 3, and Canavan, "How One Neighborhood Foils Arsonists." For Scondras quotations, see Scondras testimony in *Arson-for-Profit: Its Impact on States and Localities*, 203.

39 Barry Kluger, interview by author, July 24, 2018, New York City. Merola testimony in *"Arson-for-Profit: Its Impact on States and Localities*, 190.

40 For "first crack" quotation, see Mark Lieberman and Thomas Poster, "Arson Law Puts Banks 1st for Insurance," New York *Daily News*, October 31, 1977, 15. For "windfall" quote, see Rick Karlin, "Lobbying Legend Lester Shulklapper Dies," *Times Union*, April 3, 2017. For "the very person" quotation, see Blum and Maitland, "Arson Destroying New York Housing."

41 Robert Pesner et al., "Arson Analysis and Prevention Project Final Report," September 1981, p. 14, Box 2, General Subject Files, 1978–1984, ASF, NYMA. ASF, "Semi-Annual Report to the City Council #9," 8. "Not complying" quotation is from Blum and Maitland, "Arson Destroying New York Housing."

42 National Fire Prevention and Control Administration, *Arson: America's Malignant Crime*, 9. For "frequent antagonism" line, see Brenda E. Solomon to Haren Aronstein, August 11, 1980, Folder: Conference/Seminar; Box 4, General Subject Files, 1978–1984, ASF, NYMA. For Merola quotation, see "2 Grand Juries Indict 15 in Arson-for-Profit Ring," Gannett *Today*, July 1, 1980.

43 Jacobson, "The Enigmatic Crime," 127. Brenda Solomon (ASF), "The Role of the New York City Insurance Industry in Combatting Arson," New York Arson Strike Force, pp. 65–66, Box 3, General Subject Files, 1978–1984, ASF, NYMA.

44 Testimony of James E. Jones in *Arson-for-Profit: Its Impact on States and Localities*, December 14, 1977, 82.

45 Gelvin Stevenson, "Upsurge in Arson Calls for Insurance Reform," *New York Times*, September 11, 1977, section 8, p. 1.

46 James Brady, "Arson, Urban Economy, and Organized Crime: The Case of Boston," *Social Problems* 31, no. 1 (October 1983): 13. Advertisement printed in *U.S. News & World Report*, December 12, 1977, 47. American Insurance Association Property Claim Services Committee, "Progress Report on the Property Insurance Loss Register," January 20, 1977, Folder: Arson/Crime, Box 5, Office of the Administrator Subject File 1974–77, Records of the National Fire Control and Prevention Administration, RG 437, NARA. "Arson Costs, Incidence and Motives Highlighted in AIRAC Claim Study," *Target Arson: Update*, Folder: Newsletter #4, Box 20, General Subject Files, 1978–1984, ASF, NYMA.

47 For "patsy" quotation, see Bill Ryan, "Fighting Arson Fraud," *Hartford Courant*, March 27, 1983, B5. John Barracato with Peter Michelmore, *Arson!* (New York: W. W. Norton, 1976). Jon Land, "Arson: John Barracato's War," *Hartford Courant*, June 1, 1980, 4H. Advertisement appeared in *Ebony*, October 1979, 28.

48 "ICAC: 5 Years Fighting Arson," *Target Arson: Update*, March 1984, Box 6, General Subject Files, 1978–1984, ASF, NYMA. Weisman, "Arson Resource Directory," 111. Battelle and Insurance

Committee for Arson Control, *Arson: Ten Years Later: Report of the 1986 National Arson Forum* (Columbus, OH: Battelle, 1986), 3–4; Urban Educational Systems, "A Description of Model Arson Reporting Immunity Laws," Box 2, General Subject Files, 1978–1984, ASF, NYMA.

49 Testimony of John Wrend, *Arson-for-Profit: Its Impact on States and Localities*, December 14, 1977, 153. On the persistence of discriminatory underwriting, see Gregory Squires, ed., *Insurance Redlining: Disinvestment, Reinvestment, and the Evolving Role of Financial Institutions* (Washington, DC: Urban Institute Press, 1997). On 1976 as the peak year for arson, see New York Arson Strike Force, "Arson in New York: 1984," September 1985, accessed October 7, 2023, https://www.ncjrs.gov/pdffiles1/Digitization/99975NCJRS.pdf.

50 For "devastating effect" quotation, see Mary Lynn Tierney to Jerry Hatch, May 17, 1983, Folder: Media Correspondence, Box 20, General Subject Files, 1978–1984, ASF, NYMA. ASF, "Ownership Link Database-Specifications," Folder: Personnel/Empl, Box 1, General Subject Files, 1978–1984, ASF, NYMA. For "arson investigators" quotation, see ASF, "Semi-Annual Report to the City Council #5," July 1, 1980–December 31, 1980, Folder: ASF Report to City Council, Box 6, General Subject Files, 1978–1984, ASF, NYMA; also ASF, "Arson-for-Profit Information Center Final Review and Evaluation Report," September 1981, p. 8, accessed August 17, 2024, https://www.bjs.gov/content/pub/pdf/apic-frer.pdf. "Anti-arson zealots" is from Bruce Hoard, "Computer Link Helps Put Heat on Arsonists," *Computerworld*, August 25, 1980, 18.

51 John F. Keenan to George Zandalasini, Folder: Letters, Box 8, General Subject Files, 1978–1984, ASF, NYMA. Tanay Warerkar, "Inside the Beaux-Arts Emigrant Savings Bank Amid Its Condo Conversion," *Curbed*, June 29, 2017, accessed August 17, 2024, https://ny.curbed.com/2017/6/29/15888976/49-chambers-tribeca-chetrit-gabellini-sheppard-woods-bagot. Kaya Laterman, "Historic Bank Building Near City Hall Becoming Condos," *New York Times*, March 31, 2017, and Steve Cady, "Mayor Invests $4 on OTB Derby Choice," *New York Times*, April 29, 1971.

52 On the "image crisis," see Miriam Greenberg, *Branding New York: How a City in Crisis Was Sold to the World* (New York: Routledge, 2008), and Jonathan Soffer, *Ed Koch and the Rebuilding of New York City* (New York: Columbia University Press, 2010), 180–81. Brian Kates, "Bolshoi on Bronx: No Swan Lake," New York *Daily News*, December 14, 1978, 29; "Soviet Aid Requested for Bronx," *New York Times*, June 21, 1980, 25.

53 Jacobson, interview.

54 The ASF had something in common with the parapsychologists of *Ghostbusters* (1984), whose headquarters was, strikingly, a shuttered fire station constructed in the Beaux Arts style. Jacobson, interview. John Engel to Herbert Sturz, October 4, 1978, Folder: August 28, 1978–December 31, 1978, Box 12, General Subject Files, 1978–1984, ASF, NYMA.

55 ASF, "Arson Analysis and Prevention Project: Final Report," September 1981, pp. 2, 10, 23, 27–33, Box 2, General Subject Files, 1978–1984, ASF, NYMA.

56 For the "expressed fear" quotation, see Cherni Gillman to Milchman Management Co., August 10, 1981, Folder: C.O.U. Landlords Contacted: Bronx, Box 19, General Subject Files, 1978–1984, ASF, NYMA. Cherni Gillman memorandum, August 21, 1981, Folder: C.O.U. Landlords Contacted: Bronx, Box 19, General Subject Files, 1978–1984, ASF, NYMA.

57 John Nealon, meeting agenda and memorandum, December 16, 1980, and March 10, 1981, Folder: NW Bx Comm + Clergy Coalition, Box 19, General Subject Files, 1978–1984, ASF, NYMA. ASF, "Training Elements for the Bronx Arson Prevention and Control Project," Folder: West Bronx/LISC/Ford Fndtn, Box 19, General Subject Files, 1978–1984, ASF, NYMA.

58 On FAPP, see NWBCCC, "Program Operations—NW Bronx Fire and Arson Prevention Project," 1981, p. 2, Folder: South Bronx Prevention Project, Box 12, General Subject Files, 1978–1984, ASF, NYMA. For "threatened" quotation, see David W. Dunlap, "Fighting Arson Before the Ashes Cool," *New York Times*, November 21, 1982. NWBCCC, "Red Cap Program Honored by Northwest Bronx Community & Clergy Coalition," June 2, 1983, Folder: News Briefs June 1983, Box 2, General Subject Files, 1978–1984, ASF, NYMA.

59 Betsy Blanco, Community Outreach Unit Report, 1981, Appendix D, Box 3, General Subject Files, 1978–1984, ASF, NYMA.

60 ASF, "Proposed Anti-Arson Radio PSA's," Folder: Radio P.S.A.'s, Box 15, General Subject Files, 1978–1984, ASF, NYMA. On the racialized construction of juvenile delinquency in New York City, see Carl Suddler, *Presumed Criminal: Black Youth and the Justice System in Postwar New York* (New York: New York University Press, 2019). Sheila Sullivan, "Youth Patrols Dousing Arson in Park Slope," New York *Daily News*, November 18, 1980. For Brown Berets quotation, see "Who Are Those Kids?" *FAC Newsletter*, January 1981, Box 3, General Subject Files, 1978–1984, ASF, NYMA.

61 Muse Software, *Firebug*, pamphlet, Folder: October—Newsletter #5, Box 7, General Subject Files, 1978–1984, ASF, NYMA; Jim Hansen, "Firebug," *Microcomputing*, December 1982, 78; "Publisher's Point," *The National Fire & Arson Report*, Nov/Dec 1982, Folder: Community Publications, Box 2, General Subject Files, 1978–1984, ASF, NYMA. The game remains available for download from vintage game websites like My Abandonware. For pressure campaign, see Richard W. Harris to NYS Arson Board Members, November 17, 1982, Folder: October—Newsletter #5, Box 7, General Subject Files, 1978–1984, ASF, NYMA.

62 "Radio PSA's," *NYC Anti-Arson Update*, August 1982, p. 4, Box 8, General Subject Files, 1978–1984, ASF, NYMA. Talking Heads, "Burning Down the House," by David Byrne et al., Sire Records, 1983. Talking Heads, "Love ➔ Building on Fire," by David Byrne, Sire Records, 1977. ASF, "Proposed Anti-Arson Radio PSA's."

63 "The Omnibus Anti-Arson Law," *NYC Anti-Arson Update* 1, 1981, Folder: Newsletter, Box 3, General Subject Files, 1978–1984, ASF, NYMA.

64 "Anti-Arson Act Signed into Law," *The National Fire & Arson Report*, Nov/Dec 1982, Folder: Community Publications, Box 2, General Subject Files, 1978–1984, ASF, NYMA.

Eight: Corrective Capitalism

1 Quoted in Homefront Abandonment Committee, *Housing Abandonment in New York City* (New York: Homefront, 1977), 95.

2 Neal R. Peirce and Carol F. Steinbach, *Corrective Capitalism: The Rise of America's Community Development Corporations; A Report to the Ford Foundation* (New York: Ford Foundation, 1987), 8.

3 Citizens Committee for New York City, New York Arson Conference, October 29, 1977, Folder: Arson, Box 12, General Subject Files, 1978–1984, ASF, NYMA. Gloria Jimenez (FIA), *Flood Insurance and Crime and Riot Insurance: Hearing Before the Subcommittee on Insurance of the Committee on Banking, Housing, and Urban Affairs, U.S. Senate* (Washington, DC: U.S. Government Printing Office, 1980), February 28, 1980, 40. For "invidious redlining" quotation, see J. Robert Hunter, *Arson-for-Profit: Its Impact on States and Localities; Hearings Before the Subcommittee on Intergovernmental Relations of the Committee on Governmental Affairs, U.S. Senate* (Washington, DC: U.S. Government Printing Office, 1978), December 15, 1977, 370.

The idea of entire neighborhoods being marked as "arson-prone" recalls the geographic euphemism preferred by the Hughes Panel, "riot-prone." "Prepared Statement of National Association of Insurance Commissioners," *Arson for Profit: Hearing Before the Subcommittee on Criminal Justice of the Committee on the Judiciary, U.S. Senate* (Washington, DC: U.S. Government Printing Office 1981), September 10, 1980, 122.

4 New York Arson Strike Force and NYPIUA, "Letter of Understanding," c. 1979–1980, Folder: AFPIC, Box 14, General Subject Files, 1978–1984, ASF, NYMA. New York Arson Strike Force, "Arson in New York: 1984" (September 1985), 33, via NCJRS Virtual Library, U.S. Department of Justice, Office of Justice Programs.

5 On the multiple economic crises of these years, see Greta Krippner, *Capitalizing on Crisis: The Political Origins of the Rise of Finance* (Cambridge, MA: Harvard University Press, 2011); David P. Stein, "Fearing Inflation, Inflating Fears: The End of Full Employment and the Rise of the Carceral State" (PhD diss., University of Southern California, 2014); Meg Jacobs, *Panic at the Pump: The Energy Crisis and the Transformation of American Politics in the 1970s* (New York:

Hill and Wang, 2016); and Judith Stein, *Pivotal Decade: How the United States Traded Factories for Finance in the Seventies* (New Haven, CT: Yale University Press, 2010). For "alleviation of poverty" quotation, see Insurance Information Institute, "Survival of P/C Insurance as Free Enterprise Keyed to Residual Market Solutions, Says I.I.I. Leader," May 26, 1977, Folder: FAIR Plans, DLIA. For "dumping ground" quotation, see John Rawlins Lewis, "Property Insurance in the Urban Core: A Study of the Private Insurance Industry's Social Responsibility and the Role of Government" (PhD diss., University of Wisconsin, 1970), 1.

6 Rick Cole, "Ramon Rueda," Columbia Journalism School, 1979, Folder: People's Development Corporation, Box 3, JJ, Harry T. Johnson Collection, LLL.

7 Ibid. Thomas Glynn, "Something Good Is Growing in the South Bronx: People's Development Corporation," *Neighborhood: The Journal for City Preservation* (December 1977): 8. For an excellent and wide-ranging history of sweat equity in New York, see Benjamin Holtzman, *The Long Crisis: New York City and the Path to Neoliberalism* (New York: Oxford University Press, 2021), chapter 1, and Steve Katz, "The Faded Dream of Washington Avenue," *City Limits* (April 1983): 11.

8 Cole, "Ramon Rueda." For the "waiting to be burned" quotation, see Charles Lockwood, "Taming the South Bronx Frontier," *Quest* (December–January 1978): 38–39. For Rueda quote, see Glynn, "Something Good Is Growing in the South Bronx," 8.

9 Katz, "The Faded Dream of Washington Avenue," 12. For Velez and Benitez quotations, see Glynn, "Something Good Is Growing in the South Bronx," 8.

10 For Rueda and journalist quotations, see Lockwood, "Taming the South Bronx Frontier," 39. For Velez, see Glynn, "Something Good Is Growing in the South Bronx," 8–9.

11 Katz, "The Faded Dream of Washington Avenue," 12.

12 For "We can't depend" quotation, see Homefront Abandonment Committee, *Housing Abandonment in New York City*, 95. For "no landlords," see Katz, "The Faded Dream of Washington Avenue," 12.

13 Joseph A. Spencer, "New York City Tenant Organizations and the Post–World War I Housing Crisis," in *The Tenant Movement in New York City, 1904–1984*, ed. Ronald Lawson and Mark Naison (New Brunswick, NJ: Rutgers University Press, 1986), 77. Mark Naison, "From Eviction Resistance to Rent Control: Tenant Activism in the Great Depression," in Lawson and Naison, *The Tenant Movement in New York City, 1904–1984*, 102–30.

14 The PDC distanced itself not only from cultural nationalisms but also War on Poverty organizations. George Rodriguez, another founder, specifically distinguished the PDC from contemporary "poverty pimp" organizations (a slur frequently aimed at Ramon Velez's nearby Hunts Point Multi-Service Center). Katz, "The Faded Dream of Washington Avenue," 12. Johanna Fernández, *The Young Lords: A Radical History* (Chapel Hill: University of North Carolina Press, 2020), chapters 6 and 9; Perez quotation on p. 209. Pedro Regalado, *Nueva York: Making the Modern City* (Princeton, NJ: Princeton University Press, forthcoming), and "Where Angels Fear to Tread: Latinx Work and the Making of Postindustrial New York City" (PhD diss., Yale University, 2019). Cole, "Ramon Rueda," 12.

15 PDC member quoted in Homefront Abandonment Committee, *Housing Abandonment in New York City*, 95. Rueda quoted in Vivian Vázquez Irizarry and Gretchen Hildebran, *Decade of Fire* (Red Nut Films, 2019). Katz, "The Faded Dream of Washington Avenue," 12.

16 This was not the first time the U.S. government subsidized self-help housing. In the 1940s and 1950s, self-help housing became a worldwide phenomenon, especially in Latin America. In this period, writes Amy Offner, the federal government was "a leading promoter of self-help housing abroad but a wary opponent at home." That changed in the 1960s when the state began funding similar housing projects on Native American reservations. In the early 1970s, one of self-help's evangelists in Latin America, Don Terner, founded UHAB in New York City. Amy C. Offner, *Sorting Out the Mixed Economy: The Rise and Fall of Welfare and Developmental States in the Americas* (Princeton, NJ: Princeton University Press, 2019), 216.

Lockwood, "Taming the South Bronx Frontier," 40. Katz, "The Faded Dream of Washington

Avenue," 12. Quotations are from Roger M. Williams, "The New Urban Pioneers: Homesteading in the Slums," *Saturday Review*, July 23, 1977, 12–14.

17 Carter's people had likely learned of the PDC through Bill Moyers's documentary *The Fire Next Door*, from March 1977. "South Bronx Tour," Folder: South Bronx [1], Box 411, Jack Watson Subject Files, JC; Jill Jonnes, *South Bronx Rising: The Rise, Fall, and Resurrection of an American City* (New York: Fordham University Press, 2002), 312. Katz, "The Faded Dream of Washington Avenue," 19. "Carterized" is from Jack Flanagan, quoted in Jill Jonnes's notes, October 30, 1981, Folder: Bronx Frontier Dev Corp, Box 2, JJ, Harry T. Johnson Collection, LLL.

18 People's Development Corporation, "Neighborhood Revitalization Strategy," pp. 6–7, 12, Folder: People's Development Corporation, Box 50, Edward Joseph Logue Papers, Accession 1985-M-009, YMA. People's Development Project, "Status Report of PDC Economic Development Projects," February 1, 1979, Folder: People's Development Corporation, Box 50, Edward Joseph Logue Papers, Accession 1985-M-009, YMA.

19 For the "urban village" quotation, see Lockwood, "Taming the South Bronx Frontier," 97. Glynn, "Something Good Is Growing in the South Bronx," 14; Cole, "Ramon Rueda." For the cited study, see Institute for Local Self-Reliance, "Potentials for Immediate Open Space Development in the South Bronx," c. 1978, p. 5, Folder: South Bronx [3], Box 411, Jack Watson Subject Files, JC. People's Development Corporation, "Youth Training and Incentive Program Proposal to Department of Housing and Urban Development," p. 3, Folder: South Bronx: People's Development Corporation, Box 418, Jack Watson Subject Files, JC.

20 For Rueda quotation, see Vernetta Hill, "Receives Grant to Rehab Apartment Building," *New York Amsterdam News*, June 26, 1976. Thomas Angotti, "A Critical Assessment of Current Approaches to Housing Finance," *Black Scholar* 11, no. 2 (1979): 7.

21 Katz, "The Faded Dream of Washington Avenue," 13, 19. Martin Gottlieb, "Dream Rises, Fades in Bronx Rehab," New York *Daily News*, July 22, 1979. Cole, "Ramon Rueda," 15.

22 Katz, "The Faded Dream of Washington Avenue," 15.

23 Ibid., 20. Virginia Straus to Jack Watson, May 10, 1979, Folder: South Bronx: Memoranda and Correspondence, 1979, Box 417, Jack Watson Subject Files, JC. Jack Watson to Ramon Rueda, May 11, 1979, Folder: South Bronx: Memoranda and Correspondence, 1979, Box 417, Jack Watson Subject Files, JC.

24 Katz, "The Faded Dream of Washington Avenue," 19.

25 Brian Sahd, "Community Development Corporations and Social Capital: Lessons from the South Bronx," in *Community-Based Organizations: The Intersection of Social Capital and Local Context in Contemporary Urban Society*, ed. Robert Mark Silverman (Detroit: Wayne State University Press, 2004), 110.

26 Ibid., 106.

27 Harold DeRienzo, *The Concept of Community: Lessons from the Bronx* (Milan: IPOC, 2008), 14.

28 Ibid., 30. Janice Simpson and Derek Reveron, "Own Your Own Apartment House—for the Price of a Second-Hand Car," *New York Post*, August 1, 1977. For more on the fraught positionality of Black landlords at midcentury, see N.D.B. Connolly, *A World More Concrete: Real Estate and the Remaking of Jim Crow South Florida* (Chicago: University of Chicago Press, 2014).

29 DeRienzo, *The Concept of Community*, 30, 59. Sahd, "Community Development Corporations and Social Capital," 105.

30 DeRienzo, *The Concept of Community*, 39. Banana Kelly Community Improvement Association, "Sweat Equity Proposal," addressed to the Housing and Development Administration, Folder: South Bronx: Correspondence A–S, Box 411, Jack Watson Subject Files, JC (emphasis mine).

31 For Velez quotation, see Roberta Brandes Gratz, *The Living City: How America's Cities Are Being Revitalized by Thinking Small in a Big Way* (New York: John Wiley & Sons, 1989), 131. DeRienzo, *The Concept of Community*, 34, 58–59. For the photograph with the slogan, see New York State Division of Housing and Community Renewal, *Urban Pioneers: Don't Move, Improve!*, December 16, 1981, Folder: Banana Kelly, Box 44, Edward Joseph Logue Papers, Accession 1985-M-009, YMA.

32 Joyce Hauser, "The Bronx Is Desolate—but It's Being Rebuilt by It's People" [sic], *New York Amsterdam News*, February 7, 1981, 14.
33 DeRienzo, *The Concept of Community*, 39, 47–48.
34 Barbara Stewart, "Hunts Point: Bronx Savior or 'Slumlord'?" *New York Times*, March 29, 1998.
35 Michael Woodsworth, *Battle for Bed-Stuy: The Long War on Poverty in New York City* (Cambridge, MA: Harvard University Press, 2016), 274. Robert L. Allen, *Black Awakening in Capitalist America: An Analytic History* (New York: Doubleday, 1969), 221. Laura Warren Hill and Julia Rabig, eds., *The Business of Black Power: Community Development, Capitalism, and Corporate Responsibility in Postwar America* (Rochester, NY: University of Rochester Press, 2012), 5; Peirce and Steinbach, *Corrective Capitalism*. See also Brian Purnell, "'What We Need Is Brick and Mortar': Race, Gender, and Early Leadership of the Bedford-Stuyvesant Restoration Corporation," in Hill and Rabig, *The Business of Black Power*, 217–44.
36 DeRienzo, *The Concept of Community*, 15. For an instance of this pattern manifesting in another city, see Annelise Orleck, *Storming Caesars Palace: How Black Mothers Fought Their Own War on Poverty* (Boston: Beacon Press, 2005). Ford Foundation quotation is from Peirce and Steinbach, *Corrective Capitalism*, 8, 30.

With a few notable exceptions, urban historians have been slow to examine the origins of community development. See Woodsworth, *Battle for Bed-Stuy*; Orleck, *Storming Caesars Palace*; Julia Rabig, *The Fixers: Devolution, Development, and Civil Society in Newark, 1960–1990* (Chicago: University of Chicago Press, 2016); Brian D. Goldstein, *The Roots of Urban Renaissance: Gentrification and the Struggle over Harlem* (Cambridge, MA: Harvard University Press, 2017); Claire Dunning, *Nonprofit Neighborhoods: An Urban History of Inequality and the American State* (Chicago: University of Chicago Press, 2022); and Nicholas Dagen Bloom and Matthew Gordon Lasner, eds., *Affordable Housing in New York: The People, Places, and Policies That Transformed a City* (Princeton, NJ: Princeton University Press, 2016), chapter 6.
37 Peirce and Steinbach, *Corrective Capitalism*, 8–9.
38 Ibid., 56.
39 Banker quoted in John N. Robinson III, "Surviving Capitalism: Affordability as Racial Wage in Contemporary Housing Markets," *Social Problems* 68 no. 2 (2021): 334. Ford Foundation, "Survey of South Bronx Organizations," March 1979, Folder: Ford Foundation Reports, Box 47, Edward Joseph Logue Papers, Accession 1985-M-009, YMA. Michael Goodwin, "Controversial Father Gigante Wins Applause," *New York Times*, July 15, 1981. Michael Wilson, "One Final Twist in the Rev. Louis Gigante's Colorful Life: A Son," *New York Times*, December 26, 2022.
40 Alexander von Hoffman, *House by House, Block by Block: The Rebirth of America's Urban Neighborhoods* (Oxford: Oxford University Press, 2003), 16; Bloom and Lasner, *Affordable Housing in New York*, 251–52.
41 Keeanga-Yamahtta Taylor, *Race for Profit: How Banks and the Real Estate Industry Undermined Black Homeownership* (Chapel Hill: University of North Carolina Press, 2019), chapter 2. For the LISC quotation, see Peirce and Steinbach, *Corrective Capitalism*, 75. LISC, "A Ford Foundation Background Paper," May 1980, Folder: West Bronx/LISC/Ford Fndtn, Box 19, General Subject Files, 1978–1984, ASF, NYMA. Bloom and Lasner, *Affordable Housing in New York*, 251.
42 Ed Logue to Anita Miller, May 8, 1984, Folder: Rueda, Ramon, Box 51, Edward Joseph Logue Papers, Accession 1985-M-009, YMA. Ford Foundation Division of National Affairs, "Proposal for a Foundation Program to Help Revitalize the South Bronx," November 1979, Folder: Ford Foundation Reports, Box 47, Edward Joseph Logue Papers, Accession 1985-M-009, YMA.
43 Ford Foundation, "The Foundation in the South Bronx: A Summary of Progress and Plans," p. 1, Folder: Ford Foundation Reports, Box 47, Edward Joseph Logue Papers, Accession 1985-M-009, YMA. "Some Suggestions for the Revitalization of the South Bronx," Folder: South Bronx [2], Box 411, Jack Watson Subject Files, JC; Bloom and Lasner, *Affordable Housing in New York*, 249–51. In the early 1980s, some vacant and derelict Bronx buildings were chosen by resettlement agencies to house Cambodian refugees fleeing the aftereffects of Nixon's Cambodia campaign. The influx of refugees further stabilized some apartment houses, building on the momentum of CDCs. Eric

Tang, *Unsettled: Cambodian Refugees in the New York City Hyperghetto* (Philadelphia: Temple University Press, 2015).

44 Jonathan Soffer, "The Koch Housing Program," in Bloom and Lasner, *Affordable Housing in New York*, 273; Goldstein, *The Roots of Urban Renaissance*, chapter 5. Lizabeth Cohen, *Saving America's Cities: Ed Logue and the Struggle to Renew Urban America in the Suburban Age* (New York: Farrar, Straus and Giroux, 2019), 381.

45 Gelvin Stevenson, "The Insurance Experience of Sweat Equity Cooperatives and Non-Profit Housing Groups, 1973–1977," for the Urban Homesteading Assistance Board (UHAB), pp. 3, 6, Folder: UHAB, Gelvin Stevenson Collection, BCHS.

46 Elizabeth Holtzman, press releases, April 28 and November 2, 1977, Folder: FAIR: Congressional Testimony, Gelvin Stevenson Collection, BCHS. See also Rebecca Marchiel, *After Redlining: The Urban Reinvestment Movement in the Era of Financial Deregulation* (Chicago: University of Chicago Press, 2020).

47 Elizabeth Holtzman, press releases, April 28 and November 2, 1977, Folder: FAIR: Congressional Testimony, Gelvin Stevenson Collection, BCHS.

48 E. J. Dionne Jr., "Home Insurance Makes Redlining an Albany Issue," *New York Times*, December 27, 1978, B2.

49 Statement of George Bernstein, in *Problem of Property Insurance in Urban America: Hearing Before the Subcommittee on Housing and Urban Affairs, U.S. Senate* (Washington, DC: U.S. Government Printing Office, 1978), August 7, 1978, 57. For more on the redlining debate, see Caley Horan, *Insurance Era: Risk, Governance, and the Privatization of Security in Postwar America* (Chicago: University of Chicago Press, 2021), chapter 5. For the "pivotal role of discrimination" quotation, see Statement of Donald L. Jordan, *Problem of Property Insurance in Urban America*, 31.

50 Bernstein, *Problem of Property Insurance in Urban America*, 58.

51 Dionne, "Home Insurance Makes Redlining an Albany Issue."

52 For New York superintendent quotation, see E. J. Dionne Jr., "Carey Signs Bill to Cut Premiums for Houses in Areas of High Risk," *New York Times*, July 11, 1979, B3. Kenneth J. Meier, *The Political Economy of Regulation: The Case of Insurance* (Albany: State University of New York Press, 1988), 42.

53 As Rebecca Marchiel shows in her incisive history of NPA, the reinvestment movement's "crowning legislative achievements created a unique role for community organizations as grassroots financial regulators who policed urban redlining at the street level." The story of grassroots regulators tends to focus on savings and loan associations (or thrift banks), but property insurers were also a major target for NPA in the late 1970s. In the same way that scholarship on mortgage redlining in the postwar decades has occluded the history of insurance redlining, the historiography on the reinvestment movement has yet to address grassroots campaigns to rekindle urban insurance markets. Marchiel, *After Redlining*, 5. Beryl Satter, *Family Properties: How the Struggle over Race and Real Estate Transformed Chicago and Urban America* (New York: Picador, 2010).

William Frey, transcript of an oral history conducted by Davis Ross on April 22, 1982, p. 11, Bronx Institute Oral History Project, LLL. Northwest Bronx Community and Clergy Coalition (NWBCCC), Banking Board Hearings notes, January 25, 1978, Folder: Testimony and Statements, Box 7, JJ, Harry T. Johnson Collection, LLL. Testimony of Ted Panos (NWBCCC) before the New York State Banking Department, January 25, 1978, Folder: Testimony and Statements, Box 7, JJ, Harry T. Johnson Collection, LLL. For Devenney quotation, see John Lewis, "Heroes in the Battle for Boro," New York *Daily News*, January 16, 1983.

54 Marchiel, *After Redlining*, 135–91. Julissa Reynoso, "Putting Out Fires Before They Start: Community Organizing and Collaborative Governance in the Bronx, U.S.A.," *Law and Inequality* 24, no. 2 (2006): 232.

55 Stuart V. d'Adolf, "The Neighborhood Activists—What Do They Want?" *Independent Agent*, July 1979, 18.

56 Frey, Bronx Institute Oral History Project, 11.

57 Ibid. NWBCCC Reinvestment Committee, "Redlining, Credit Needs, and the Future: A Study of Bank Investment Policy in the Northwest Bronx," August 9, 1978, Hearing Before the Subcommittee on the Oversight of Financial Institutions, Folder: Testimony and Statements, Box 7, JJ, Harry T. Johnson Collection, LLL.

58 For the "patterned response" quotation, see Frey, Bronx Institute Oral History Project, 11. Aetna, "A Neighborhood Reinvestment Partnership," November 1982, Folder: Reinvestment Comm—NWBCCC, Box 7, JJ, Harry T. Johnson Collection, LLL. "Insurance Redlining: Eight Danger Signs," *Northwest Bronx Neighborhood Action*, August 31, 1978, p. 4, Box 16, JJ, Harry T. Johnson Collection, LLL.

59 Aetna, "A Neighborhood Reinvestment Partnership," November 1982, Folder: Reinvestment Comm—NWBCCC, Box 7, JJ, Harry T. Johnson Collection, LLL. Frey, Bronx Institute Oral History Project, 7. LISC, "Request for Program Action, NWBCCC," March 20, 1981, p. 4, Folder: Arson: South Bronx Prevention Project, Box 12, General Subject Files, 1978–1984, ASF, NYMA. On the politics of "choice," see Nikolas Rose, *Powers of Freedom: Reframing Political Thought* (Cambridge: Cambridge University Press, 1999).

60 "Insurance Companies Promise to Combat Arson and Redlining," *Riverdale Press*, c. January 24, 1981.

61 Frey, Bronx Institute Oral History Project, 9. See also Marchiel, *After Redlining*, chapters 4–5.

62 D'Adolf, "The Neighborhood Activists—What Do They Want?" 17.

63 Gregory D. Squires, "Race, Politics, and the Law: Recurring Themes in the Insurance Redlining Debate," in *Insurance Redlining: Disinvestment, Reinvestment, and the Evolving Role of Financial Institutions*, ed. Gregory D. Squires (Washington, DC: Urban Institute Press, 1997), 7. Peter Kerr, "Did Insurers Abandon the Inner City?" *New York Times*, May 31, 1992; James A. Carlson, "$14.5 Million Settlement Reached in Insurance Suit," Associated Press, March 29, 1995. For the "ugly duckling" quote, see Squires, *Insurance Redlining: Disinvestment, Reinvestment, and the Evolving Role of Financial Institutions*, vii.

64 Matthew Kahn, "Insurance Redlining Needs to End," *Risk & Insurance*, June 25, 2020. Guy Faulconbridge and Kate Holton, "Lloyd's of London Apologizes for Its 'Shameful' Role in Atlantic Slave Trade," *Insurance Journal*, June 18, 2020, accessed November 26, 2020. "The New, New Black Swan," *Risk Market News*, May 31, 2020.

Epilogue: The Ashes of History

1 Robin D. G. Kelley, *Freedom Dreams: The Black Radical Imagination* (Boston: Beacon Press, 2002), 196.

2 Thomas Frank, "Climate Change Is Destabilizing Insurance Industry," *Scientific American*, March 23, 2023. Thomas Johansmeyer, "How 2020 Protests Changed Insurance Forever," World Economic Forum, February 22, 2021; Kate Smith, "Who Was Prepared for This?" *Best's Review*, November 2020.

3 For the State Farm quotation, see Christopher Flavelle, Jill Cowan, and Ivan Penn, "Climate Shocks Are Making Parts of America Uninsurable: It Just Got Worse." *New York Times*, May 31, 2023. Ryan Mac, "Allstate Is No Longer Offering New Policies in California," *New York Times*, June 4, 2023. Sam Sachs, "Florida's Citizens Property Insurance Premium Volume Nearly Doubles," WFLA (Tampa), January 9, 2023; "Another Insolvent Florida Property Insurer Headed to Receivership," *Tampa Bay Times*, February 17, 2023. Insurance Information Institute, "Louisiana Insurance Crisis," March 2023. New York Assembly Committee on Insurance, "The Case for a Permanent Property Insurance Safety Net in New York," March 2005. Emily Flitter, "How a Small Group of Firms Changed the Math for Insuring Against Natural Disasters," *New York Times*, August 16, 2023.

4 Insurers themselves have described the climate crisis as a potential boon to the industry. In the words of Lloyd's CEO John Neal, "Climate is the biggest single opportunity the insurance indus-

try has ever seen." Anmar Frangoul, "Climate Is the 'Biggest Single Opportunity' the Insurance Industry Has Ever Seen, CEO Says," CNBC, November 9, 2021.

For Aon quotation, see Frank, "Climate Change Is Destabilizing Insurance Industry," and testimony of Eric Andersen, *Senate Budget Committee's Hearings on "Risky Business: How Climate Change Is Changing Insurance Markets": Hearing Before the Committee on the Budget, U.S. Senate* (Washington, DC: U.S. Government Publishing Office, 2023), March 22, 2023, 2 (emphasis mine); also available here: https://www.iii.org/sites/default/files/docs/pdf/triple-i_trends_and_insights_louisiana_03282023.pdf. For "unpredictability" in the 1960s context, see Richard Roddis's statement in *Hearings Before the President's National Advisory Panel on Insurance in Riot-Affected Areas* [Hughes Panel], November 8, 1967 (Washington, DC: U.S. Government Printing Office, 1968), 52.

5 Robert P. Hartwig and Claire Wilkinson, "Residual Market Property Plans: From Markets of Last Resort to Markets of First Choice," Insurance Information Institute, May 2016, 6.

6 Saskia Sassen, "Expanding the Terrain for Global Capital: When Local Housing Becomes an Electronic Instrument," in *Subprime Cities: The Political Economy of Mortgage Markets*, ed. Manuel B. Aalbers (West Sussex, UK: Wiley-Blackwell, 2012), 83–84.

7 Michael Kamber, quoted in Denis Slattery, "It's High Time to Talk About the Anticipated Gentrification of the South Bronx," New York *Daily News*, December 4, 2013. On the history of gentrification in New York City, see Suleiman Osman, *The Invention of Brownstone Brooklyn: Gentrification and the Search for Authenticity in Postwar New York* (New York: Oxford University Press, 2011), 265–76; Christopher Mele, *Selling the Lower East Side: Culture, Real Estate, and Resistance in New York City* (Minneapolis: University of Minnesota Press, 2000), chapters 7–8; and Neil Smith, *The New Urban Frontier: Gentrification and the Revanchist City* (New York: Routledge, 1996), chapter 1.

8 Winnie Hu, "Fighting the Image of the 'Burning' Borough," *New York Times*, June 2, 2013.

A typical example of the long shadow of the arson years: during the 2016 presidential campaign, in response to then-candidate Donald Trump's racist dog whistles about the "inner city," the *New York Times* urban critic shot back, "It often sounds as if he is describing the Bronx in the 1970s." Emily Badger, "Actually, Many 'Inner Cities' Are Doing Great," *New York Times*, October 11, 2016.

9 Carolyn McLaughlin, *South Bronx Battles: Stories of Resistance, Resilience, and Renewal* (Oakland: University of California Press, 2019), 248–49; Julie Sze, *Noxious New York* (Cambridge, MA: MIT Press, 2007), chapter 4; Richard Sisk, "South Bronx Is Poorest District in Nation, U.S. Census Bureau Finds," New York *Daily News*, September 29, 2010.

10 Denis Slattery, "It's High Time to Talk About the Anticipated Gentrification." Katherine Clarke, "South Bronx Sizzle," New York *Daily News*, April 8, 2015.

11 Yet another bridge to the history chronicled herein was the event's co-curator, Jeanne Greenberg Rohatyn, the daughter-in-law of Felix Rohatyn, who was the chairman of the Municipal Assistance Corporation—the budget-cutting executor of austerity during the New York fiscal crisis. Winnie Hu, "Bronx Pop-Up Art Show Prompts Criticism That It Invoked Borough's Painful Past," *New York Times*, November 6, 2015.

On the Macabre Suite, see Peter L'Official, *Urban Legends: The South Bronx in Representation and Ruin* (Cambridge, MA: Harvard University Press, 2020), 247–48; Ed García Conde, "Developers, Celebrities Celebrate a Tale of Two Cities at a 'Macabre' Halloween Party in the South Bronx," Welcome2TheBronx, October 31, 2015. Joshua Chaffin, "Not Burning but Building: The Bronx on the Rise," *Financial Times*, December 28, 2019.

12 For an extended critique of the cultural politics behind the Macabre Suite, see Shellyne Rodriguez, "How the Bronx Was Branded," *New Inquiry*, December 12, 2018. The sushi, served at Ceetay in Mott Haven, was later renamed "Bronx Boogie Down Roll." E. B. Solomont, "Chetrit, Somerset Throw A-List Blowout for Mott Haven Warehouse Blowup," *The Real Deal*, October 30, 2015.

13. Hu, "Bronx Pop-Up Art Show Prompts Criticism." As the *Times* reported, "DJ Kool Herc said he had no objections to the show, and was glad to have helped bring more people to the Bronx. 'It was entertainment and art and tourism, that's the bottom line.'" L'Official, *Urban Legends*, 247–48.

The hashtagging of the burning Bronx tapped into a broader nostalgia for the 1970s that bloomed in the 2010s, a pining often expressed through the metaphor of fire. Book titles like *City on Fire*, *The Flamethrowers*, *Love Goes to Buildings on Fire*, and *Ladies and Gentlemen, the Bronx Is Burning* have hardened the link between the inflationary and the inflammatory 1970s. Though anti-arson organizing took the profit out of fire decades ago, fire apparently remains a profitable mode for narrating history. For an incisive review of some of the works listed below, see Nicholas Dames, "Seventies Throwback Fiction: A Decade in Review," *N+1* 21 (Winter 2015): 147–57. Garth Risk Hallberg's *City on Fire* (New York: Alfred A. Knopf, 2015), for example, earned one of the highest-ever advances for a debut novel. Rachel Kushner, *The Flamethrowers* (New York: Scribner, 2013); Will Hermes, *Love Goes to Buildings on Fire* (New York: Faber and Faber, 2011); Jonathan Mahler, *Ladies and Gentlemen, the Bronx Is Burning: 1977, Baseball, Politics, and the Battle for the Soul of a City* (New York: Picador, 2005). Julie Bosman, "'City on Fire,' a Debut Novel, Fetches Nearly $2 Million," *New York Times*, November 10, 2013. Jill Jonnes, *South Bronx Rising: The Rise, Fall, and Resurrection of an American City* (New York: Fordham University Press, 2002), 398–406. Clarke, "South Bronx Sizzle."

14. Hu, "Bronx Pop-Up Art Show Prompts Criticism."
15. Rodriguez, "How the Bronx Was Branded." Take Back the Bronx (@takebackBX and @TakeBackTheBX), Twitter, accessed January 21, 2021. Take Back the Bronx, Facebook, January 26, 2016, accessed January 21, 2021, https://www.facebook.com/takebackthebx/posts/1201309259898535. For more on Nos Quedamos, see https://www.nosquedamos.org and McLaughlin, *South Bronx Battles*, 161–62.

On the ongoing cycle of dispossession, see Jodi A. Byrd, Alyosha Goldstein, Jodi Melamed, and Chandan Reddy, "Predatory Value: Economies of Dispossession and Disturbed Relationalities," *Social Text* 36, no. 2 (June 2018): 1–18, and David Harvey, *The New Imperialism* (New York: Oxford University Press, 2003), 116–51.

16. Virginia K. Smith, "Confessions of a Neighborhood Blogger: The Blogger Behind 'Welcome 2 the Bronx' Dishes on the REAL Little Italy, Why the Borough Shouldn't Be 'Colonized,' and More" (Ed García Conde interview), Brick Underground, November 15, 2016.
17. Vivian Vázquez Irizarry and Gretchen Hildebran, *Decade of Fire* (Red Nut Films, 2019). Quoted in Conde, "Developers, Celebrities Celebrate a Tale of Two Cities." For more on Antonetty, see Sonia Song-Ha Lee, *Building a Latino Civil Rights Movement: Puerto Ricans, African Americans, and the Pursuit of Racial Justice in New York City* (Chapel Hill: University of North Carolina Press, 2014) and Lana Dee Povitz, *Stirrings: How Activist New Yorkers Ignited a Movement for Food Justice* (Chapel Hill: University of North Carolina Press, 2019).
18. Kelley, *Freedom Dreams*.

A Note on Arson Statistics

1. Committee on Governmental Affairs of the U.S. Senate, *Arson in America* (Washington, DC: U.S. Government Printing Office, 1979), 3.
2. Testimony of Michael J. O'Connor (chief fire marshal of FDNY), in *Arson-for-Profit: Its Impact on States and Localities; Hearings Before the Subcommittee on Intergovernmental Relations of the Committee on Governmental Affairs, U.S. Senate* (Washington, DC: U.S. Government Printing Office, 1978), December 15, 1977, 226.
3. Michael Jacobson, "The Enigmatic Crime: A Study of Arson in New York City" (PhD diss., City University of New York, 1985), 15–18.
4. Ibid., 19.
5. Arson Strike Force memorandum, "Reporting and Investigations of Suspicious Fires by Police and Fire Marshals 1976–1977," October 1978, Folder: BCAP and Arson, Box 10, General Subject Files, 1978–1984, ASF, NYMA.

6 Jacobson, "The Enigmatic Crime," 26–27.
7 Ibid., 20.
8 Ibid.
9 Ibid. Michael Jacobson, interview by author, September 18, 2017, New Haven, CT.
10 Anne Winslow Murphy and Andrew Maneval, "Arson Fraud: Criminal Prosecution and Insurance Law," *Fordham Urban Law Journal* 7, no. 3 (1978): 543.
11 Jacobson, "The Enigmatic Crime," 22–24.
12 Texas Insurance Information Center, "Texas Insurance Fact File No. 65b," April 25, 1979, Folder: Ins. Co. Responses, Box 10, General Subject Files, 1978–1984, ASF, NYMA.
13 Reported in Michael Graham and Jim Neubacher, "Fire Fraud Spreads Statewide," *Detroit Free Press*, July 18, 1974.
14 Jacobson, "The Enigmatic Crime," 1.
15 Joe Flood, *The Fires: How a Computer Formula, Big Ideas, and the Best of Intentions Burned Down New York City—and Determined the Future of Cities* (New York: Riverhead Books, 2010), 19.
16 Ibid., 19–20. In the Bronx, he writes, "Aging electrical wiring and outlets, as well as leaky oil- and gas-burning furnaces and water heaters, sparked thousands of blazes." Flood's claims have been contentious, with one online report dedicated to enumerating its "instances of errors, misrepresentations, speculation, and analytic deficiencies." Catherine O'Hagan Wolfe, "'The Fires . . .' by Joe Flood: Instances of Errors, Misrepresentations, Speculation and Analytic Deficiencies," accessed January 27, 2020, https://static1.squarespace.com/static/5b3a8a2aa2772c2f141d7d2f/t/5c255a63c2241b57cbd384a4/1545951843721/Instances+of+errors%2C+misrepresentations%2C+speculation+and+analytical+deficiencies.pdf.
17 Urban Educational Systems, "Profiles: A Handbook on Community Arson Prevention," 1981, p. 1, Box 3, General Subject Files, 1978–1984, ASF, NYMA.
18 Patrick W. Sullivan, "S. Bronx: A Line of Fire," *New York Post*, April 27, 1977, 41.
19 Address by Howard Tipton, April 29, 1976, Folder: Arson/Crime, Box 5, Office of the Administrator Subject File 1974–77, Records of the National Fire Control and Prevention Administration, RG 437, NARA.
20 "Arson for Hate and Profit," *Time*, October 31, 1977, 22.
21 Saidiya Hartman, *Wayward Lives, Beautiful Experiments: Intimate Histories of Social Upheaval* (New York: W. W. Norton, 2019), 155.

CREDITS

1 © Tim Rollins and K.O.S.
3 Tim Rollins and K.O.S., *Untitiled (brick)*, 1984 (screenshot from Whitney.org Online Collection). Oil on brick, 8⅛ × 3½ × 2½ in. (20.6 × 8.9 × 6.4 cm). Whitney Museum of American Art, New York; promised gift of Thea Westreich Wagner and Ethan Wagner P.2011.348. © Tim Rollins and K.O.S.
4 New York Daily News / Tribune Content Agency
5 Wesley Pearman
7 Map adapted from "Burning Down, Rising Up: The Bronx in the Seventies," in *Nonstop Metropolis: A New York City Atlas*, edited by Joshua Jelly-Schapiro and Rebecca Solnit (University of California Press, 2016); cartography by Molly Roy, research by Jonathan Tarleton, design by Lia Tjandra
19 LBJ Library
32 LBJ Library
39 LBJ Library / The President's National Advisory Panel on Insurance in Riot-Affected Areas
47 Getty / New York Daily News
50 New York Municipal Archives
73 Copyright Camilo José Vergara
79 Larry Morris / The New York Times / Redux
83 Electragraphics
85 Cartoon by Paul Rigby, appeared in the *New York Post*
90 National Fire Protection and Control Administration
101 Perla de Leon, *Good Morning Teacher* © 1980
105 Jill Freedman Estate
112 New York Daily News / Tribune Content Agency
114 Rodrick Wallace
118 Electragraphics
122 Copyright Martin Wong Foundation; Courtesy of the Martin Wong Foundation and P·P·O·W, New York
136 Electragraphics
140 Getty / Evening Standard
161 Eddie Hausner / The New York Times / Redux
170 Copyright Time-Life Films
175 Copyright Jerry Kearns
177 Copyright Jerry Kearns
182 *The Boston Globe*, January 7, 1979. © Boston Globe Media Partners
187 Philip Zimbardo, Nebraska Symposium on Motivation (1969). Courtesy of the University of Nebraska Press.

189 The Morris Justice Project
191 New York Department of Housing Preservation and Development, October 1980
193 © Aetna
212 © The Travelers Insurance Company
214 Electragraphics
219 Northwest Bronx Community and Clergy Coalition
222 Copyright Muse Software
225 Photograph © Allen Tannenbaum / SoHoBlues.com
233 Jimmy Carter Library
235 Getty / Bettmann
240 New York State Division of Housing and Community Renewal
255 Copyright Joe Conzo Archive / TATS Cru

INDEX

Page numbers in *italics* refer to illustrations/photos and accompanying captions.
Page numbers after 281 refer to endnotes.

abandonment, 7, 62–67, 69, *73*, 81, 107, 131–32, 197, 201, 230, 238
abolitionism, 135
Abrams, Robert, 66, 202, 205
absentee landlords, 13, 38, 68, 82, 119
accelerants, fire, 125, 204
ACT UP, 180
Action (NWBCCC bulletin), 252
"acts of God," 30
actuaries (actuarial science), 12, 33–35, 38, 42, 59, 60, 85, 86, 91, 123–24, 143, 146, 226, 252, 254, 257, 263
adjusters. *See* insurance adjusters
aerial photography, 32, *32*
Aetna, 8, 27, 95, *193*, 212–13, 218, 220, 245, 252
affirmative action, 37, 38, 44
affordable housing, 83, 198, 228, 237, 242–46
AFL-CIO, 43
Ahern, Patrick V., 200
Albany, New York, 221; *see also* New York State
Albuquerque, New Mexico, 179
Alinsky, Saul, 199, 249–50
Allen, Robert L., 242
Alliance Insurance Company, 35
Alliance of American Insurers, 249
Allstate, 218, 252, 256
America Burning (report), 89, *90*, 164
American dream, 52, 116, 183
American Insurance Association (AIA), 35
American Mutual Insurance Alliance, 214
amortization, recapture of, 64
Amsterdam News, 58
Anchorage, Alaska, 117
Andersen, Eric, 257
Anderson, South Carolina, 194

anonymity, sense of, 186–87
Anti-Arson Act (1982), 222–23
anti-arson initiatives (anti-arson movement), 14, 82, 94, 94, 117, *118*, 153, 166, 195, 206, 210–15, *212*, 217–19, 226, 247, 263, 276, 328
anti-fraud measures, 207, 210–11, 213–14
anti-gentrification activism, 261–63
anti-Semitism, 8, *85*, 85–86, *86*, 178, 282
anti-trust laws, 30
Aon, 257
Apple II, 220, *222*
Arab-Israeli War (1973), 142
aristocracy, British, 146, 155, 158
arson; *see also* arson wave (1970s)
  as conspiracy, 4, 76–77, 85–86, 131, 136–37, 153, 202–3
  deaths related to, 6, 110, 120, 302
  injuries related to, 110–11
  predicting, 82, 208, 217–18
  prevalence/rates of, 2, 29, 83, *83*, 89, 92, 118–20, 124, 157, 196–97, 205–6, 214, *214*, 226–27, 252, 275–76
  psychological effects of, 102–15
  scapegoating of, 14, 104, 120, 121, 127, 131, 144–45, 155, 238, 239, 284
  "trailers" of, 204
  welfare, 9, 104, 127–31, 207
Arson! (Barracato), 213
arson arrests, 76, 78, 79, *79*, 204, 209
arson databases, 275
"arson for profit," 74, 77, 78, 92, 98, 121, 124–26, 130, 131, 135–36, 166, 176, *193*, 196, 197, 202, 208–11, 215–17, 220, 221
Arson in America (report), 126

arson investigators (arson investigations), 76–77, 80, 87, 93–94, 96, 121, 123, 125, 127, 139, 166, 196, 202–5, 208, 210–11, 214–16, 218, 221, 222, 275
arson research, 145, 302
Arson Resource Directory, 117
arson rings, 76–77, 135–37, 144–48, 150–54, 204, 209, 215
Arson Risk Prediction Index, 217, 218
"arson squad," 210
Arson Strike Force (ASF), 77, 82, 92, 96, 125, 129, 166, 207, 210–12, *214*, 215–23, 217–23, *219*, *222*, 226, 275, 320
arson wave (1970s)
 blaming of residents for, 2, 7–8, 14, 29, 104, 120, 125, 127, 129, 131, 144–45, 155, 175–76, 185, 238, 239, 306
 and Bronx exceptionalism, 7, 117
 deaths from, 6, 110, 120, 302
 destruction caused by, 6
 downplaying of, 276
 end of, 193–224
 peak of, 89
 profit as driver of, 4–5, 82–84, 87–88, 92–97
 psychic toll of, 102–15
 and race, 6–9, 12
 and shifts in political economy, 9, 92–97
 and urban renewal, 14
Arson-for-Profit Information Center, 215–16
"arson-prone areas," 42, 96, 226, 321
Art Deco, 184
Artforum, 177
ASF. *See* Arson Strike Force
Asner, Ed, 169
asphyxiation, arson-related, 110
assigned-risk auto insurance, 292
Association of Lloyd's Members, 157
Atlantic Monthly, 185, 188, 190
Auletta, Ken, 197
austerity measures (austerity politics), 54–56, 59, 97, 116, 165, 174–75, 242
auto insurance, 292
Ayala, Luis, 150–53, 210

Back in the Bronx magazine, 52
"back of the bus" insurance, 41, 137, 252
Badillo, Herman, 247
Bailey, William O., 252
Bailey Avenue (Bronx), 66
Bainbridge, John, 19
Baker, Ella, 183–84
Bald, Joe, 152–54, 210

"Bald ring," 151–54
Baldwin, James, 19
Baltimore, Maryland, 220
Baltimore Sun, 182
Bambaataa, Afrika, 131
Banana Kelly Community Improvement Association, 237–42, *240*
banks and banking, 8, 10, 25, 54, 64–65, 74–76, 84, 85, 95, 128, 141, 142, 199, 209, 220, 250–51
Barclay, Mrs., 66
Barracato, John, 128, 205, 212–13
Bartlesville, Oklahoma, 90
Bateman, J. Carroll, 68
Beame, Abe, 162, 166, 207
Bedford Stuyvesant Restoration Corporation, 242
Bedford-Stuyvesant neighborhood (Brooklyn), 151–52
Belmont Avenue (Bronx), 74–76, 81, 87, 90, 98
Benitez, Jane, 229–30
Bentley, James, 33
Berkman, Alexander, 34
Berman, Marshall, 54, 120, 125
Bernstein, George, 43–44, 248
Best's Weekly, 34
"Bicentennial Blues" (song), 134, 155
Bicentennial celebration (1976), 134
Biden, Joseph R., and administration, 87, 126, 290
Big Heat (painting), 122, *122*
"binding agents," 145, 146
Birmingham, Alabama, 6, 290
Black Americans, 1, 6–9, 12, 20–22, 27–29, 31, 33–35, 38, 41–42, 45, 49, 52, 52, 53, 53, 55–57, 60, 61, 65, 67, 78, 107–8, 110, 123–25, 128, 134–35, 155, 162, 165–67, 169, 171, 173–76, 183, 194, 195, 221, 229, 231, 236, 238, 240, 253, 254
Black and Latino Coalition Against Police Brutality, 173
Black Awakening in Capitalist America (Allen), 242
Black capitalism, 242
Black Liberation Army, 169
Black militancy (Black power movement), 13, 38, 242
Black Panthers (Black Panther Party), 169, 228, 231
Black United Front, 174
blackface, 3, 4, *4*, 8, 9, 282
Blackness, 8, 42, 123–24, 282

blackout (New York City, 1977), 164–66, 181, 207, 209, 211
block associations, 104, 194, 197, 199, 215, 217–18, 223, 251
blockbusting, 28, 107
Bloomington, Illinois, 253
blues, the, 134, 155
Bolshoi Ballet, 216
bombs (bombings), 34, 143–45, 148, 205
bonds, 54, 94, 96, 97
Boner Realty, 153
Bonet, Roberto, 79
Bonfire of the Vanities (Wolfe), 133, 309
Borden, Lizzie, 14–15
Born in Flames (film), 14–15
Boston, Massachusetts, 5, 14, 27, 36, 95, 117, 119, 121, 126, 179, 207–9, 212, 217
Boston Globe, 119, 124, 181–82, *182*
Boulevard of Dreams: Heady Times, Heartbreak, and Hope Along the Grand Concourse in the Bronx (Rosenblum), 52
Bouza, Anthony, 202
Boyd, Rosetta, 110–11
Brady, James, 212
Brando, Marlon, 21
Brant, Paul, 199–201
brass salvaging, 126
Braudel, Fernand, 10
Brazil, 13, 135, *136*, 148
breakdancing, 198
Brenner, Lynn, 142–43
Bretton Woods system, 141
Bricks series, *1*, 2–3, *3*, 260
Briggs Avenue (Bronx), 251
Britain. *See* aristocracy, British; United Kingdom
British Empire, 10
Brody, Adrien, 260
broken windows (broken windows policing), 9, 14, 61, 163, 180–81, 183–92, *189*, 199, 200, 261, 315
"Broken Windows: The Police and Neighborhood Policy" (Wilson and Kelling), 185–88
Bronx; *see also* South Bronx; *specific neighborhoods*
 arson by small-time landlords in, 77
 arson rings in, 145, 148, 151–54
 average arson loss in, 92
 brownlining in, 49, 61–62
 Co-op City's effect on, 52–54
 exceptionalism of, 7, 117–19
 and financialization, 97
 fireproof housing construction in, 80–81, 88
 firewatching in, *101*, 102–9, *105*
 gentrification in, 259–63
 landlord abandonment in, 63
 loss of housing stock in, *7*
 mortgage redlining in, 65
 nostalgia surrounding the past, 51–52, 183, 328
 NYPIUA's effect on, 59–62
 population loss during 1970s, *114*, 114–15
 rate of arson in, 276
 risk communities in, 86
 scapegoating of residents of, 12, 29
 subprime lending in, 258
 tenant movement in, 198–202, 217–20, 227, 250–53
 in triangular trade, 135–37, *136*, 145, 158
 upper-floor fire in (photo), *5*
 welfare recipients in, 127–30
Bronx Arson Task Force, 195–96, 202
Bronx County Courthouse, 202
Bronx D.A. office, 202; *see also* Merola, Mario
Bronx in the Innocent Years, 1890–1925, The (Bronx County Historical Society), 52
Bronx Is Burning, The (ESPN series), 166
"Bronx miracle," 246
Bronx Office of Rent Control, 84
Bronx pastoral, 51–52
Bronx People's Development Corporation. *See* People's Development Corporation
Bronx Realty Advisory Board, 49–51, 63
Bronx River Houses, 131
Bronx Savings Bank, 250
"Bronx Slave Market, The" (Cooke), 183–84
Bronx Tenant League, 231
Bronx Warriors, The (film), 167
Bronxploitation films, 9, 14, 167; *see also Fort Apache, the Bronx* (1981 film)
Brooklyn, New York, 27, 53, 62, 63, 102, 151–54, 173, *191*, 218, 220, 242, 247, 260
Brooks, Emily, 311–12
Brooks, Genevieve. *See* Brown, Genevieve Brooks
Brooks, Herbert, 194
Brown, Genevieve Brooks, 106, 108, 115, 194–95, 202, 203, 207, 238
Brown Berets, 220
brownlining, 13, 49, 59, 61–62, 66, 69, 70, 75, 86, 87, 97, 135, 147, 196, 201, 219, 226, 227, 239, 246–47, 249, 251, 252, 254, 256, 258, 299
Brueckner, Richard G., 67
building codes, 88, 89, 217, 241

Bumpurs, Eleanor Gray, 301
Burn Out: How to Beat the High Cost of Success (Freudenberger), 116–17
"burning" (DJ technique), 198
"Burning Down the House" (song), 221
burnout, 14, 115–17
burns, arson-related, 110
Bushwick neighborhood (Brooklyn), 107
Butch Cassidy and the Sundance Kid (film), 168, 170
Byrd, Hedy, 48–49, 49, 59, 110, 130, 196
Byrne, David, 221

Caballero, Diana, 173, 180
CAFA. *See* Committee Against Fort Apache
Cairo, Egypt, 120
California, 34, 84, 256
Cambodian refugees, 324
Campbell, Cindy, 198
Campbell, Clive. *See* Herc, DJ Cool
Campbell, Naomi, 260
Campbell, Rita, 251
Campbell family, 197–98
Canada, 120
cancer metaphors, 107–8
Capital (Marx), 309
capitalism, 9, 11, *19*, 20, 24, 28, 33, 75, 84, 85, 97, 133, 209, 212, 216, 242, 263; *see also* racial capitalism
Capitalism and Slavery (Williams), 139
carbon emissions, 257
carceral state, 57, 60, 61, 163
Carlos (Bronx resident), 55–56
Caro, Robert, 52–53, 181
Carruthers, Francis, 202
Carter, Jimmy, and administration, 114, 123, 162–63, 166, 168, 178, 181, 211, *233*, 233–34, 237, 239, 245–46, 248
cash-flow underwriting, 95
cash-out refinancing, 64
Casita Maria Settlement House, 237–38
Catholic Church, 199–200, 202–3
Cauldwell Avenue (Bronx), 105
Cavalry and Guards Club, 156
Caz, Grandmaster, 164–65
CBS, 164
CDCs. *See* community development corporations
Cedardale Drug Company, 61–62
Center for Urban Policy Research, 64
CETA (Comprehensive Employment and Training Act), 241

Charlotte Street (Bronx), 114–15, 162–63, 167–69, 171, 195, *225*, 229
Chicago, Illinois, 41–42, 60, 88, 123, 199, 203, 250, 252, 253, 289–90
Chicago Law Review, 40–41
Chicanos, 179
children, 48–49, 104–5, 108–11, 194–95, 220–21, 228
China, 234
Chisholm, Shirley, 247
Christian, Samuel, 106
Cincotta, Gale, 251, 252
Citibank, 220
City on Fire (Hallberg), 292
City Planning Commission (New York), 190
civil rights movement, 6, 12, 42, 188
Civil War, 123
Civilization and Its Discontents (Freud), 121
claims, settlement of, 5, 87, 93–94, 144, 211, 273
Cleveland, Ohio, 36, 117
climate change, 30, 44, 256–58
Clinton, Bill, 163
Coalition of Asians to Nix Charlie Chan, 174
coastal property, 43–44, 256–57
cocaine, 172
Cockettes, 122
cocklofts, 81, 127, 143–44, 150–51
Cold War, 4, 215
Colon, Angelo, 78–79
Colorado, 34
"color-blind" racial politics, 42
Colored Orphan Asylum (New York City), 123
Columbian Brokerage, *136*, 145, 154
Comiskey Park (Chicago), 123
Committee Against Fort Apache (CAFA), 172–80, *175*, *177*, 231, 261
Committee on General Welfare (New York City Council), 179
Communism, 183, 231
Community Action Program, 242, 243
community development corporations (CDCs), 195, 227–28, 237–47, 259
Community Reinvestment Act (CRA) (1977), 250, 253, 295
Comprehensive Employment and Training Act (CETA), 241
Concourse Plaza Hotel, 131
condo conversions, 126, 129
Congress, 12, 36, 80, 91, 93, 107, 164, 245, 247, 248; *see also* U.S. Senate
Connecticut, 115, 119, 228
Connolly, Neil A., 196, 202–3, 205, 207

INDEX

Consolidated Edison (Con Ed), 164, 217
conspiracy, arson as, 4, 76–77, 85–86, 131, 136–37, 153, 202–3
Cooke, Marvel Jackson, 183–84
Cooke, Terence, 106
Cool Hand Luke (film), 170
Co-op City, 52–54, 194
Cooper, Robert B., 56
copper salvaging, 126
Coral Gables, Florida, 147
corporate bonds, 94
Corrective Capitalism (Peirce and Steinbach), 225, 243
Cosell, Howard, 166, 259
counterinsurgency, 38
CRA. *See* Community Reinvestment Act
crime insurance, 61, 294
crimes of passion, 124–25
Criminal Justice Coordinating Council, 232
criminalization, 163–64, 174–75, 188, 221
criminology, 123–24, 185–190
Crisis, The (journal), 183
Cross Bronx Expressway, 52–53, 55, 115, 181, 190, 197–98, 232
Crotona Park East neighborhood (Bronx), 194
crowd mentality, 186
Cultural Revolution, 234

Daily News, 74, 75, 112, *112*, 113, 124–25, 127–28, 220, 260
"Dance (Disco Heat)" (disco song), 122
dance clubs, 102, 121–22
David Susskind Show, The, 167
Davidson Avenue (Bronx), 66
Dazhai, China, 234
deaths, arson-related, 6, 110, 120, 207–8, 302
Decade of Fire (documentary), 125, 263
Def Jam Recordings, 131
deficit spending (federal budget), 141–42
deindustrialization, 158; *see also* industrial relocation
Democratic National Convention (1980), 225
Democratic Party, 162
Denenberg, Herbert, 285
Den-Har Underwriters, *136*, 145, 147–51, 153, 156–58
Department for the Aging (New York City), 215
Department of City Planning (New York City), 217
Department of Finance (New York City), 217
Department of Housing and Urban Development (HUD), 24–25, 35, 162, 231, 232, 244

Department of Housing Preservation and Development (HPD) (New York City), 83, 190, *191*, 207, 217, 245–46
Department of Relocation and Management Services (New York City), 129
Department of the Treasury, 35
"depopulation" (insurance industry term), 138, 139, 148
depreciation, 64, 244
deregulation, 10, 24, 65, 95
DeRienzo, Harry, 29, 108, 115, 200, 237–41
derivatives, 142
desegregation, 53, 107, 201, 247
Detroit, Michigan, 6, 30–32, *32*, 34–37, 45, 118
Devenney, Anne, 239, 250
Diario, El, 58, 176
Dime Savings Bank, 76
Dirty Harry (film), 171, 178
disco, 14, 102–3, 122–23, 221
Disco Demolition Night, 123
"Disco Inferno," 14
Disco Wiz, 164–65
displacement, from fires, *47*, 48–49, 90, 97, 104, 113–15, 128, 130, 158, 208, 239
Division of Emergency Housing (NYC Department of Relocation and Management Services), 129
DJs (DJing), 122, 130–31, 164–65, 198; *see also* hip-hop
Dollar Savings Bank, 65, 128
Douglas, Nigel, 146
down payments, 230–31
Downer, Sylvia, 27
draft evasion, 228–29
draft riots (New York City), 123
Dresden, Germany, 245
drug enforcement, racially targeted, 126
Dumbo neighborhood (Brooklyn), 260
Dykhouse, David, 33

early warning systems, 14, 208–9, 217–18, 223
East Bronx, 217
East Harlem, 53, 128, 184, 229
East Tremont neighborhood (Bronx), 53, 74, 143–44, 197
East Village (New York City), 116, 117, 122
Eastern Savings Bank, 250
Ebony, *193*, 213
economies of scale, 25, 153
80 Blocks from Tiffany's (film), 167
Emergency Financial Control Board (EFCB), 54

Emigrant Industrial Savings Bank Building (Manhattan), 215–16
empires, declining, 9–10
employment (employment training), 6, 12, 20, 28, 43, 44, 54, 61, 62, 241; *see also* unemployment
Equal Employment Opportunity Commission, 37
E&S markets. *See* excess and surplus markets
Escape from the Bronx (film), 167
Espinal, Jacquelin, 111
ESPN, 166
ethical dilemmas, of "torches," 75, 78–80
Eton School, 156
Eurodollar, 141
Europe, 120, 139
evictions, 9, 48, 104, 116, 126, 183, 208, 227, 260
exceptionalism, Bronx, 7, 117–19
excess and surplus (E&S) markets, 138–40, 145, 147, 215, 246, 308

FAIR (Fair Access to Insurance Requirements) plans
and climate change, 256–58
creation of, 12–13, 22, 24, 135, 137, 188, 245
Den-Har Underwriters and, 147–48
and "depopulation," 138
expansion of, around the country, 38–39, 58
failure and inadvertent effects of, 60, 67–70, 91–94, 96–97, 118–19, 210
Hughes Panel and, 35–38, 41–45, 56
Illinois, 41–42, 68, 87, 91
Maryland, 87
Massachusetts, 57, 87, 119
New York State. *See* New York FAIR plan
Ohio, 94
Pennsylvania, 87
property insurance industry and, 39–40, 253, 256
rates lowered by, 226
restrictions on, 294, 298
Washington, D.C., 87
Falcone, Elisa, 110
Fanon, Frantz, *1*
FAPP (Northwest Bronx Fire and Arson Prevention Project), 218, 218
Farwell, Frank, 43
FBI. *See* Federal Bureau of Investigation
FDNY. *See* Fire Department of New York
"fear of riots," 23
Federal Bureau of Investigation (FBI), 202, 205–6, 223, 228–29, 275

Federal Housing Administration (FHA), 23, 25, 44, 65
Federal Insurance Administration (FIA), 26, 36, 41–43, 58–59, 91, 226, 248, 273, 294, 299
Federal Reserve, 10, 141, 227, 289–90
Fenway neighborhood (Boston), 117, 121, 126, 207–8
Ferrer, Fernando, 111
FHA. *See* Federal Housing Administration
FIA. *See* Federal Insurance Administration
film, 9, 14–15, 103, 167–71, 178; *see also Fort Apache, the Bronx* (1981 film)
Financial Times, 155
financialization, 9–11, 13, 22, 49, 57, 65, 69, 75, 94–95, 97, 135, 141–43, 146, 158, 228, 230–31, 239, 242, 246, 283, 284, 301; *see also* FIRE (finance, insurance, and real estate) industries
"finishers," 76, 154; *see also* strippers
Fiorello, Tim, 176
Fire, Safety, and Educational Program, 195
"Fire" (song), 102
FIRE capitalism, 75, 212
Fire Department of New York (FDNY), 80, 91, *112*, 125, 126, 128, 144, 151, 164, 202–5, 207, 212, 216–19, 275
fire departments (in general), 76, 88, 89, 106, 205, 275; *see also* firefighters (firefighting)
"fire diaspora," 114–15
"Fire Down Below" party, 122
fire escapes, 75, 105, 110, 143
FIRE (finance, insurance, and real estate) industries, 11–12, 75, 97, 120, 196, 210, 212, 254
fire insurance (fire insurance industry), 6–8, 13, 19, 24, 26, 34, 38, 41, 49, *50*, 56, 59, 61, 67, 74, 86, 88–90, 93, 97, 120, 124, 145, 155, 157, 207, 209–10, 219, 222, 226, 239
Fire Insurance Proceeds Law (1977), 209–10
fire marshals, 80, 81, 91, 93, 111, 121, 128, 130, 144, 151, 195–96, 203–5, 209, 212–13, 216, 218, 221, 275, 276
Fire Next Door, The (television documentary), 164, 167, 323
fire prevention, 88–90, 120, 164
Fire Prevention Week, 89
fire protection services, 54–55, 59, 75, 80, 89
fire safety, 75, 82, 88–90, 89, *90*, 97, 170–71, 195
fire watching, *101*, 102–9, *105*
firebombs, 4, 143–45, 148
Firebug (video game), 220–21, *222*, 321

firefighters (firefighting), 2, *47*, 55, 88, 110, 111, 113, 122, 125, 126, 144, 171, 184, 206; *see also* Fire Department of New York (FDNY)
Firehouse (New York dance club), 121
fireproof housing construction, 61, 80–82, 88, 197
Fires, The: How a Computer Formula, Big Ideas, and the Best of Intentions Burned Down New York City—and Determined the Future of Cities (Flood), 276
firesetting, 80, 82, 91, 120–21, 123–25, 130, 199, 207, 220, 221; *see also* incendiarism; torches
501(c)(3) status, 243–44
Flood, Joe, 276
Flood, The (painting), *133*
flood insurance, 43–44
Florida, 26, 147, 256
Floyd, George, 253–54, 256
Ford, Gerald, and administration, 89–90, 169
Ford, John, 167
Ford Foundation, 165, 218, 243–45
Fordham Road (Bronx), 107, 251
Fordham University, 60–61, 200
Fordism, 11, 283; *see also* post-Fordism
foreclosures, 9, 218, 250, 258
Forest Houses (Bronx), 53
Forest Neighborhood Committee, 53
Fort Apache (1948 film), 169
Fort Apache (memoir by Tom Walker), 312
Fort Apache, the Bronx (1981 film), 14, 167–80, *170, 175, 177*, 188, 192, 200, 202, 229, 245
Fortescue, Earl, 146, 155
Fortunato, Joyce, 67
Foucault, Michel, 296
Fox, Hetty, 60, 111, 192
Fox Street (Bronx), 127, 169
Fox Street Relocation Shelter, 113
France, 120
fraud, 8, 12, 77, 86–88, 126, 131, 139, 149, 202, 207, 210–11, 213–14, 220, 222, 226
Fraunces Tavern (New York), 205
Freud, Sigmund, 121
Freudenberger, Herbert, 115–17
Frey, Bill, 252, 253
From the War on Poverty to the War on Crime (Hinton), 306
Fuerzas Armadas de Liberación Nacional, 205
"Fulton Mines," 232
Funches, Peter, 173
Furness, Betty, 38

GAB. *See* General Adjustment Bureau
Garcia, Edwin Julio, 152–53
García Conde, Ed, 261, 262
gas chromatography, 204
Gay Activist Alliance, 121
gay clubs, 121–22
Gear, Juanita, 59, 60
GEICO, 119
Gemini II Theater (New York), 179
General Adjustment Bureau (GAB), *19*, 20, 32
General Electric, 95
Genoa, 10
gentrification, 126, 190, 208, 259–63, 298
Gerena Valentín, Gilberto, 216
Germany, 163
Get Down, The (Netflix series), 261
ghettos, 38, 56, 109, 163
Ghostbusters (film), 320
GI Bill, 44
Gigante, Father Louis, 106, 202, 238, 244
Gilmore, Ruth Wilson, 11
Glazer, Nathan, 124, 304
Glen Cove, New York, 228
Glenn, John, 119, 209
Gliedman, Anthony, 190, *191*
Global South, 142
globalization (global economy), 10, 11, 31, 75, 84, 117, 120, 134–37, 141–42, 148, 153, 158, 258
Goepfert, John, 147
Gold, Bernard, 144–45
"Gold ring," 144–45, 148, 151
gold standard, 84, 95, 141
Golem Realty Corporation, 153
Gonzalez, David, 192
González, Juan, 180
Gonzalez family, 113
"good repair clauses," 250
Government Accountability Office, 41; *see also* U.S. General Accounting Office
government bonds, 54, 94
graffiti, 185, 190–91, *255*
Grand Concourse (Bronx), 54, 66, 109, 154, 162
Grandmaster Flash and the Furious Five, 161
Great Depression, 183–84, 231
Great Fire of London, 120
Great Rent Strike War (1932), 231
Great Society, 29, 163
greenlining, 13, 49
Grier, Pam, 168–69
Guardian, 155
Gumbs, Robert, 53, 111

Hallberg, Garth Risk, 292
Hands Up (anti-arson organization), 117

INDEX

Hansberry, Lorraine, 178
Harlem, 48–49, 53, 150; *see also* East Harlem
Harlem River, 197, 259
Harris, LaShawn, 301
Harris, Patricia Roberts, 162
Harrison, Dennis, 147
Hart, Philip, 29
Hartford, Connecticut, 96, 212
Hartford Courant, 213
Hartford Insurance Company (The Hartford), 8, 138
Hartman, Saidiya, 9, 134, 276, 291
Harvard University, 191
Harvey, David, 133, 141, 309
HDA. *See* Housing and Development Administration
health care, 54, 55, 59, 173, 175
Henderson, James, 111
Herc, DJ Cool, 198, 261
Highbridge neighborhood (Bronx), 111
Hinton, Elizabeth, 163, 306
hip-hop, 14, 73, 81, 134, 143, 161, 164–65, 314
HIV/AIDS epidemic, 246
HMDA. *See* Home Mortgage Disclosure Act
Hoboken, New Jersey, 126
Hodgson, Godfrey, 143, 155
Hoffman, Frederick L., 123–24
HOLC. *See* Home Owners' Loan Corporation
Holland Avenue (Bronx), 217
Holocaust, 163, 261
Holtzman, Elizabeth, 247–49
Holtzman Amendment, 248–50, 253
Home Mortgage Disclosure Act (HMDA) (1975), 250, 295
Home Owners' Loan Corporation (HOLC), 23, 65
Homefront: Citywide Action Group Against Neighborhood Destruction and for Low-Rent Housing, 64–66
homelessness, 9, 57
homeowners policies, 12, 25–28, 147
homesteading, urban. *See* urban homesteading
homosexuality (incl. homophobia), 121–23, *122*
Hôtel de Paris (Monte Carlo), 142
housing abandonment. *See* abandonment
Housing Abandonment in New York City (report), 64
Housing and Community Development Act (1978), 248
Housing and Development Administration (HDA), 55, 231, 232
Housing and Urban Development Act (1968), 36
housing boom, post–World War II, 24, 25
housing organizations. *See* tenant organizations (tenant associations)
Houston, Texas, 63, 203
HPD. *See* Department of Housing Preservation and Development
HUD. *See* Department of Housing and Urban Development
Hughes, Richard, 21, 35–36, 44
Hughes Panel (The President's National Advisory Panel on Insurance in Riot-Affected Areas), 21–22, 35–38, *39*, 41–45, 56, 58, 67, 69, 211, 247, 248, 257, 288, 321
Human Resources Administration (New York City), 207, 217
Hunts Point Multi-Service Center, 322
Hunts Point neighborhood (Bronx), 107, 202, 237, 244
Hurricane Andrew, 257
Hurricane Betsy, 31, 33, 287
Hurricane Katrina, 257

ICAC. *See* Insurance Committee for Arson Control
Illinois, 41–42, 43, 68, 87, 91
in rem buildings, 245
incendiarism, 8, 120, 121, 123–24, 131, 175–76, 210, 275; *see also* firesetting
industrial capitalism, 11, 97
industrial relocation, 22, 28, 54, 61, 69, 97, 119, 120, 158
Industrial Workers of the World, 34
industrialization (industrial expansion), 88, 120, 123, 148, 216
inspections, property, 62, 91, 96
"instant liquidity," 12
Institute for Urban Studies, 60–61
Instituto de Resseguros do Brasil (IRB), *136,* 145, 148–50, 154, 156
insurance, definition of, 33
insurance adjusters, *19,* 20, 32, 81, 136, 144, 148, 214
Insurance Advocate, 118
insurance cancellations, 22–23, 31, 35, 61, 147, 150, 151, 154, 156, 214, 219, 251
Insurance Committee (Northwest Bronx Community and Clergy Coalition), 252
insurance fraud. *See* fraud
insurance gap, 84, *85,* 86–88, 97, 98, 119, 120, 126, 127, 148, 197, 213–14, 247, 273, 298

insurance industry (in general), 8, 36; *see also* FIRE industries; fire insurance (fire insurance industry); property insurance industry
"Insurance Industry, The: It Redlines Too" (report), 66
Insurance Information Institute, 68, 257
insurance redlining, 6, 11–13, 22, 23, 24, 27–30, 35–38, 40, 41, 44, 49, 56, 58–60, 74, 86, 124, 138, 214, 226–27, 238, 247–54, 257–58, 325; *see also* brownlining
interest rates, 10, 95–96, 141, 227
Intermediate School 52 (Bronx), *1*
Internal Revenue Service (IRS), 64, 244
international insurance market, 31
international monetary system, 141
involuntary markets, 68
IRB. *See* Instituto de Resseguros do Brasil
Irish Americans, 51, 53, 123
Italian Americans, 51, 53

J-51 program, 129
Jackson, Jesse, 163
Jacobson, Matthew Frye, 282
Jacobson, Michael, 92, 96, 125, 140, 216–17, 275
Jacobson, Robert, 190
Japan, 163
Jay, Jazzy, 130–31
Jazz Singer, The (film), 282
Jenner, Kendall, 260
Jersey City, New Jersey, 179
"Jew risk," 8, 86
"Jewish lightning," 8, 86
Jews, 8, 51, 52, 53, 85–86, 86, 194; *see also* anti-Semitism
Jim Crow (Jim Crowification), 24, 41, 67, 123
Jimenez, Gloria, 91, 299
jobs. *See* employment (employment training)
Johnson, Carrie B., 35
Johnson, Lyndon Baines, and administration, 20–21, 29, 38, 242
Joint Committee on Urban Problems, 245
Jolson, Al, 282
Jones, Millie, 184
Jonnes, Jill, 306, 317–18
Jordan, Vernon, 166
jurisdiction (jurisdictional conflicts), 202, 203, 205, 218–19, 222–23, 244
juvenile delinquency, 220
Juvenile Offender Law (New York State), 78

Katz, Steve, 232, 233, 235–36
Kelley, Clarence, 205
Kelley, Robin D. G., 255
Kelling, George L., 185–88
Kelly Street (Bronx), 238, 241; *see also* Banana Kelly Community Improvement Association
Kennedy, John F., and administration, 37
Kennedy, Robert F., 242
Kennedy, Ted, 163
Kent State shootings, 228
Kerner, Otto, Jr., 21
Kerner Commission (National Advisory Commission on Civil Disorders), 21, 29, 44, 163, 285, 288
Kerner Report, 21
Kids of Survival (K.O.S.), 2–3, *3*, 260
King, Martin Luther, Jr., 6, 165, 228, 293
King, Rodney, 253
Kingsbridge neighborhood (Bronx), 105
Kish, Zenia, 307
Klein, Ruben, 49–51, 63
Kluger, Barry, 152–54, 204, 209
K.O. areas, 27
Koch, Ed, 163, 190, 191, 216, 246
Koch Housing Plan, 246
K.O.S. *See* Kids of Survival
Kunstler, William, 176

La Guardia, Fiorello, 311
labor force (labor unrest), 11, 34, 51, 123, 131, 143, 183–84
landlords
 abandonment by, 7, 62–67, 69, *73*, 81, 107, 131–32, 197, 201, 230, 238
 absentee, 13, 38, 68, 82, 119
 blackface worn by, 3, 4, *4*, 8, 9
 "milking" by, 28, 66, 74, 127, 199
Lanni, Carmine, 74–78, 87, 90, 98, 124–25, 130
"last resort" residual market, 26, 257–58
Law Enforcement Assistance Administration, 29, 208–9, 217
law-and-order liberalism, 126, *161*, 163–64, 171, 311–12
Lederman, Sol, 61–62
Lehman College, 15
Leroy, Justin, 307
Levan, Larry, 122
Levy, Jonathan, 86
Lewis, Oscar, 305
liability lag, 137, 149

liberalism, 174; *see also* law-and-order liberalism
life insurance, 42, 124, 245, 288
LIHTC (Low-Income Housing Tax Credit), 244
Lima, Alfred J., 145
Lima memo (Lima report), 145–49, 309
Limits to Capital, The (Harvey), 133
Lincoln Hospital (Bronx), 173, 231
Liquid Smoke (Manhattan dance club), 102
liquidity, 10, 12
LISC. *See* Local Initiatives Support Corporation
Lloyd's Act (U.K., 1982), 157
Lloyd's of London, 31, 33, 35, 135–37, *136*, 139–41, *140*, 143–51, 153–58, 215, 216, 249, 251, 252, 254; *see also* Sasse syndicate
Local Initiatives Support Corporation (LISC), 218, 245
Local Law 45 (New York City), 245
L'Official, Pete, 168
Logue, Ed, 181–82, *182*, 245
Logue, Frank, 94, 204
London, England, 120, 141, 148, 158; *see also* Lloyd's of London
Long Island, 256–57
Long Island University, 228
Longwood neighborhood (Bronx), 202
looting, 128, 164–66
López Antonetty, Evelina, 174, *255*, 263
Lorde, Audre, 103
Los Angeles, California, 118, 253; *see also* Watts uprising
Los Angeles Times, 107, 116, 183
loss ratio, 94
Louisiana, 256
Lower East Side (New York City), 63, 184, 259
Low-Income Housing Tax Credit (LIHTC), 244
Lowndes, Joseph E., 305
Ludlow Massacre, 34
Luhrmann, Baz, 261
lynchings, 124

MAC (Municipal Assistance Corporation), 54
Macabre Suite, 260–61
Madison Square Garden, *225*
maintenance, building, 28, 66–69, 152, 194, 258
Manhattan, 51, 53, 62, 63, 96, 97, 102, 148, 176, 179, 184, 218, 229, 259–60; *see also specific locations, e.g.:* Harlem
manufacturing, 10, 22, 28, 54, 61, 62, 216
Mao Zedong (Maoism), 231, 234, *235*
Marchiel, Rebecca, 325
Marcuse, Peter, 62
Marcy Place (Bronx), 154

Margaret, Princess, 146
Martinez HoSang, Daniel, 305
Marx, Karl, 309
Maryland, 87
mass consumption, 11
mass incarceration. *See* carceral state
mass production, 11
Massachusetts, 57, 87, 119, 121, 209
Mayor's Arson Task Force (New York), 207
McCarran-Ferguson Act (1945), 25, 30, 212, 253
MEChA, 179
media coverage, 21, 60, 77, 127, 145, 149, 155–56, 163–64, 166, 173, 178, 181–84, *193*, 207, 210, 211, 213, 221, 245, 259
Medwin, Charles, 52
Meeting the Insurance Crisis of Our Cities (Hughes Panel report), 21–22, 38, *39*
Mel, Melle, 143
Melrose neighborhood (Bronx), 189, 262
Mendoza, John, 2
Merola, Mario, 5, 76–77, 81–83, 92, 93, 106, 154, 202–6, 209, 210, 215, 216
Merritt Committee, 286
"Message, The" (hip-hop song), 161
MHNIA (Morris Heights Neighborhood Improvement Association), 198–201
Miami, Florida, *136*, 145
Michigan, 29, 33, 39, 119
Michigan Chronicle, 37
Mid-Bronx Desperadoes, 195, 238, 241
Milchman, Ernest, 217
"milking," 28, 66, 74, 127, 199
Miller, Arthur, 75
Milwaukee, Wisconsin, 253
Minneapolis, Minnesota, 253–54
Mitchell-Lama development (Bronx), 198
money markets, 94–96
Monte Carlo, Monaco, 142
Montrose, George, 110
moral hazard, 84–87
Morris Avenue (Bronx), 189
Morris Heights neighborhood (Bronx), 48–49, 102, 197–202, 218, 219
Morris Heights Neighborhood Improvement Association (MHNIA), 198–201
Morris High School, 111
Morris Justice Project, *189*, 190
Morrisania neighborhood (Bronx), 97, 107, 108, 111, 115, 229, 234–35, *235*, 258
mortgage lending, 23, 25, 250; *see also* subprime lending (subprime mortgages)

mortgage redlining, 7, 54, 64–65, 67, 75, 84, 87, 128, 176, 250, 253, 325
Moscow, U.S.S.R., 140, 216
Moses, Robert, 52–54, 115, 197–98, 244
Mott Haven neighborhood (Bronx), 107, 189
Moyers, Bill, 164, 323
Moynihan, Daniel Patrick, 29, 120, 124
multinational corporations, 10, 141
multiple-line insurance, 25–26, 286
Municipal Assistance Corporation (MAC), 54, 327
municipal bonds, 54
Murphy, Margaret, 113–14
MUSE Company, 221
Muse Software, 220–21
music, 102–3, 130–31, 134, 155; *see also* hip-hop
Mutual Fire, Marine and Inland Insurance Company, 22–23
mutual savings banks, 65

NAACP, 183, 253
"Names" (Lloyd's of London), 156–57
napalm, 103, 182
Napier, Lord, 146
Nation magazine, 95, 141, 143–45, 148
National Advisory Commission on Civil Disorders. *See* Kerner Commission
National Association of Fire Engineers, 88
National Association of Insurance Commissioners, 33, 226
National Board of Fire Underwriters (NBFU), 88, 210
National Commission on Fire Prevention and Control (NFPCA), 89, *90*, 120, 164
National Congress of Puerto Rican Rights (NCPRR), 180
National Fire Academy (NFA), 123
National Fire Prevention and Control Administration, 121, 126
National Fire Protection Association, 81, 89, 204
National Flood Insurance Program (NFIP), 43–44
National Gay Task Force, 123
National Guard, 20
National People's Action (NPA), 59, 249–53, 325
National Urban League, 65, 166
Nazism, 85, 163
NBC, 213
NBFU. *See* National Board of Fire Underwriters
NCPRR (National Congress of Puerto Rican Rights), 180

Near West Side Neighbors in Action (anti-arson organization), 117
neo-Keynesianism, 231
neoliberalism, 11, 57, 141; *see also* post-Fordism
Netflix, 261
Netherlands, 10
New Deal, 11, 25, 63, 283
New Haven, Connecticut, 94, 228
"New Haven Nine," 228
New Jersey, 115, 147
New Orleans, Louisiana, 121
New York City; *see also specific headings, e.g.:* Bronx; Fire Department of New York (FDNY); Wall Street
  anti-arson efforts in, 226
  arson fires in, 75, 76, 78, 82, *83*, 90
  arson investigation in, 203
  arson rings in, 135
  arson-related deaths in, 110
  attempts to counter "image crisis" of, 167
  Bicentennial celebration in, 134
  blackout (1977), 164–66, 181, 207, 209, 211
  blaming of residents for fires in, 120–24
  decline of arson in, 223
  draft riots in, 123
  fiscal crisis in, 54–55, 62, 275
  gentrification in, 190, 259–62
  as global financial center, 10, 96–7, 142
  housing displacements in, 48–49, 90, 97, 104, 113–15, 128, 130, 158, 208, 239
  insurance gap in, 148
  K.O areas on, 27
  landlord abandonment in, 62–66
  law-and-order liberalism in, 163
  loss of tax base by, 28
  NYPIUA's effect on, 56, 59, 137–38
  redevelopment efforts in, 181–82
  rent control in, 64–65
  structural arsons in (1968-1984), *214*
  subprime lending in, 258
  and tax-lien legislation, 207–10
  tenant activism in, 64
  Triangle Shirtwaist Factory fire in, 10–11
  in triangular trade, *136*, 142, 149
  uninvestigated arsons in, 76
New York City Arson Strike Force. *See* Arson Strike Force (ASF)
New York City Housing Authority (NYCHA), 53, 82, 108, 128, 129, 131
New York City Public Housing Authority, 128
New York Department of Insurance, 67

New York FAIR plan, 42, 49, *50*, 58, 67–70, 91–92, 135, 139, 150, 205–6, 247–48; *see also* New York Property Insurance Underwriters Association (NYPIUA)
New York Head Shop and Museum (Lorde), 103
New York Herald, 86
New York magazine, 63
New York Metropolitan Brokers Association, 139
New York Municipal Archives, 217
New York Police Department (NYPD), 50–51, 60, 61, 76, 81, 168, 172, 173, 177, 178, 189, 190, 202, 205, 207
New York Post, 107
New York Property Insurance Underwriters Association (NYPIUA), *50*, 56, 58–62, 66–68, 70, 74, 84, 86, 87, 91–92, 96, 97, 117–18, 124–25, 137–39, 145, 147, 148, 150, 153, 164, 205–6, 210–11, 215, 217, 219–20, 226–27, 246–49, 252, 256–57, 273, 275, 293–96, 298–300
New York State, 25, 34, 55–56, 58, 65, 67, 78, 92, 94, 120, 128, 137, 145, 147, 207, 209–11, 213, 246–49, 256–57
New York State Omnibus Anti-Arson Law (1981), 221–22
New York State Supreme Court, 176
New York Times, 4, 6, 52, 58, *79*, 80, 93, 107–9, 126, 128, 129, 134, 151, 163, 166, 181, 182, 185, 190, 195, 199, 204, 205, 211, 256, 259, 261
New York University, 317
New York Urban Coalition, 28, 66, 114, 138
Newark, New Jersey, 6, 21, 28, 30–32, 34, 36, 67, 123–24, 150
Newman, Paul, 161, 168–73, 178
Newsday, 38
Newsweek, 93, *193*, 213
NFA (National Fire Academy), 123
NFIP (National Flood Insurance Program), 43–44
NFPCA. *See* National Commission on Fire Prevention and Control
Nixon, Richard, and administration, 29, 84, 124, 127, 141, 242, 324
"non-economic firesetting," 124, 125
North Carolina Mutual Life Insurance Company, 288
North New York Savings Bank, 65
North Omaha, Nebraska, 35
North Side Savings Bank, 74–75
Northeastern University, 208

Northwest Bronx Community and Clergy Coalition (NWBCCC), 14, 60, 74, 98–99, 200–1, 218–19, *219*, 221, 239, 250–53
Northwest Bronx Fire and Arson Prevention Project (FAPP), 218
Nos Quedamos, 262
NPA. *See* National People's Action
Nuñez, Mike, 128
NWBCCC. *See* Northwest Bronx Community and Clergy Coalition
NYCHA. *See* New York City Housing Authority
NYPD. *See* New York Police Department
NYPIUA. *See* New York Property Insurance Underwriters Association

Oakar, Mary Rose, 94
Oakland, California, 36
Obama, Barack, and administration, 290
Oberlander, Imre, 3–5, *4*, 8
Occupied Look program, 190–92, *191*
Office of Code Enforcement (New York City), 217
Office of Fire Prevention and Control (New York State), 221
Offner, Amy, 322
offshoring, 135, 158; *see also* industrial relocation
Ogden Avenue (Bronx), *47*, 110
Ohio, 94, 94, 119, 213
Ohio Players, 102, 106
Oliver, Jesse, 208
Olshan, Morton, 66
158th Street (Bronx), 128
163rd Street (Bronx), 55
178th Street (Bronx), *73*
OPEC oil embargo, 84, 95, 142
Orange, Joe, 108
organized crime, 77
Orlando, Florida, 121
Ortiz, José, 108–9
overinsurance, 87–88, 153; *see also* insurance gap

Padilla, Lorine, 78, 80
Palo Alto, California, 186–88
Paradise Garage nightclub (New York City), 122
Park Slope neighborhood (Brooklyn), 220, 259
Parking Violations Bureau (New York City), 216
paternalism, state, 235
Patrolmen's Benevolent Association, 178
Patterson, Orlando, 174
PDC. *See* People's Development Corporation

INDEX

Peirce, Neal, 225
Pelham Bay neighborhood (Bronx), 154
Pelham Parkway (Bronx), 250
Pennsylvania, 87
people of color, 41, 110, 188, 189, 226; *see also* Black Americans; Puerto Ricans (Puerto Rico)
People's Convention, *225*
People's Development Corporation (PDC), 62, 131–32, 225, 229–39, *233, 235,* 245, 246, 322, 323
Perez, Richie, 173, 176, 177, 180, 231
Perla de Leon, *101*
Perry Avenue (Bronx), 110
Persian Gulf, 103
Petrie, Dan, 177–79
petrodollars, 142
Philadelphia, Pennsylvania, 22–24, 27, 80, 179
Philadelphia Housing Authority (PHA), 22–23
Philadelphia Inquirer, 22
Phillips-Fein, Kim, 55, 165
PIPSO (Property Insurance Plans Service Office), 68
"planned shrinkage," 55–56
"plantationism," 232
police (police departments), 6, 20, 61, 188–90, 205, 216; *see also* broken windows (broken windows policing); New York Police Department (NYPD)
police brutality (police violence), 45, 173–75, 253–54
Police Tapes, The (documentary), 167
pooling (insurance), 39, 67, 86, 91
pop psychology, 115
Port Morris neighborhood (Bronx), 260
Posner, Sy, 130
post-Fordism, 11, 97, 168, 216, 227
Potts, Frank, 238
Potts, Leon, 238, *240,* 241
Potts, Nancy, 238
poverty, 54, 78, 97, 184, 227; *see also* War on Poverty
Power Broker, The (Caro), 52–53, 181
Prairie Fire (Weather Underground manifesto), 103
"predatory inclusion," 42, 290
premiums, insurance, 22, 25, 26, 33, 42, 58, 62, 66–68, 89, 92–96, 135, 137–39, 141–43, 146–49, 158, 251
presidential campaign (2016), 327
presidential debates (1980), 181

President's National Advisory Panel on Insurance in Riot-Affected Areas, The. *See* Hughes Panel
privacy laws, 296
private property, enshrining of. *See* property rights
Prix de l'Arc de Triomphe, 146
profit, as driver of arson wave, 4–5, 82–84; *see also* "arson for profit"; insurance gap
Progressive Era, 215, 231
property insurance; *see also* fire insurance (fire insurance industry); property insurance industry
    "back of the bus," 41, 137, 252
    as civil rights issue, 38, 252
    and climate change, 256–58, 263
    as "disciplinary device," 296
    homeowners policies, 12, 25–28, 147
    and mitigation of risk, 69, 93, 211, 263
    and moral hazards, 84–5, 87
    as prerequisite for mortgage loans, 23
    and racial capitalism, 227
    racially stratified market of, 6, 12–13, 49, 258
    residual market for, 26–27, 38–41, 56, 57, 59, 119, 147, 206, 251–52, 256–58
    as roadblock to revitalization, 246–47, 251
    via FAIR plans. *See* FAIR (Fair Access to Insurance Requirements) plans
property insurance industry
    adjusters in, *19,* 20, 32, 81, 136, 144, 148, 214
    and anti-arson initiatives, 210–15, *212*
    anti-Semitism in, 86
    and arson investigations, 210–11
    arson-related losses willingly absorbed by, 75
    bailout of, 12
    "depopulation" by, 138, 139, 148
    deregulation of, 24
    FAIR plans and, 39–40, 253, 256; *see also* FAIR (Fair Access to Insurance Requirements) plans
    financialization of. *See* financialization
    and Holtzman Amendment, 247–49
    jargon of risk in, 42
    Jim Crowification of, 24
    profitability of, 59
    public relations by, 40, *193,* 212–13
    redlining by. *See* insurance redlining
    and reinvestment movement, 252–53
    role of, in arson wave, 90–91
    shift to investing by, 94–95
    state regulation of, 25, 30, 253
    and subsidized housing, 244–45

property insurance industry (*continued*)
  ultimate use of claims paid by, 69
  urban uprisings' effect on, 20, 29–30, *32*, 33–37
Property Insurance Loss Register, 212–14
Property Insurance Plans Service Office (PIPSO), 68
property rights, 36, 210, 228, 230, 258
property taxes, 66, 207, 236, 237, 245
Prudential, 42, 124, 245
PSAs (public-service announcements), 221
public housing, 13–14, 53, 82–84, 104, 105, 108, 109, 113, 128, 130, 130–31, 229, 240
public relations, by insurance industry, 40, *193*, 212–13
public-private partnerships, 243–44, 257
public-service announcements (PSAs), 221
Puerto Rican Social Club Fire (1976), 305
Puerto Ricans (Puerto Rico), 6, 27, 28, 38–39, 52, 53, 56, 65, 77, 78, 102, 107, 116, 124, 128–30, 151, 152, 171, 173, 174, 176, 180, 194, 205, 229, 236, 288, 305
Pulse nightclub massacre (Orlando), 121
pyromaniacs (pyromania), 9, 120, 121, 125, 220

Queens, New York, 60, 144, 218, 276

racial capitalism, 11, 22, 34, 45, 49, 55, 96, 130, 135–37, 139, 165, 183, 202, 227, 232, 257, 263, 283–84
racial segregation. *See* segregation
"racial succession," 107
"racial transposition," 124, 305
racially tiered (racially stratified) insurance market, 6, 12, 24, 26, 35, 40, 41, 49, 89, 97, 147–48, 249, 286
radicalism, 38, 231
Raisin in the Sun, A (film), 178
Ramirez, Roberto, *1*, 2
Rangel, Charles, 247
rap music. *See* hip-hop
"Rapper's Delight" (song), 180
Reagan, Ronald, and administration, 141–42, 163, 181, 222, 244, 249
Reaganomics, 243
real estate market (real estate industry), 8–9, 11–13, 27, 36, 49, 51, 54, 57, 62–64, 67, 78, 84, 86–87, 97, 107, 119, 126, 127, 130, 131, 136, 152, 154, 176, 196, 199, 201, 208, 209, 227, 239, 251, 259–62
Real Estate Record and Builders' Guide, 183
Recession of 1973-1974, 84, 95

Reconstruction, 123
Red Cap program, 218–19
redevelopment, 27, 126, 181, 234, 260–62
redlining. *See* insurance redlining; mortgage redlining
refinancing, cash-out, 64
reinsurance, 31, 36–41, 93, 126, 135, 137, 140–43, 145, 148–50, 153, 154, 156, 158, 211, 249, 256, 257; *see also* riot reinsurance
Reinvestment Committee (Northwest Bronx Community and Clergy Coalition), 251–52
reinvestment movement, 249–53, 256, 259
Renegades, 229
Reno, Nevada, 7
renovations, 27, 28, 55, 229, 230, 232, *233*, 234, 239, 246
rent control, 9, 50, 63–64, 84, 128, 208, 231
rent gap, 298
rent strikes, 183, 218, 231
renter's insurance, 28, 287
replacement cost, 298
Report from Engine Co. 82 (Smith), 125
residual market, 26–27, 38–41, 56, 57, 59, 119, 147, 206, 251–52, 256–58
Reyes, Raoul, 232
Rhode Island, 43
Richmond, Virginia, 7
Rio de Janeiro, Brazil, *136*, 145, 149, 158
riot insurance, 34–35
riot reinsurance, 12, 22, 35–40, 44, 226, 248, 249, 254
"riot-affected areas," 21, 37, 41, 42, 58–59, 257
"riot-prone areas," 22, 41–42, 45, 57, 59, 75, 137, 188, 293, 321
"risk communities," 86
Rivera, Virginia, 79
Rivers, Darney "K-Born," 109, 115
Rivieccio, Anthony, 102, 103
Robbins, Idaho, 99
Roberts, A. A., 37, 40
Rock Master Scott & the Dynamic Three, 14, 73, 81
Rockefeller, John D., 34
Rockefeller, Nelson, 56
Rodriguez, Alberto, 112
Rodriguez, George, 322
Rodriguez, Lucy, 112, *112*
Rodriguez, Luis, 173
Rodriguez, Miguel, 78–79
Rodriguez, Shellyne, 261–62
Rohatyn, Felix, 327
Rohatyn, Jeanne Greenberg, 327

Rollins, Tim, 2, *3*
"Roof Is On Fire, The" (hop-hop song), 14
Roosevelt Gardens (Bronx apartment complex), 66, 109
Rosen, Harry, 151–54, 210
Rosen, Willie, 152–53
Roy, Molly, *7*
Rubenstein, Keith, 260–61
Rueda, Leslie, 228
Rueda, Ramón, 228–36
Ruiz, Richard, 108–9
rust belt states, 119
Rutgers University, 64

safety net, social, 57, 69
safety violations, 68
St. Louis, Missouri, 36
St. Mark's Free Clinic, 116
Saint Mary's Park Houses, 105, 108
Salt Lake City, Utah, 117
salvaging, 126–27
San Francisco, California, 88
San Juan Hill (New York City), 53
Sanchez, Ivan, 105
Sanchez, Sonia, 47
Sanderson, Shelley, 108
Sarah Lawrence College, 169
Sarris, Andrew, 172
Sasse, Frederick "Tim," 145–49, 157, 158, 216, 309
Sasse syndicate (Sasse scandal), 145–50, 148, 149, 153–58, 163, 215, 254
Sassen, Saskia, 142
savings and loan associations, 65
savings banks, 65
SBDO. *See* South Bronx Development Organization
scapegoating of arson, 14, 104, 120, 121, 127, 131, 144–45, 155, 238, 239, 284
Scarsdale, New York, 169
Schneiderman, Rose, 10–11
Schumacher, E. F., 231
Scondras, David, 193, 208, 209
Scott-Heron, Gil, 134, 155
Scranton, William, 20–21
Seabury Daycare Center, 194–95
Seabury Place (Bronx), 194
Seattle, Washington, 5, 118
SEBCO. *See* South East Bronx Community Organization
Section 8 housing units, 55, 83
Sedgwick Avenue (Bronx), 198

segregation, 26, 53, 67, 86, 155; *see also* desegregation
Selemoncsak, Frank, 144
self-determination, 231–32, 242
self-help, 227, 230, 231, 240, 246
self-incrimination, 125
self-reliance, 231
Senate Budget Committee, 257
Senate Committee on Governmental Affairs, 196, 203–4
Senate Consumer Subcommittee, 95
Senate Subcommittee on Criminal Justice, 119
Senate Subcommittee on Insurance, 59
Senate Subcommittee on Investigations, 48–49, 126
sensitivity training (for police), 188
Sepeda, Jose, 110
Seventh Avenue (Harlem), 150
sexuality, 121–23, 125
Shakespeare Avenue (Bronx), 113–14
shareholder value, prioritization of, 11
shell corporations, 153–54
single-line insurance, 25, 286
slavery (slave trade), 11, 123, 134, 135, 139–40, 155, 194, 254, 296, 307
Slevin, James M., 126
Slotkin, Richard, 169
"small is beautiful" philosophy, 231
Smith, Dennis, 125
Smith, Jack, 183
Smith, Lucien, 260
Smith, Neil, 298
Smith, Seymour, 30
smoke inhalation, arson-related, 110–11
smoke machines, 102
sniffers, 204
SoBro. *See* South Bronx Overall Economic Development Corporation
social housing, 83–84; *see also* public housing
social services, 28, 54, 57, 128, 234
socialism, 209, 231
Socialist Women's Consumers League, 231
SoHo neighborhood (Manhattan), 260
solar power, 232, 234, 241
Somerset Partners, 260–62
South Africa, 284
South Bronx, *1, 255; see also specific locations, e.g.:* Grand Concourse; Morrisania neighborhood
arson blamed on residents of, 29, 120, 124
Jimmy Carter's visit to, 114, 162–63, 166, 168, 178, 181, 211, *233*, 233–34, 237, 239, 245

South Bronx (*continued*)
   extraction by landlords in, 84
   fire watching in, *101*, 102–9, *105*
   fireproof housing in, 80–81
   gentrification of, 190
   landlord abandonment in, 62–63, 229
   legacy of interracial solidarity in, 53
   New York FAIR plan in, 49
   NYPIUA payouts for losses in, 92
   Occupied Look program in, 190–92
   and "planned shrinkage," 55–56
   police presence in, 189
   refugees in and from, 113–15
   revitalization efforts in, 200–2, 240, 245–46
   as symbol of America's urban ruin, 107–9, 162, 163, 166, 168, 185, 261, 303; *see also Fort Apache, the Bronx* (1981 film)
   tourism in, 163, 168, 216
   as tourist destination, 163, 216
   unemployment in, 78
   as uninsurable area, 248, 251
   vandalism in, 185
   as welfare dumping ground, 128
   Philip Zimbardo's "anonymity" experiment in, 186–87
South Bronx Development Organization (SBDO), *182*, 245
South Bronx Overall Economic Development Corporation (SoBro), 260, 261
South Bronx Rising (Jonnes), 306
South East Bronx Community Organization (SEBCO), 106, 238, 241, 244
South Fordham neighborhood (Bronx), 98, 219
South Fordham Organization, 98
Southeast Asian refugees, 316, 324
Southern Boulevard (Bronx), 3–4
Southern District of New York, 147, 202
Soviet Union, 4, 216
Special Portfolio, 147, 148
Spielberg, Morris, 31
squatters, 229
Stanford prison experiment, 186
Stanford Research Institute, 204
Stanford University, 186, *187*, 276
Star-Ledger (Newark), 31
Starr, Roger, 55, 185, 232
State Farm, 252, 253, 256
state-based insurance regulation, 25, 30, 253; *See also* McCarran-Ferguson Act (1945)
statistics, 42, 86, 119, 124, 125, 129, 223, 275–76
Statue of Liberty, *133*, 134
Steinbach, Carol, 225

Sterling, Lee, 63
Sternlieb, George, 64
Stevenson, Gelvin, 84
STOP. *See* Symphony Tenants Organizing Project
straw ownerships, 153–54
strikes, 34, 143, 183, 218, 231
strippers, 126–27
subprime lending (subprime mortgages), 258–59, 284
subsidized housing, 55, 83, 128, 231, 244–45
suburbs, 11, 12, 24–27, 41, 49, 54, 61, 65, 89, 117, 139, 147
Sugar Hill Gang, 180
Sugar Hill Neighborhood (Harlem), 48–49
Sunbelt states, 54, 65
supply chains, transnational, 11
"suspicious" fires, 80, 82, 119, 125, 203, 207–8, 219, 275, 276
Susskind, David, 167, 171, 177–78
sweat equity (sweat equity movement), 99, 131, 227–41, 245–47, 262; *see also* Banana Kelly Community Improvement Association
Sylvester, 122
Symphony Road (Boston), 207–8
Symphony Tenants Organizing Project (STOP), 14, 208–9, 217

Take Back the Bronx, 261–62
Talking Heads, 73, 221
Tancl, Richard, 53
Tang, Eric, 316
Tarleton, Jonathan, *7*
Tate, Greg, 314
Tate, James, 27–28
Tats Cru, *255*
tax arrears, 82, 84, 98, 207, 209, 210
tax base, loss of, 28, 54–55
tax credits, 244, 245
tax lien legislation, 207–11, 222, 223
Tax Reform Act (1986), 244
tax shelters (tax abatements), 64, 129, 198, 228, 242, 244
Taylor, Keeanga-Yamahtta, 42, 290
Teichner, David, 66
Tenant Interim Lease Program, 99
tenant movement, 98–99, 198–202, 207–8, 223, 227, 231, 259; *see also* tenant organizations
tenant organizations (tenant unions and associations), 14, 64, 98–99, 139, 183, 194, 198, 199, 201, 208, 217–19, 236, 251; *see*

also specific organizations, e.g.: Northwest Bronx Community and Clergy Coalition
tenants, blaming of, 2, 7–8, 14, 29, 104, 120, 125, 127, 129, 131, 144–45, 155, 175–76, 185, 238, 239
Tennessee Valley Authority (TVA), 43
Texas, 275–76
Theme on a Pipe Dream: A Formula for Buying, Breeding, and Backing the Derby Winner (Sasse), 146
threat equity, 262
Ticotin, Rachel, 168, 172–73
Tiffany Street (Bronx), 78
Time-Life Films, 167, 172–74, 176–79
Times (London), 31, 33
tip offs, 108, 149, 172, 220
Tipton, Howard, 88, 89
Tokyo, Japan, 119–20
torches (paid firesetters), 9, 74, 75, 78–82, *79*, 98, 104, 116, 136, 143, 144, 150–54, 204, 220
Torres, Lourdes, 174
"totaling" the building, 81
tours and tourism, 163, 168, 216
Towering Inferno, The (film), 14, 103, 170–71
"trailers," arson, 204
trauma, of fire survivors, 48–49, 104–15
Travelers Insurance Company, 27, 30, 33, 212, *212*, 252
Tremont Avenue (Bronx), 102; *see also* East Tremont neighborhood
Triangle Shirtwaist Factory fire, 10–11
triangular trade, 13, 135–37, *136*, 139–43, 145, 149, 158, 254
tribunalization, 147
Truman, Harry S., and administration, 44
Trump, Donald, 327
TVA (Tennessee Valley Authority), 43
213th Street (Bronx), 78

underwriters and underwriting, 8, 9, 13, 25, 27, 30, 30, 33–35, 40–45, *50*, 56, 68, 85, 87, 88, 91–97, 116–18, 135, 136, *140*, 143–48, 155–57, 206, 210, 211, 213–14, 226, 248, 252–54, 257; *see also* Den-Har Underwriters; insurance redlining
unemployment, 10, 54, 57, 74, 78, 129, 158, 165, 227, 236; *see also* employment (employment training)
Uniform Crime Reports, 223
Union of Patriotic Puerto Ricans, 174
United Bronx Parents, 174, 263

United Kingdom, 13, 135, 143, 157; *see also* Lloyd's of London
University Heights neighborhood (Bronx), 219, 258
Up Stairs Lounge (New Orleans), 121
Upper West Side (New York City), 63
"urban crisis," 14, 28–29, 57, *161*, 162, 163, 166, 171, 172, 258
Urban Educational Systems, 95, 208
urban homesteading, 14, 227, 230, 232, 234, 236
Urban Homesteading Assistance Board (UHAB), 232
Urban Homesteading Demonstration Program, 234
Urban Property Protection and Reinsurance Act (1968), 36–38, 40–41, 289
urban renewal, 14, 28, 53, 107, 115, 128
urban triage, 55
urban uprisings (1960s), 6, 12, *19*, 20–22, 24, 28–38, *32*, *39*, 40, 42, 43, 45, 57, 59–60, 124, 125, 135, 143, 165, 257, 293; *see also specific headings, e.g.:* Hughes Panel; Watts uprising
urban villages, 234, *235*
urination, 121
U.S. dollar, 10, 141, 142
U.S. Fire Administration, 25, 77, 107, 117, *118*, 145, 208
U.S. General Accounting Office, 93, 95; *see also* Government Accountability Office
U.S. Navy, 103
U.S. Senate, 41, 48–49, 59, 77, 91, 95, 113, 119, 126, 166, 196, 203–4, 209, 257
U.S. Steel, 10

Valentine Avenue (Bronx), 76, 98–99
valuations, building, 75, 84, *85*, 87, 214
vandalism, 25, 29, 60, 124–25, 184–87, 209
Variety, 179
Vázquez, Irizarry, Vivian, 125, 132, 263; *see also Decade of Fire* (documentary)
Vega, Adrian "Popo," 74–76, 78, 81, 98
Velez, Eladio, 229, 230
Velez, Mildred, 240
Velez, Ramon, 322
vengeance, fires set out of, 121, 125
Vera Institute of Justice, 206
Vergara, Camilo José, *73*
video games, 220–21, *222*
Vietnam War, 134, 141, 173, 243, 288, 324
Village Voice, 84, 152, 172
Volcker shock, 227

voluntary market, 38, 60, 61, 66, 67, 93, 139, 147, 249, 251–52, 294, 300
von Hoffman, Alexander, 200
Vyse Avenue (Bronx), *73*, 110

Wade, Chrystal, 112–13, 115
Walker, Alice, 101
Walker, Tom, 312
Wall Street, 10, 12, 58, 96, 97, 205
Wall Street Journal, 181
Wallace, Mike, 283
War on Crime, 285
War on Poverty, 127, 242, 243, 322
Warriors, The (film), 167
Washington, D.C., 39, 87
Washington Avenue (Bronx), 229–39, *233*
Washington Post, 149, 185
water damage, 81, 112–14
Watergate, 155
Watson, Jack, 237
Watts uprising, 6, *19*, 20, 32, 34
WBAI-FM, 180
Weather Underground, 103
Webber, Yishai, 3–4, *4*, 8
welfare arson, 9, 104, 127–31, 207
"welfare queens," 127, 306
welfare system (welfare state), 54, 57, 69, 104, 127–31, 146, 165, 174, 202, 207, 238
Westchester Avenue (Bronx), 145
Westchester County, New York, 75, 115
Westport, Connecticut, 168
White, Kevin, 209
white flight, 12, 26, 28, 52–54, 65, 107, 119, 200

white supremacy, 6, 21, 123
whiteness, 8, 52, 182, 286
Whitney Museum of American Art, 3, *3*
Wichita, Kansas, 117
Wild Style (film), 167
Will, George F., 191
William the Conqueror, 146
Williams, Eric, 139
Williamsburg neighborhood (Brooklyn), 4
Wilson, James Q., 185–88, 191
window, broken. *See* broken windows (broken windows policing)
WKTU-FM, 221
Wolfe, Tom, 133, 309
Wolfen (film), 167
Wolfenstein (video game), 220
Women Against Pornography, 174
Women's City Club of New York, 63
Wong, Martin, 122, *122*, *133*
Woods, Clyde, 287
Worcester, Massachusetts, 119
World Series (1977), 259
Wozencraft, Frank, 36
Wynter, Sylvia, 174

Yankee Stadium, *47*, 166
Young, Karen, 122
Young Lords (Young Lords Party), 169, 173, 179, 220, 228, 231, 232, 262

Zarem, Bobby, 176–77
Zimbardo, Philip, 186–87, *187*, 315
Zong (British slave ship), 135, 140, 307